ANIMAL KINGDOMS

Animal Kingdoms

HUNTING, THE ENVIRONMENT,
AND POWER IN THE
INDIAN PRINCELY STATES

Julie E. Hughes

HARVARD UNIVERSITY PRESS
Cambridge, Massachusetts
2013

First published in India by Permanent Black, 2012

First Harvard University Press edition, 2013

Typeset in Adobe Garamond by Guru Typograph Technology,
Dwarka, New Delhi 110075

Library of Congress Cataloging-in-Publication Data

Hughes, Julie E., 1978–
Animal kingdoms : hunting, the environment, and power in the Indian princely
states / Julie E. Hughes. — First Harvard University Press edition.
pages   cm
Includes bibliographical references and index.
ISBN 978-0-674-07280-0 (cloth : alk. paper)
1. Hunting—India—History.   2. Hunting—Political aspects—India—
History.   3. India—History—British occupation, 1765–1947.   I. Title.
SK235.H84 2013
639′.10954—dc23   2012033402

for

Panthera tigris tigris
Pterocles orientalis

and

Sus scrofa

Contents

ILLUSTRATIONS AND MAPS

Illustrations (*between pp. 132 and 133*)

Maps

Abbreviations

AGG	Agent to the Governor-General
BA	Bundelkhand Agency
BL	British Library
BMK	Bikaner Mahakma Khas
CI	Central India
CP	Central Provinces
FD	Foreign Department
FPD	Foreign and Political Department
GOI	Government of India
MJ	Mewar Jangalat
MMK	Mewar Mahakma Khas
MMSL	Maharana Mewar Special Library
MR	Mewar Resident
NAI	National Archives of India
PA	Political Agent
PB	Political Branch
PD	Political Department
PFD	Political and Foreign Department
PSP	Pratap Shodh Pratistan
PWD	Public Works Department

RA	Rajputana Agency
RD	Revenue Department
RMK	Revenue and Mahakma Khas
RSA	Rajasthan State Archives
SM-MGST	Sadul Museum, Maharaja Ganga Singhji Trust
SRSA	Southern Rajputana States Agency
UP	United Provinces
UPSA	Uttar Pradesh State Archives

Acknowledgments

For institutional and financial support: American Institute of Indian Studies; Centre for Historical Studies, Jawaharlal Nehru University; University of Texas at Austin; Environmental Studies Program, Vassar College, Mellon Research Funds; History Department, Vassar College, for a warm welcome.

For granting me access, helping me use it, and sharing expertise: Maharana Mewar Charitable Foundation and Maharana Mewar Special Library (especially Arvind Singh Mewar and Bhupendra Singh Auwa); Sri Sadul Museum and Maharaja Ganga Singhji Trust (especially Rajyashree Kumari and Dalip Singh); Pratap Shodh Pratisthan (especially Tej Singh Shaktawat, Mohabbat Singh Rathore, Ishvar Singh Ranawat, and Rajmati Datt); Alkazi Foundation for the Arts (especially Pramod Kumar); Kalka Mata Botanical Nursery; National Archives of India; Rajasthan State Archives (especially Mahendra Khadgawat and P.C. Joiya); Rajasthan State Archives Intermediary Depository, Udaipur (especially M.L. Mundra and Sohanlal Damor); Old Secretariat Archives, Banganga Marg, and State Museum libraries, Madhya Pradesh Directorate of Archeology, Archives, and Museums (especially Gita Saberwal, M.K. Khan, S. Naimuddin, and B.L. Lokhandhe); Uttar Pradesh State Archives; British Library; Cambridge South Asian Archive; and British Empire and Commonwealth Museum.

For opening doors and sharing knowledge: Salauddin Ahmed; Raza H. Tehsin and family; Lav Bhargava; Karni Singh Parihar of Hotel Panna Vilas Palace, Udaipur, and Gajendra Singh Parihar of The Curious House, Pvt., Ltd., Udaipur; the Boheda family of Hotel

Mahendra Prakash, Udaipur; the Sardargarh family of the Sardargarh Heritage Hotel, Sardargarh; and Billu, who got me from Khas Odi to Nahar Odi.

For expert advice and more: Mahesh Rangarajan, Divyabhanusinh, Gail Minault, Cynthia Talbot, K. Sivaramakrishnan, Ann Grodzins Gold, Janet Davis, Dan Klingensmith, Kathleen Morris, Rohan D'Souza, Brian P. Caton, Arupjyoti Saikia, Neeladri Bhattacharya, Indivar Kamtekar, Silvio Calabi, Steve Helsley, Roger Sanger, and Pushpendra Singh Ranawat.

For vital feedback along the way: participants and organizers of the AAS Dissertation Workshop on Art and Politics (2007); Workshop on Political Ecology (Delhi University, 2007); Workshop on Interdisciplinary Directions in Modern South Asia (Tufts University, 2007); 37th and 38th Annual Conferences on South Asia (University of Wisconsin, 2008 and 2009); and 125th Annual Meeting of the AHA (2011).

My editors Rukun Advani and Michael Fisher for smoothing the way; Phil Schwartzberg for the fabulous maps.

Naheed, Raj, and Simran Varma of Lucknow Home Stay, for my home away from home; Sunayana Walia; Richard Bingle; Shakti Kak and family.

Josh for everything; Mom and Dad, Brian, and the Hughes family at large, for love, personality, and education.

1

Introduction: A Leopard
in the Garden

On a late summer evening in 1918, in one of the many princely states of Rajasthan in northwestern India, a leopard wandered into a verdant lakeside garden crowded with spent mango and ripening jackfruit trees.[1] Perhaps seeking a comfortable resting place, or else retreating from the excited shouts of gardeners tending the local prince's private grounds, the leopard scaled the upper branches of a fantastically overgrown Malabar nut tree, or possibly a towering neem.[2] Safely out of reach and with the commotion below fading off towards the north, in the direction of the nearby royal palace, the animal draped itself over the tree's twisting limbs in a way only a leopard could find comfortable and dozed off.

Not long afterwards—as depicted in a formal court painting of the incident—a small party of huntsmen entered the garden. Some

[1] August 9, 1918; see G.N. Sharma, ed., *Haqiqat Bahida: H.H. Maharana Fateh Singhji 24 Dec., 1884 to 24 May, 1930* (Udaipur: Maharana Mewar Research Institute, 1992–7), 5:198.

[2] The tree looks like a neem (*Azadirachta indica*), but is identified as an *adusa* or Malabar nut (*Justicia adhatoda*) in Dhaibhai Tulsinath Singh Tanwar, *Shikari aur Shikar* (Udaipur: privately printed, 1956), 345. Malabar nuts are evergreen shrubs that grow up to eight feet tall. The tree as painted is considerably taller and has foliage unlike a Malabar nut, a plant in any event incapable of housing a leopard: Ann Grodzins Gold, personal communication, August 20, 2010.

came on foot, accompanied by dogs. Others from the palace rode in style on elephant-back. They took their places a few yards from the sleeping leopard. A shot rang out. The animal dropped like a stone, dead before it hit the ground.

When this particular leopard walked into this particular garden, it sparked an immediate response from the palace, initiating a predictable sequence of events and flurry of documentation centered on the resident prince's armed pursuit of it. Soon after the shoot—which the sovereign in question would generously delegate to his heir-apparent—palace scribes recorded the tale in their official daily register or *haqiqat bahida*. Within a few years, court artists too memorialized the incident in a miniature painting showing the leopard three times in narrative sequence: asleep in the tree, falling through the air, and dead on the ground (Fig. 1). Three decades after entering the tale in his Rajasthani diary, a Mewar State *shikari* or huntsman recounted the story once more for a wider Hindi-speaking audience in his published memoirs, copies of which are available just a few steps from where the miniature painting now hangs on display in the Udaipur City Palace Museum, within half a mile of the garden where the leopard died.[3]

The domesticated garden setting, the nobly choreographed extermination of the leopard, and the targeting of a sleeping animal from a nearly impregnable post are all sharply at odds with the familiar ideals of colonial *shikar* and sportsmanship. Under the British Raj, standards of so-called true sportsmanship were allegedly universal and self-evident. By these standards, sitting securely on a trained elephant in a garden while shooting unsuspecting quarry was a questionable practice: there was little danger, the stakes were patently uneven, and the surroundings too tame. Nevertheless, few Indian princes would have judged the leopard shoot that evening entirely out of place or wholly beyond the pale of sportsmanship. The ruling family, artists, and royal huntsmen of Mewar, in fact, considered the event worthy of special commemoration: not every leopard shoot received such notice. Why, then, was this particular hunt so carefully memorialized?

[3] At the time of my research, this Hindi memoir could be purchased from the City Palace Museum's gift shop in Udaipur.

The explanation emerges from its localized, princely context: the brown summer peaks of the nearby Aravalli hills and the well watered, carefully manicured greenery in the foreground; the richness of fine turbans and elephant tusks accented in gold; the utilitarian practicality of khaki howdah cloths and unadorned rifles; the complementary characters and overlapping contexts of wild beasts and Rajput princes. Confirmed and expanded through representative examples and illustrations drawn from a selection of Indian princely states, this picture forms the basis of a distinct colonial era princely ecology—identified and described for the first time in these pages.

Princely ecology in the late-nineteenth and early-twentieth centuries perceived no sharp divisions between human and animal, or between the so-called artificial and natural environments. Operating within the constraints imposed by British paramountcy, it encompassed the animals, grounds, and practitioners of the hunt within a subtly shifting web of local histories, state traditions, lineal and regional identities, elite hierarchies, diplomatic relations, political aims, and personal ambitions. It allowed sovereign power and princely identity to be constructed as originating simultaneously from, and contested with reference to, hunting practices, animal characteristics, and environmental conditions that varied contextually and temporally, and whose meanings could be negotiated on the local, regional, all-India, and British imperial stages. Drawing on the Bundelkhandi context, one historian has argued that "[Rajput] identities were constantly contested and required continuous revalidation;" so too, I argue, were the qualities of Rajput environments and game.[4]

In fact, notwithstanding notions of permissibility within the hegemonic ethic of sportsmanship, it was quite natural that an Indian prince, or his designated representative, should sally forth to slay a big cat wandering in his gardens during the high era of the Raj. Arriving on the scene with rifle in hand, a princely gun could demonstrate dominion over nature and membership in an elite cadre of imperial

---

[4] Malavika Kasturi, *Embattled Identities: Rajput Lineages and the Colonial State in Nineteenth Century North India* (New York: Oxford University Press, 2002), viii–ix.

sportsmen while seemingly protecting his subjects heroically from potential danger. This was no simple assertion of despotic authority over a state and its environment, nor some pale imitation of late-Victorian codes of British imperial masculinity grounded in rationality, paternalism, self-control, and pluck. Indian princes used their sporting exploits, within their gardens and in the jungles beyond, to show themselves simultaneously akin to, yet distinct from, local game, rival princes, and elite Englishmen, and to illustrate their personal influence over and intimate association with state environments.

Much more transpired that evening than the celebrated death of a wild animal. In killing the leopard, this princely sportsman suggested the ways he was and was not leopard-like. He defined the predator's relationship to the garden, as well as his own association with state hunting grounds. He reaffirmed and strengthened connections between his heroic action and noble character, and the history and legitimacy of his lineage. Riding out at his father's bidding, he consolidated his status in numerous hierarchies: between himself and worthy beasts, within his own family, in comparison with the nobles of his state, peers in neighboring realms, government officials, British royalty, and European elites.

The physical and psychological boundaries that nominally distinguished Indian princes from *jangli* (wild) beasts, and domesticated environments from dense jungle, were surprisingly permeable. This characteristic of princely ecology is unfamiliar conceptual terrain in modern Europe and North America, and perhaps among all heavily urbanized populations, where far sharper divisions have developed between the civilized and the wild. In these regions, it is common sense that bears do not belong in backyards, alligators in swimming pools, wolves in urban parks, and leopards in gardens.

At first glance, the Mewari landscape in which this leopard was shot looks like a thoroughly domesticated space, carpeted with English lawns, dotted with fruit trees, and bounded by low walls. Yet, not far away, another section of the garden doubled as a nursery for selectively bred wild boar with which to stock the state's *shikargahs* or royal hunting reserves. Like the leopard in the Malabar nut tree, these corn-fed creatures complicated the categories, the supposed oppositions between domestic and wild, calling the exact character of the landscape into question. What the garden was on any given day—jungle, shikargah, zoological ground, pleasure park, orchard, or hybrid space—depended on human perception, princely activity, and the nature of the animals in it. All landscapes in the princely states had similarly layered, multiple, and changeable identities, paralleling those of the people and other animals that visited and inhabited them. In particular, India's princes understood their hunting grounds, whether formal or *ad hoc*, as intimately associated with and productive of the regionally distinct physical and psychological characteristics of their game, and, indeed, of themselves.

Within princely ecology, there was no popularly accepted and fundamental divide between people and wilderness of the sort famously identified and critiqued by William Cronon.[5] Whether Rajput elites approached them as locations or concepts, they saw neither the wilderness nor the garden as devoid of human mediation. This did not necessarily compromise the qualities that constituted wilderness— although some interventions and certain humans certainly could. Princely gardens in colonial India never lacked some measure of wildness. A leopard in such a garden was not foreign, but rather a rare and valuable enhancement of something that in a sense was already there. The animal might be a dangerous transient, a welcome guest, or a tolerated wayfarer; however viewed, it remained a creature whose potency could be harvested by the king, and that could be hunted on the same terms as those that prevailed in the forest. Akin to leopards in gardens, kings were no strangers in forests. On the contrary, it has been suggested that Indian princes were symbolically as well as literally rooted in the forest, their very legitimacy and physical substance nourished on its fruit and meat.[6]

If little separated kings and leopards, a deep chasm divided

---

[5] William Cronon, "The Trouble with Wilderness; or, Getting Back to the Wrong Nature," in *Uncommon Ground: Rethinking the Human Place in Nature* (New York: W.W. Norton & Co., 1995), 80–1.

[6] Joanne Punzo Waghorne, *The Raja's Magic Clothes: Re-Visioning Kingship and Divinity in England's India* (University Park: Pennsylvania State University Press, 1994), 181.

peasants from kings and leopards alike. The ability to move safely and successfully between forest and garden was largely restricted to the elite. To the extent that princes and princely character overlapped with wild animals and wilderness, it is impossible to segregate the human from the wild in princely India. And yet, socio-economic and political rank and identity severely constrained the idyllic possibilities at the heart of princely ecology. Agricultural peasants could enter a forest's margins, but its depths remained beyond their scope; adivasi communities like the Bhils belonged in the jungle, but the garden was out of bounds. Kings, leopards, and their ilk alone reigned transcendent. Cronon's hope—"if wildness can stop being (just) out there and start being (also) in here, if it can start being as humane as it is natural, then perhaps we can get on with the unending task of struggling to live rightly in the world—not just in the garden, not just in the wilderness, but in the home that encompasses them both"— finds no validation in princely ecology. Here, divisions between the human and the wild are complicated by hierarchies of class, caste, and sovereign privilege.[7]

The recently coined term "cosmopolitan tiger" describes this animal as it is perceived by contemporary Indian city-dwellers, international wildlife foundations, and foreign elites. It suggests that knowledge about tigers in these cosmopolitan populations comes primarily from Animal Planet television and visits to zoos or wildlife sanctuaries.[8] Bengali villagers in the Sundarbans who actually live in the midst of tigers face an entirely different animal—an uncaged creature of flesh and blood—yet do not consider tigers implacably dangerous by nature. This is, rather, an animal that can be negotiated with through the diplomatic services of local deities; it can be appeased if villagers regulate their behavior while in the forest (by avoiding strife and temporarily suspending caste hierarchies) to avoid causing it offense. Tigers only withdraw from such negotiations and become uncontrollably violent when they realize the privileges of being seen

---

[7] Ibid., 90.

[8] The term was coined by Annu Jalais, in idem, *Forest of Tigers: People, Politics and Environment in the Sundarbans* (New Delhi: Routledge, 2010), 196–201.

from a cosmopolitan perspective by unconditionally supportive elites, governments, and NGOs, all of whom condemn villagers as environmental trespassers deserving their fate as "tiger food."[9]

Not so long ago, there were princely tigers. Like their cosmopolitan cousins, princely tigers were conceived of at comparatively safe distances. Those who imagined them and maintained their importance—and tried to conserve their numbers—were elite, powerful, and all-too-frequently unreceptive to popular petitions and policy demands based on countervailing visions of prosaically dangerous carnivores. The villagers of princely Rajputana and Bundelkhand, unlike those in contemporary Bengal, may not have maintained close diplomatic relations with local tigers, but it is unlikely that they, or the tigers, failed to practice basic "strategies of avoidance . . . [that] allowed for coexistence if not total harmony."[10] Still, the modern breed of "cosmopolitan tigers" in the Sundarbans are not far removed from their Rajput state predecessors. Princely tigers and other royal game acted on their near-sovereign immunity by attacking people, killing livestock, and destroying crops. The extent of damage in the states is unclear, but tigers in British India reportedly killed 828 people in 1877 and similar numbers annually throughout the late 1800s and early 1900s.[11]

Under British paramountcy, Indian princes could no longer declare war, they could not engage in direct diplomatic relations with other states, and their freedom to undertake most sovereign activities was severely circumscribed. Many princes responded by focusing their energies on the few means that remained of exercising royal influence and asserting status. Shikar was one of these means. Partha Chatterjee has suggested that British colonialism deeply affected the political and social landscape of South Asia, provoking Indians to modify how they expressed and exercised power in their own homes and the

[9] Annu Jalais, "Dwelling on Morichjhanpi: When Tigers Became 'Citizens,' Refugees 'Tiger-Food'," *Economic and Political Weekly* 40, 17 (April 2005): 1759.

[10] Mahesh Rangarajan, "The Raj and the Natural World: The War against 'Dangerous Beasts' in Colonial India," *Studies in History* 14, 2 (1998): 288.

[11] Ibid., 289.

world beyond.[12] According to Chatterjee, Indian men, as the relatively powerless subjects of the colonial state in the public sphere, found their agency spatially restricted to—and thus concentrated in—the domestic sphere, where Indian women became their objects of reform. For Indian princes, an analogous space was the shikargah. As one of the few locations remaining beyond the reach of direct colonial interference, hunting grounds provided an arena for articulations of power—with wildlife and the environment as the objects of control—now impossible in the wider political sphere. Under these circumstances, even if the resultant environmental controls elicited protests from the most vulnerable segments of the population, elite Rajput princes, undeterred, found compensating advantages in the socio-economic and political assets they gained from the hunt.

By the late nineteenth century, sporting princes, pigsticking British officers, and tiger hunting officials *all* understood the hunt as a prime measure of martial ability and, by extension, an important factor in gauging the legitimacy and nobility of those who ruled. Viewed as a field of knowledge, the hunt as a legitimizing martial activity thus invites investigation into its origins, either as a foreign implant or a dialogic production of colonizer and colonized. The evidence here forces us beyond the standard positions in the debate on colonialism and knowledge. The British could not have introduced the hunt's martial associations to India because these were already well known in the subcontinent, and likely had been for millennia. In addition, British hunting methods and martial tactics were not static but continued developing in the colonies. These basic facts suggest a dialogic production. Yet, princes and colonizers did not work together or in parallel, knowingly or unknowingly, to create a *single* colonial vision of the hunt. Rather, a wide range of actors—from princes through peasants and viceroys through subalterns, inhabiting their several related but varying colonial contexts—produced *multiple* spheres of knowledge. They agreed on certain fundamentals (hunting was martial), but differed on the particulars (whether shooting boar

---

[12] Partha Chatterjee, "The Nationalist Resolution of the Women's Question" (1989), reprinted in idem, *Empire and Nation: Essential Writings 1985–2005* (Ranikhet: Permanent Black, 2010).

counted). So the colonial hunt did not emerge from a simple binary of British and Indian, but was an ongoing production of innumerable conversations—public and private, official and informal, in English, Hindi, Rajasthani, etc.—conducted amongst the interested parties and individuals.

Because they viewed shikar as a martial activity, the hunt became something more than a pale imitation of war for these militarily dispossessed princes.[13] In the colonial context, shikar supplanted war as the universally recognized marker of martial prowess and sovereign power. British civil servants, potentially having skipped military service, needed a means of proving their authority without participating in battle just as much as Indian princes did. British military officers, too, had fewer opportunities to put their active service on display, the major conflicts having shifted towards the northwest and east along with the frontiers. So they went pigsticking and blackbuck shooting in the populous Indo-Gangetic plains and the Deccan, and tiger hunting wherever possible to metaphorically conquer the remaining jungle tracts.

The hunt's martial and sovereign potential thus suggests the need for a fresh evaluation of just how autonomous and influential Indian princes and their states were during the colonial period. Was the princely crown hollow?[14] Did the British preserve princely states only to avoid the costs of administering isolated, unremunerative, "problem" provinces? While it is true enough that "no state at Delhi ever sought to govern directly the Thar desert area of Rajasthan, the remote salt flats of Cutch, or the jungly tracts of central India and Orissa," any explanation that grants exclusive agency to economically minded and politically savvy British administrators, and to their control of select Indian environments, is partial.[15] India's princes were better off, better placed, and better educated than the vast majority of their compatriots. And, as Hira Singh insists, the British Raj was never

[13] Thanks to Divyabhanusinh for suggesting this possibility.

[14] Nicholas B. Dirks, *The Hollow Crown: An Ethnohistory of an Indian Kingdom* (New York: Cambridge University Press, 1987).

[15] Barbara N. Ramusack, *The Indian Princes and Their States* (New York: Cambridge University Press, 2004), 86–7.

able to rely on these sovereigns to obligingly fulfill their "functional requirements" for allies, legitimacy, and local knowledge. Rather than a system of "indirect rule," the princely state was a process of "resistance, negotiation, and mutual accommodation."[16]

Indian rulers used hunting, wild animals, and shikargahs to improve their positions and define themselves variously as defiant kings, loyal peers, modern administrators, and traditional Indian rulers. Through shikar they revisited the more favorable political and environmental conditions that supposedly had prevailed in former times: during the reigns of their immediate predecessors, before their ancestors had signed treaties with the East India Company in the early 1800s, antecedent to the rise of the Maratha Confederacy in the 1700s, or even prior to their states' subordination under the Mughal empire in the 1500s and 1600s. Sport linked princes with the noble deeds of their glorious forefathers on the same grounds: in shikargahs, on the battlefield, or in the midst of precipitous hills, dense jungles, and cooling lakes. Killing impressive beasts in stately landscapes helped produce and maintain superior sovereigns.

Hunting, however, was not only a means of displaying stereotypically masculine attributes and heroic exertions. Indian rulers equally strove to present a picture of privileged ease, whether seated on elephant-back or perched within a lavishly outfitted shooting box or in a comparatively simple (but still carpet-strewn) tree-based *machan*. Their interest in being sumptuously sovereign played no small part in elevating the worth of garden-dwelling leopards alongside that of free-ranging big cats. Attempts to balance the brashly heroic warrior and the serene consumer of luxuries were defining features of princely shikar, as well as points of departure from the so-called true sportsmanship of the British.

Within the bounds of their shikargahs, princes could reshape, reject, or participate in "Western" ideals of sportsmanship, all the while displaying the natural bounty of their states as outward manifestations of their competence as rulers. Shikargahs provided a space for

[16] Hira Singh, "Colonial and Postcolonial Historiography and the Princely States: Relations of Power and Rituals of Legitimation," in *India's Princely States: People, Princes and Colonialism*, ed. Waltraud Ernst and Biswamoy Pati (Delhi: Primus Books, 2010), 16.

informality, a momentarily valorized position for princely hosts, and an element of chance within the relatively unpredictable context of the hunt. Shooting excursions in state grounds carried the potential for inversions of hierarchy that could make Indian rulers temporarily but memorably equal or superior to their British guests. This volatility also made shikargahs among the least risky sites for princes to contest British dominance. What happened in them did not necessarily reflect on or impact outside political or social realities, just as the comparatively lush grounds of princely reserves did not necessarily bear much resemblance to less privileged landscapes elsewhere in the state. Shikargahs similarly hosted hierarchical contests between Indian princes, and between princes and their subordinate nobles.

When we think of the hunt in princely India, more often than not we picture tigers as the quarry. Tigers were the most emblematic of colonial game, their skins among the most prized trophies obtainable. But they were by no means the only important Indian game. Princes pursued wildfowl, wild boar, and blackbuck antelope with gusto, not to mention sambar deer, chinkara gazelle, crocodiles, and a plethora of other creatures large and small. The meanings of royal sport were not constant through wildfowl shoots and tiger hunts. Princes attributed different qualities to different species, associated different characteristics with different habitats and shooting landscapes, and differentially valued the hunting methods they used to pursue different kinds of prey. If we investigate only tiger shikar, we will understand nothing but tiger shikar. "[O]ur obsession with big game of the four-footed kind blinds us to how much of shikar consisted of tracking and shooting birds" and small game, argues one eminent wildlife historian.[17] This blind spot has obscured the importance of almost all hunting in colonial India other than the pursuit of big cats. In addition to the leopard and the tiger, this book considers wild boar,

[17] Mahesh Rangarajan, preface to J.H. Baldwin, "Hunting the Houbara," in *Oxford Anthology of Indian Wildlife: Hunting and Shooting*, ed. Mahesh Rangarajan, vol. 1 (New York: Oxford University Press, 1999), 61.

wildfowl, and blackbuck—all species that ranked among the princes' favorite prey. These animals provide access to a diverse range of habitats, including rocky hillsides, seasonal wetlands, and open plains, in addition to the jungles and scrub most associated with big cats. The diversity embodied in this selection of animals reveals the multiplicities that characterized princely shikar, as well as the underlying core values and interests that tied everything together across the particularities of species, landscapes, states, and princely individualities.

Natural and man-made features (and everything in between) adjusted the meanings of princely shikar. A mountain state's undulating hills, thorny brush, and lush trees signified as much as its tigers and boar. A desert realm's irrigation tanks and arid wastes were as relevant as its wildfowl and antelope. Environmental features intersected and interacted with the political identities and historical profiles of the grounds. Tigers that a prince killed in his own territory meant something different from those he pursued in British India, and the big cats he hoped to bag in the famous forts of his ancestors were unlike the animals he could shoot in his own less (or differently) distinguished surroundings. The past too was more than a passive point of reference, for, beginning in the sixteenth and seventeenth centuries, the Mughal empire had been instrumental in the development of the Rajput royal hunt.

The most influential exposition of a rationale behind Mughal shikar comes from the sixteenth-century courtier and scholar Abu al-Fazl, who wrote of his patron, the emperor Akbar, that "superficial, worldly observers see in killing an animal a sort of pleasure ... [and] think that His Majesty has no other object in view but hunting, but the wise and experienced know that he pursues higher aims."[18] The chase ideally facilitated surprise inspections of the army and inquiries into the "condition of the people," allowing the emperor to expand his knowledge, discover and alleviate oppression, and punish wrongdoers. Rudradeva, the Raja of Kumaon, likewise wrote in his sixteenth-century *Syainikasastram*, a Sanskrit treatise on falconry,

---

[18] Abul al-Fazl 'Allami, *The Ain i Akbari*, trans. H. Blochmann, vol. 1 (Calcutta: Asiatic Society of Bengal, 1878), 282.

that royal shikar inculcated the skills necessary for maintaining power and winning wars, while also conditioning elite bodies for battle.[19] Rudradeva's martial understanding of sport resonated with contemporary Mughal pastimes like the *qamargah*, a hunt in which game was surrounded within a progressively tightening ring of beaters and then slaughtered in large numbers at close range in imitation of the bloodshed and chaos of battle.[20]

Scholars seeking to explain how Mughal emperors and their apologists conceived of the links between rulership and shikar have relied on Abu al-Fazl's vindication of royal sport.[21] Assuming a significant continuity between Mughal sport and princely hunting, and between aspects of Mughal sport and British imperial shikar, Abu al-Fazl's argument has also appeared in scholarship on hunting in the colonial era. There is some justification for this. Late-nineteenth and early-twentieth-century princes themselves echoed this courtier's line of thought—itself apparently borrowed from Persian sources—by claiming that shikar familiarized them with problems in their realms while bringing them into beneficial contact with their subjects.[22]

At first glance, the Persian origin of words like shikar, shikargah, and shikarkhana supports a significant degree of continuity between Mughal and Rajput sport, especially given the comparative rarity of the Rajasthani term for the hunt, *akhet*.[23] Yet, a number of Persian expressions share the spotlight with their Rajasthani counterparts,

---

[19] Mohan Chand, preface, *Syainikasastram: The Art of Hunting in Ancient India of Raja Rudradeva of Kumaon* by Rudradeva, ed. Mohan Chand, trans. Haraprasad Shastri (Delhi: Eastern Book Linkers, 1982), 1; ibid., 104 and 82–3.

[20] Thomas T. Allsen, *The Royal Hunt in Eurasian History* (Philadelphia: University of Pennsylvania Press, 2006), 26–33.

[21] For example, see ibid., 193.

[22] Dhaibhai Tulsinath Singh Tanwar, *Samsmaran: Maharana Fateh Singhji, Maharana Bhupal Singhji, Maharana Bhagvat Singhji Mewar* (Udaipur: privately printed, 1982), 65; Maharawal Lachman Singhji of Dungarpur, quoted in Charles Allen and Sharada Dwivedi, *Lives of the Indian Princes* (New York: Crown Publishers, Inc., in association with the Taj Hotel Group, 1984), 127–8.

[23] Thanks to Divyabhanusinh for reminding me of this.

like the Persian for lion or tiger, *sher*, and the equally flexible
Rajasthani *nahar*. As the primary language of the imperial court
from the sixteenth century, Persian balanced its renowned literary
refinements with a sophisticated vocabulary for Mughal innovations
in governance, centralized power, ceremonial, and courtly conduct.
The local preference for shikar over *akhet* existed against this wider
backdrop of *darbar, zamindar, darkhvast,* and *sar o pa.*[24] This select
Persian lexicon was emblematic of Mughal prestige and power, but
the words' precise meanings were mutable to local needs and by no
means limited to hunting terminology. No simple continuity between
Mughal and Rajput sport can be posited on this basis, any more than
it can between the specifics of any other aspect of their respective
courtly cultures.

The hunting practices and related interests of the emperor Jahangir
(r. 1605–27) provide a clearer picture of the potential continuities
between Mughal and Rajput sport. According to Ebba Koch, Jahangir
approached "his dominions scientifically," by observing, weighing, and
measuring slain and captured game, unusual flora, and other objects
of interest.[25] The investigations he conducted and the selective data
he compiled recall contemporary developments in Baconian empiri-
cism in Europe. Jahangir's approach to the natural world, however,
shares less with the more systematic and specialized methods employed
by the newly professional botanists, ornithologists, and biologists that
had emerged in the colonies and the metropole by the late nineteenth
century.[26] At the turn of the century, even when elite Rajput and
British sportsmen identified themselves as amateur natural historians,
few presumed anymore to count their casual field observations and
measuring tapes as the stuff of science. Nevertheless, the particular

[24] Royal court; land holder; petition; robe of honor.

[25] Ebba Koch, "Jahangir as Francis Bacon's Ideal of the King as an Observer
and Investigator of Nature," *Journal of the Royal Asiatic Society, Series 3,*
19, 3 (2009): 327–8.

[26] Narisara Murray, "From Birds of Paradise to *Drosophila*: The Changing
Roles of Scientific Specimens to 1920," in *A Cultural History of Animals in
the Age of Empire,* ed. Kathleen Kete (New York: Berg, 2007), 122, 126, and
131.

animal dimensions that mattered most to these sportsmen, and the precise methods they used to obtain and confirm "correct" measurements, showed—at least in theory—a remarkable degree of standardization.

Size mattered to colonial Rajputs and Britons. It had mattered to the Mughals too, but in somewhat different ways. The scientific questions integral to Jahangir's activities had faded from the hunt as the centuries advanced and science transformed from its origins as a cultured pastime into a specialized profession. In their place, amateurish echoes of scientific methodology came to the forefront in modern measures of shikar, especially among the British. According to Rowland Ward's authoritative *Records of Big Game*, for the antlers of the sambar stag these measures included length on outside curve, circumference above brow tine, tip to tip, widest inside, and number of points. For the tiger, they were length before skinned, length of body, length dressed, girth of body, upper arm, forearm, and head, height at shoulder, and weight.[27] While Rajput princes often used these numbers, they also measured their game by criteria that differed in focus from both British and Mughal approaches, but which fell short of being entirely foreign to either. For the Indian princes, environmental context and local character balanced out these supposedly more empirical weights and measures.

The emperor Jahangir, equally, had claimed attractive or unusual aspects of "nature as his own by making a permanent imprint on it with architectural features, sculptures and dynastic inscriptions."[28] While formal gardens were the Mughals' most characteristic means of marking favored sites, shikar additionally inspired palaces and minars. A few miles east of Delhi, the emperor Shah Jahan (r. 1627–57) built a hunting palace and the imposing Hashtsal Minar, which may have functioned as a shooting tower. Jahangir built a hunting complex and raised a minar at Sheikhapura in memory of a favorite captive hunting antelope. Akbar (r. 1556–1605) completed similar

[27] Rowland Ward, *Records of Big Game*, 4th ed. (London: Rowland Ward, Ltd., 1903), 70 and 468.

[28] Koch, "Jahangir as Bacon's Ideal," 326.

projects, including the distinctive elephant-tusk-studded Hiran Minar at Fatehpur Sikri.[29] Despite these amenities, the Mughals preferred hunting on foot or from the saddle (or the elephant howdah) over shooting towers.

Rajput trends would have responded to Mughal constructions in the field, just as they did to other imperial genres of architecture—from which they freely adapted forms to challenge centralized control and express local power.[30] But the Mughals' wan interest in shooting towers, in contrast with their zeal for shikar palaces and memorials, would have left sub-imperial rulers largely free of architectural influence in this area. Besides the scant Mughal stimulus, Rajput patronage of masonry shooting boxes in the forested and hilly regions of Rajputana actually appears to have peaked *after* Mughal decline, i.e. during the eighteenth, nineteenth, and early twentieth centuries. If so, the royal Rajput shooting box postdates the seventeenth-century developments in arts and architecture that have been identified as consciously sampling, referencing, and challenging Mughal works to assert the power and status of local kingdoms, particularly Mewar.[31] The context of these structures, and of the royal hunt in princely India, appears to be more colonial than Mughal.

Pleasure and duty operated in tandem to motivate the ideal sovereign, and no inevitable conflict of interest existed between a king's enjoyment of sport and service to his people: "a life of bhoga [appetite] had long been a Rajput ideal—or rather bhoga on display; bhoga as a public ideal of kingship."[32] Royal consumption indicated a ruler's privileged access to resources. Calculated bouts of overconsumption

[29] Ebba Koch, "The Copies of the Qutb Minar," *Iran* 29 (1991): 95 and 98.

[30] On Rajput and Mughal connections, see Catherine Asher, "The Architecture of Raja Man Singh: A Study of Sub-Imperial Patronage," in *The Powers of Art: Patronage in Indian Culture*, ed. Barbara Stoler Miller (New Delhi: Oxford University Press, 1992), and Jennifer Beth Joffee, "Art, Architecture and Politics in Mewar, 1628–1710" (PhD diss., University of Minnesota, 2005).

[31] Joffee, "Art, Architecture and Politics," 2–3.

[32] Molly Emma Aitken, *The Intelligence of Tradition in Rajput Court Painting* (New Haven: Yale University Press, 2010), 220.

further suggested a king's superhuman capacities for collecting and controlling assets, savoring and digesting produce, pleasing and ferti- lizing wives and concubines, and subduing or destroying wild animals and untamed environments. The "massive" appetites of ideal Rajput kings, however, jarred with Victorian ideals of sound governance and self-control. Stereotype by the late nineteenth century asserted that English sportsmen could hunt within limits, whereas Indian princes habitually transgressed the bounds of decency by amassing immoderate bags of unsuitable animals, shooting out of season, and pursuing the most unsporting practices in relation to game and the rural peasantry.

Besides their purported excesses in the field, princely motives too were suspect when it came to shikar. Tension arose because Britons and Indian sovereigns increasingly competed through the hunt to embody the colonial ideal of "predatory care," which relied on "public specta- cles of terror ... to produce identity with the state by constituting subjects as passive and feminized spectators." This happened most often through a ruling elite's "heroic" destruction of man-eating tigers and other dangerous beasts.[33] But despite the shared British and Rajput espousal of the ethic of predatory care, and despite the venerable thesis of royal sport as an enjoyable yet altruistic occupation ultimately pur- sued for the people's benefit, princely shikar remained vulnerable to negative interpretations as a selfish and morally suspect activity.

Difficulties arose as well because princely approaches to shikar and rulership spanned colonial and Mughal styles of predatory care. The latter aimed at "[conveying] the fearful grandeur of the emperor, and his capacity to capture and subdue lesser predators ... [enabling] the pursuit and punishment of seditious officers and chiefs ... [and staging] the forgiveness and incorporation of these insurgents into the hierarchical order of empire."[34] Predatory care by the Mughals provided an elegant and flexible means of managing multiple sover- eignties, overlapping hierarchies, and fluid reconfigurations of

[33] Anand S. Pandian, "Predatory Care: The Imperial Hunt in Mughal and British India," *Journal of Historical Sociology* 14, 1 (March 2001): 88.
[34] Ibid., 90.

allegiance and dissent. The colonial approach made allowances for sovereign and subordinate, clear and fixed hierarchies, and a simple binary of loyalist and traitor. Neither style could satisfy princely needs and desires by the early twentieth century, and so they often operated, uneasily and disconcertingly, in between.

Unsurprisingly, the idea that Indian princes could balance pleasure and public service, or even that they might have been interested in doing so, rarely found its way into the commentaries Englishmen wrote on princely shikar. In part because these widely available English-language sources are easier to access than archival materials on the subject, they are the most commonly consulted. As a result, scholars have relied too much on imperial interpretations when constructing their own arguments about princely sport in colonial India. In line with their views on other princely activities and concerns, the British, with few exceptions, judged elite Indian hunting as inferior, decadent, based on trickery rather than skill, and indicative of an unsavory preference for show over substance. By and large, princely shikar continues to be judged according to these imperial stereotypes.

The reputation of princes who appeared to enjoy sport at the expense of good governance is, if anything, more vulnerable today. Sharp divisions in the ways hunting has been thought of since India's independence in 1947 have presented serious challenges to princely descendants; this is particularly true of the popular tendency to link shikar with elite profligacy, moral degeneracy, and un-Indian practices. The descendants of several princely houses, who now manage major archival collections of state documents, have been long reluctant to grant access to those researching princely shikar.[35] Some feel their ancestors have been blamed unfairly for environmental degradation in modern India and for the challenges faced by endangered species like the tiger. The great-granddaughter of Maharaja Ganga Singh of Bikaner, in particular, defends her family's legacy by asserting that all "problems that exist today, deforestation, poaching and the disturbing of animal habitats ... [and] tapering numbers are due entirely to selfish commercial development, deforestation and human greed

[35] Divyabhanusinh, personal communication, spring 2008.

and have nothing whatever to do with the Indian Princes and their hunting pastimes." When Ganga Singh ruled and hunted in Bikaner, she insists, the "animals and birds thrived."[36]

For those with a scholarly interest in princely shikar outside the subcontinent, the situation can be rife with controversy as well. In the United States, modern opponents of hunting tend to visualize "a drooling, all-powerful, sadistic male armed to the teeth with survival and assault weaponry, 'blasting' a Bambi or another Disneyified animal with saucer-sized eyes to death."[37] One influential book even concludes that "some of the feelings that many hunters express—the murderous love and other incoherent emotions, the Hemingwayesque anxiety about sexual identity, the relish for doing delicious evil, the false and contemptuous affection for the victim, the refusal to think of the victim as an individual—are also common feelings among rapists."[38] Meanwhile, proponents insist that "hunting ennobles boy and man (and girl and woman) . . . by introducing them to the virtues of sportsmanship, patience, and physical hardiness, and the pleasures of nature study, camaraderie, and social solidarity." Between these hostile standpoints, it seems, there is "little or no opportunity for reconciliation."[39]

My book neither endorses princely shikar nor denounces it as some insidious "pathology of princes."[40] The evidence cannot exonerate elite Indian sportsmen, but neither can it demonstrate their responsibility for the crisis that tigers and other endangered species face in the shrunken forests and fragmented habitats of modern South

[36] Rajyashree Kumari, "Foreword," in L.S. Rathore, *Maharaja Sadul Singh of Bikaner (A Biography of the Co-Architect of India's Unity)* (Bikaner: Books Treasure and Maharaja Ganga Singhji Trust, 2005), vii–viii.

[37] Thomas L. Altherr and John F. Reiger, "Academic Historians and Hunting: A Call for More and Better Scholarship," *Environmental History Review* 19, 3 (Fall 1995): 39.

[38] Matt Cartmill, *A View to a Death in the Morning: Hunting and Nature through History* (Cambridge: Harvard University Press, 1993), 240.

[39] Altherr and Reiger, "Historians and Hunting," 39–40.

[40] Khalid Latif Gauba, *H.H., or the Pathology of Princes* (Lahore: Times Publishing Company, 1930).

Asia. I do not seek to answer whether princely ecology and shikar were good or bad for the states or their people. Rather, I show that the princes themselves believed their actions justifiable and even beneficial. It is important to recall, however, that the growing scholarship on forests and shooting reserves in colonial times, when read in parallel with investigations into the human costs of conservation efforts like Project Tiger in independent India, must suggest otherwise. On the other hand, Gold and Gujar's studies of one erstwhile Rajput realm remind us of the complexities of the situation: "the past achievement of environmental well-being in Sawar was evidently at the expense of some—for example, farmers whose crops were threatened by wild animals. It also opposed the needs of herders, and of women. But it resulted in recognizable ecological common good on which almost everyone would agree."[41]

It is well known that the histories of hunting and conservation are closely intertwined. Looking to southern Africa's Cape Colony, Lance van Sittert has argued convincingly that John M. MacKenzie's canonical thesis that "wild animals were transformed from *res nullius* (a thing which has no owner) into public property... is wrong in almost every respect, completely obscuring the primary trajectory towards the 'privatization' of game and the commercialization of all wild animals... and all hunting." Likewise, wildlife in princely India did not become public property over the course of the nineteenth century, even if game conferred public benefits through the medium of sporting kings. It is additionally unclear if wild animals were ever *res nullius* in the states during the nineteenth century, or indeed at any time within the several preceding centuries. Finally, the game laws that MacKenzie sees as marking "the transformation of hunting into 'the Hunt'" in British India and Africa primarily operated within princely India as formalizations of and elaborations on existing orders.[42] Nevertheless, MacKenzie's timeline for the canonization of "true" sportsmanship remains invaluable (Indian princes did know

---

[41] Ann Grodzins Gold and Bhoju Ram Gujar, *In the Time of Trees and Sorrows: Nature, Power, and Memory in Rajasthan* (Durham: Duke University Press, 2002), 259.

[42] Lance van Sittert, "Bringing in the Wild: The Commodification of

the rules even if they chose to reinvent them), as does his recognition of the vital role played in the emergence of conservationism by elite hunters' apprehensions of disappearing game (Indian princes entertained similar fears and undertook their own fixes).

The British often assumed that elite Indian sport had remained relatively untouched by outside influence and unchanged in its fundamental values, methods, and meanings since medieval times. Dismissing even those substantial improvements in weaponry that continued to revolutionize hunting and its norms throughout the nineteenth and early twentieth centuries, they perceived a core of antiquity lurking beneath an ephemeral veneer of princely modernity. When an Indian prince shot a tiger from elephant-back, the scene revealed the shooter's medieval character, by turns splendid and repugnant. Other views dominated when an Englishman performed comparable acts. He was humoring "native" tastes for spectacle or reluctantly but politely acquiescing to a princely host's desire to treat him to a grand shikar in the state's distinctive style. Viewed according to these stereotypes, princes could only *act* the part of a true sportsman, while Englishmen naturally exemplified the role.

The representations of princes and their apologists, insisting there were no fundamental differences between their shooting and the sportsmanship of the British—even if Rajput traditions ornamented the proceedings—cannot be taken at face value either. British colonial and princely representations did agree, however, on the fact that the states offered lavish entertainment to high-ranking officials while subjecting them to skillful manipulation, whereby fine tiger skins and blackbuck trophies served as informal currency for government concessions, unofficial favors, and indulgences for princely peccadilloes. Yet most princely sport took place with no powerful Englishmen present to be flattered or manipulated. The meanings and aims of such sport extended beyond the British.

If historians are increasingly reluctant to admit the existence of a universal and unchanging true sportsmanship among British imperialists, it is doubly imperative that we question princely norms. Indian rulers were neither just like the British, nor were they precisely their opposite. Because the British themselves had multiple approaches to hunting beneath the monolithic façade of true sportsmanship, we cannot make simplistic comparisons between their standards and those of the princes. What we can do is investigate what Indian princes were trying to accomplish as sportsmen and how they understood their actions. British imperial sportsmanship, with all its complexities, represented only one ideal among many that the princes—individually, lineally, or collectively—could selectively internalize, imitate, or improve upon. We must remember too that the lines of influence were multidirectional: even MacKenzie recognized that British imperial sportsmanship was a hybrid of English shooting practices, Mughal-style shikar, and innovations arrived at in the colonial context.[43]

Ruled by an imposing collection of maharajas, maharaos, maha-rawals, and maharanas, some two-fifths of the subcontinent remained under princely control throughout the colonial period. All told, there were some five hundred states, great and small. Situated in North, Central, and peninsular India as well as everywhere in between, there were Sikh and Maratha territories, Jat and Rajput kingdoms, and realms ruled by Muslim nawabs, nizams, and begums. These diverse polities featured a correspondingly wide array of landscapes and game, ranging from Himalayan foothills where the one-horned Indian rhinoceros still roamed, through the Thar desert with its blackbuck herds and great Indian bustards. To manage such diversity, this book narrows the field to a single category of princes, the Rajputs, while investigating a wider selection of game and environments. The states under consideration were located in India's Desert and Semi-Arid biogeographic zones. They had rulers who were able, if

[43] John M. MacKenzie, *The Empire of Nature: Hunting, Conservation and British Imperialism* (New York: Manchester University Press, 1988), 169–70.

they so chose, to use their connections to access hunting reserves in the Central Highlands biotic province of the Deccan zone and, on occasion, sporting grounds in the Gangetic Plain and Himalayan zones as well.[44]

Comprising a set of clans belonging to the *kshatriya* or warrior caste, the Rajputs' alleged progenitors have been identified by various authorities as everyone from the Persians through men and women of the purest Indo-Aryan stock. The most likely scenario is that they descended not from any single ethnic group, but rather from historical processes of identity formation linked to gradual transitions from tribal to state polities.[45] By adopting the martial and regnal styles of pre-existing kshatriya classes, from which kings ideally derived, and the title "Rajput," meaning sons of kings, newly powerful groups and individuals are likely to have legitimized their claims to sovereignty. Rajput polities were prominent throughout the medieval and early modern periods in North India, particularly in the western and central regions, and they retained much of their fame in the colonial period. As a group, the Rajputs claimed martial origins and enjoyed a reputation as avid sportsmen.

Before the advent of British colonialism in Rajputana in the early nineteenth century, the various Rajput lineages had already developed or begun developing detailed oral traditions and literatures to explain and justify their unique regional identities, local rivalries, and political fortunes. After the establishment of treaties between the East India Company and the states in 1818, British orientalists and Rajputs together refined, adapted, and canonized these identities. Most notable in this process was the collaborative effort of the Company's first

[44] On biogeographic zones and biotic provinces, see W. Alan Rodgers, Hemendra S. Panwar, and Vinod B. Mathur, *Wildlife Protected Area Network in India: A Review, Executive Summary* (Dehra Dun: Wildlife Institute of India, *c.* 2002).

[45] B.D. Chattopadhyaya, "The Emergence of the Rajputs as a Historical Process in Early Medieval Rajasthan," in *The Idea of Rajasthan: Explorations in Regional Identity*, ed. Karine Schomer, Joan L. Erdman, Deryck O. Lodrick, and Lloyd I. Rudolph, vol. 2 (New Delhi: Manohar; American Institute of Indian Studies, 1994), 162.

agent in Rajputana, James Tod, and his Jain assistant Gyanchandra, who maintained close connections with Mewar State. Tod and Gyanchandra together amassed and interpreted the vast collection of inscriptions, legends, and other documentation—much of it with a distinct Mewari slant—that formed the basis of Tod's massive two-volume *Annals and Antiquities of Rajasthan, or the Central and Western Rajput States* (1829–32).

Rajput identities were embedded in ancestral lands, called *bhum*, and claims on various land rights, including the rights to hunt, levy taxes, and command forced labor or *begar*.[46] Nevertheless, as late as the eighteenth century, "Rajput kingdoms had not achieved absolute territorial integrity," even though they "had begun to emphasize their ancient bonds with the lands they ruled" by the 1500s.[47] The fact that the colonial project begun by Tod went far beyond merely writing about the Rajputs to actually reorganizing their internal and external boundaries is, therefore, extremely pertinent to the ongoing processes of identity formation in the nineteenth-century central and western Rajput states. It is clear that Tod's "romantic premises" found fertile ground as he continued the work, already well underway in these states, of "linking the identity of the Rajputs as a 'nation,' to an indissoluble bond with their declared territories."[48]

The weight of British popular opinion in colonial India would swing against the Rajputs by the late nineteenth century, judging them more irresponsible than daring and more unsteady than passionate. But the princes themselves clung to the early-nineteenth-century vision of Tod's *Annals*, reading in it their ancestors' own ideals and flattering self-valuations, filtered through Gyanchandra's research and reportage and validated by Tod's authoritative voice. Positive stereotypes here described the Rajputs as natural sportsmen, chivalrous warriors, instinctive horsemen, generous hosts, honorable rulers, loyal liegemen, and fierce independents with an innate consciousness of and respect for lineage and tradition. Rajput princes

[46] Kasturi, *Embattled Identities*, 7.

[47] Ramya Sreenivasan, *The Many Lives of a Rajput Queen: Heroic Pasts in India, c. 1500–1900* (Seattle: University of Washington Press, 2007), 134.

[48] Ibid.

naturally agreed with these stereotypes and other qualities they judged attractive or useful, affirming them through their hunting practices and interactions with game animals and sporting landscapes.

Evidence from several western and central Rajput states underpins the arguments and chapters that follow, but three dominate the narrative. These are Mewar in semi-arid southern Rajputana under Maharana Fateh Singh, Orchha in semi-arid Bundelkhand in Central India under Maharaja Pratap Singh, and Bikaner in northern Rajputana's Thar desert under Maharaja Ganga Singh.[49] Similar political challenges, lineage histories, and social concerns united these polities and princes, but the relative importance and particular associations of these issues with shikar varied between realms. In fact, the Mewar, Orchha, and Bikaner states together present a startling show of diversity as a representative cross-section of the Rajput states. Not one looked much like the next in its hunting environments, wildlife, size, or regional status. Fateh Singh, Pratap Singh, and Ganga Singh likewise had their own political concerns and social ambitions, and they adopted strikingly different tactics when dealing with their peers and the British paramountcy.

Underlying consistencies between princely states resulted from parallels in their cultural, historical, political, and geographical settings, and from similarities their rulers shared in ancestry, status, and personality. Likewise, differences between Mewar, Orchha, and Bikaner grew out of contrasts in these same fields. This amalgam of diversity and equivalence suggests that Rajput identity in the colonial period allowed for significant local variation. It is probable that overlaps relied as well on these rulers' shared status as elites, on their similar rights and privileges over land, and comparable experiences of subordination under the British. Besides their Rajput identities, these rulers reigned during the high imperial period, *circa* 1870 to 1930.

Stories of pigsticking or spearing wild boar from horseback in Mewar's variegated grasslands, wildfowling over man-made lakes in

---

[49] Rodgers, *et al.*, *Wildlife Protected Area*, Figs. 3–4. Mewar was also known as Udaipur. I use Mewar to avoid confusion with Udaipur city.

Bikaner, and tiger poaching beyond Orchha's borders in the British Indian jungles of greater Bundelkhand make their appearance in these pages, as do illustrations from Dungarpur, Rewah, and other central and western Rajput states. Landscape-specific hunting experiences like these were shared widely amongst the ranks of elite Indian rulers. All sporting princes sought out the hunting landscapes they considered most conducive to their particular needs. If the shikargahs available in their own states fell short of their requirements, rulers accessed more suitable grounds elsewhere. In addition, they endeavored to improve landscapes in their own territories by building up state shooting infrastructure, as well as by controlling the lives of local flora and fauna, and the activities of their subjects.

Born the youngest son of the head of the Shivrati branch of the royal line in 1849, Fateh Singh (r. 1884–1930) became the adoptive heir to the throne of Mewar at the age of 35. Like his predecessors since the mid-seventeenth century, Maharana Fateh Singh claimed preeminent status for his state and lineage on the all-India stage.[50] As Sisodia Rajputs, the rulers of Mewar had long believed their origins could be traced "back thousands of years to the ancient race of warriors born of the sun, the surya-vamsha or solar clan, through a direct line of descent from the eldest son of the great god-king Rama."[51] Fateh Singh and his predecessors found additional reason for pride in their political and military history. They celebrated their ancestors' heroic efforts to resist Mughal domination at Chittor in 1568, at the Battle of Haldighati in 1576, and throughout the length and breadth of the Aravalli hills in the late sixteenth and early seventeenth centuries. Even though Fateh Singh's ancestor Rana Amar Singh I (r. 1597–1620) ultimately surrendered to the Mughal emperor Jahangir in 1615, the Sisodias insisted that Mewar and its rulers maintained a level of independence and dignity unmatched by any other Rajput state.

[50] Cynthia Talbot, "The Mewar Court's Construction of History," *Kingdom of the Sun: Indian Court and Village Art from the Princely State of Mewar,* ed. Joanna Gottfried Williams (San Francisco: Asian Art Museum, Chong-Moon Lee Center for Asian Art and Culture, 2007), 15.

[51] Ibid., 15–16.

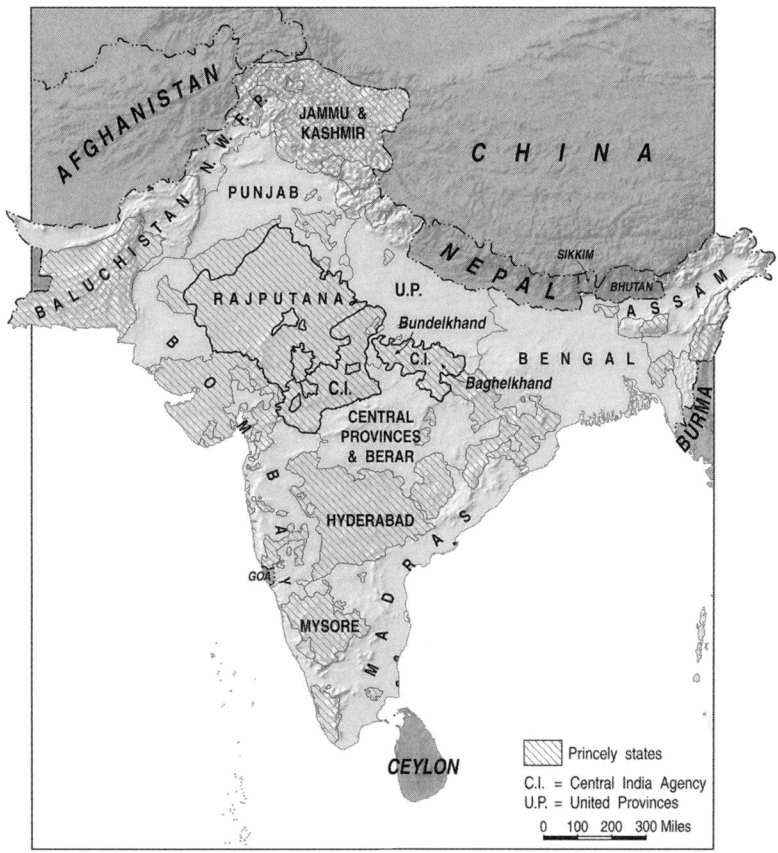

Map 1: Princely and British India

Consistent with this deep-seated pride in his Sisodia ancestry and state history, Fateh Singh shunned activities and situations that he believed might compromise Mewar's reputation or his personal dignity. Most famously he avoided participating in the 1903 and 1911 Delhi durbars, held to celebrate the coronations of the King-Emperors Edward VII and George V, because he objected to his placement below the rulers of Hyderabad, Mysore, Kashmir, and Baroda in the planned processions and official rankings.[52] Often interpreted as an

---

[52] G.N. Sharma, "Life and Achievements of H.H. Maharana Fateh Singhji (1884–1930 A.D.)," in Sharma, ed., *Haqiqat Bahida*, 1:20–1.

effort to keep outside influences at bay, Fateh Singh's policies also delayed the introduction of railways and other "progressive" works in his state. Many have described Fateh Singh as pious, intelligent, deliberative, proud, hospitable—the quintessential Rajput.[53] On the other hand, many British officials considered him difficult, out of touch, uneducated, excessively conservative, and potentially disloyal. In 1921, the Government of India forced him to abdicate most of his sovereign powers—although not his title—in favor of his son Bhupal Singh.

Mewar's territories in southern Rajputana were defined on the one hand by welcoming lakes and verdant trees, and on the other by protective hills and thorny brush. The major lakes were man-made and expansive, including Jaisamand, Rajsamand, and Udai Sagar in the countryside, and Lake Pichola, Sarup Sagar, and Fateh Sagar in Udaipur city. In 1908, approximately one-third of the state was forested. Vegetation ranged from lofty mango, mahua, and pipal trees through scrub and undergrowth best suited to arid regions, like acacias and cactus-like *thuhars*. Numerous branches and isolated peaks of the Aravallis dotted the state, while the main range delineated Mewar's western border, beyond which the inhospitable desert plains of Jodhpur State began: a landscape poetically termed Marwar or "the region of death."[54]

A wide selection of game flourished in Mewar's variegated environment. The 1908 *Imperial Gazetteer of India* reported that

> antelope and "ravine deer" [*Gazella bennettii*] abound in the open country and in the cold season the numerous tanks are usually thronged with wild-fowl. Leopards and wild hog are common in and near the hills. Tigers, bears, and *sambar* (*Cervus unicolor*) are found in the Aravallis from Kumbhalgarh to Kotra, in the Chhoti Sadri district in the south-east, and

---

[53] For examples, see Sharma, "Life and Achievements," 1:12–13; Brian Masters, *Maharana: The Story of the Rulers of Udaipur* (Ahmedabad: Mapin Publishing Pvt., Ltd., 1990), 21–2.

[54] James Tod, *Annals and Antiquities of Rajasthan, or the Central and Western Rajput States of India*, ed. William Crooke, vol. 1 (1829–32; New York: Humphrey Milford, 1920), 19.

in the Bhainsrorgarh and Bijolia estates in the east. *Chital* (*Cervus axis*) confine themselves to the vicinity of the Jakam river.[55]

Nilgai (*Boselaphus tragocamelus*) lived in the state too, along with the "usual small game," including hare and the grey partridge.[56] Mewar's natural riches enabled the maharana, who was an enthusiastic and discriminating sportsman, to shoot as he pleased.

Maharaja Pratap Singh of Orchha (r. 1874–1930) enjoyed far less flexibility when it came to shikar. There were, however, significant parallels between the princes of Orchha and Mewar. Both were born around 1850 and grew up with little exposure to the English tutors and college education that became common amongst the princely elite from the 1870s.[57] Save for the first decade of Pratap Singh's reign, their tenures on the throne exactly overlapped. Like Mewar, Orchha's ruling lineage hailed from the *surya-vamsha* clan of Rajputs. Whereas Mewar's Sisodias claimed direct descent from Rama's elder son Lava, the Bundelas said they had issued from the god-king's younger son Kusa, and thence by way of Kusa's distant descendant, the younger son of Raja Virabhadra of Benares.[58] In accordance with their lesser derivation, Orchha's ruling house occupied a distinctly lower hierarchical status. Although this line of Bundela Rajputs was well known, it was primarily of regional note as "the parent ruling house from which the other Bundela kingdoms subsequently separated."[59] Pratap Singh was nevertheless "very proud of his descent" and small kingdom.[60]

Orchha's history featured numerous fine examples of honor and

[55] *Imperial Gazetteer of India*, vol. 24 (Oxford: Clarendon Press, 1908), 87.

[56] K.D. Erskine, *A Gazetteer of the Udaipur State, with a Chapter on the Bhils and Some Statistical Tables* (Ajmer: Scottish Mission Industries, Co., Ltd., 1908), 11.

[57] Ramusack, *Indian Princes*, 110–11.

[58] Ravindra K. Jain, *Between History and Legend: Status and Power in Bundelkhand* (New Delhi: Orient Longman Private Limited, 2002), 9–10.

[59] Ibid., 5.

[60] F.G. Beville (PA-Bundelkhand), to V. Gabriel, October 11, 1902, GOI, BA, 42 of 1902, NAI.

regional influence, tempered by some uncomfortable episodes. Several ancestors had rebelled against expanding Mughal control; others had opted to serve the emperors "much to their own advantage," and not always with unimpeachable integrity.[61] Most jarring was Raja Bir Singh Deo's 1602 murder of the famed Abu al-Fazl, carried out at the behest of Prince Salim, who later became the emperor Jahangir. For many years Orchha as a distinct polity even lapsed into non-existence. In the eighteenth century, the remaining Bundela Rajputs ceded great swathes of territory to the Marathas, although their descendants would claim their forebears technically had never submitted to the Peshwa.[62] According to the *Imperial Gazetteer of India*, Pratap Singh's realm in fact enjoyed "no independent existence till comparatively modern times, and its early history is that of British Bundelkhand."[63] The Bundelas remembered things differently. When the ruler of Orchha entered into a subordinate alliance with the British in 1812, he "remarked that never before had his family acknowledged another Power as supreme."[64]

If Orchha's past was problematic, the present was not entirely comfortable either. There were significant discrepancies between what the realm had been at its height and the realities in Pratap Singh's day, when the state's territorial extent and overall importance were vastly reduced from their sixteenth-century apogee. Although Orchha had suffered a sporadically interrupted political existence, the royal line had been dominant in the Bundelkhand region for hundreds of years. The princes of nearly every Bundelkhand state in colonial times traced their ancestry back to the Orchha line. These glaring divergences between Orchha State's debased political situation and the family's elevated royal reputation gave Pratap Singh ample reason for concern.

[61] *Imperial Gazetteer*, 19:243.

[62] Sorabji Jehangir, *Princes and Chiefs of India, a Collection of Biographies, with Portraits of the Indian Princes and Chiefs and Brief Historical Surveys of their Territories*, vol. 1 (London: Waterlow and Sons, Limited, 1903), 1. This is an optimistic interpretation of Chhatrasal's relationship with the Peshwa: see *Imperial Gazetteer*, 9:71 and 14:148.

[63] Ibid., 19:242.

[64] Jehangir, *Princes and Chiefs*, 1.

Although he shared a reputation for excessive conservatism with Mewar's maharana, Pratap Singh was the better ruler in British eyes. It is difficult to say if this reflected actual administrative achievements on the maharaja's part, or if British appreciation resulted from his somewhat greater efforts to maintain good relations with them. For example, whereas Fateh Singh resisted the railways as long as possible, Pratap Singh in 1884 readily ceded the small amount of land required for the construction of the Indian Midland Railway.[65] Unlike Mewar's ruler, who considered his lineage at least equal to the House of Windsor and superior to all other Englishmen and elite Indians, Pratap Singh accepted his assigned place in imperial processions and refrained from exalting himself or his state so obviously. On the other hand, he shared Fateh Singh's reluctance towards disclosing state administrative and financial details.[66] Officials judged, however, that Orchha was "well-ruled on old fashioned principles" and that some of its institutions were as good as could be found in adjoining British districts.[67]

Visibility certainly mattered, too. Mewar was a frequent destination for British VIPs. Its high profile and exalted rank ensured that Fateh Singh's smallest insubordinations and slightest inadequacies would be noticed sooner rather than later. Orchha's diminutive size and relative unimportance made any failings or quiet dissent on Pratap Singh's part less conspicuous and more forgivable.

In matters of shikar, Pratap Singh's state again was less notable than Fateh Singh's. Orchha had few tigers and jungles inferior even in comparison with some of its Bundelkhandi neighbors. While the entire region reportedly had been heavily forested at least through the seventeenth century, Orchha by 1900 could boast only of some "scanty scrub jungle and low trees." Most of the realm afforded "no cover for large animals," and big game like tigers were "scarcely ever met with."[68] Some respectable but lesser game was fairly common,

[65] *Imperial Gazetteer*, 19:244.
[66] Ibid., 19:247.
[67] Beville, to Gabriel, October 11, 1902, GOI, BA, 42 of 1902, NAI.
[68] Charles Eckford Luard, *Gazetteer of India Eastern States (Bundelkhand)* (Bhopal: Gazetteers Department, Government of India, 1995), 1 and 3.

including blackbuck, chinkara gazelle, and the ubiquitous leopard. Orchha was middling in its landscape as well, lacking the distinction of Mewar's rugged hills. Riverine islands along the course of the Betwa occasionally offered some satisfactory tiger shooting, but Pratap Singh's grounds on the whole were undistinguished and best known for small game. In particular, some of the state's man-made lakes were suitable for wildfowling, including Bir Sagar and the tanks at Jatara.[69] Because Orchha was deficient in big game, its prince often crossed state borders in pursuit of shikar.

Our third prince, Maharaja Ganga Singh of Bikaner (r. 1887–1943), was born in 1880. A generation or so younger than Pratap Singh and Fateh Singh, his reign nevertheless roughly coincided with those of his elder peers. While the princes of Orchha and Mewar came to their thrones as adults, Ganga Singh became maharaja while still a minor. As a result, British officials involved themselves in Bikaner's administration to an extent not seen in Orchha or Mewar (although Fateh Singh too endured several years of direct interference, both at the beginning and end of his reign). Bikaner was governed by a British-dominated Regency Council appointed by the Government of India, leaving the young prince no independent powers and little influence. In addition, the council appointed tutors for him, sent him to Mayo College, arranged for instruction in riding and shooting, and sanctioned his training with an Indian Army regiment. Even after coming of age in 1898, Ganga Singh had to labor to convince British officials that he was a modern prince capable of governing effectively and independently. His ambitions to regulate British influence and opinions were lifelong obsessions that he expressed in part on the hunting ground.

British officials by and large considered Bikaner a well-governed and progressive state on account of its railroads, financial reforms, and vigorous public works program, all of which the Regency Council claimed partial credit for initiating.[70] Some considered Ganga Singh an appropriate role model for all Indian princes. Others deemed

---

[69] *Imperial Gazetteer*, 19:242.

[70] K.D. Erskine, *The Western Rajputana States Residency and The Bikaner Agency*, vol. 1 (1908; repr., Gurgaon: Vintage Books, 1992), 329.

him insufferable and opinionated, finding particularly distasteful the campaigns that he undertook in the 1920s and 1930s in favor of the states' collective interests and individual rights.[71] Certainly, the maharaja was unusually keen on securing control, but all agreed on his energetic and detail-oriented nature, supreme discipline, and graciousness as a host. He appears to have cared genuinely about his subjects' welfare and the improvement of his state.

Like the princes of Mewar and Orchha, Ganga Singh's lineage was included in the extended surya-vamsha clan. While the royal Sisodias were preeminent on the national stage and the Bundelas claimed regional precedence, the Rathor Rajputs of Bikaner were an offshoot of the ruling family of their somewhat higher-ranking neighbor, Jodhpur. Bikaner was founded by the sixth son of a sixteenth-century king of Jodhpur, but Bikaneris insisted the main line had continued through that sixth son, making their state's lineal branch the senior and Jodhpur's the junior. In subsequent centuries, and especially during the eighteenth century, Ganga Singh's ancestors repeatedly found themselves defending their sovereignty and status against Jodhpur.[72] Relations normalized in the colonial era, but Ganga Singh still felt that Bikaner's rank, honor, and importance were underestimated and underappreciated in comparison with Jodhpur and other Rajput realms.

The problem was not Bikaner's military or political history, which featured "a record of heroic exploits, epic feats of arms, and magnificent gallantry."[73] Rather, it was the way history had been recorded and interpreted by outsiders. Tod never visited Bikaner and allegedly relied on biased Jodhpuri sources when writing about the state. His account was distorted by Mewari biases too, which favored lineages like the Sisodias that had remained aloof from the Mughals. Ganga Singh maintained that the Rathor Rajputs of Bikaner had not been lax in repelling Mughal invasions nor in standing against the unreasonable

---

[71] Ian Copland, *The Princes of India in the Endgame of Empire, 1917–1947* (New Delhi: Cambridge University Press, 1999), 49.

[72] *Imperial Gazetteer*, 8:205–6.

[73] *Four Decades of Progress in Bikaner* (Bikaner: Government Press, 1937), 1.

demands of controversial emperors like Aurangzeb. At the same time, he took pride in the fact that his ancestors had served several emperors with loyalty and distinction, and that his immediate predecessors had been faithful to their 1818 treaty with the East India Company, supporting the British during the Rebellion of 1857.

There was also Bikaner's harsh and seemingly inferior landscape to contend with. Judged by its vast area of 23,331 square miles, Bikaner came out ahead of Mewar with its 12,691 square miles and Orchha with its mere 2080 square miles. But Mewar enjoyed a balanced landscape of hills and plains carpeted in a rich variety of vegetation. Even Orchha occupied a fairly fertile and partially forested plain bounded by rivers. Located in the extreme northwestern corner of Rajputana, the desert state of Bikaner in contrast was "dreary and desolate in the extreme."[74] It was covered in sand, had no proper forests, and suffered from poor rainfall. Its rivers were scanty and seasonal at best. Yet, when sufficient water was available, there were good prospects for animal husbandry, limited agriculture, and wildfowling. As a result, Ganga Singh focused his personal efforts and government expenditure on expanding and improving Bikaner's irrigation facilities, both in the arable northern marches and in the south near the man-made Gajner lake and wildfowling grounds.

Mewar abounded in royal sport and Orchha had some desirable game, but Bikaner was distinguished as a land without tigers. There was no dangerous game (shorthand for big cats) in the state at all. Among the state's "not very varied" wildlife around the turn of the century,

> the ravine deer (*chinkara*) is fairly common everywhere, and hyenas and wolves are not altogether rare; there are fine herds of blackbuck in the north, where, as also in the eastern districts, the *nilgai* ... is sometimes met with. Wild hogs are plentiful ... Among small game may be mentioned the hare; the partridge (of the grey variety only); the florican (rare and practically confined to the north); the great Indian bustard or *gurahn* (*Eupodobara Macqueeni*); wild duck and teal (on the tanks and marshes in the winter); and several species of sand-grouse.[75]

[74] *Imperial Gazetteer*, 8:202, 19:241, 24:85, and 8:203.
[75] Erskine, *Western Rajputana*, 311–12.

What Bikaner lacked in variety, it made up for in the quality and volume of select species. The local blackbuck and chinkara achieved record sizes, and excellent stocks of wildfowl made Ganga Singh's annual sandgrouse and duck shoots world famous. Like his peers in Orchha and Mewar, Ganga Singh was an enthusiastic sportsman. He made the most of his state's mixed shooting and actively courted opportunities to pursue big game in other realms.

Indian princes usually maintained a special office or department devoted to shikar called a *shikarkhana*. Officers attached to state shikarkhanas made all the necessary arrangements for royal sport. They maintained hunting grounds, monitored game populations, oversaw the distribution of grain to support wild game, enforced shooting regulations, and reported violations. When a prince or state guest went hunting, shikar officers procured (or coerced) the assistance of local residents, arranged for baiting and tracking, and conducted the beat in accordance with orders and as suggested by the lay of the land. Shikarkhana records detailing the day-to-day activities of state huntsmen are unevenly informative and sporadically available. Shikaris and their work were most important, and most thoroughly documented, when extraordinary events interrupted their routines, as when VIPs visited or major problems surfaced.

Sporting princes took a keen interest in shikarkhana operations. Fateh Singh of Mewar and Pratap Singh of Orchha apparently gave the bulk of their directions verbally, although Mewari records do document basic shikargah maintenance and policies relating to wildlife in the state. Ganga Singh of Bikaner, on the other hand, preferred to issue written notices. He was a prolific composer of detailed letters, orders, and programs relating to his shooting entertainments and planned hunting ground improvements. He accented his compositions with frequent underlinings and crammed his notes with exhaustive specifications governing every aspect of his plans.[76]

---

[76] A typical memorandum: "we must <u>not</u> have <u>wasps</u> at Gajner when the Viceroy goes there. They are <u>always</u> bad early in November. Please see to this and have all <u>Chhattas</u> etc. burnt at once and keep on seeing to this." Ganga Singh, to K. Bhairun Singh, [Oct. or Nov. 1908?], BMK, s. no. 138, file 926-I of 1906–10, RSA.

Princely hunting made its mark in government records produced outside the state shikarkhanas as well. In Mewar, Fateh Singh's administrative officials recorded the maharana's daily activities in the *haqiqat bahida* registers, which provide a detailed picture of the maharana's yearly hunting rounds, shikargah improvements, and shooting successes. While most entries convey little more than the basic triad of place, date, and species killed, others are minutely detailed, even recording what variety of tree supported the maharana's shooting platform.

Many sportsmen maintained game diaries, including Ganga Singh of Bikaner and his eldest son Sadul Singh. Written as personal records for limited circulation among friends, the big game diaries of these two men detail the dates, locations, and quarry of their shooting excursions.[77] They comment on the shikar practices and infrastructure observed in the princely states that they visited in pursuit of big game. Every animal that Ganga Singh killed between July 21, 1920 and July 20, 1942 is listed in his separate general shooting diary, along with a brief summary of yearly bags prior to 1920. When he judged an animal or a day's shooting exceptional, he added a brief note or, less frequently, a detailed memorandum. Besides his own successes, Ganga Singh occasionally recorded the content and quality of the bags obtained by his shooting companions, including his sons, peers, and European guests.

Among the most illuminating sources for Mewar are the memoirs of Dhaibhai Tulsinath Singh Tanwar, the state shikari responsible for recording the tale of the leopard in the garden. Born in 1903 and attached to Fateh Singh's shikar department from the tender age of 5, Tanwar accompanied the prince on innumerable shooting expeditions throughout the state, beginning in the 1910s. The maharana personally supervised his education in riding, shooting, and sword fighting. Tanwar's two published memoirs, *Shikari aur Shikar* (1956) and *Samsmaran: Maharana Fateh Singhji, Maharana Bhupal Singhji, Maharana Bhagvat Singhji Mewar* (1982), provide a detailed record of the Mewar court's sporting culture.[78]

[77] Ganga Singh, *Extracts from His Highness' Diary* (Bikaner, n.d.), 1.
[78] *Shikari aur Shikar* is Tanwar's Hindi adaptation of his Rajasthani diary.

Perhaps the most striking records of sport from Mewar are the miniature paintings of historical hunts produced by court artists for the maharanas. Idealized representations of royal shooting experiences, these paintings illustrate the court's understanding of game animals and hunting landscapes. Often annotated with narrative accounts of the specific episodes they recorded, these miniatures corroborate and add detail to the landscape visions and shooting values described in other sources. In addition to the large corpus of published miniatures, there are extensive and previously unstudied wall paintings of shikar inside the Nahar Odi shooting box, just south of Lake Pichola.[79]

The first three chapters of this book examine topics exemplified by Orchha, Mewar, and Bikaner states with the goal of highlighting the unique concerns and approaches of their rulers and the specific environments—natural, political, and historical—that characterized each realm. Taken collectively, these chapters reveal significant similarities and telling differences in the ways Rajput princes evaluated game and shooting grounds, and how each ruler expected to profit from his state's particular assets or compensate for its perceived disadvantages. "Princely Sport and Good Tiger Grounds" examines conditions in Orchha to reveal what made princely hunting unique in ideals, methods, and understandings of the most desirable qualities

---

Tanwar served Fateh Singh, Bhupal Singh, and their post-colonial successors. He aimed to publicize glorious episodes from their sporting lives and counter-complaints against royal hunting and its alleged legacies. His book questions the 1921 reduction of Fateh Singh's powers, elevates Mewar above rivals, and educates readers in Mewari history and heroism. Post-1947 developments shaped *Samsmaran*. In 1956, Tanwar trusted his audience to have fairly positive views on his subject matter. With the abolition of privy purses and anti-hunting sentiment in the 1970s, Tanwar assumed the worst. He defends against charges of environmental mismanagement: ibid. 75, 82, and 83, and rejects allegations that sport hurt state subjects: ibid. 51, 73–4, and 88–9.

[79] Andrew Topsfield, personal communication, January 15, 2009.

of specific grounds and prey. "Exceptional Game in Powerful Places" uses examples from Mewar to illustrate the links between a state's coveted reputation of superiority and the peculiar benefits of local wildlife and sporting landscapes. "Controlling Environments for Progressive Sport" describes conditions in Bikaner to explore the strategies princes could pursue to physically alter or rhetorically exalt a state's shooting to compensate for perceived environmental deficiencies.

The final two chapters explore themes transcending differences in landscape, game, and status. Adopting a more comparative approach, they draw on evidence from Mewar, Orchha, Bikaner, and other Rajput territories and subordinate noble estates. This produces a broader perspective on the place of shikar and shikargahs in elite Rajput identity, and a better sense of the general difficulties associated with princely sporting practices and policies in the late colonial context. "Martial Pasts and Combative Presents" discusses how princes used the hunt to establish meaningful links with historic battlefields and the remembered heroics of their ancestors. "Threatened Kingdoms of Dwindling Beasts" details the common urge towards referencing, reinventing, and reinstating desirable aspects of the better political and environmental conditions that these rulers imagined their predecessors had enjoyed. By tracing the connections princes saw between environmental degradation in their states and their progressive loss of political power, this chapter exposes parallels between princely hunting and the sport as practiced by their most intimate rivals, the state nobles.

2

Princely Sport and
Good Tiger Grounds

Over the summer months in the early years of the twentieth century, tigers used to cross the dried-up channels of the Betwa river in Central India to visit Karkigarh island. There they roamed along boulder-strewn shorelines, through intermittently cultivated flats, scrub jungle, and isolated stands of teak that lightly forested the interior. Karkigarh's itinerant tigers shared their 800-acre island habitat with wild boar, sambar, chital, leopard, and a variety of smaller beasts and birds. Peasant cultivators came here seasonally to plant and tend their crops and, less frequently, foresters to harvest the valuable teak. From time to time, princely shooting parties visited to pursue and kill Karkigarh's tigers and any other game they could find.

Karkigarh was a "first class" preserved forest and royal shikargah in Orchha State through the early 1900s. Today it is largely submerged beneath the dammed-up waters of the Betwa river. The negotiations that effected Karkigarh's dramatic transformation from being one of Maharaja Pratap Singh's most valued shooting preserves to the "wretched island" of a series of government officials took place in Orchha State and the neighboring region of British Bundelkhand between 1904 and 1916.[1] Karkigarh's metamorphosis proceeded

---

[1] Collector of Jhansi, to PA-Bundelkhand, October 17, 1907, GOI, CI, 129-A of 1905–8, NAI.

in step with the ascendancy of colonial definitions of good tiger grounds and "true" sportsmanship over the maharaja's own princely practices, needs, and ideals. Beyond its material impact on the local environment, the Karkigarh affair was an ideological debate between a Rajput prince and representatives of the government of British India over what the landscape and its tigers meant, and how they figured in administrative concerns and sovereign identities.

For Pratap Singh of Orchha and his princely peers, good tiger grounds were more than plots of land harboring suitable prey that they could successfully track and bag. They were equally places governed by shooting rules and regulations that neither restricted nor subverted princely sovereignty, but which instead supported their desired positions within a variety of social and political hierarchies inside their own states and in relation to other realms and British India. The princes did not require, nor did they consider it necessary to create, level playing fields for their fellow sportsmen and quarry. When it came to other guns, princes like the Maharaja of Orchha rejected the relatively democratic ideals of true sportsmanship as fundamentally at odds with their own social and political interests. As for royal prey, tigers and Rajputs were already sufficiently similar in their fierce abilities to render additional leveling unnecessary.

It was in 1905 that the Public Works Department (PWD) of the government of the United Provinces first informed Maharaja Pratap Singh that Karkigarh, one of his best tiger grounds and an isolated pocket of state territory situated just inside the British district of Jhansi, was slated to be submerged in favor of an irrigation scheme. The work was already well underway: a state of affairs resulting from a flawed reading of a map some years before, which had led government surveyors to believe Karkigarh was a British possession. The prince's island would be submerged soon—shooting grounds and some 800 acres of revenue-producing land alike—regardless of any objections Pratap Singh could possibly raise.

Good tiger grounds were scarce in Orchha State. It was, in fact, debatable if any existed at all. But, as recently as 1903, the maharaja had bagged two tigers on Karkigarh over the course of three days. This was perhaps the only place in the state where these animals could be found. If the maharaja's meager resources became even more inadequate through Karkigarh's submergence, the state itself risked drowning in ignominy. Karkigarh's loss would be incontrovertible evidence of Orchha's subordination to British power and the vagaries of the PWD. It would also force the maharaja to become a supplicant, petitioning outsiders to pursue almost every tiger he bagged.

Even with Karkigarh, circumstances already compelled the prince to go beyond Orchha's borders and into neighboring realms to find many of the shooting opportunities he required to sustain himself and his state. And so, in 1905, Pratap Singh went on the offensive, campaigning for the right to extend his sport into British territory and receive due compensation for Karkigarh. Over the course of a decade, he negotiated for the reparations he deemed consistent with his status as the premier Bundela Rajput chief, scorning a cash settlement and demanding not only an equitable exchange of land for Karkigarh but a replacement tiger jungle.

Shikargahs like Karkigarh were necessary components of a princely landscape. Any forced reduction in their number or area by rival powers damaged a king's sovereignty in ways not dissimilar to that caused by the loss of other lands. Land of *any* kind was relatively scarce in a small state like Orchha, so tiger grounds were even less common and proportionately more valuable. Writing of his island to the British political agent for Bundelkhand in 1906, the maharaja explained that "the parting [with] of pieces of land one after another for the consideration of money only will certainly lower my reputation in the eyes of my successors."[2] Money was beside the point. Pratap Singh assessed Karkigarh above and beyond its monetary value and other assets, and viewed British offers of cash compensation as something of an insult.

As the years advanced, the maharaja sent proposal after proposal to the Bundelkhand Agency Office, putting forward a string of tiger jungles, first in the Central Provinces and then in the United Provinces, as more or less acceptable replacements for his island. If

[2] Pratap Singh, to PA-Bundelkhand, December 19, 1906, GOI, CI, 129-A of 1905–8, NAI.

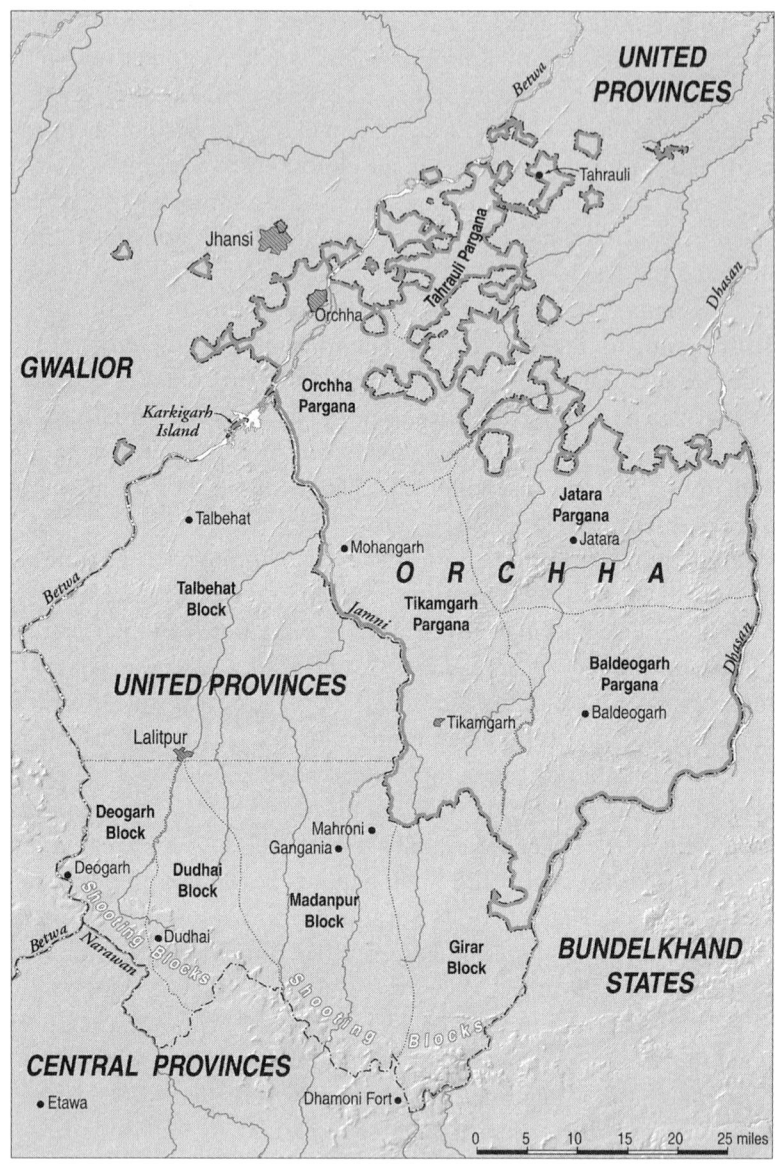

Map 2: Princely and British Bundelkhand

the British would not grant him ownership of the land itself, he hinted at his willingness to consider a perpetual lease on some good hunting blocks that his successors could inherit or, as a last resort, guaranteed yearly shooting rights and special privileges for himself and his heirs in British territory. A succession of political agents dutifully forwarded his requests to their superiors. Then they dutifully forwarded their superiors' responses to the maharaja: a series of firm refusals, polite regrets, and ruminations on the virtues of cash settlements. Caught without a reliable hunting ground in the meantime, Pratap Singh began applying for temporary licenses to shoot in those very same British jungles, seeking to fulfill his ongoing need to bag tigers in what he judged to be good tiger grounds.

Indian rulers had been losing ground, quite literally, ever since the establishment of British power in the subcontinent. While some princely houses had forfeited portions of their holdings through battles and treaties in the eighteenth and early-nineteenth centuries, other lineages had failed to produce heirs, resulting in the much resented annexure of their states through the controversial Doctrine of Lapse.[3] Even after the reassurances offered in Queen Victoria's 1858 Proclamation to the Princes, Chiefs, and the People of India— that "We desire no extension of our present territorial possessions" and "We shall respect the rights, dignity and honour of native princes as our own"—the government still could and did "request" princes to cede territory for military cantonments and, not infrequently, tracts of land like Karkigarh for PWD projects designed to benefit British India.[4]

Pratap Singh's preference for territorial exchange was a typical princely reaction in Bundelkhand, even when shooting grounds were not at stake. Just as the Karkigarh affair was drawing to a close in 1916, the British were breaking ground on a new irrigation project requiring territorial concessions from the Rajput princes of Chhatarpur, Panna, and Charkhari. All three rulers demanded compensation

---

[3] The GOI began granting the right of adoption only from the 1860s.

[4] *Speeches and Documents on Indian Policy, 1750–1921*, ed. A. Berriedale Keith, vol. 1 (New York: Humphrey Milford, 1922), 383.

in land rather than cash. The relatively small sizes of their states magnified their collective desire for exchanges: Charkhari was only 745 sq. mi., Chhatarpur had 1118 sq. mi., and Panna claimed 2492 sq. mi. The Maharaja of Orchha likewise felt that his state, which covered only 2080 sq. mi., had no land to spare. Indeed, writing to the political agent in 1906, Pratap Singh had declared himself "anxious to preserve what little is mine."[5]

Wealth ultimately came from the land, so territorial reduction held serious ramifications for the princes, but revenue was not the only consideration. Princes derived different benefits from varying categories of land. A mixture of cultivated and urbanized zones along with managed wilderness areas, like enclosed hunting grounds, provided spaces both controlled enough and sufficiently dangerous to highlight a chief's legitimacy and power from multiple perspectives. Desiccated terrain and jaundiced forests devoid of game reflected poorly on princes seeking to confirm their status in a culture where the righteousness of kings guaranteed the health and prosperity of the landscape.[6] While fertile and rainfed agricultural fields were the primary markers of sovereign success, other landscapes, especially hunting grounds, signified as well.

Mystical qualities reached their highest concentration in uncultivated areas. In addition to housing tigers, dense forests and isolated wildernesses contained religious shrines, sages of repute, and sites of historic and legendary importance.[7] Together, these features made jungles potent places, alternately hazardous and advantageous to those who entered. A worthy king would naturally withstand the physical and spiritual dangers of the wilderness; lesser individuals just as surely would succumb.[8]

---

[5] P. Singh, to PA-Bundelkhand, December 19, 1906, GOI, CI, 129-A of 1905–8, NAI.

[6] Gold and Gujar, *In the Time of Trees and Sorrows*, 246 and 253.

[7] One of Fateh Singh's hunting grounds hosted a colony of sages: see Tanwar, *Samsmaran*, 71. Maharana Sangram Singh too visited sages while hunting: see Andrew Topsfield, *Court Painting at Udaipur: Art Under the Patronage of the Maharanas of Mewar* (Zurich: Artibus Asiae Publishers and Museum Rietberg Zurich, 2001), Fig. 154a.

[8] Waghorne, *Raja's Magic Clothes*, 181.

Having entered the forest, a legitimate sovereign could commune with tigers and reap benefits for himself and his realm. Princes constituted the link between the cultivated and the wild, confidently moving back and forth between these landscapes and cyclically restoring their precarious balance.[9] Extreme experiences, like the legendary forest exile of the god-king Rama, set the standard, but lesser austerities and sporting excursions too had their advantages. Uneventful walks in the woods are not likely to have sufficed to affect the necessary transfers.

While the entry of kings into the forest and their activities there were often violent and always associated with power, the relationship was not fundamentally adversarial. Writing of the southern state of Pudukkottai during colonial times, Waghorne has critiqued the "language of 'conquest' and 'ordering' of the forest" that tends to dominate discussions of princely interactions with "wild people," wild animals, and wilderness areas.[10] She perceptively argues that to use such language "is to see the forest from outside in. But the Pudukkottai rajas and many other forest lords like them instead looked at the forest from the inside out."[11] Kings were not separate from the jungle. Instead, their "very bodies arose from the forest" and they were "kissing-cousins" with its inhabitants.[12] The testimony of Rajput shikar confirms the view that it is more appropriate to speak of princely management, or perhaps even hierarchical partnership, and maintenance of the forest. Pushing beyond Waghorne, it is apparent too that kings were just as closely related to wild animals as they were to "wild people."

Perhaps following Abu al-Fazl's lead, modern princes like Pratap Singh insisted that the benefits of their forest sojourns and hunting reserves extended well beyond themselves. Superior shooting grounds promoted the common good, improving the happiness of subjects and the prosperity of states. Properly maintained wildernesses with

---

[9] Ibid.; Nancy E. Falk, "Wilderness and Kingship in Ancient South Asia," *History of Religions* 13, 1 (August 1973): 1.

[10] Waghorne, *Raja's Magic Clothes*, 184.

[11] Ibid., 185.

[12] Ibid., 184.

abundant stocks of game, grass, timber, and other forest produce provided additional sources of income and constituted effective buffers against famine. They offered proof that a ruler's authority and protective power extended into even the remotest of regions. Anything less provided evidence of a ruler's immorality, weakness, and mismanagement.

Just as landscapes intimated a sovereign's achievements, or betrayed his failures, so too did the number, condition, and behavior of wild animals living in those places. While tigers stereotypically behaved themselves in the green expanses produced by righteous kings, they became treacherous in the arid wastes created by unqualified or immoral regimes. Environmental degradation is supposed to have naturally resulted in a heightened incidence of man-eaters and cattle-killers. Tigers do, in fact, trouble people most during periods of drought.[13] They prey on a limited set of suitably large ungulates, including wild boar, chital, and sambar, as well as domestic cattle and buffalo.[14] While the evidence indicates their preference for wild species, the most important factor in tiger predation is availability. During droughts, the number of livestock found in tiger habitats increases as conditions force herds to range farther in search of fodder and water. Any downward shift in a tiger's wild prey base, such as one occasioned by a prolonged drought, can result in a higher reliance on livestock kills and more conflicts with humans, whose presence in the jungle correlates with that of their animals.[15] Agricultural expansion in the nineteenth and early-twentieth centuries

[13] Rosie Woodroffe, Simon Thirgood, and Alan Rabinowitz, "The Future of Coexistence: Resolving Human–Wildlife Conflicts in a Changing World," in *People and Wildlife: Conflict or Coexistence?*, ed. Rosie Woodroffe, Simon Thirgood, and Alan Rabinowitz (New York: Cambridge University Press, 2005), 393.

[14] John Seidensticker, "Tigers: Top Carnivores and Controlling Processes in Asian Forests," in *Terrestrial Ecoregions of the Indo-Pacific, a Conservation Assessment*, ed. Eric Wikramanayake, Eric Dinerstein, Colby J. Loucks (Washington, DC: Island Press, 2002), 56–9.

[15] On man-eating and cattle-lifting, see Mahesh Rangarajan, "The 'Raj' and the Natural World: The War Against 'Dangerous Beasts' in Colonial India," *Studies in History* 14 (1998): 282–3.

may have intensified conditions as well by reducing the size of buffer zones between tiger habitats and people, livestock, and crops.

More than that of other wild animals in the colonial period, the presence of tigers indicated a prince's worth as a ruler. Killing tigers demonstrated kingly authority over otherwise invincible beasts, indicating a sovereign's possession of near supernatural powers.[16] The ferocity and legendary supremacy of tigers over other animals were qualities particularly attractive to rulers who aspired to the same sort of ascendancy over their rivals. The practice of associating kings with tigers was well established in the Bundelkhand region. In the *Chhatraprakasha*, an eighteenth-century panegyric written by the Bundelkhandi poet Lal Kavi (b. 1658) for his patron, the Bundela Rajput king and warrior Chhatrasal (1649–1731), powerful sovereigns were as imposing as enraged tigers, their voices matched the roar of tigers, and they were as terrifying as ferocious tigers.[17] Lineage histories maintained by other Rajput houses made similar connections, likening effective kings and impressive warriors to tigers and the subcontinent's other royal felid, the lion.

Any controlled contact with these impressive creatures—whether they were hunted and shot in the wilderness, captured and held in state menageries, stuffed and displayed next to the throne during state festivals, or even dressed and eaten—was held to have a similarly positive impact on rulers who could thereby claim to have assimilated the animals' vitality into their own bodies. Since the classical period, South Asian medical treatises and commentaries had credited the flesh of game with potent healing properties and the capacity to nurture kings into ideal physical form.[18] Tigers were superior to other animals, just as kings were superior to other men, and so their tissue constituted the most appropriate royal remedy. Because tigers were at the top of the food chain they incorporated

[16] Allsen, *The Royal Hunt*, 10.

[17] W.R. Pogson, *A History of the Boondelas* (1828; repr., Delhi: B.R. Publishing Corporation, 1974), 11, 20, 45, 48, 54, 67, and 83.

[18] Francis Zimmermann, *The Jungle and the Aroma of Meats: An Ecological Theme in Hindu Medicine* (Berkeley: University of California Press, 1987), 101–4.

the benefits of every animal they preyed on into their own bodies, making their flesh the supposed panacea for all ailments not curable by the consumption of lesser meat.

While the tiger's special therapeutic connection with kings does not appear to have persisted into the twentieth century, its associations with vitality, masculinity, and healing did. A wide array of salutary applications, including cures for cloudy vision and hemorrhoids, were derived from various parts of a tiger's body and recommended by state residents, including Dhaibhai Tulsinath Singh Tanwar.[19] Ointments made from tiger's fat allegedly cured erectile dysfunction, kebabs made from the male animal's genitalia enhanced masculinity, and the rest of the meat, although difficult to digest, fostered courage.[20] The very presence of tigers in Orchha State suggested the fertility of the countryside. When the maharaja shot tigers his actions publicized his physical prowess, the health of the ecosystem, and the superior condition of his state.

Princes welcomed tigers so long as—from a royal sportsman's perspective but not always from a peasant's—their numbers were reasonable and they refrained from causing too many problems. A sovereign's reputation did not suffer on account of depredations by the occasional aggressive tiger or leopard because the benefits of eventually killing the animal could outweigh the drawbacks. Man-eaters made a negative impression on state visitors, but they gave Indian princes, and Englishmen in British India, the opportunity to appear masculine, capable, and responsive to their subjects' concerns.[21] Ultimately, a ruler needed to find an appropriate balance

---

[19] Tanwar, *Shikari aur Shikar*, 7.

[20] Ibid., and S.R. Gupta, *Shikari Dost* (Ratlam: 1903), 176. It is unclear if such therapies were in use. For a contemporary shikari doubting their efficacy, see Kesri Singh, *Hints on Tiger Shooting (Tiger by Tiger)* (Bombay: Jaico Publishing House, 1965), 26–7. But, compare with Kesri Singh, *The Tiger of Rajasthan* (London: Robert Hale Limited, 1959), 164–5. British hunters reported popular (but not princely) use of tiger whiskers, claws, and bones: see Charles Hardinge, *My Indian Years, 1910–1916: The Reminiscences of Lord Hardinge of Penshurst* (London: John Murray, 1948), 71.

[21] See Pandian, "Predatory Care," 79–107.

between having enough ferocious beasts to protect his subjects from, thereby appearing heroic, and not having so many that state residents and foreign observers might begin doubting his competence as their sovereign. Well-behaved cats that showed themselves only to be shot were most desirable as their docility reflected favorably on a sovereign's righteousness; it took a truly great king to intimidate tigers into obedience. Even tame cats, however, were potential threats to life and property, and so kings who killed them could also appear heroic.

Of the larger Eurasian context, from ancient through modern times, it has been remarked that the "special powers attributed to successful hunters derive, in no small measure, from the special powers and properties attributed to the animals they vanquish. Fabulous beasts can only be slain by fabulous humans."[22] In late-nineteenth-century India, these supernatural powers had devolved for the most part into more mundane qualities, like princely monopolies over state hunting rights and privileged access to weapons that reliably killed big game. Though the loss of status and power under British paramountcy had undermined the supposed potency of their forest sojourns and tiger conquests, Rajput rulers continued well into the twentieth century to derive legitimacy from associating with wilderness harboring dangerous beasts. Ultimately, tiger grounds were special because they produced and were graced by tigers, and because the royal tiger hunt was a ritual harnessing and internalization of the vital power of fierce beasts and wild places into the body of the ruler.[23]

Princes who enjoyed an abundance of verdant jungles and well-behaved tigers possessed obvious advantages. They could use their resources to impress their subjects, outdo their rivals, and curry favor with the powerful. They also faced fewer impediments when pursuing animals for themselves. It was a point of pride for Pratap Singh that he could kill tigers within the bounds of his own realm and, each time he did, a suitable notation was made in his state's

[22]Allsen, *Royal Hunt*, 10.
[23]Waghorne, *Raja's Magic Clothes*, 169.

administration reports.[24] Through the early 1900s, Karkigarh was one of the most reliable places in Orchha to find tigers and, while the island hardly compared with Shivpuri in Gwalior or the forests of Kotah and Bundi, any state shikargah that had yielded tigers to Pratap Singh's gun within recent memory counted as a fine jungle indeed by Bundelkhandi standards.[25]

Tigers were scarce in Orchha, but they showed themselves frequently enough that the maharaja's servants managed to compile a list of the animals' favorite haunts in 1928.[26] While the list included 38 named reserves in the Orchha, Jatara, Baldeogarh, and Tikamgarh Ranges, Pratap Singh's officials did not consider any of these locations to be reliably productive of the big cats. They identified several less-desirable game species as being somewhat more common, including wild boar, nilgai, four-horned antelope, sambar, chital, and leopard. The Orchha Division had the smallest forests out of all the maharaja's ranges but it contained the best tiger habitat, besides producing the highest quality timber in the state.[27] The comparatively rich hunting available in the Orchha Range was reflected in its 14 shikargahs. Before being submerged by the waters of the Betwa, Karkigarh had been the range's 15th preserve. In contrast, the much larger Jatara Range had 11 game preserves, Baldeogarh 8, and Tikamgarh only 5.[28]

Pratap Singh's sovereignty over the island augmented its natural riches. Prior to its destruction, Karkigarh was essential for maintaining Pratap Singh's position because he could shoot tigers there

[24] *Administration Report of the Orchha State for 1912–13 (July to June)* (Allahabad: Pioneer Press, 1916), 2.

[25] P. Singh, to H. Daly, April 29, 1908, GOI, CI, 129-A of 1905–8, NAI.

[26] Madur-ul-Moham, Orchha, to PA-Bundelkhand, October 6, 1928, GOI, BA, 81-D of 1928, NAI.

[27] *Administration Report of the Orchha State for 1912–13*, 33.

[28] Madur-ul-Moham, Orchha, to PA-Bundelkhand, October 6, 1928, GOI, BA, 81-D of 1928, NAI; P. Singh, to Daly, April 29, 1908, GOI, CI, 129-A of 1905–8, NAI. In 1912, Orchha had 1021 *bigha*s of "forest proper," Tikamgarh 43,837 *bigha*s, Jatara 35,164 *bigha*s, and Baldeogarh 50,155 *bigha*s. A *bigha* is about half an acre.

without reference to foreign rules and without having to interact with any external authority. In his correspondence with the political agent, the prince stressed that he required a replacement jungle "so that I may go shooting there whenever it pleases me and nobody may disturb my shooting arrangement."[29] Accustomed to hunting within Orchha, where no sportsman's rights could supersede his own, Pratap Singh aimed to guarantee his enjoyment of a similar situation in British territory. Indeed, the maharaja's correspondence with the Bundelkhand Agency Office and the tenor of his demands threw into sharp relief his intention not just of hunting in British India but of hunting there like a prince.

This was difficult to achieve in British districts, where hunting was policed by a vast corpus of regulations that institutionalized certain enforceable aspects of true sportsmanship. These included norms and rules designed to preserve wildlife from over-shooting, such as closed seasons and limits on the size, gender, and species of legitimate game. Most sporting principles, however, were informally and inconsistently upheld by a slew of British sportsmen-officials. These well-placed enthusiasts had the power to approve or deny shooting permits and requests for prohibited bore weapons, parcel out forest blocks, and generally make shikar in British territory more or less difficult for individual princes and other elites.

Conveniently summarized by MacKenzie, the canonical code of sportsmanship as fully developed by the late nineteenth century in Britain's colonies held that

> the hunter should appreciate the beauty and respect the life force of the animals he set out to shoot. He should never succumb to 'buck fever' or ever fire indiscriminately into herds. The true hunter spoored and stalked his prey to a point at which the age, sex and quality of the trophy could be identified, a point which would offer the best chance of a mortal shot. Females and their young should be left alone [except select species including big cats], and ... the hunted animal should have a 'sporting chance.' If any animal were merely wounded, then the

---

[29] P. Singh, to PA-Bundelkhand, July 14, 1907, GOI, CI, 129-A of 1905–8, NAI.

hunter should follow to deliver the *coup de grace* at whatever cost in time and discomfort to himself ... No one should shoot from railway carriages, river steamers ... motor vehicles or aeroplanes.[30]

Certainly, there was much in the code that Pratap Singh and his peers would have agreed with, or at least not have objected to. On the whole, Indian princes were less likely to condemn shooting from moving vehicles, at night, or over watering holes. While they admired animals that put up a good fight, particularly wild boar, they seem to have had fewer illusions about giving their prey a "sporting chance," a somewhat hollow claim at any rate when armed with a rifle. None of this necessarily set them apart. After all, Englishmen too were known to transgress the sporting code, which no doubt was honored more consistently in literary works than in the field.[31]

One aspect of true sportsmanship that Pratap Singh and many of his peers disagreed with was its valorization of fairness between fellow sportsmen. They found it difficult to believe and impossible to accept that, regardless of rank and identity, no sportsman was entitled to special consideration and every shooter was required to be considerate of "the next man."[32] Shooting like a true sportsman under those conditions would have reduced Pratap Singh to the level of a commoner.

According to British officials, Pratap Singh indeed ranked the same as every other sportsman in British India. Shooting licenses were guaranteed to no one and there was every chance that the most desirable shooting blocks would be unavailable when they were wanted. Like every elite citizen of a princely state, Pratap Singh had to obtain special permits for his followers to carry weapons when accompanying him into British India. The process was routine, but it was an additional inconvenience and yet another galling concession to foreign dictates. It was also insulting and potentially injurious. The rules had been framed in the first place to suppress

[30] MacKenzie, *Empire of Nature*, 299.

[31] Ibid., 300.

[32] H. Pritchard (PA-Bundelkhand), to P. Singh, March 25, 1914, GOI, CI, 898 of 1913, NAI.

armed banditry in the Jhansi District, and their enforcement suggested that Pratap Singh's followers, on the basis of shared Rajput lineage, might lend their weapons to Bundelkhand-based dacoits.[33] It was in the maharaja's best interests, in order to avoid British interference in his administration, to dispel any notion that might be current in government circles that he or his followers might aid or abet these criminals. So long as the Karkigarh affair went unresolved, however, Pratap Singh's access to tiger shooting in Orchha itself remained unbearably limited. Therefore, despite the drawbacks of sport in British territories, the prince began submitting frequent requests to hunt at Dhamoni fort in the Central Provinces, and in the forest blocks of the Jhansi District's Lalitpur subdivision.[34]

An enterprising prince could find ways to mitigate and compensate for the disadvantages of shooting by permit in British territory. Pratap Singh did his best to avoid submitting to government regulations, particularly the galling limitations imposed by shooting licenses and game laws. To ensure that his experiences in British Bundelkhand would be in accord with his sovereign need for undisputed superiority in the field, he had to find ways to place himself as far beyond the reach of the rules as possible, through the killing of tigers on his own terms in reserved blocks, or, more boldly, through obtaining ownership of land by proxy in the vicinity of British preserves.

Obtaining a lease or ownership of property in British India was the most attractive option, and one that Pratap Singh had pursued to augment his shooting even before the onset of the Karkigarh affair. One method of doing so was by circumventing the rule that prevented close relatives and high officials of ruling chiefs, and princes themselves, from possessing private property in British territory.[35]

[33] Kasturi, *Embattled Identities*, 218.

[34] Lalitpur: P. Singh, to Pritchard, December 11, 1913, GOI, CI, 898 of 1913, NAI; Mohammad Zaman Khan, to P.T.A. Spence, October 12, 1914, GOI, CI, 898 of 1913, NAI; Dhamoni: Khan, to Spence, December 19, 1915, GOI, CI, 898 of 1913, NAI.

[35] Variations on the policy preventing rulers from owning land in British India had been in place since 1867: see O. Bosanquet, to J.B. Wood, July 9, 1917, GOI, FPD, Secret I, 4–6 of October 1917, NAI.

Eventually relaxed in 1922, this regulation was a long-standing source
of discontent in the states, including Orchha.[36] In 1903, Madho
Singh, brother-in-law of the maharaja and Diwan (prime minister)
of Orchha State, acquired a partial interest in Gangania village in the
Jhansi District, in contravention of the law. Although the government of the United Provinces ordered him to sell the property as soon
as they discovered the purchase, Madho Singh quietly transferred
ownership to his illegitimate son.[37]

When Madho Singh's continuing claim on Gangania came to light
a few years later, H.G. Warburton, Collector of Jhansi, concluded
that the whole affair was a pretense meant to obscure Pratap Singh's
personal interest in the place as a staging point for yearly shooting
parties. Gangania was just north of one of the premier shooting
blocks around Lalitpur, and Warburton claimed to have evidence
that the maharaja had hunted there, without a license, on several
occasions. The partial interest in Gangania enjoyed by Madho Singh's
son established a claim to residence in the United Provinces. This
gave him and his guests greater latitude to shoot without licenses in
Gangania than they ever could have hoped to receive as foreigners
and non-owners. As guests of Madho Singh's illegitimate son, the
maharaja and his heir exploited a legal grey area and hunted not just
in Gangania but in nearby villages.[38] The phenomenon of *bhumeawat*,
a desperate and violent struggle undertaken by elite Rajputs of this
time and place for "identity, status and power ... arising out of a sense
of commitment and attachment to territory," helps contextualize
the Maharaja of Orchha's struggle to regain free access to hunting

[36] Acquisition of residential property by Ruling Princes and Chiefs in British
India, FPD resolution 2563, December 19, 1922, GOI, PD, UP, 1 of 1923,
UPSA.

[37] Translation of a vernacular communication, Orchha Darbar, to PA-Bundelkhand, March 4, 1904, in C.S. Bayley, to FD Secretary, April 14, 1904,
GOI, FD, Internal B, 161–7 of August 1905, NAI; and H.G. Warburton,
to Commissioner of Allahabad, December 20, 1906, GOI, PD, 24 of 1907,
UPSA.

[38] Warburton, to Commissioner of Allahabad, December 20, 1906, GOI,
PD, 24 of 1907, UPSA.

grounds in his ancestral territory, or *bhum*, which extended far beyond his state's modern boundaries and into the Jhansi District of British Bundelkhand.[39]

In pre-colonial Bundelkhand, sovereignty over land was never singular but always plural, "because complicated revenue and political interactions rendered intricate the distribution of proprietal rights and boundaries."[40] Numerous stake-holders, and not just the local prince, shared in the rights and privileges associated with land, which might include occupancy, cultivation, and taxation. The example of Pratap Singh demonstrates that shikar too must be seen as a basic territorial asset in Bundelkhand, and in princely India more generally.[41] Hunting without the king's permission arrogated a specific and transferable right associated with land to the (nominally) illegitimate hunter, constituting a very serious sovereign challenge. The principle held regardless of whether the animals poached were wildfowl or big game, but the severity of the offense increased in step with the desirability of the prey. A nobleman killing a brace of duck out of turn would have merited a stern reprimand, but a *thakur* hunting tigers on his own recognizance was another matter entirely.[42]

The territorial redistributions enacted by the British in the early- and mid-nineteenth century further complicated the situation. Jhansi and Jalaun were "once part and parcel of the Bundela states," and Pratap Singh's ancestors had "watched with dismay" when they became British districts in the 1840s. Although government officials assumed that all rights and privileges were transferred along with the land, Rajput connections to ancestral bhum were not necessarily severed when territory changed hands.[43] Even if Rajputs agreed that certain rights had been transferred, they might not concede that all had, or that negotiations on the matter were closed. Their

[39] Kasturi, *Embattled Identities*, 21.

[40] Ibid., 66.

[41] Waghorne, *Raja's Magic Clothes*, 180–1.

[42] For poaching in Mewar, see files 555 and 631 of 1942 (VS 1999), MJ-Shikar, RSA.

[43] Kasturi, *Embattled Identities*, 184 and 66.

understanding of sovereignty was "processual," not static.[44] So long as the government claimed Jhansi and Jalaun, it would face continual pressure from Bundela Rajputs—both those living in the states and in British Bundelkhand—asserting their stake in those lands, including the rights and privileges of shikar.

Attachment to bhum permeated Diwan Madho Singh's interests in the village of Gangania, even if he never used violence (beyond the hunt) to press his claims. According to an official *rubkar* to the government from the Orchha darbar, Madho Singh's ancestors had owned a number of properties around Gangania in what was now British territory. Furthermore, his contemporary landed relatives held properties in adjacent British Lalitpur, and were allowed to do so because of their lower rank and comparatively remote association with ruling princes. As for Madho Singh's abilities as a proprietor, the rubkar attested that he had "lately brought under cultivation and settled cultivators in [his] share of the village at the sacrifice of personal money."[45] While it is clear that shikar helped draw Madho Singh to Gangania, it is equally obvious that the noble's connections to the region were deep and multifaceted.

Madho Singh's interests in Jhansi and Lalitpur were common amongst the Bundela Rajputs of Orchha State; he even shared them with Pratap Singh. The prince's ancestors had held Jhansi along with Karkigarh and numerous other sites, just as Madho Singh's once managed their territories around Gangania. As for Lalitpur, Pratap Singh and his nobles as a whole were reportedly "of the same race and brotherhood" as the Rajputs of that region, suggesting potential interests there as well.[46] The spirit of bhumeawat thus helped shape

[44] Norbert Peabody, "*Kota Mahajagat*, or the Great Universe of Kota: Sovereignty and Territory in 18th Century Rajasthan," *Contributions to Indian Sociology* 25, 1 (1991): 33.

[45] Translation of Orchha Darbar to PA-Bundelkhand, March 4, 1904, in Bayley, AGG-CI, to FD Secretary, April 14, 1904, GOI, FD, Internal B, 161–7 of August 1905, NAI.

[46] Malavika Kasturi, "Rajput Lineages, Banditry and the Colonial State in Nineteenth-Century 'British' Bundelkhand," *Studies in History* 15, 1 (1999): 92.

the Karkigarh affair and the nature of Pratap Singh's proposed exchanges, just as it played its role in the controversy over Gangania.

While sporting abroad was always problematic, even when accomplished from a place like Gangania, the animals that princes could shoot in British India contributed to their sovereignty in unique and desirable ways. The successful pursuit and destruction of "British" animals, especially tigers, posited a ruler's symbolic dominance over an enlarged territory. By extending their legitimizing activities beyond the constraints of official state borders, princes literally poached the paramount power's sovereignty. Local British officials felt threatened by these incursions that broke the spirit, if not always the letter, of the law. They also objected to what they understood as Pratap Singh's unsporting insistence on shooting in British territory without going through official channels and without a proper license, particularly when Englishmen were regularly denied access to hunting grounds in Orchha State. According to the collector of Jhansi, the maharaja's selfishness as a "jealous game preserver" was a source of deep dissatisfaction in British Bundelkhand, especially in light of the prince's alleged habit of encouraging his heir and dependents to visit Gangania as well. Because the situation constituted an outright negation of sporting fairness, British officials, officers, and sportsmen of the Jhansi District agreed that it was "undesirable to let him think he can keep people out of his State as much as he likes and at the same time make what use he pleases of adjoining districts."[47]

Even as Pratap Singh tried to extend his sovereignty by shooting in foreign territory, he defended his legitimacy within Orchha's borders by carefully limiting the ability of outsiders to hunt in his realm. The prince had to regulate British shooting in part because Indian princes and Europeans generally agreed on a standard hierarchy of prey, running from small game through a succession of ever larger and more dangerous beasts, with tigers, followed by lions and then leopards, topping the list. This meant that elite Indian and British sportsmen

[47] Warburton, to Brownrigg, February 23, 1907, GOI, PD, 24 of 1907, UPSA.

were competing for the same scarce resources. Princely associations between shikar and sovereignty naturally heightened the stakes.

The field was even narrower for Pratap Singh, and proportionately more competitive. Because he was not just a maharaja but also the premier sovereign in Bundelkhand and the head of his Rajput clan, he maintained that he would shoot only the highest class of game: "carnivora such as tigers, leopards, and bears."[48] To elevate him above his subordinates and rivals in princely and British India, the game he pursued had to match his status and be exclusive to him. To emphasize his point, Pratap Singh restricted Orchha's nobles to shooting the state's blackbuck antelope and chital deer. State elites nevertheless could content themselves with the knowledge that they outranked visiting British officers, who were restricted to wildfowl, small game, and fish.[49] Pratap Singh wisely made exceptions for government VIPs and princely peers. Anything less would have been construed as a serious insult. Besides, good hospitality was a matter of pride in the Rajput states, and flattery had its advantages.

British hunting parties in Orchha could detract from the maharaja's sovereignty not only by giving Europeans access to the same game and landscapes that Pratap Singh based his reputation on, but by exposing state laws and judicial processes to government interference. British officers were often insufficiently acquainted with local boundaries, customs, and dialects. As a result, their shooting parties occasionally ended in altercations with state subjects.[50] The maharaja's goal in limiting their sport was not only to protect his people

[48] P. Singh, to Pritchard, December 11, 1913, GOI, CI, 898 of 1913, NAI.

[49] L.M. Crump, to Impey, June 8, 1911, GOI, CI, BA, 614 of 1910, NAI.

[50] A 1903 affray occurred when officers ignorant of tank cultivation shot a villager while wildfowling: see Court of Sessions, Orchha, to F.G. Beville, translation of *rubkar*, August 9, 1903, GOI, FD, Internal B, 238–43 of December 1903, NAI. A 1905 affray occurred when officers asking after local game approached a dwelling decorated for a bride: see Special Magistrate, Orchha, translation of judgment, April 8, 1905, GOI, FD, Internal B, 437–53 of August 1905, NAI.

from stray bullets and other transgressions, but to avoid the inevitable British interference in his jurisdiction and sovereignty that resulted from these "shooting affrays." When Orchha's citizens attacked officers out hunting, as they allegedly did in 1903 near Arjar tank and again in 1905 near Chakrapur, the Government of India was reluctant to stand back and let Pratap Singh's courts settle the matter, as they assumed judgments would be biased against the officers and that villagers would receive undue leniency.[51]

British military commanders too were disinclined to allow princely officials to arrest or punish European officers who violated state shooting rules.[52] Cantonment officials cautioned Pratap Singh through the political agent, after several disturbances in the early 1920s, that the state must "not make any attempt to detain persons trespassing but will inform [the Commanding Officer] as soon as possible in order that [he] may take suitable action." The communication ended with a stern warning that "any attempt at forcible detention ... might lead to an unfortunate incident."[53] Pratap Singh and other princes may have had jurisdiction in their own territories, but they were powerless when the transgressors were British officers. Little wonder, then, that the line between protecting sovereignty and preserving wildlife was indistinct.

Under these circumstances, Pratap Singh might have liked to ban British shooting parties altogether, but doing so would have been disastrous from a diplomatic standpoint. In the end, he chose to restrict the officers' activities as far as possible. If he could not wholly exclude British sportsmen, he did prevent them from penetrating more than a few miles into his state, and from getting anything better

[51] Major A.H. Block, to Adjutant, Royal Artillery, March 11, 1903, GOI, FD, 238–43 of December 1903, NAI; W.E. Jardine, to E.H. Kealy, March 18, 1905, GOI, FD, Internal B, 437–53 of August 1905, NAI.

[52] For Orchha and Indore examples, see Headquarters, 20th Infantry Brigade, Jhansi, to PA-Bundelkhand, October 13, 1921, GOI, CI, BA, 212-D of 1921–34, NAI, and Superintendent, AGG-CI, to Diwan Bahadur R. Ragunath Rao, Indore, May 27, 1887, GOI, CI, 3 of 1887, NAI.

[53] Headquarters, 20th Infantry Brigade, Jhansi, to PA-Bundelkhand, October 13, 1921, GOI, CI, BA, 212-D of 1921–34, NAI.

than small game. British officers (unlike the occasional European VIP), could never bag royal prey in Orchha State. On the other hand, so long as he followed the rules and obtained a valid license, Pratap Singh could get permission to shoot tigers in British India.

The perceived shortage of tigers that Pratap Singh faced in his state was hardly unique in the late-nineteenth and early-twentieth centuries. It is important to keep in mind, however, that princely perceptions were relative. They formed their expectations with reference to imagined utopian pasts and jealous estimations of conditions in rival territories. The exact population of tigers in India during Pratap Singh's lifetime is unknown, but it must have been substantial. Some idea may be had from the numbers killed for government bounties in British India, which have been shown to be at least 16,573 between the years 1879 and 1888, with another estimated 65,000 killed between 1875 and 1925.[54] By comparison, the most recent tiger census in India has returned approximately 1706 animals in the wild as of 2010.[55] Although the species was not in danger of extinction at the turn of the twentieth century, it was scarce in Bundelkhand and becoming rare enough in British India to facilitate the gradual transition of tigers in official estimations from dangerous vermin to creatures worthy of conservation.

Besides shooting in British districts, rulers with few tigers of their own, like the Maharaja of Orchha, and those whose states lacked them entirely, like the Maharaja of Bikaner, relied on the hospitality of other princes. Princely legitimacy in these years was in fact rarely serviced by hunting exclusively within one's own state. As when shooting in British territory, princely sportsmen had to ensure that their experiences in other states did not detract from the benefits of obtaining tiger trophies. It seems to have been most common, and probably wisest, to shoot in states closely connected with one's own house, or in those that were indisputably higher or lower in status,

---

[54] Rangarajan, "Raj and the Natural World," 285.

[55] Y.V. Jhala, Q. Qureshi, R. Gopal, and P.R. Sinha, eds, *Status of Tigers, Co-predators, and Prey in India, 2010* (New Delhi and Dehradun: National Tiger Conservation Authority and Wildlife Institute of India, 2011), Table ES.1, p. xiii.

thereby limiting the risk of awkward diplomatic incidents.[56] A sort of "professional courtesy" existed among Indian rulers according to which a friendly prince would support his guest's sovereign image by supplying some shooting, while simultaneously bolstering his own reputation by playing the ideal host or dutiful relative.[57] Pratap Singh frequently visited Bijawar State to hunt, both taking advantage of and cementing his close relationship with that ruler—who was in fact his younger son. More distant lineage-based relationships, like that with the Datia ruling family, proved useful as well. The Maharaja of Orchha got a tiger or two from their famous grounds at Seonda, while Datia's Bundela Rajput ruler no doubt gained from the prestige of hosting the premier chief of Bundelkhand.[58]

Hunting in foreign landscapes, and not just in foreign lands, could benefit princes as well. Datia and Bijawar states had somewhat denser and more mountainous jungles than Orchha, but the differences were probably insufficient to matter to Pratap Singh. The situation was different for other rulers. Sojourns in lush tiger jungles contrasted favorably with what was available to Ganga Singh in his arid Bikaner State. While the Rathore Rajputs saw their state's harsh environment as a positive factor shaping their distinctive local character, Ganga Singh's annual excursions to hunt big game in places like Nepal, Gwalior, and the Central and United Provinces of British India reinvigorated him through contact with the potent animals and habitats that his own realm lacked.[59]

Attractive foreign hunting grounds notwithstanding, Pratap Singh wanted his own tiger jungles in Orchha. To obtain the compensation he desired for his Karkigarh island shikargah, however, he first had

---

[56] For a Rajput noble's complaints about Mewari arrangements for the Kishangarh wedding party, see Susanne Hoeber Rudolph and Lloyd I. Rudolph, eds, with Mohan Singh Kanota, *Reversing the Gaze: Amar Singh's Diary, A Colonial Subject's Narrative of Imperial India* (Boulder, CO: Westview Press, 2002), 461.

[57] Allsen, *Royal Hunt*, 235.

[58] *Report on the Administration of Orchha State for 1907–1908* (Tikamgarh: Shri Pratap Prabhukar State Press, 1913), 2.

[59] *Four Decades of Progress in Bikaner* (Bikaner: Government Press, 1937), 17–18.

to convince the British of the legitimacy of his claims and the severity of his loss. This proved difficult as the majority of British officials refused to see Karkigarh island as good tiger ground, and because they increasingly entertained doubts about Pratap Singh's personal qualifications as an upstanding prince and sportsman. Even allowing for the obvious incentives on the government's side to understate, and on Pratap Singh's to exaggerate, their disparate evaluations of the quality of Karkigarh as a tiger jungle indicate a fundamental disagreement over what constituted good tiger ground and, by extension, good sportsmanship.

The maharaja measured Karkigarh's worth by standards foreign to the British and declared on numerous occasions that his island was not just a good tiger ground but in fact "the best of its kind in the Orchha Pargana."[60] One of the island's chief attractions was as a site where the maharaja had killed tigers previously, not just in an ordinary fashion, but two within the space of three days in a sequence of events well known throughout the region.[61] The fame produced by these kills guaranteed Karkigarh's importance. While princes could benefit from any tiger they bagged, unusual kills stood out in local memory. A hunter's celebrity was not based solely on his sportsmanship, nor a ruler's reputation entirely on the quality of his governance; it mattered equally how extraordinary their exploits appeared. Because Karkigarh had helped a hunter-king like the Maharaja of Orchha transcend the mundane, and because it might do so again, it was a valuable shikargah.

Karkigarh island and its possible replacements, namely the forests associated with Dhamoni fort in the Central Provinces and the jungles south of Lalitpur in the Jhansi District of the United Provinces, all appealed to Pratap Singh because they came close to satisfying his definition of ideal hunting grounds. Like his island shikargah, he could rely on Dhamoni fort to produce memorable kills.

---

[60] P. Singh, to H. Daly, April 29, 1908, GOI, CI, 129-A of 1905–8, NAI.
[61] H.Z. Darrah, November 27, 1906, in Chief Secretary to Governor, UP, to FD Secretary, March 15, 1913, encl. 1, GOI, FPD, 32–9 of September 1914, NAI.

At Dhamoni, sport took place within the fortifications themselves, where the walls enclosed an area of fifty-two acres and reached higher than a tiger could jump.[62] Gaps could be closed by carefully positioned stops during a hunt, ensuring that animals would follow a predictable path directly to the maharaja's station.[63] The comparative ease of the beat, however, was offset by the singularity of the place, described in 1844 by William H. Sleeman as a "magnificent fortress ... built upon a small projection of the Vindhya range, looking down on each side into two enormously deep glens."[64]

The layout of the hunting grounds in southern Lalitpur does not seem to have been as conducive to celebrity. This helps account for Pratap Singh's preference for Dhamoni over the Madanpur, Girar, Dudhai, and Deogarh shooting blocks, despite the fact that they offered similar prospects for successful shoots and were in the same hills and stretch of jungle as the fort. Although the Lalitpur blocks were relatively convenient to the maharaja's primary place of residence and capital at Tikamgarh, ease of access does not appear to have been a primary consideration, and the slightly more distant Dhamoni remained more attractive.

Pratap Singh especially valued shikargahs that allowed him to associate with the environmentally-based legitimacy of his dynastic forebears. Just as battlegrounds became hallowed sites by absorbing the blood of slain heroes, the "sovereign substance" found in hunting grounds compounded over time as successive rulers saturated these places with the blood of slain tigers and the energy released through royal contact with them and their habitat.[65] The hunting grounds of the Orchha Pargana, possibly including Karkigarh itself, had been providing Bundela Rajput rulers with tigers for centuries.

---

[62] Jardine, to Reynolds, September 25, 1905, GOI, CI, 129-A of 1905–8, NAI; Charles Grant, ed., *The Gazetteer of the Central Provinces of India* (1870; repr., New Delhi: Usha, 1984), 186.

[63] Stops kept tigers in beats by startling them with a sudden noise.

[64] W.H. Sleeman, *Rambles and Recollections of an Indian Official*, ed. Vincent A. Smith (London: Oxford University Press, 1915), 110.

[65] Peabody, "*Kota Mahajagat,*" 52.

According to legend, the famous Bundela chief and avid hunter Raja Rudra Pratap (r. 1501–31) had died a hero's death while defending a cow from a tiger in a nearby forest.[66] The historical presence of big game in the area is corroborated by paintings on a nobleman's *chhatri* or cenotaph near the fort complex.[67] Dating to the sixteenth or seventeenth century, the images include a lion hunted from horseback and a tiger pursued from elephant-back. Similar images adorn the fort.[68] The continued centrality of the locale in Pratap Singh's period is evident from his construction in the late nineteenth century of a hunting lodge in the area.[69] The locality figured in the history of the Orchha lineage as a repeatedly visited hunting ground. New kills on the site were proportionately more significant than the slaughter of animals anywhere else lacking in comparable context.

The importance of a shooting locale's lineal connections is evident in examples taken from other states as well. Princes and their followers consistently took notice when they met with success in places made significant by prior shooting exploits. Dhaibhai Tulsinath Singh Tanwar recorded in his memoirs that Maharana Fateh Singh of Mewar once hunted on a hill where Maharana Raj Singh (r. 1652–80) had made a particularly impressive shot at a sambar, in commemoration of which a monument had been erected that still stood on the site.[70] Also in Mewar, Fateh Singh in about 1888 lavishly restored Nahar Odi, a small shooting box where another of his predecessors, Maharana Jagat Singh II (r. 1734–51), had famously killed a tiger. Recalling hunting successes within his own lifetime, the Maharaja of Bikaner's eldest son carefully recorded in his game diary when he shot from locations

[66] Pogson, *History of the Boondelas*, 10; *Administration Report of the Orchha State for 1931–32* (Jhansi: Union Press, n.d.), 2.

[67] At the Bundelkhand Riverside, owned by Madhukar Shah of the Orchha family.

[68] Alok Srivastava, *Orchha: An Ode to the Bundelas* (Bhopal: Directorate of Archaeology, Archives and Museums, Government of Madhya Pradesh, 1999), 30.

[69] See http://www.bundelkhandriverside.com/ret.html, accessed April 24, 2009.

[70] Tanwar, *Shikari aur Shikar*, 279.

where his father had achieved notable successes before him.[71] There is no evidence that physical markers ever embellished Karkigarh, but momentous events like Pratap Singh's shooting of the two tigers in 1903 were orally preserved and reinscribed in letters.

Assuming the island continued to host tigers, visits by future generations would have taken on the feel of sovereign pilgrimages, piling up layer after layer of power and legitimacy. This suggests that Peabody's important concept, expanding on Inden's insights, of "processual kingship" actually telescoped out beyond a king's "perpetual reestablishment and reconstitution" of sovereignty in the present to the repeat performances of his ancestors and descendants.[72] Future, past, and present folded into one another in the singular talismanic spaces offered by famous hunting grounds, forts, and darbars.

A place like Karkigarh had the potential to allow an ancestor's exploits to be internalized and re-experienced through imitative hunts. As his descendants sported where he himself had shot, Pratap Singh's prowess against tigers would be recalled as legendary deeds, inspired time and again by the landscapes in which they had occurred. Shooting over the same ground as one's predecessors boosted a modern maharaja's reputation while stressing the antiquity and continuity of his lineage, cementing his authority by association. Without memorable, accessible, and controllable grounds as reminders, Pratap Singh's exploits, and therefore his reputation as a good sovereign, could fall out of currency.

The broad channels of the Betwa around Karkigarh island and the walls of Dhamoni fort rendered tiger beats at these places relatively predictable by restricting the ability of game to escape unnoticed. Pratap Singh's enthusiasm for shooting in enclosed areas like Dhamoni or naturally delimited ones like Karkigarh was not unique among the princes. When visiting the Dholpur State in 1928, the Maharaja of Bikaner's son and heir Sadul Singh enthusiastically described the

---

[71] Sadul Singh, *Big Game Diary of Maharaj Kumar Shri Sadul Singhji of Bikaner, Rajasthan* (Bikaner: privately printed, *c.* 1930), 19, 49, 99, and 109.

[72] Peabody, "*Kota Mahajagat,*" 33–4.

hunting grounds near Tal Shahi in his game diary as "a beautiful *Kho*
[hill] with nice jungle and sheer cliffs on either side, so that the tiger
when driven out had to come along in this valley, either along the nulla
[ravine] immediately below us or on either side of the steep sides of
the hill below the cliffs."[73] Some hunting grounds in Rewah State
featured masonry walls to guide prey directly to the desired location,
while the Maharana of Mewar occasionally set up temporary boundaries
using cloth screens to achieve the same effect.[74] Princes conse-
crated their favorite landscapes with frequent visits and permanent
shooting boxes, called *odi*, *burj*, or *mul*. In recognition of Dhamoni's
attractions, Pratap Singh had hoped to build a shooting box there
even before the onset of the Karkigarh affair.[75]

Despite Pratap Singh's partiality for Dhamoni, the government
of the Central Provinces, which had jurisdiction over the fort,
vetoed his idea of exchanging Karkigarh for it early in 1906, citing
the interests of officers stationed at the nearby Saugor cantonment,
administrative inconvenience, and their desire to remain uninvolved
in a case that properly concerned the United Provinces.[76] Pratap
Singh continued to state his preference for Dhamoni through 1915,
but he heeded the political agent's warning that there was little hope
of success. Looking to the United Provinces, the prince next raised
the Nimkhera jungles around Lalitpur in the Jhansi District as a viable
albeit lesser alternative.

Like Karkigarh and Dhamoni, Nimkhera was familiar to the
prince, and he deemed it more desirable than untried jungles.
Formerly stationed in the area as a government official, a Mr Rand

---

[73] Singh, *Big Game*, 109.

[74] Louis Rousselet, *India and its Native Princes, Travels in Central India and
in the Presidencies of Bombay and Bengal* (Delhi: B.R. Publishing Corporation,
1975), 394; Tanwar, *Shikari aur Shikar*, 312. Eighteenth-century miniatures
suggest Umed Singh I of Kotah preferred nets: see Stuart Cary Welch, ed.,
Gods, Kings, and Tigers: The Art of Kotah (New York: Prestel, 1997), Figs 45–6
and 48–9.

[75] Jardine, to Beville, April 15, 1904, GOI, BA, 185 of 1904, NAI.

[76] Chief Commissioner, CP, to AGG-CI, January 18, 1906, GOI, CI, 129-A
of 1905–8, NAI.

reported that he once had hosted the maharaja and his son there on a tiger shoot, and "it was in that capacity that they got to know the jungles they now want."[77] While there is no indication that Pratap Singh had bagged a tiger on this initial visit to the area with Mr Rand, the prince had reason to hope he would in the future because, of all the shooting blocks in the area, Nimkhera was known to be the "more certain place for a tiger to live." Due once again in part to the strenuous objections of local officers, this proposal fared no better than the one for Dhamoni had.

The most important stumbling block, however, was Karkigarh itself. While Pratap Singh insisted on defining Karkigarh as good tiger ground, local government officials and PWD employees contended from the beginning that the island was not a real tiger jungle and that it was undeserving of the compensation demanded. In order to evaluate the maharaja's claims to the contrary, the government of the United Provinces solicited the opinion of the Commissioner of Allahabad, H.Z. Darrah. The commissioner was "an authority on such questions" by virtue of being the author of *Sport in the Highlands of Kashmir*, which he had published a few years earlier under the auspices of Rowland Ward, the world-famous London taxidermist and compiler of game records.[78] Darrah's assignment, after weighing factors ranging from timber values to shooting prospects, was to produce an award statement setting the cash amount government should offer the maharaja for the island without territorial exchange. After personally walking over Karkigarh on November 9, 1906, the commissioner reported unequivocally that "no one acquainted with the sort of cover in which tigers are found would ever speak of the island as a tiger preserve."[79] The

[77] W. Rand, to PA-Bundelkhand, November 26, 1905, GOI, BA, 261 of 1904, NAI.

[78] Chief Secretary to Governor, UP, to FD Secretary, March 15, 1913, GOI, FPD, 32–9 of September 1914, NAI; H.Z. Darrah, *Sport in the Highlands of Kashmir* (London: Rowland Ward, 1898).

[79] Darrah, November 27, 1906, in Chief Secretary to Governor, UP, to FD Secretary, March 15, 1913, encl. 1, GOI, FPD, 32–9 of September 1914, NAI.

undergrowth was too thin, and, while nilgai had left their mark, there was no sign of pig and only a suggestion of sambar; all in all there was "nothing living ... except a few *langurs*." Darrah added that according to Mr Blanchfield, a Divisional Forest Officer with "considerable experience" of neighboring Jhansi District, only two tigers had been shot on Karkigarh over the past nine and a half years, the ones Pratap Singh had bagged in 1903. The Collector of Jhansi asserted that even those had been "in the nature of a happy accident" and that the maharaja had little reason to expect he would be so fortunate again.[80]

As the primary goals of the PWD and local government were to obtain a settlement, proceed with the work free from all complications, and avoid the question of territorial exchange altogether, it is hardly surprising that they would wish to discredit Pratap Singh's claim to shooting rights by devaluing Karkigarh. In addition, government officials were used to operating under the laws in effect in British territory and liked to follow the same guidelines in their interactions with the princely states. Numerous precedents backed them up, although cases could also be cited where exchanges had taken place or were in the process of being negotiated.[81] Still, the Land Acquisition Act with its preference for simple cash settlements was the acknowledged norm, despite the fact that it was not technically applicable in princely India and was unpopular enough to later be debated in the Chamber of Princes.[82]

The application of the Act by the PWD to the Maharaja of Orchha's case even led W.E. Jardine, political agent in Bundelkhand, to protest

[80] Darrah, quoting Collector of Jhansi, November 27, 1906, in Chief Secretary to Governor, UP, to FD Secretary, March 15, 1913, encl. 1, GOI, FPD, 32–9 of September 1914, NAI.

[81] See office notes, GOI, FPD, Internal B, 208–11 of September 1915, NAI. Datia and Baoni states in Central India received exchanges in connection with canal works around 1890. Rewah would in connection with the Belan Canal between 1902 and 1917, Alipura for the Dhassan Canal between 1906 and 1912, and Samthar for the Betwa Canal in 1917.

[82] At the February 1928 session: see Agendum 7, GOI, FPD, 30-R of 1928, nos. 1–5, NAI.

on the prince's behalf: "it happens repeatedly that [government officials] take and use land first and then fix compensation afterwards at rates which the Durbars consider inadequate but are practically powerless to question."[83] Jardine, however, did not advocate a land exchange because he agreed with the maharaja's high opinion of Karkigarh or the prince's sporting ideals, although he was sympathetic to Pratap Singh's desire to retain free access to good sport. Rather, he pursued a quick resolution to satisfy his own aims, hoping to establish a precedent for dealing with Central India's numerous troublesome pockets of land which languished in a neighbor's territory and impeded efficient administration.[84] If Pratap Singh made too many demands or the government of the United Provinces proved too inflexible, his pet project risked being scratched before it ever got off the ground. Jardine's personal ambitions for advancement, his vision for the region as a whole, and his apparently genuine belief that the prince deserved a replacement jungle on account of being an enthusiastic sportsman, led him to champion the maharaja's cause.

Indeed, a widespread awareness of the maharaja's fondness for sport did influence responses to his demands. The collector of Jhansi grudgingly conceded in 1909 that "it is important to remember that the Durbar is of [the] opinion that it is losing some fair shooting in losing the island."[85] Regardless of what they considered Karkigarh's actual merits, some Englishmen were willing to take Pratap Singh's opinions into account because they recognized his sincere attachment to the place. In line with a growing trend in policy, they believed there were significant advantages in keeping princes content.[86] They applied the same reasoning to the Karkigarh affair as was aired in 1908 in relation to the Mir of Khairpur's request for a prohibited bore sporting rifle, namely that "more is to be gained by granting the

[83] Jardine, to Daly, July 1905, GOI, BA, 261 of 1904, NAI.

[84] Jardine, to Daly, April 24, 1905, GOI, CI, 129-A of 1905–8, NAI.

[85] Collector of Jhansi, to Commissioner, Bundelkhand Division, January 15, 1909, GOI, CI, 85 of 1908, NAI.

[86] The major public expression of a new *laissez faire* policy was Lord Minto's 1909 speech: see Copland, *The Princes of India*, 31.

request than is to be gained by refusing it. It is these concessions—there are few only—that go far to keep chiefs contented and happy."[87] In light of these factors, some individuals, particularly those in the Foreign Department, urged the United Provinces to consider yielding a little sport to the maharaja. Nevertheless, British officials in general remained condescending towards Pratap Singh's sentiments even when they deigned to admit them into discussion. With the possible exception of individuals like Jardine, they either failed to appreciate or chose to ignore the fact that pragmatic considerations relating to sovereignty and royal reputation were at stake.

The Maharaja of Orchha's sporting values were not, in any case, entirely at variance with those of the British. Pratap Singh recognized that his exploits on Karkigarh would fade from memory if shooting was discontinued there due to an absence of game. So, in broad agreement with British definitions of good hunting ground, he assessed Karkigarh's merits in accordance with its actual number of tigers and suitability as a tiger habitat. Recognizing the attributes of a good tiger jungle, he could see that Karkigarh fell short at the time of Darrah's visit in 1906. Nevertheless, he insisted the evaluation was flawed, because it relied on impressions gathered after the commencement of the canal works. The influx of surveyors and PWD employees had disturbed the grounds, displacing the game and rendering the island's condition unrepresentative. Additionally, inspections of the island had been "limited to such occasions only when the forest has been devoid of shrubs owing to scanty rain fall in the past two years; moreover it had been ... laid open to the public, by removing all restriction in famine days of 1906, that forest area being the only relief in that locality. Under such circumstances it is impossible that the forest may retain its former condition."[88] Undervaluing Karkigarh's assets, he implied, was tantamount to punishing him for having been a good and merciful ruler who had sacrificed his hunting interests and the integrity of his island reserve to save his subjects from starvation.

[87] Sir Harcourt Butler, May 19, 1908, GOI, FD, Internal B, 82 of September 1908, NAI.

[88] P. Singh, to PA-Bundelkhand, July 14, 1907, GOI, CI, 129-A of 1905–8, NAI.

He hoped to force British officials to weigh not only Karkigarh's present worth, but evidence of its former verdancy and his own record of good stewardship.

One of the major flaws of the Land Acquisition Act from the princely perspective was that assessments routinely ignored a location's potential, resulting in disappointingly low settlements. The maharaja judged his island on the basis of its past glory and future prospects, not its present lackluster appearance. He anticipated the return of tigers to the area, as well as the maturation of lucrative stands of teak. The conflict thus came down to a matter of perspective. By most measures, Karkigarh was not an impressive shikargah. But within Orchha, where there was little to begin with and none of it particularly productive, Karkigarh was quite simply the best tiger jungle there was.

Conventional wisdom in late-nineteenth- and early-twentieth-century colonial India held that British sportsmanship had triumphed over princely norms, so that European and Indian elites universally acknowledged the validity of a single code of true sportsmanship.[89] While Englishmen had no trouble accepting and following its precepts by virtue of their Englishness, Indian princes lacked the necessary moral compass. Their supposed failures revealed a host of faults, including selfishness, degeneracy, inconstancy, and substandard masculinity. In fact, the tenets of elite sportsmanship in India remained unsettled and contested well into the twentieth century. True sportsmanship was not so much a timeless precept as an orientalist construct used to define and reinforce difference between ruler and ruled.[90] Many princes who appeared to be transgressors, including Pratap Singh during the Karkigarh negotiations, were simply operating under a different set of rules commensurate with their Rajput identity, political situation, and social standing.

[89] Codification of true sportsmanship in India occurred between the 1870s and 1890s: see MacKenzie, *Empire of Nature*, 170.

[90] M.S.S. Pandian, "Hunting and Colonialism in the 19th Century Nilgiri Hills of South India," *Nature and the Orient: The Environmental History of South and Southeast Asia*, ed. Richard H. Grove, Vinita Damodaran, and Satpal Sangwan (Delhi: Oxford University Press, 1998), 273.

In 1914, two years before the end of the Karkigarh island affair, Pratap Singh applied for a license to go tiger shooting in the forests of Jhansi District. His desire to hunt in the Madanpur block near Lalitpur quickly became tied up in the ongoing attempts to settle the Karkigarh question, despite the ostensibly separate nature of the application. Shooting rights in the Madanpur block had already been identified as a concession likely to be included in the maharaja's eventual compensation package. A temporary license allowing him immediate access to Madanpur was, therefore, an attractive interim solution, as well as a means of personally evaluating the tiger grounds and their capacity to fulfill his needs. The maharaja's requests to shoot in Madanpur, however, solicited British officials to relax or disregard established shooting rules and regulations in his favor. His petitions led to diplomatic difficulties that exposed the differences between them in their conceptions of sportsmanship.

Much to official distress, Pratap Singh seemed determined not to follow the rules—issued by the Forest Department—to regulate hunting, shooting, and fishing in the reserved forests of the United Provinces. These rules stated that no one could reserve a shooting block for more than fifteen consecutive days.[91] From the start, the maharaja insisted on a month. A barrage of correspondence ensued, eventually reaching the desk of the lieutenant-governor of the United Provinces, who interceded on the prince's behalf. The maharaja could have his month's shooting, but not when he wanted it. Another rule stood in the way, one that required a two-week waiting period between bookings to allow disturbed game to return to shot-over areas. Anything less would be unfair to the next man. The timing was bad and another reservation stood in Pratap Singh's way. Surely, the lieutenant-governor wrote to the Agent to the Governor General of Central India, the Maharaja of Orchha "is a sufficiently good sportsman to appreciate the reasonableness of this."[92] He passed the message on to the local political agent, who wrote to the maharaja

[91] Bosanquet, to Political Secretary, August 6, 1914, GOI, FPD, 32–9 of September 1914, NAI.

[92] Lt Governor, UP, to AGG-CI, March 7, 1914, GOI, CI, 898 of 1913, NAI.

in like terms: surely, he admonished, "Your Highness is so good a sportsman."[93] After an initial conciliatory letter accepting the lesser booking, the prince almost immediately resumed his campaign when state huntsmen sent word of a tiger in his reserved block, just before his fifteen-day permit was set to expire and not long enough for him to reach Madanpur in time.[94] The political agent reminded him of the standing objections and again denied his request. Subsequent applications followed for first a two-month and then a six-month shooting period, all seemingly insensate to the interests of fellow sportsmen. How are we to interpret these progressive demands? Had the lieutenant-governor's appeal fallen on deaf ears? Was Pratap Singh less than a true sportsman?

The supposedly unsporting character that Pratap Singh displayed as he tried to regain good tiger ground or get licenses to shoot in Lalitpur, was, in fact, a nuanced response to a political situation that threatened his sovereignty. While the British prided themselves on placing all sportsmen on an equal footing, the maharaja viewed most other hunters as his inferiors in terms of their rights, privileges, and status. It was this attitude, perfectly in accord with princely sportsmanship, which enabled Pratap Singh to insist that his own desire to get the tiger that appeared in Madanpur at the end of his fifteen days ought to outweigh the interests of the next man. Because the royal hunt was intended to uphold a ruler's sovereignty, it would have been contradictory for the maharaja to admit the equality of a social and political inferior on the basis of British sporting ideals of fairness. While it was common practice for rulers to hunt in the company of their nobles, hierarchy was carefully maintained. Some relaxation was possible in the company of other princes, but even then it was case by case. It was unthinkable for a prince to concede parity with some unknown British shooter.

By exhorting the maharaja to exhibit good sportsmanship, the British were requesting him to play by their rules and subsume his sovereign status to the imperial agenda. Their pseudo-democratic

[93] PA-Bundelkhand, to P. Singh, March 25, 1914, GOI, CI, 898 of 1913, NAI.
[94] P. Singh, to Pritchard, April 16, 1914, GOI, CI, 898 of 1913, NAI.

standard of sport was meant to recall the best characteristics of the much idealized English fox-hunt.[95] The salubrious effect of British principles was taken as a given; the mere mention of good sportsmanship called up images of fair play, manliness, honor, and honesty. Besides signifying all that was Western, modern, and masculine, good sportsmanship was widely acknowledged as demonstrating loyalty to the empire. In consequence, princes who were consistently unsporting by British standards were automatically categorized as stereotypically Oriental, backward, effeminate, greedy, petty, and potentially disloyal.

The maharaja's failure to adhere entirely to their rules of sportsmanship was a source of continual distress to government officials. Pratap Singh's perceived deficiencies as a sportsman were read as shortcomings unbecoming a loyal sovereign. Officials were careful to forward a 1921 amendment to the shooting regulations of the United Provinces to the maharaja, which admonished all sportsmen to "cooperate loyally in carrying out [the] rules."[96] Regulated sports and organized games helped make good citizens in Victorian England.[97] In India, the British hoped they could produce relatively competent princes whose devotion to the crown was unquestionable.

Realizing that princely hunting was linked to sovereignty, the British felt a need to control and shape elite Indian practices in line with their own lofty ideals which, they believed, were capable of inculcating good governance and loyalty in the same way proper English education could.[98] Princes hunting independently and by their own rules were a threat to the empire. Seemingly aware of this, rulers like the Maharaja of Orchha walked a fine line between doing as they pleased and acting in accordance with British strictures. Pursuing the goal of hunting in ways that were alternately *almost but not*

[95] On fox-hunting, see David C. Itzkowitz, *Peculiar Privilege: A Social History of English Foxhunting, 1753–1885* (Hassocks: Harvester Press, 1977).

[96] Secretary to Governor, UP, to Chief Commissioner of Forests, UP, June 10, 1921, GOI, BA, 125-D of 1921, NAI.

[97] J.A. Mangan, *The Games Ethic and Imperialism: Aspects of the Diffusion of an Ideal* (New York: Viking, 1986), 18.

[98] Ibid.

quite Indian, and *almost but not quite* British, gave them the ability to navigate the paradoxes and conundrums fostered by the imperial milieu.[99]

Even if the Maharaja of Orchha preferred to shoot like a prince, he was aware of British standards, and of the diplomatic advantages of projecting an aura of loyalty. He presented some of his arguments for hunting privileges and replacement tiger jungles within the framework of true sportsmanship by strategically adapting the rhetoric of good sporting behavior, particularly that of fairness, to his own needs. Because fairness was a quality that the British consistently sought to project and which they believed marked the superiority of European civilization, Pratap Singh went out of his way to portray government officials and their decisions regarding his island as entirely unfair. In 1906 he declared that "if the Government with its vast dominions over which the sun never sets, thinks of giving a thousand times the territorial compensation like that of Karkigarh I do not think that there will be any perceptible effect on it whatsoever, while my State with its limited area shall certainly have to suffer for the loss of this area of 820 acres."[100] By portraying Orchha as a small, defenseless, and undeserving victim of circumstance whose treaty protected sovereignty and territorial rights were being compromised unjustly, the maharaja hoped to shame the British into magnanimity. Rather than conceding the maharaja's point, government officials responded by framing their critiques of Pratap Singh in terms of his own alleged failure to demonstrate fair play.[101]

As far as the British were concerned, the issue of fairness went beyond the question of sportsmanship. The common good itself hung in the balance because PWD engineers and surveyors had concluded that scientifically regulated irrigation waters would protect the people of the Jalaun District of the United Provinces from the dual threat

[99] Homi Bhabha, "Of Mimicry and Man: The Ambivalence of Colonial Discourse," *October* 28, (Spring, 1984): 125–33.

[100] P. Singh, to PA-Bundelkhand, December 19, 1906, GOI, CI, 129-A of 1905–8, NAI.

[101] Pritchard, to P. Singh, March 25, 1914, GOI, CI, 898 of 1913, NAI.

of drought and famine. Karkigarh's inundation would help provide those waters. Pratap Singh's pleas on behalf of his personal shooting and land rights, therefore, were trivial, even downright distasteful and obstructionist, an unseemly exercise of residual power tantamount to disloyalty. The entire affair smacked of selfishness to officials in the same way the Maharaja of Chhatarpur's short-lived ban on shooting within his territory would a few years later.[102] Having personally eschewed violence, that prince did not hunt and yet denied locally stationed British officers the much-sought-after recreation. Because Karkigarh was nothing special and had no tigers, officials believed the ruler of Orchha, like Chhatarpur's prince, had no cause to inconvenience everyone simply to suit his own misguided fancy.

Local government officials and military men had a long history of conflict with the princely states of Central India over sportsmanship, manifest in bitter rivalry over access to the limited number of first-rate shooting blocks in the British districts. The general feeling was that if a prince was unwilling to throw open his tanks and jungles for the benefit of locally stationed British officers, he had no right to partake of what was regarded as British shooting.[103] It was a matter of accepted notions of sportsmanship coming into conflict with princely sovereignty, as vested in proprietary, juridical, and shooting rights. So, if a ruler excluded or over-zealously regulated officers desiring sport in his state, he was no true sportsman and his requests to shoot in British districts were likely to be hindered or denied.

The idea was that every sportsman, by virtue of being a sportsman, was entitled to his fair share of game above and beyond that which would be used by the landowner. Popular opinion held that no reasonable objection could exist, for without sufficient hunters game would simply go to waste; sensible shooting would never eat into a proprietor's rightful share. Thus, princes who insisted on acting like

---

[102] G.D. Ogilvie, in [illeg.], to Impey, May 23, 1911, GOI, CI, BA, 614 of 1910, NAI.

[103] Mahesh Rangarajan, *Fencing the Forest: Conservation and Ecological Change in India's Central Provinces 1860–1914* (Delhi: Oxford University Press, 1996), 167.

independent sovereigns by keeping their shooting to themselves and maintaining the integrity of their boundaries were unsporting, disloyal, or both. For years, the Maharaja of Orchha had required all outsiders to obtain special licenses to shoot in his territory. As he had a reputation for granting such requests only to officers personally known to him, sympathy was short in the cantonment town of Jhansi when he focused his sights on the Madanpur shooting block in 1914.[104]

Pratap Singh had as much trouble tolerating the limitations British shooting licenses imposed on him as English officers had accepting Orchha State regulations. In particular, the maharaja resented the fifteen-day rule. Pratap Singh prized predictable hunting experiences and controllable hunting grounds. His standards of sportsmanship allowed for an exclusive interest in shoots where positive outcomes were virtually guaranteed, and a mere two weeks was insufficient for his shikaris to minimize the chance of failure.[105] Like other princes, he maintained a network of informants who kept him apprised of the game available in his state. When reserving a block in British territory, he likewise preferred to send shikaris ahead to mark down any tigers so that, if none were found, he could stay home or go elsewhere.[106] In doing so he avoided the ignominy of blank outings.

After receiving his 1914 shooting license but a few days before shikaris belatedly discovered evidence of a tiger in Madanpur, Pratap Singh actually announced his intention of returning his permit. Citing his huntsmen's initial reports, the prince complained that "there is no water in those jungles and ... no tiger can live or remain in them; in such a case there is no certainty of finding any tiger there."[107] The element of chance and the illusion of a matched battle of wits between predator and prey was a central feature of British sport, but

[104] Ogilvie, in [illeg.], to Impey, May 23, 1911, GOI, CI, BA, 614 of 1910, NAI.

[105] P. Singh, to Pritchard, December 11, 1913, GOI, CI, 898 of 1913, NAI.

[106] P. Singh, to H. Spencer, February 17, 1914, GOI, CI, 898 of 1913, NAI.

[107] P. Singh, to PA-Bundelkhand, March 29, 1914, GOI, CI, 898 of 1913, NAI.

less so for this maharaja who desired a greater measure of certainty and hunting grounds that could deliver it. The royal hunt was designed to reinforce the idea that righteous and legitimate sovereigns had a special connection with wilderness and wild animals, on account of which they generally got their tigers. Rulers who repeatedly endured blank days, missed their shots, or suffered tigers to slip through their beats risked betraying a distinctly ignoble inability to commune with the "dark power" of the forest and its beasts.[108]

British sportsmen too considered "hilly country, dense homogenous forests and other surroundings indicating no definite line of retreat ... most difficult and often impossible to beat."[109] Like the princes, they benefited far more from successful beats than failed ones, both personally and as representatives of the empire eager to impress the locals. All sportsmen recognized the necessity and desirability of achieving some degree of predictability in tiger shooting, and finding manageable grounds was an integral part of the process. While princes tended to make significant temporary alterations or permanent additions to landscapes to facilitate sport, many British shooters clung to an ideal of self-sufficiency and endurance that was better served by shooting from a rickety machan in a tree. This meant going without the benefit of artificial walls, and minus the luxuries princely sportsmen used to soften their seats, please their palates, and maintain their sovereign aura while hunting. Elite British sportsmen—most notably viceroys and visiting royalty—often hunted in the princely fashion, however, relegating their supposedly higher shooting standards to the realm of rhetoric rather than reality.

Pratap Singh and his fellow princes were not alone in their desire to hunt without undue restrictions, project an aura of legitimacy through sport, and maximize their chances of bagging tigers. English sportsmen shared these hopes, but even as they gratefully benefited from the princes' efforts on their behalf when visiting the states, they criticized Indian rulers for going too far. Tales that featured

---

[108] Waghorne, *Raja's Magic Clothes*, 184.

[109] J. W. Best, *Indian Shikar Notes*, 2nd ed. (Allahabad: Pioneer Press, 1922), 52.

drugged tigers or animals transported in cages to hunting grounds direct from state menageries were prolific, while the fabulous size of animals shot by important VIPs spawned rumors of deceptively numbered measuring tapes capable of transforming a normal beast into a gargantuan "viceroy's tiger."[110] Such stories played on stereotypes of "wily Orientals" and cast aspersions on the sportsmanship and legitimacy of Indian sovereigns. Nevertheless, there is evidence that some princes did engage in these tricks.[111] Most who used these tactics simply wanted to avoid any eventuality that would result in being "looked upon ... as a third-rate state that couldn't produce a tiger for a VIP."[112] Some rulers may have meant to pay public compliments to their guests while furtively insulting them with the suggestion—true enough for certain VIPs—that they were unequal to the task of bagging unimpaired animals. The implication was that British superiority was an illusion, based not on paper tigers but drugged ones.

Despite the impression given by Pratap Singh's troubles with the British, there was a great deal of overlap between imperial orthodoxy and the prince's rogue sportsmanship. The invention and delineation of so-called true sportsmanship was the product of the colonial experience. Since arriving in India and up through the mid-nineteenth century, Europeans had hunted with Indian elites in accordance with local norms.[113] The presence of prey species and habitats that were

[110]Arthur Cunningham Lothian, *Kingdoms of Yesterday* (London: John Murray, 1951), 129–31; Lawrence M. Stubbs, "Gossip about Tigers," [1930s–1940s], 2–3, J. and L.M. Stubbs Papers, Centre for South Asian Studies; Bernard C. Ellison, *H.R.H. The Prince of Wales's Sport in India* (London: William Heinemann, Ltd., 1925), 182 and 184.

[111]On drugging tigers, see Singh, *Hints*, 20–1. One prince claimed to have tigers ranging from wild to grain-fed, meted out according to a VIP's abilities: see Stubbs, "Gossip."

[112]Allen and Dwivedi, *Lives of the Indian Princes*, 140.

[113]See François Bernier, *Travels in the Mogul Empire, A.D. 1656–1668*, 2nd ed., trans. Archibald Constable, ed. Vincent A. Smith (Delhi: Low Price Publications, 1999), 374–83; see also William Blane, *An Account of the Hunting Excursions of Asoph ul Doulah, Visier of the Mogul Empire, and Nabob of Oude* (London: John Stockdale, 1788).

initially exotic to them but familiar to the princes, like tigers and tiger jungles, meant that local practices had helped shape what became the canonical standards. Like many princes, the British had loosely followed Mughal examples in their quest to establish legitimacy, enact superiority, and look sovereign, whether in court or field.[114] British officials and Indian princes, therefore, helped each other towards the conclusion that tiger shooting, when done correctly, was a masculine activity that could augment social standing and political clout.

Even after the codification of true sportsmanship in the late Victorian period, British elites continued to participate in Indian-style hunts. In the late-nineteenth and early-twentieth centuries, they were hunting tigers less in line with their own celebrated ideals—which called for stalking the animals on foot with minimal protection and little support—and instead firing almost exclusively from secure platforms in lofty trees, padded howdahs perched on elephant-back, and shooting boxes stocked with iced lemonade and cigarettes.[115] These practices gained acceptance as the British retreated from un-regulated daring or recklessness as measures of masculinity—now firmly ascribed to supposedly non-modern and inferior races like the Rajputs—and began to elevate values typical of the newly vaunted middle class, like discipline and practicality.[116] Now it was the ability to suffer stoically inside a cramped shooting box for hours on end that mattered—never mind the cooling lemonade—alongside the restraint necessary to wait for the perfect shot, and the willingness to sacrifice one's own interests to sportsmen better positioned to make the kill. These were the new measures of imperial masculinity. Excessive risk, on the other hand, cracked the civilized veneer differentiating Englishmen from Indians and threatened the European's aura of superiority and infallibility.

---

[114] Bernard S. Cohn, "Representing Authority in Victorian India," in *The Invention of Tradition*, ed. Eric Hobsbawm and Terence Ranger (New York: Cambridge University Press, 1992), 168 and 172; MacKenzie, *Empire of Nature*, 169.

[115] See Rousselet, *India*, 174. Not all Englishmen partook: see Best, *Indian Shikar Notes*, 93.

[116] Satadru Sen, *Migrant Races: Empire, Identity and K.S. Ranjitsinhji* (New York: Manchester University Press, 2004), 179.

As a result, ironically, British elites after the 1870s adopted the luxurious and safety-conscious hunting style associated with princes, even as they continued to insist it was fundamentally foreign and less than sporting.[117] Because hyper-masculinity and the element of danger in sport remained celebrated in imperial lore—reflected in the continuing stream of popular shikar memoirs that seems to have abated only in the 1930s—British VIPs had to dissociate themselves from the very practices they were now espousing.[118] Despite their protests, few Englishmen managed to dispense with luxuries in an era defined by the proliferation of novel camp equipage and servants. An uncomfortable dissonance existed between the brawny sportsman-imperialist of legend and the comparatively effete bureaucrat-huntsman of reality: an unappealing figure who was, moreover, "unfairly" aided after 1911 by the power and accuracy of newly available high velocity small bore rifles.[119] British elites tried to resolve the tension created by engaging in and publicly enjoying princely hunting by casting themselves in their conversations, letters, and memoirs as amused observers, critical participants, and good sports who managed to endure the proceedings with a stiff upper lip and a wry sense of humor.[120] These rhetorical strategies helped transform their temporary transgressions, recast as stark contrasts with normality, into reaffirmations of British difference and superiority.

[117]British sportsmen in colonial Kenya similarly adopted aspects of African hunting while continuing to denigrate local methods: see Edward I. Steinhart, "Safari Hunting, 1909–1939," in *Black Poachers, White Hunters: A Social History of Hunting in Colonial Kenya* (Athens: Ohio University Press, 2006), 113–37.

[118]There were exceptions to this trend of abatement, notably those authored by Jim Corbett.

[119]S.R. Truesdell, *The Rifle: Its Development for Big Game Hunting* (Harrisburg, PA: Military Service Publishing Co., 1947), 126–7. Rapid developments in the power, precision, and reliability of firearms ensured that concepts of sportsmanship remained open to adjustment through the 1910s, when the rate of change leveled off after the invention of high-velocity small bore weapons, combining the penetration and power of earlier large bores with greater accuracy and convenience.

[120]For a viceroy doing so, see Hardinge, *My Indian Years*, 73 and 75; for a former political agent, see Lothian, *Kingdoms*, 27.

Although British elites explained their participation in terms of humoring their Indian hosts' backward ways and childish desires, many recognized advantages for themselves in the proceedings.[121] Some enjoyed the opportunity to hunt in an atmosphere that sanctioned or even encouraged departures from the standards of true sportsmanship.[122] In the states, they could shoot wild boar with impunity and pursue blackbuck antelope from speeding automobiles. Outside princely India, Englishmen who engaged in these activities had no excuse for their actions. Only "pork butchers" shot boar when the proper method was to spear them from horseback.[123] A group of British sportsmen in Mewar State, however, allegedly reacted to the sight of an approaching herd in 1887 by rising "in their places, forgetting that each and all had merely come 'to see the fun,' and [beginning] to fumble among ... [their] little mounds of cartridges."[124] Façades crumbled and British sportsmen lost their reserve when princes armed them with rifles, posted them in shooting towers, and confronted them with fast-moving sounders of wild boar.

It was more consistent with the Maharaja of Orchha's sovereign image and no contradiction of his standards of sportsmanship to be surrounded by luxuries while hunting. The amenities Pratap Singh enjoyed on the trail were not meant to suggest that he was soft. Such conveniences naturally surrounded sovereigns, though genuine kings were immune to them. They might sit on cushions, but they could withstand bare rocks. This was nothing new. In the sixteenth century, Raja Rudradeva of Kumaon had categorized hunting among eighteen vices which included the enjoyment of women, meat, and liquor.[125] The addictive nature of these pastimes meant

---

[121] Waghorne, *Raja's Magic Clothes*, 34.

[122] Englishmen could embrace state pageantries: see ibid., 36.

[123] Rudyard Kipling, "Of the Pig-Drive Which was a Panther-Killing, and of the Departure to Chitor," in *From Sea to Sea: Letters of Travel*, vol. 1 (New York: Doubleday and McClure Company, 1899), 71. MacKenzie dates the elevation of pigsticking over pig shooting to about 1890: see *Empire of Nature*, 299–300.

[124] Kipling, "Pig-Drive," 73.

[125] Rudradeva, *Syainikasastram*, 66 and 78.

that only kings had the necessary strength of will to indulge in them without running the risk of corruption. They were in fact expected to hunt for the good of their states, just as Abu al-Fazl had posited. Conspicuous consumption of taboo yet powerful luxuries like sport invigorated rulers and promoted a kingdom's prosperity.[126] Opulence was not testament to a prince's need, but a tribute to his greatness. While all Rajput rulers shared Pratap Singh's biases, most harbored a complementary desire to display reckless feats of masculinity or publicly endure extreme hardships in their pursuit of game. Such trials validated the utility of the hunt as a conditioner of royal bodies while also serving as a link to the military traditions and legendary privations suffered by Rajput heroes. What rulers in the late-nineteenth and early-twentieth centuries hoped to achieve was the appearance of accomplishing great deeds against great odds with even greater ease.

Although Pratap Singh eventually did receive yearly shooting privileges in the Lalitpur forest blocks, no land whatsoever was given as compensation for Karkigarh, and there would be no inheritable guarantees for his heirs. His success in regaining ground after the PWD's encroachment, therefore, was partial at best. The Karkigarh island affair was more than a conflict between two unequal powers over their respective territorial rights, however they defined them; it was also a clash of ideals. The maharaja's image of good tiger grounds, along with the shooting arrangements and behavior he deemed appropriate for Rajput princes like himself, shaped his demands and sporting campaigns, as did his understanding of shooting as a sovereign right and privilege associated with his ancestral territories. Likewise, British sporting criteria and their understandings of sovereignty and property ownership framed their counter-offers and justified their refusals. Caught somewhere in the middle, Karkigarh island itself simply retreated under the rising waters, and its tigers moved on.

[126] Velcheru Narayana Rao, David Shulman, and Sanjay Subrahmanyam, *Symbols of Substance: Court and State in Nayaka Period Tamilnadu* (New York: Oxford University Press, 1992), 120, 124, and 188.

3

Exceptional Game in
Powerful Places

A small bunker-like structure, weathered into streaks of red ochre, cement grey, and lime white, stands on the grounds of the Kalka Mata botanical nursery just south of the Pichola lake. Lightly shaded by an open canopy of drought-resistant foliage and completely surrounded by exposed earth and parched grass, the building's door opens onto a different world. Inside, brilliant blue and green pigments shine against a backdrop painted in rich browns and warm tans. Beautifully maintained shooting towers in diverse shapes and sizes, embellished with colored-glass window panes and architectural flourishes, dot the forested hillsides and open plains that cover the walls. In this painted environment, wild boar and leopards crowd the verdant shoreline, while tigers and bears slip through the trees. On the ceiling, birds and butterflies float through softly clouded skies. Throughout this Mewari landscape in miniature, Maharana Fateh Singh and his huntsmen immerse themselves in their state's characteristic environments to pursue its distinctive local game.

Today the sharpest visual contrasts at this former royal shooting box, known as Nahar Odi, are between the building's muted exterior and drab surroundings, and its vibrantly painted, if faded and flaking, interior. Yet, when Fateh Singh's court artists completed their work in the late 1880s a few years after the maharana's coronation, the most important contrasts at the site were inside the shooting box itself. The

Nahar Odi paintings portray Mewar's hunting grounds as marked by severity, complemented and tempered by an almost omnipresent fertility. On every wall, the reds and browns of the partially exposed hillsides indicate the region's aridity. Just as prominently, scattered uplands vegetation and ubiquitous lowland greens suggest the overall complexity of Mewar's environment.

The landscape most identified with Mewar during Fateh Singh's reign was the one depicted on the walls of Nahar Odi, namely, the hill-bound setting of the Pichola lake and the capital city, Udaipur. Closely associated with the royal Sisodia Rajputs since the late sixteenth century, Udaipur's surroundings embodied its sovereigns' military might in the defensive capacity of rugged hills augmented by fortifications, while the city's gardens, lake palaces, and accumulated waters of its man-made lakes suggested a life of luxury and cultural refinement appropriate to kings. At Nahar Odi, the maharana's artists chose to depict this specific landscape not only because it represented the actual environs of the royal shooting box, but also because its composite nature epitomized a fundamental Mewari environmental ideal.

The best possible environment for Rajput princes, and for their prey, was one that balanced nurturing attributes with suitably challenging aspects. While cultivators preferred fertile fields and merchants wanted open roads, Rajput sovereigns and nobles needed imposing hills and dense forests alongside their pleasure gardens. These same salubrious hills, forests, and grasslands produced and housed better classes of game, which in turn required bigger, better, and braver sportsmen to kill them.

Like their Rajput peers throughout North India, the princes of Mewar saw close connections, and even causal relationships, between the landscapes of their individual states, and the nature and worth of their royal lineages. As a consequence of their contacts with local topography and plant life, Rajputs either grew soft and degenerate in overly paradisiacal surroundings, or else became hardened and formidable as they struggled within challenging environments. Likewise, the state's most celebrated hunting grounds were those that balanced difficulty with ease, and severity with abundance.

The fine balance of fecundity and ruggedness in Mewar's ideal hunting grounds found expression in steep hillsides softened with foliage, the proliferation of dangerous game, and an abundance of vegetation tipped with thorns. It also found echoes in the cultural refinement and undiluted Rajput masculinity claimed by the house of Mewar and its maharana. Fateh Singh's self-image as a possessor of admirable game and fine shikargahs, and as a keen yet discriminating hunter, coincided with his understanding of a Mewari sovereign's ideal sophistication, strength, and status *vis-à-vis* his nobles, other princes, and the British. Even though environmental severity was a feature shared widely amongst the Rajput states, many of which had more arid or forbidding territories, Mewaris managed to excel by stressing the advantages unique to their homeland, where environmental challenges coexisted with fields of plenty.

The most significant game animals in Mewar were wild boar, tigers, and leopards. Mewaris drew on an established set of qualities that they ascribed to each species, habitat, and hunting method to support flattering conclusions about themselves and their realm. While they based their assessments on criteria similar to those used by other Rajputs and to a lesser degree akin to those accepted by the British, their judgments remained subjective and aligned with local interests. As a result, what made Mewar great and validated its proud heritage of independence in local opinion could undermine the state's image before hostile audiences reluctant either to credit the maharana's claims of preeminence, or accept his avowed reliance on tradition—both of which he used to justify transgressions against British paramountcy and slights against princely houses that he viewed as inferior.

Fateh Singh endeavored throughout his reign to engage with Mewar's environment and hunting landscapes in authoritative ways. He built better shooting towers, promoted thicker forests, and fostered game to create opportunities for hunting in a manner consistent with and constitutive of Rajput sovereignty and legitimacy. Like Pratap Singh of Orchha, Fateh Singh needed well-stocked shikargahs where he could obtain abundant game with minimal risk of failure. Unlike Orchha's prince, Mewar's maharana required more ostentatious links with hardship and danger while hunting. Fateh Singh's preeminent rank and the perceived dignity of his office as Maharana of Mewar forced him to outclass every prince in India, not just his immediate rivals. In addition, the maharana's nobles were more independent and powerful than their counterparts in Orchha, and some of them tended towards outright defiance. As a result, Fateh Singh's displays of strength and skill had to be that much more impressive.

In line with the maharana's requirements, the wall paintings at Nahar Odi touted the full range of habitats available in the immediate vicinity, each conducive to different game and sporting styles, and each capable of making its own unique contribution to the constitution of Mewar's Rajputs through the particular difficulties and advantages it posed. Both the lowlands and the hills around Udaipur were conveniently accessible to the prince as he went about his daily routine, which included mounted excursions along the shores of the Pichola lake, and target practice at the rifle range just west of Tikhalya Magra.

The lower reaches around Udaipur housed the maharana's wild boar. The gentle contours of these grounds were suitable for pigsticking from horseback, or for shooting from the roofs of low-profile boxes like Nahar Odi. Hunters at such sites came into intimate contact with their prey, often dispatching animals by hand with spears or swords. These places and their signature prey showcased a hunter's strength, daring, and superior horsemanship or marksmanship. The hillier regions with their thicker vegetation contained leopards and tigers. These landscapes required elaborate beats to guide an animal's movements through ravines and over slopes. Such places also encouraged the use of multi-storied shooting boxes, which provided sportsmen with security and a clear line of sight over tall bushes and trees. As a result, the hills foregrounded tactical skill and leadership.

Apportioned out between the lowlands and the highlands, wild boar, tiger, leopard, sambar, blackbuck, bear, wildfowl, and hare populated the ruggedly bountiful Mewari landscapes inside Nahar Odi. The almost implausible abundance of wildlife in these paintings represented Udaipur's immediate surroundings as a hunter's paradise. The conflation of every kind of game occasionally seen in these hills into one sprawling illustration, along with every method used to hunt them, conveyed the false impression that each animal was available concurrently and continuously. In fact, appearances in the closest hills of certain game, like tigers, could be separated by months or even years.

Fateh Singh's artists painted an exaggerated environment to suggest that Udaipur's natural surroundings, by virtue of their proximity to the center of power and regular contact with the maharana, were ideal. Fateh Singh's policies, righteousness, and presence unlocked the potential of Mewar's topography, giving the land fecundity and the game distinction. One lowland scene in particular stands out as a fantastic overstatement: a pair of rhinoceros in the same panel as a deer and two wild boar. The Indian rhinoceros is a species that inhabits riverine grasslands, adjacent swamps, and forests.[1] While their famously tough hides were once prized for shields in the area, no wild rhinoceros lived in arid Rajasthan, making their inclusion in Nahar Odi an environmental hyperbole. Of course, it is not inconceivable that Fateh Singh had acquired a rhinoceros or two for his menagerie, which he was building up from an existing collection that reportedly included "a terrace-full of tigers, bears, and Guzerat [*sic*] lions bought from the Nawab of Oudh's sale."[2] Nevertheless it seems likely that his artists' depiction of a lone huntsman and hounds approaching the rhinoceros on foot suggests some naiveté regarding these animals.

The maharana's artists did not necessarily believe that their ruler could transform Udaipur's countryside into a lush environment suited to rhinoceros, assuming they even knew what sort of habitat rhinoceros required. More likely, they tailored their art to Fateh

[1] B.K. Talukdar, R. Emslie, S.S. Bist, A. Choudhury, S. Ellis, B.S. Bonal, M.C. Malakar, B.N. Talukdar, and M. Barua, "*Rhinoceros unicornis*" (2008), in *IUCN Red List of Threatened Species*, Version 2011.2, accessed March 24, 2012, http://www.iucnredlist.org/apps/redlist/details/19496/0.

[2] Sharma, ed., *Haqiqat Bahida*, 2:5; there was a new zoo by 1897: ibid., 3:71; Rudyard Kipling, "Diverse Passages of Speech and Action Whence the Nature, Arts, and Disposition of the King and His Subjects may be Observed," *From Sea to Sea*, vol. 1, 69.

Singh's sporting tastes and association of Mewari exceptionalism with the hunting state landscapes offered. Their painting asserted the maharana's prowess, therefore, by showing an abundance of game rather than fields of sprouting grain. The images inside Nahar Odi would have appealed far less to the general populace, which was more likely to associate plentiful game with damaged crops and decimated livestock. But Nahar Odi was not designed for them. Instead, "the relevant 'public' whose loyalty had to be regulated and ordered was [the prince's] kinsmen, the nobles and 'aristocrats' of the state."[3]

Hills dominate the Nahar Odi paintings by providing backdrops for most hunting scenes. The same is true of the well-known Mewari miniatures executed on paper, which depict royal sport around Nahar Magra, Udai Sagar, Jaisamand, and Chittorgarh. The basic features of the state's hunting landscapes remain constant between the wall and miniature paintings, indicating that Mewar's shikargahs shared a similar aesthetic either in fact or in the imagination of local artists. Few hunting miniatures violate these standards, which prescribe tiger or leopard beats in intimate amphitheaters of undulating green-brown hills dominated by *anwal* or Indian gooseberry (*Phyllanthus emblica*), acacias, and cactus-like thuhar (*Euphorbia caducifolia*). These often feature exposed rocks and are cut here and there by ravines or stream-fed valleys carpeted with banyan, pipal, mango, and mahua trees. Wild boar appear in the same settings as the big cats or in more open forests with smaller brush and lower hills. Paintings that differ from the norm do so only slightly. In some, the field of view spills out between the foregrounded slopes into distant hilly plains. In others dating to the end of Fateh Singh's reign, barren summer landscapes full of skeletal trees and bleached grass replace the usual greens and warm earthen tones.[4]

Although hills occupied a place of prominence in almost all Mewari paintings of the hunt, Fateh Singh's shikari Dhaibhai Tulsinath Singh Tanwar reported that around the Jaisamand shikargah most animals

[3] Edward S. Haynes, "Rajput Ceremonial Interactions as a Mirror of a Dying Indian State System, 1820–1947," *Modern Asian Studies* 24, 3 (1990): 468.

[4] Topsfield, *City Palace*, Figs. 54–6, 58–9, and 61.

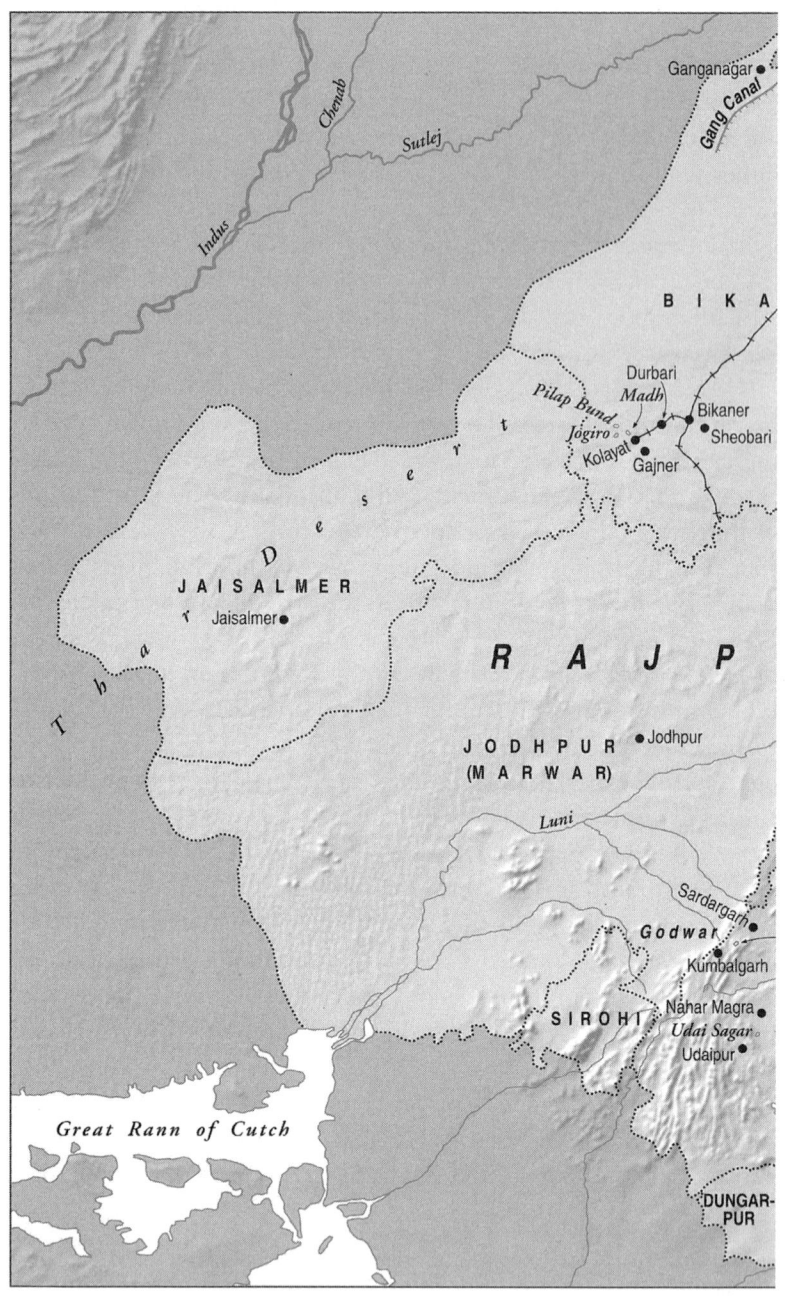

Map 3: The Rajputana States (left side)

Map 3: The Rajputana States (right side)

lived not on the slopes or summits but at the base of the hills and along their margins in the plains below.[5] The occasional placement of shooting boxes in the flats, and of many more halfway down the hillsides and overlooking ravines around Udaipur and at Nahar Magra, suggests that the same was true of game at these sites. But Fateh Singh's artists did not frame the action so narrowly as to exclude the hilltops, even though the pictured events usually took place at least partway down or at the bottom of the hills. The geographical scale of hunts, during which the prey had ranged far and wide in its attempts to escape, certainly would have encouraged them to show skies and hills alike; but they did not limit their panoramic depictions to such scenes. In Mewar, it was consistently as important to document the landscape as to detail the animals, actions, and human participants.

These were not hunts like any other, transpiring anonymously in unimportant places. These were exceptional kills of exceptional prey by an exceptional ruler accomplished in an exceptional and specifically Mewari setting. For Fateh Singh and his followers, immediately recognizable formations like Machhla Magra and Nahar Magra set the scene as effectively as glimpses of the royal reservoir at Rajsamand or the victorious Vijay Stambha at Chittorgarh. One state shikari even claimed such thorough familiarity with his prince's favorite hunting grounds that "the hill slopes, the trees, and even the stones, nothing is unknown."[6] Cloaked in the same vegetation and rendered in a consistent style, even the less distinctive contours around the Koriyat, Hinglajya, and Amjhar hunting grounds looked fundamentally Mewari.

The importance of Mewar's landscape helps explain Fateh Singh's apparent preference for miniature paintings of the hunt over photographs. Even after improved technology eliminated many of the problems associated with the long exposure times and bulky cameras of the mid-to-late nineteenth century, the maharana remained

[5] Tanwar, *Shikari aur Shikar*, 312.
[6] Ibid., 141. All translations from this source are my own.

indifferent to photography's particular documentary abilities when it came to royal sport. In order to capture the lay of the land during a hunt in Mewar's hills, photographers needed to situate themselves at some distance from the action, preferably at a height. In retreating far enough to get the big picture, intervening foliage and other landscape features could obscure the action. Accurately but undesirably, wider perspectives invariably diminished the central figures of the maharana, his nobles, and their prey, rendering the sportsmen's identities indeterminate and the game invisible. While brightly attired nobles and orange tigers stood out against hills in green and tan, black-and-white figures disappeared against black-and-white backgrounds. The quick pace and unpredictability of royal shikar made it challenging to artfully encompass participants, action, and setting in a single frame or series. Fateh Singh's court painters, on the other hand, were practiced in overcoming these difficulties, commonly depicting the prey and other figures repeatedly in sequence to indicate each stage of the action. They could also manipulate perspective, color, and relative sizes to render important individuals and animals suitably prominent without sacrificing a sharp sense of place.

In line with common assumptions about Fateh Singh, it is tempting to conclude that the maharana's alleged hostility to the stereotypical trappings of modernity and anything European must have figured in his preference for shikar miniatures over photographs. But Mewar's prince did not blindly reject everything that was new or that originated in the West. He had electric boats on the Pichola lake by 1908 and apparently owned automobiles by 1909.[7] He was a well-known aficionado and collector of the finest European sporting rifles, including a .450 double-barreled high-velocity Rigby that was good enough to lend out to the Prince of Wales in 1921.[8] The problem was not the advanced and foreign technology of the camera, but its inadequacy for his purposes.

Nevertheless, photography had a place in Fateh Singh's court because the maharana found himself at the intersection of several distinct cultures that all valued the production and gifting of portraits, from

[7] Sharma, *Haqiqat Bahida*, 4:391 and 4:537.
[8] Ellison, *H.R.H. The Prince of Wales's Sport in India*, 138 and 186.

the photographic Victorian *carte de visite* to the painted portraiture of the Mughal court and its subsequent adaptations to Rajput aesthetics. Patronizing famous photographic firms like Johnston & Hoffman of Calcutta and Herzog & Higgins of Mhow, Fateh Singh had his portrait taken in 1885 after his coronation and several times afterwards in the 1890s and early 1900s.[9] He presented these formal portraits to his peers, state nobles, and foreign dignitaries. Like other Rajput princes, he evidently preferred photography over miniature paintings for these purposes because photo-artists could add color to multiple prints produced from a single negative or photographic plate with greater speed, ease, and economy than court artists could replicate miniature paintings. In addition, photographs may have met the expectations of Europeans and other recipients better than miniatures executed in the Mewari style.

Most princely states had embraced photography for their visual documentary needs by 1900. The earliest Indian hunting photographs from the mid-to-late 1800s showed British sportsmen posing inside or in front of buildings with pelts, horns, or bare skulls. Photographic equipment was fragile, bulky, and heavy; travel was slow, and preservation difficult in the field. As cameras grew more common and increasingly mobile, and as field preservation became more feasible, photographers began shooting in the camps of their elite clients, which now included more Indian princes. Genre standards soon developed: the carcass laid out in front; the gun credited with the kill at center with rifle in hand and a foot on the animal's flank; hunting companions next to and behind the shooter in orderly rows, their placement dictated by rank and degree of participation in the kill. Further technological advances would allow "candid" shots by the early 1900s.

Judging by their ubiquity, however, the most successful shikar photographs in princely India remained those that showed the shooter and his companions standing triumphantly behind the body of their prey, which they generally arranged in a lifelike fashion. Yet, even these images were not particularly common at the Mewari court during Fateh Singh's reign. Few posed shikar photographs of the maharana exist and, in nearly every case, the image immortalizes the successes of Fateh Singh's state guests, not his own trophies. Seemingly only one photograph, possibly dating to 1888, shows the maharana with his own tiger kill.[10] Significantly, it includes a sizeable hill in the background.

Either Fateh Singh himself, or, more likely, his photography enthusiast son Bhupal Singh, approved of this particular image enough to commission a firm of photo-artists in Jaipur, K.R. Sharma & Sons, to prepare a tinted print, probably around 1930 (Fig. 2).[11] While both the original and the painted-over versions demonstrate that photography could capture Mewar's distinctive landscape along with the prince and his prey, the technology still fell short of accomplishing these ends as well as miniature paintings could. Against this single photographic image, the court artists at Mewar produced at least sixteen large-scale miniatures of Fateh Singh's shikar exploits, besides the extensive wall paintings at Nahar Odi.[12] From the maharana's perspective, the photographic experiment had failed when it came to documenting his sport.

The 1888 image, however, was not the only shikar photograph to record Fateh Singh's early tiger kills, even if it does seem to have been the only one reproduced and, possibly, gifted to state nobles and other deserving recipients. Inside Nahar Odi, there is a very large painting of a lone shikari seated behind a slain tiger (Fig. 3) that appears to have been based on a photograph, and possibly even on an alternate frame of the same tiger seen in the 1888 picture. Photographers often took multiple frames, experimenting with different groupings and exposures. If they did so for Fateh Singh's 1888 kill, then alternate

[10] James C. Ivory, *Autobiography of a Princess, Also Being the Adventures of an American Film Director in the Land of the Maharajas* (New York: Harper & Row, Publishers, 1975), 18–19.

[11] The tinted print is undated; photographs similarly prepared by K.R. Sharma & Sons depicting Bhupal Singh's tiger shoots date to the early 1930s.

[12] Additional photographs may come to light as the City Palace collection is cataloged: Pramod Kumar, personal communication, July 2008.

views might have been available for the Nahar Odi painters to reference as they completed their work in 1888 or 1889. The slight angle of the tiger's body relative to the horizon, with its head a little lower than its tail, along with its open mouth and exposed fangs are consistent between the 1888 photograph and the painting. The positioning of the animal's legs, however, is reversed: the Nahar Odi tiger's left forepaw crosses over its right, while the opposite is true in the photograph. The rear legs show an equivalent difference. The stripes on the Nahar Odi animal are impressionistic and do not accord with the photographed one any better than they would with any other genuine tiger.

The substantive differences between Mewari paintings and shikar photography reveal how Fateh Singh's artists tried to improve on photographic representations to make them conform to Mewari court aesthetics and princely aims. Where photography failed in its attempts to delineate the hunting landscape, Fateh Singh's painters simply drew it in. This is evident in the sharp contrast between both versions of the 1888 photograph and the Nahar Odi painting. Although visible in the original photograph, the hills behind the maharana are out of focus, the brush and trees barely discernible, and the contours hazy. In preparing their tinted product, the Jaipur firm of photo-artists failed to enhance these features, instead rendering the hills as a series of indistinct green and ecru smudges that reproduced the fuzziness of the original image.

Inside Nahar Odi, Fateh Singh's artists produced a far more robust backdrop. They made the hills more prominent, more extensive, and more detailed. Clearly defined in bold colors, individual trees and multiple peaks cluster above and behind the shikari and the dead tiger. The particular hills shown may be those just west of the Pichola lake, or some other specific grouping that Fateh Singh and his followers would have recognized. Indeed, many landscapes on Nahar Odi's walls are readily identifiable, including Machhla Magra and Banki Magra.

While K.R. Sharma & Sons did little for the 1888 photograph's background, they did improve the foreground. When a few individuals spoiled a large group shot by moving during the exposure, as clearly happened here, photo-artists could correct the resultant blurring. They did so here for the young man on the far right, the slightly portly figure at the left, and the white-bearded gentleman in the back.[13] As attested by the often encyclopedic inscriptions on Mewari hunting miniatures that name the pictured VIPs, noblemen, shikaris, and sometimes even the horses and elephants, visual records of the maharana's sport documented not just the prince's prowess and the landscapes he sported in, but also the attendance and participation of his followers. Just as the hills had to be in focus, everyone pictured in shikar images—whether painted or photographic—needed to be identifiable.

Besides enhancing the hills, the Nahar Odi painters likely departed from their reference photograph to make the slain tiger appear as impressive as possible. To begin with, they skewed the tiger's face towards the viewer, thereby rendering one eye visible. Assuming Fateh Singh's artists did replicate the overall positioning of the tiger's body from an alternate frame of the 1888 photograph, then the angles suggest that the animal's entire face would have been obscured. By distorting the image, the artists made it possible for Fateh Singh and his followers to meet the painted tiger's gaze and re-experience something of the animal's intimidating presence. They underscored this sensation of immediacy by highlighting the tiger's lolling red tongue and bared canines, and by producing an exceptionally large painting. The tiger in the 1888 photograph, in contrast, is a necessarily smaller and less assertive figure. Its sharp white teeth may stand out against the black coloration around its gaping mouth, but its head turns away and its averted eyes do not return the viewer's gaze.

Beyond showcasing painted commentaries on Mewar's ideal environments and royal game, Nahar Odi functioned as a regular shooting box. In order to emphasize and harness the attributes of Mewar's formidable hills and inviting plains, and to facilitate the maharana's entry into these landscapes to hunt, superior shooting infrastructure needed to complement the shooting grounds. Early in his reign,

[13] See Ivory, *Autobiography of a Princess*, 18–19.

Fateh Singh embarked on an ambitious program of restoring and improving Mewar's existing *odi*s and *mul*s, and constructing new shooting boxes across the state. The prince started close to his capital city, and his court artists immediately began incorporating his most impressive works into their miniature paintings and onto the walls of Nahar Odi.

Inside the recently refurbished Nahar Odi, they painted a miniature of Nahar Odi itself. Barely discernible now, three well-armed Rajputs stand on the box's roof and confer with a fourth man on the ground, while a bear approaches from the west. In 1886, Kala Odi too underwent renovations.[14] This striking black tower was constructed sometime between the 1830s and the early 1850s, when it first appeared in a painting of Maharana Sarup Singh hunting a tiger just south of the city walls on Tikhalya Magra.[15] Oddly, it does not appear in the Nahar Odi paintings, although its location is pictured and it was in use in the late 1880s. Just south of Udaipur and a little lower than Kala Odi on Tikhalya Magra, Maj Mul incorporated a special ladies' compartment after Fateh Singh's renovations.[16] When completed, its ground floor featured an open courtyard and an attached room with small lattice-work windows, while its luxurious first-floor apartment had a built-in bench, shuttered windows, and a small balcony. Fateh Singh and his followers would have shot from the rifle loops on either floor, from the staircase, or from the split-level roof. Like Kala Odi, however, Maj Mul does not appear in the Nahar Odi paintings.

Perhaps the most important building shown in the Nahar Odi paintings is Khas Odi. Renovated by 1888, Khas Odi was a site of importance throughout the maharana's reign that he used for hosting wild animal fights and observing the local wild boar, which gathered daily at the base of the structure to feed.[17] The building contained elegant interior apartments, holding cells for wild animals, and an attached courtyard that functioned as an arena. Just as Khas Odi

---

[14] Sharma, *Haqiqat Bahida*, 2:33.

[15] See Topsfield, *City Palace*, Fig. 31.

[16] Sharma, *Haqiqat Bahida*, 3:129. Maj Mul was also called Tikhalya re Maj Mul and Tikhalya re Mul.

[17] It was used for fights as early as 1885: see ibid., 1:169 and 1:190.

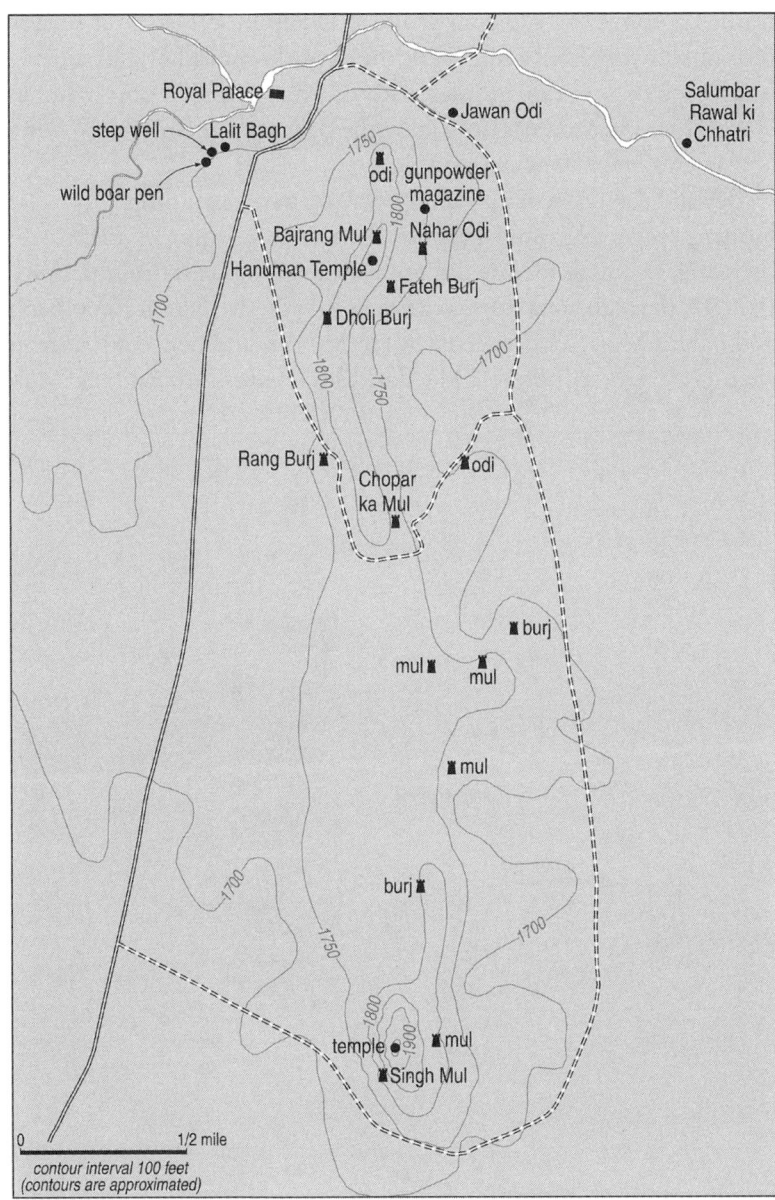

Map 4: Hunting Grounds at Udaipur

featured prominently in courtly life at Udaipur, so too did it feature prominently in Nahar Odi. While the entire lower half of the painting is now missing, the image of a restored Khas Odi still dominates as one of three major scenes (including the tiger and shikari) illuminating Nahar Odi's northwestern wall.

Beyond the immediate vicinity of Udaipur, Fateh Singh's favorite hunting seat at Nahar Magra too saw numerous improvements over the years, although the site did not feature in his artists' productions. In 1897, the maharana inspected works in progress there at Kesar Bagh and Lakhu Mul.[18] A decade later, renovations and new construction were underway at Diwan Odi, Bari Odi, Rang Burj, Bajrang Mul,

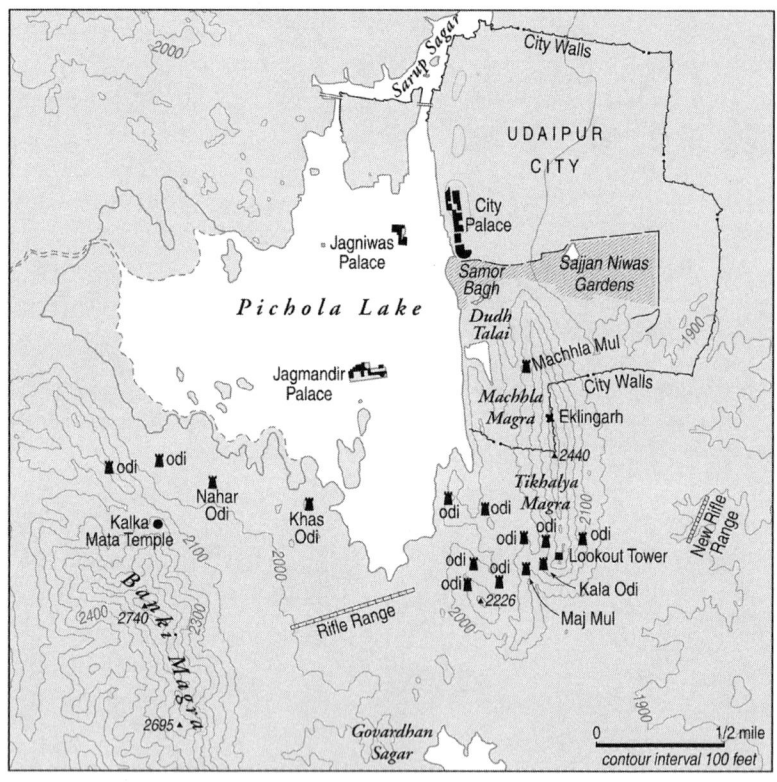

Map 5: Hunting Grounds at Nahar Magra

[18] Ibid., 3:81 and 3:99.

Nahar Odi, Fateh Burj, and Chopar ka Mul.[19] Some of these boxes
were elaborate structures with courtyards and towers meant for
shooting, while others were staging grounds for hunts or outposts
for feeding wild boar. It is likely that many featured extensive decorations. Inside Bajrang Mul, faded poppies in red and green still adorn
the walls, oval piercings once fitted with colored glass surround some
of the windows, and painted embellishments in black and white
remain visible on the ochre-colored exterior. Fateh Singh arranged
for the upkeep of his new and improved *odi*s and *mul*s too. In 1908,
for example, shikar department employees were visiting and cleaning
the shooting boxes at Nahar Magra, Kamlod, and Bagdara every eight
to twelve days.[20]

Mewar's renovated shooting towers provided acceptable alter-
natives to hills in photographs of game bagged by foreign VIPs,
which were intended for inclusion in souvenir presentation albums.
If Fateh Singh chose or influenced the choice of background, then
he likely hoped his European guests would comprehend the import
of magnificently restored and newly built shooting boxes better than
they would the meaning of a Mewari landscape. While locals could
interpret the state's distinctive contours, viceroys and commanders-
in-chief could not easily discern the identity or import of hills like
Machhla Magra, Hinglajya Magra, or even the grounds at Jaisamand.
But they might grasp the powerful message of three-storied shooting
boxes with courtyards, towers, rifle loops, and elegant decorations—
like the particularly fine Dhimra Bagh at Jaisamand most often
pictured in VIP shikar photographs (Fig. 4). Even if British officials
admired these structures, they did not accept them as substitutes
for modern roads and railways. Far from authenticating a princely
balance between refinement and practicality, these buildings instead
reinforced British impressions that Fateh Singh was hopelessly old-
fashioned, obsessed with hunting to the detriment of his administration, and out of touch with the populace.

[19] Ibid., 4:368, 4:376, 4:379, and 4:383.
[20] Gamir Singh Chauhan, circular 235, *samvat 1965 asar sud 14*, book of
MMK circulars beginning VS 1951, RSA-Udaipur.

Often located in inhospitable surroundings on steep hillsides covered with thorns, Fateh Singh's elegantly restored shooting towers reaffirmed this royal sportsman's sophistication to local audiences while facilitating complementary displays of his practical talents and princely abilities. At the same time, an array of newly-built and comparatively plain shooting boxes and temporary structures, like machans, expanded his options and offset the luxury of sites like Khas Odi and Maj Mul. In fact, very few miniatures show the maharana in tall, elaborate, white towers like the ones at Hinglajya and Amjhar where he shot tigers in 1885.[21] The prince's artists usually pictured him in tree machans, on lightly cushioned rocky outcroppings, or in comparatively squat boxes like those in paintings of Chittor, Kamlod, and Bagdara.[22] In these simpler structures, the maharana's confident demeanor, royal nimbus, and generally exquisite dress maintained the requisite aura of refinement in the midst of Mewar's hilly environment.

Mewaris were acutely aware that their state's landscape had played a vital role in preserving their independence throughout history. In addition to keeping the realm isolated from imperial power centers, the local hills had sheltered royal family members from Mughal forces centuries ago. Mewar had fought its most famous battles from hill forts and passes in various branches of the Aravalli range, so that

----

[21] Topsfield, *City Palace*, Figs. 37 and 39. Topsfield incorrectly dates these hunts, and possibly a third (ibid., Fig. 38), to before Fateh Singh's December 1884 coronation. Confirmed in Sharma, *Haqiqat Bahida*, 1:236–327 and 1:199–200, the Hinglajya hunt occurred on May 30, 1885, and the Amjhar hunt on April 25, 1885. The inscription for the third hunt indicates that two tigers were marked down at Koriyat on *samvat 1941 ka asoj sud 6*, unsuccessfully hunted on *asoj sud 8*, and the male killed on *kati sud 1*. Topsfield accurately assigns these dates to autumn 1884, but the inscription's *1941* may be an error for *1942*, putting the hunt after the coronation. If so, it may be the hunt recorded in ibid., 2:220: two tigers were marked down at Koriyat on *samvat 1942 asoj sud 5*, unsuccessfully hunted on *asoj sud 11*, and the male killed on *kati vid* [*sic*] *1*.

[22] For *machan*s, see Topsfield, *City Palace*, Figs. 40, 42–3, 53, 55–6, and 59; for rocks, Figs. 54 and 61; for plain *odi*s, figs. 41, 44, and 58.

local Rajputs associated defiance and glory with their state's elevated districts. The lowlands had neither seen nor fostered heroism to the same degree. Because of lessons learned from living in the hills and due to the protection afforded by such surroundings, Mewar's rulers claimed to have resisted Mughal encroachment more effectively than other Rajput kingdoms. The supposed gulf between their own heroic landscape and the comparatively lackluster grounds and lesser dignity of neighboring states, particularly Jodhpur, helped cement local identity and offered a partial explanation for Mewar's perceived successes.

As early as the mid-seventeenth century, Mewar's maharanas began claiming that their ancestors' refusal to marry women of the royal family to Mughal emperors had confirmed Mewari exceptionalism.[23] From their perspective, inferior landscapes in other states had rendered those places less protected, their Rajputs less prepared to resist, and their rulers lamentably more willing to send a daughter or sister to the emperor. Jodhpur, for instance, had become "closely linked to the Mughal house" through marriage ties early in the seventeenth century.[24] Perpetuated by the Mewar court with Tod's complicity in the early 1800s, these past failures remained fresh in the nineteenth and twentieth centuries.

For the maharanas and their subjects, the arid expanses of Marwar or Jodhpur State, visible from the summits of the Aravallis, provided the perfect foil for their own typically hilly countryside. This sharp distinction had deep roots. Heavily influenced by his Mewari informants and European understandings of the confluence between national character and territory, Tod noted in the early 1800s that natural barriers coincided with differences in customs and manners, so that "whoever passes from upland Mewar, the country of the Sesodias [*sic*], into the sandy flats of Marwar, the abode of the Rathors,

---

[23] Cynthia Talbot, "The Mewar Court's Construction of History," in Joanna Gottfried Williams, ed., *Kingdom of the Sun: Indian Court and Village Art from the Princely State of Mewar* (San Francisco: Asian Art Museum, Chong-Moon Lee Center for Asian Art and Culture, 2007), 15.

[24] Frances H. Taft, "Honor and Alliance: Reconsidering Mughal–Rajput Marriages," in *The Idea of Rajasthan*, ed. Karine Schomer, *et al.*, vol. 2, 230.

would feel the force of this remark."[25] He had learned from an envoy of Maharana Bhim Singh that plants marked the territorial divide too, sometimes more accurately than the hills. According to this Mewari informant, the region of Godwar, then included in Marwari territory, properly belonged to Mewar because "wherever the anwal puts forth its yellow blossoms, the land is of right ours ... Let [Marwaris] enjoy their stunted babuls [*Acacia nilotica*], their karil [*Capparis decidua*], and the ak [*Calotropis gigantea*]; but give us back our sacred pipal [*Ficus religiosa*], and the anwal of the border."[26] According to Tod, a common saying in Mewar reiterated this distinction "*Anwal, anwal Mewar; Bawal, bawal Marwar.*"

While there was some truth to these generalizations, the contrasts were overdrawn. Visitors describing the Mewari countryside in the nineteenth and early-twentieth centuries consistently noted the dominance of cacti, dry scrub, and thorny acacias.[27] These were the same plants Mewaris considered emblematic of Jodhpur, even if they were offset in Mewar by pipal trees and yellow-flowering *anwal*. Besides, Jodhpur was not entirely a flat, sandy expanse. There were low hills around the capital and at Jawantpura and Jalor, while portions of the Aravalli range extended into the state's territory. In the early-twentieth century, Jodhpur had some 345 square miles of forest (admittedly just 1 per cent of the total area), and a smattering of ravines, rivers, and seasonal marshes, along with numerous reservoirs and several lakes (the latter admittedly salt).[28] Considering their self-image, it is not surprising that Mewaris ignored this limited variety and instead saw unrelenting hardship with restricted opportunities for cultural refinement and no hope of independence in the Jodhpuri environment. In contrast, Mewar's felicitous mixture of impervious hills and open valleys crowned with protective thorns and succulent foliage insulated the state from outside forces while preserving its

[25] Tod, *Annals and Antiquities of Rajasthan,* 2:708.

[26] Ibid., 2:803. Other editions render *anwal* as *aonla*.

[27] For examples, see David Walker, *The Prince in India. A Record of the Indian Tour of His Royal Highness The Prince of Wales – Nov. 1921 to March 1922* (Bombay: Bennett, Coleman & Co., Ltd., 1923), 42, and Rousselet, *India and its Native Princes,* 172.

[28] Erskine, *Western Rajputana,* 50 and 113.

inhabitants from provinciality and undue deprivation.[29] Mewar's environment literally elevated the region above Jodhpur.

Some of Mewar's best landscapes were at Nahar Magra, where Mewari foliage grew large and thick in the royal pigsticking grounds at Rana Kui ka Bir and Bara Bir. Paintings from the 1850s and 1860s depicting the hills and lowlands around Nahar Magra, including Rana Kui ka Bir and Bara Bir, show the region as a largely unbroken expanse of green regularly dotted with trees.[30] The unofficial buffer zones between these grounds and areas under cultivation narrowed over the years—resulting in conflicts between the maharana and local villagers plagued by boar—but, at least through 1930, both preserves retained significant grass, shrub, and small tree coverage.[31] This reduced the range of sight and forced huntsmen on horseback to make quick turns in their pursuit of boar. Aside from dense vegetation, the grounds at Nahar Magra were full of stones that could trip or injure a galloping horse.

For its pigsticking, Jodhpur could boast of smooth and treeless plains that offered horse and rider few obstacles and minimal danger. According to the Mewari huntsman Tanwar, Marwar in fact had the more suitable landscape for pigsticking.[32] In contrast, he judged Rana Kui ka Bir a dangerous run and called Bara Bir a "very bad place."[33] At least one English pigsticking enthusiast agreed, declaring in 1930 that the "country round Udaipur itself, though abounding in pig, does not lend itself to pigsticking like Jodhpur and Jaipur; it is hilly and rough."[34]

Tanwar, however, was actually proud of the difficulties posed by the denser foliage and sharper contours of his Mewari homeland. Pigsticking was at its best when somewhat hazardous and he bragged

---

[29] Compare with the "moral decline" of deforestation, Gold and Gujar, *In the Time of Trees and Sorrows*, 255.

[30] For examples, see Topsfield, *City Palace*, Figs. 32 and 34.

[31] Tanwar, *Shikari aur Shikar*, 271–2, 184, 299, and 304.

[32] Ibid., 54–5.

[33] Ibid., 299 and 284.

[34] F.W. Caton Jones, "A Glance at Udaipur," in *The Hoghunter's Annual*, ed. H. Nugent Head and J. Scott Cockburn (Bombay: Times of India Press, 1930), 80.

that in Mewar, unlike in Marwar, "on account of the thuhar, bushes, trees, steep water channels, and plenty of rocks, it was not possible to kill a boar easily even if one worked very hard to do so."[35] Jodhpur's undemanding grounds, on the other hand, detracted from the potential merit of the experience. Tanwar and his peers saw Marwar's Rajputs as softer and less skilled men, despite their fame as pigstickers. In Mewari eyes, Rajputs who regularly went pigsticking in the hills of Mewar demonstrated superior talents as horsemen and hunters. They also revealed greater courage by facing the dangers of their state's more challenging and thus more rewarding landscape.

Even as Mewaris imagined that their grounds produced superior Rajputs and a better class of game, the vegetation they hailed as most conducive to wildlife in the state were desert flora like those associated with Jodhpur. It was not Mewar's broad-leafed pipals and banyan trees, but its woody scrub that sheltered and fed the local fauna. One such plant was the so-called "leafless" spurge or thuhar, a thorny cactus-like shrub found in the drier portions of Mewar and throughout western Rajasthan, especially Jodhpur (Fig. 5).[36] The thuhar "flourishes in extreme conditions of water scarcity," to the extent that its seeds fail to germinate in overly moist conditions. This plant's ideal habitat in Rajasthan is marked by the Aravalli range, where the steep, rocky slopes allow excess water to run off. With stems ranging in color from dark green through deep yellow and seasonal sprays of blossoms in green, buff, or red, the most noticeable feature of a thuhar's morphology are its sharp spiny thorns. These are "strong, somewhat curved outward at the tip, about a centimeter long, and ... persistent [i.e., ever-present]."[37]

[35] Tanwar, *Shikari aur Shikar*, 277.

[36] *Euphorbia caducifolia*, as it is described in David N. Sen, "Leafless Euphorbia on Rajasthan Rocks, India 1. Ecological Life-History," *Folia Geobotanica and Phytotaxonomica* 3, 1 (1968): 1–15.

[37] S. Sadr-Uddin Hussain and S.A. Qadir, "An Autecological Study of *Euphorbia caducifolia* Haines," *Vegetation* 20, 5/6 (1970): 329–80.

While villagers occasionally rely on the thuhar's seasonal leaves for edible, if sour, sustenance, and gather its branches for fuel (breaking them down with stones thrown from a respectable distance), the plant's natural defenses make it "unpalatable and unapproachable to animals."[38] Like the trained botanists who would later describe the plant and its ecology, Mewari sportsmen did not think wild boar ate thuhar. Unlike later botanists, however, and on the basis of their own observations and collective hunting experiences, they believed Mewari boar readily approached and took refuge in the midst of these prickly plants. Tanwar credited the thuhar with providing ideal habitat for wild animals and preventing the spread of civilization into wilderness regions in his youth.[39] In defending the wilds, thuhar preserved game for the chase.[40] The plant even made Mewari sport more challenging. In 1899, at Koriyat, a leopard hid in a thick clump of the stuff that defied entry, testing Fateh Singh's organizational skills and the ability of his beaters, who had to approach close enough to throw stones and fire blank shots to flush the animal out.[41] As a result, locals viewed the thuhar as contributing to the tough character, physical superiority, and overall competency of Mewaris.

Another drought-resistant plant associated with local wildlife was a bush closely related if not identical to Jodhpur's signature acacias. A few years prior to Fateh Singh's coronation, a European traveler noticed that the slopes around the royal hunting seat at Nahar Magra were "entirely covered with a thick underwood of thorny dwarf acacias," producing abundant fruit that the resident boar thrived on.[42]

---

[38] Sen, "Leafless Euphorbia," 11.

[39] Tanwar, *Shikari aur Shikar*, 350.

[40] The thuhar was not appreciated by all. Mohan Lal, Assistant Conservator of Forests in Mewar, complained of a "wretched growth of 'Thors,' thorny shrubs, and absence of grass" in the Udaipur hills. Given that his brief was to meet "fuel and fodder requirements," he could ignore the thuhar's relationship with game. Mohan Lal, to E.V.P. Pillai, January 10, 1942, MJ, 441 of 1942, RSA.

[41] Sharma, *Haqiqat Bahida*, 3:267. For a tiger taking cover in thuhar, see Topsfield, *City Palace*, Fig. 64.

[42] Rousselet, *India and its Native Princes*, 172. Rousselet called them berries; fruit or pods is more appropriate.

Nahar Magra boasted some of the few good pigsticking grounds in the state, and its well-nourished boar made for larger trophies, longer runs, and tougher fights. Mewar's maharana and any others who pursued these animals had to be equally well conditioned. It is no coincidence that Nahar Magra doubled as a health resort for Mewar's rulers, who benefited from the same wholesome surroundings as their prey.[43]

Mewari plants could be as prickly as their Marwari counterparts, but they signaled the greater fertility of their state by producing more fruit and blossoms, growing in greater numbers, and achieving higher densities. They also shared ground with shade trees and ornamentals. In Mewar, severity existed in proper proportion with fecundity, mirroring the maharana's superior qualities as a refined Rajput prince who ruled over a prosperous and settled land that had not lost its defiant edge. This was a helpful narrative not just in drawing comparisons with Jodhpur, but also when it came to rationalizing Mewar's uncomfortable subordination to the British. Mewar was pacific, but more than capable of effective resistance should the need arise.

It was not just the wild flora and the forage it provided that determined the relative quality of boar in Marwar and Mewar, however. It was also the grain that shikar officers gave them. In Mewar, the state had been feeding wild boar at least since the eighteenth century, when a painting of Pratap Singh II (r. 1751–4) recorded the maharana slaying boar attracted to the Sadri Odi with grain.[44] A later painting of Maharana Jawan Singh (r. 1828–38) showed a great mass of boar feeding on corn provided by a servant outside a shooting box, while the prince and his followers took their own meal inside an attached courtyard.[45] In Fateh Singh's time, wild boar received corn at numerous sites including Diwan Odi, Rang Burj, Kesar Bagh, and Bari Odi at Nahar Magra, and at Khas Odi near Udaipur.[46] At all of

---

[43] Fateh Singh, to Lord Reading, *c.* 1924, p.4, acc. no. 27262, MMSL.

[44] Topsfield, *City Palace*, Fig. 14.

[45] Anjan Chakraverty, *Indian Miniature Painting* (Delhi: Lustre Press, 1996), 61.

[46] Kamdar of Nahar Magra, to Hakim of Girwa, *samvat 1962 kati sud 10,*

these locations, they received larger portions in the winter months.[47] This may have compensated for a decrease during the winter months in the availability of energy-rich plant foods, such as nuts, seeds, and cereal grains, but aimed primarily at fixing game to known locations during the height of the hunting season.[48] Indeed, when Fateh Singh went to Nahar Magra in March 1906, local shikaris received orders to increase the pigs' daily rations at both Diwan Odi and Kesar Bagh by ten *ser* in anticipation of his arrival.[49]

Jodhpur's wild boar received handouts as well. Unlike Mewar's corn-fed animals, Tanwar reported that Marwari boar in the early 1940s were feasting on a more drought-tolerant crop: lentils. The results failed to impress Mewari huntsmen when they visited the state. Marwari boar looked "fat in body, but upon being weighed, it didn't come out. By appearance, they were thought to be six or seven *man*. Upon investigation, it turned out that their bodies were bloated on account of living in the desert and eating lentils."[50] Mewar's invigorating landscape and succulent corn produced the real thing. Jodhpur's rough lentils failed to nourish and its desert conjured up disappointing mirages.

A boar's quality derived from the landscape it lived in and the vegetation it consumed. Yet, just as lineage mattered among Rajputs, pedigree counted among boar. From a princely perspective, genuine wild boar were an endangered species due to the readiness with which they interbred with domestic pigs. There is no evidence from Fateh

---

MMK-RD, 269 of VS 1962, RSA-Udaipur; Padam Singh, to Kesri Singh, March 5, 1907, MMK-RD, 269 of VS 1962, RSA-Udaipur.

[47] Kamdar of Nahar Magra, to Hakim of Girwa, *samvat 1962 kati sud 10*, MMK-RD, 269 of VS 1962, RSA-Udaipur.

[48] Studies in the European context have found that *Sus scrofa* "always consumed at least one energy-rich plant food," Laurent Schley and Timothy J. Roper, "Diet of Wild Boar *Sus scrofa* in Western Europe, with Particular Reference to Consumption of Agricultural Crops," *Mammal Review* 33, 1 (2003): 43–56. Maize is used similarly in Europe: ibid., 45.

[49] Motilal Boheda, to Manohar Singh, *samvat 1932 chet vid 11*, MMK-RD, 269 of VS 1962, RSA-Udaipur. A *ser* is approximately one kilogram.

[50] Tanwar, *Shikari aur Shikar*, 221. There are forty *ser* in a *man*.

Singh's period to suggest that he agonized over illicit interbreeding, but he did attempt to enumerate and increase the population of (presumably) pure-blooded animals in his preserves. As wilderness areas contracted and human settlements expanded in the early twentieth century, the integrity of wild bloodlines became an ever greater concern. In 1942, during the reign of Bhupal Singh, one particularly troublesome wild boar repeatedly broke into a village near Udaipur to kill domestic males and mate with the sows.[51] The shikar department was charged with destroying it. Around the same time, Maharana Bhupal Singh was directing breeding programs for wild boar at Samor Bagh and Dudh Talai in Udaipur, and possibly at Lalit Bagh near Nahar Magra as well.[52]

Unlike Bhupal Singh's huntsmen in the 1940s, Fateh Singh apparently saw nothing wrong with Jodhpuri animals in terms of breeding or environment when he killed two and injured another from horseback in the Masuriyo and Kayalano shikargahs while visiting the state in 1892.[53] Relations between Mewar and Marwar at the time were cordial beyond the hunting ground too, and a few years later the Mewari prince made a condolence visit to Jodhpur when Maharaja Jaswant Singh died.[54] In 1908, the maharana's daughter married into the house of Jodhpur. In addition, Fateh Singh was on friendly terms with Sir Pratap Singh, sometime regent of Jodhpur State and third son of Maharaja Takht Singh (r. 1843–73). None of this seems to have affected Mewari confidence in their own superiority.

Jodhpur's fame throughout India for pigsticking and other peculiarly Rajput feats of horsemanship like polo suggests that Mewari prejudice was based less on Marwari inferiority than Mewari feelings of superiority. In fact, Mewari dignity required that Jodhpuri visitors be remembered as somehow having conceded the superiority of local prey, grounds, and hunting methods. Sir Pratap Singh (who

[51] Ibid., 292–3.

[52] Ibid., 297; employees at the former royal estate of Lalit Bagh near Nahar Magra showed me stone enclosures once used to raise wild boar. Tanwar mentions similar practices in Jodhpur, adding that in Mewar the Thakur of Bednor too kept tame boar: see ibid., 293.

[53] Sharma, *Haqiqat Bahida*, 3:170.

[54] Ibid., 3:225.

later ruled Idar State) appears in Tanwar's memoirs as an ardent admirer of Mewari sport who praised Fateh Singh for having attained the highest Rajput standards in pigsticking.[55] Given Sir Pratap's fame as "the best pig-sticker in India" and as one "trained to fight a boar on foot with only a knife in hand," his high opinion would have done much to validate Fateh Singh's reputation.[56]

Jodhpuri princes were known for enjoying superior sport in Mewar during Fateh Singh's reign. In 1895, the maharana entertained Jodhpur's heir apparent with a hunt in the Aravallis near Kumbhalgarh.[57] In 1914, Maharaja Sumar Singh (r. 1911–18) killed two leopards and a sambar in the hills around Jaisamand.[58] Following Fateh Singh's death in 1930, Maharaja Umaid Singh (r. 1918–47) hunted tiger near Chittor. Afterwards, he extolled "the bravery and courage of the shikaris ... trained in the time of the late maharana."[59] According to Tanwar, this prince believed Mewar State huntsmen had taken unusual risks and shown considerable skill in turning the tiger towards his station; their actions reflected well on Fateh Singh specifically and on Mewari practices in general. When a foreign prince politely (but not necessarily falsely) praised some aspect of the state's sport, it was construed as yet another affirmation of Mewari exceptionalism.[60]

In an apparent continuation of Tanwar's prejudices, some modern-day Mewaris remain inordinately proud of their local wild boar, and dismissive of animals living in Rajasthan's erstwhile desert kingdoms. More than one scoffed at my assertion that I had seen several sizeable animals in a wildlife preserve at Gajner in the former Bikaner State. Those boar, they claimed, were no better than domestic pigs. Yet, not unlike the maharanas of Mewar, the princes of Bikaner had held their state's boar in high esteem. Maharaja Ganga Singh once claimed that his Bikaneri "boars are very plucky and fight bravely to

[55] Tanwar, *Shikari aur Shikar*, 272, and Tanwar, *Samsmaran*, 86.

[56] Hardinge, *My Indian Years*, 34.

[57] Sharma, *Haqiqat Bahida*, 3:220.

[58] Ibid., 5:252–3.

[59] Tanwar, *Shikari aur Shikar*, 77–9.

[60] Tanwar also remembered Ganga Singh of Bikaner lavishing high praise in 1938: ibid., 98.

the end as a rule—often charging before they are speared."[61] But these boar, like the Jodhpuri ones Tanwar maligned, were desert animals. They hailed from a state ruled by Rathor Rajputs whose status was similar to Jodhpur's but much lower than Mewar's, and which had a level and sparsely vegetated landscape that was, in Ganga Singh's words, "<u>almost</u> like a Billiard Table." Flat grounds did not impress people who were accustomed to exalting mountainous terrain and the virtues it instilled in humans and animals.

The modern assertions I heard, of the comparative excellence of Mewari animals decades after the dissolution of the states, offer eloquent if anecdotal evidence of the persistent confidence in local superiority and the power of past maharanas.[62] As the anthropological investigations of Gold and Gujar have demonstrated, wild boar clearly remain "emblems of royal power and nature's abundance" in another former Rajput realm not too distant from Mewar, though smaller and less powerful.[63] Alongside wild boar, pigsticking grounds and their flora communicated similar messages.

And so did a state's distinctive ways of approaching the sport of tiger hunting. This can be seen from Maharaja Madhav Rao II Scindia of Gwalior's visit to Mewar State, during which he joined Fateh Singh on a shooting excursion. While out hunting with his host, the higher-ranking (by British reckoning) but low-born (by Rajput standards) Maratha prince entered into a discussion with his Rajput host about the relative merits of shooting structures. The maharana particularly praised a local rope-built platform called a *mande*. When his guest asked how they were made, "right then and there the maharana ... had

[61] Ganga Singh, "Programme, cont'd," [Oct. or Nov. 1901?], BMK, item 30, s. no. 736, file 68 of 1901, RSA.

[62] Those I spoke with believed, however, that Mewari stock had declined since the days of Fateh Singh and Bhupal Singh.

[63] Ann Grodzins Gold, with Bhoju Ram Gujar, "Wild Pigs and Kings: Remembered Landscapes in Rajasthan," *American Anthropologist* 99, 1 (1997): 70. See also idem, *In the Time of Trees and Sorrows*.

one set up in a mango tree."[64] Fateh Singh then presented Madhav Rao II with rope and a ladder so that he could make Mewari-style mandes in his own state.

Madhav Rao II, however, was no novice when it came to tiger hunting. Gwalior had some of the finest tiger grounds in all of India and the hunting methods in vogue there had reliably produced kills for countless VIPs, including Lord Curzon's first tiger in 1899 and the record animals Lord Hardinge and Lord Reading shot respectively in 1914 and 1923.[65] Madhav Rao II even published his own guide to tiger shooting in 1920.[66] All of this was of little account to Mewari Rajputs. What concerned them was the fact that an upstart and uncultured Maratha state, which they considered Gwalior to be, enjoyed a 21-gun salute while their own venerable realm had to make do with just 19. It did not help that the Gwalior maharaja's ancestors had targeted Mewari territory and revenues in the eighteenth and early-nineteenth centuries. In Mewari eyes, the importance of the meeting between Madhav Rao II and the maharana was that Scindia's interest in a specifically Mewari hunting technique constituted satisfying acknowledgement of Fateh Singh's greater expertise and excellence in the field.

When the chronicler was not Mewari, Fateh Singh and his state's hunting norms could appear in a less flattering light. During his visit to Mewar as part of the Kishangarh State marriage party in 1904, the young Rajput noble Amar Singh (whose family had close ties to Jodhpur and whose brother Kesri Singh was a well-known shikari in Gwalior and then Jaipur) recorded his impression of a conversation between his father and the maharana:

> At one time the maharana sahib wanted to turn the talk on eating and dressing with a purpose to mock us, but my father took the conversation in his own hands ... [He said that] dress should be worn as best suited

[64] Tanwar, *Shikari aur Shikar*, 221.

[65] Lord Hardinge's tiger was 11 ft 6.5 in. Lord Reading's was 11 ft 5.5 in. Both measurements have been disputed: see Kesri Singh, *Tiger of Rajasthan* (London: Robert Hale Limited, 1959), 33.

[66] Tanwar was unimpressed with advice in Madhav Rao Scindia, *A Guide to Tiger Shooting* (Gwalior: Alijah Darbar Press, 1920): see Tanwar, *Shikari aur Shikar*, 221.

to the occasion; for instance, at the present moment there ought to be achkans and jewels and such like things while there was a durbar being held, but this won't answer the purpose of shooting, for on that occasion we ought to have a strong cloth and coats, otherwise the long skirts of the achkans would get entangled in the thorny bushes ... [He] said these things because the other day when we had gone out shooting the maharana sahib and his followers were wearing achkans.[67]

While Fateh Singh's sartorial preferences in the context of the hunt were consistent with Mewari ideals, in that his chosen garb helped balance his show of physical prowess with evidence of sophistication, Amar Singh and his father failed to appreciate the message. They either refused to credit the maharana's performance or chose to reject the basis upon which he asserted Mewari superiority. When it came to sport, the emphasis on refinement as understood at the Mewar court was passé in many states by the turn of the century. Modern practicality and innovative conveniences mattered more, and rulers who surrounded themselves with such things were seen in some circles as truer sportsmen and better Rajputs.

Fateh Singh's hunting achkans, in fact, were innovations as much as they were "traditional." Apparently inspired by the sporting outfits worn by maharanas in the late-eighteenth and early-nineteenth centuries, Fateh Singh instituted his hunting achkans as the most appropriate dress for royal hunting parties in Mewar. Only the maharana and one courtier sported long dress in the 1888 photograph (Fig. 2), while their companions opted for coats and pants. Around the same time, Fateh Singh's artists clothed many of the huntsmen and courtiers inside Nahar Odi in achkans, but used coats and pants for a number of sportsmen. Twentieth-century photographs show the maharana and his companions more uniformly outfitted in long dress (Fig. 4). Fateh Singh was fashioning a distinct Mewari modernity on the hunting ground, patterned on what he considered his state's most appropriate and unique traditions.

He also tried to assert his personal superiority as Maharana of Mewar through his selective hunting habits, restricting himself for

[67] Rudolph and Rudolph, eds, *Reversing the Gaze*, 461.

the most part to big game including tiger, leopard, and wild boar, and avoiding killing females and immature animals.[68] In his reign, he reportedly killed 375 tigers and 991 leopards, also shooting 990 boar and spearing another 275 from horseback. To keep his hunting commensurate with his status, he concentrated on species widely viewed as among the best in India while shooting only paltry numbers of the more common game varieties. Other Rajput rulers, including Pratap Singh of Orchha, similarly claimed superiority on the basis of their nearly exclusive pursuit of big game.[69] Presumably even Amar Singh and his father would have been impressed.

The maharana's chosen emphasis also allowed for favorable comparisons within Mewar with state nobles, whose tallies were vastly smaller than his own. By 1898, Fateh Singh had accounted for forty-nine tigers. Generally unable to obtain these animals without their maharana's express permission, important nobles including Thakur Manohar Singh of Sardargarh had shot only one in the state, while others like Rawat Shivnath Singh of Amet had not shot any.[70] By the end of his reign, Fateh Singh could boast of having killed more tigers than any previous maharana.[71]

His selectiveness when it came to personal sport included territorial considerations. After his single foray into Jodhpur in 1892 for wild boar, the maharana apparently never again hunted as a guest in a foreign realm. An official record of game shot by the prince prior to 1898 reported with pride that, of the animals listed, he had obtained "only three or four" outside the state.[72] Apparently unaware of the Jodhpur excursion, Tanwar boasted more than once that Fateh Singh had never shot anywhere but in his own state.[73] The maharana's fidelity

[68] Tanwar, *Shikari aur Shikar*, 197.

[69] Pratap Singh, to H. Pritchard (PA-Bundelkhand), December 11, 1913, GOI, CIA, 898 of 1913, NAI.

[70] *Shikar ka Naksha* (Udaipur, *c.* 1921), 27 and 29. This source only tallies kills made as the maharana's guest.

[71] Tanwar, *Samsmaran*, 63. Tanwar here puts Fateh Singh's lifetime total of tigers at 300–350.

[72] *Shikar ka Naksha*, 3. All translations from this source are my own.

[73] Tanwar, *Shikari aur Shikar*, 197; idem, *Samsmaran*, 81.

advertised that Mewar's hunting was of a caliber sufficient to obviate any need for external supplement: nothing in other realms could tempt him because his game, shikargahs, and state were inevitably superior. Sharply contrasting with princely practices in Bundelkhand, the maharana's exclusivity reiterated Mewar's reputation for self-sufficiency and independence.

Fateh Singh's decision to limit his activities to Mewar when his high rank would have granted him easy access to shikar elsewhere was atypical. Most Rajput rulers were happy to hunt as guests in one another's states, especially to pursue game varieties unavailable in their own states. Their visits reflected and reinforced the existence of close relations between princely families linked by marriage, friendship, and shared interest.[74] Nor was it unheard of for a ruler of Mewar to hunt in neighboring realms, although precedents involving Bundi State had resulted in the assassination of former maharanas on more than one occasion, most recently in the eighteenth century.[75] This would hardly have recommended the practice to subsequent rulers and, for Fateh Singh, there appears to have been more to lose than gain from shooting abroad.

There was certainly more than enough wild boar in Mewar to satisfy Fateh Singh's considerable needs: he killed well over 1000 during his reign. The absence of miniature paintings and photographs showing him out pigsticking or standing over trophy animals, however, requires some explanation. While there are photographs of his heir Bhupal Singh with slain boar, including one where the young man evidently made his kill from elephant-back, Fateh Singh neither hunts nor poses with the animals even in Nahar Odi's encyclopedic paintings.[76] We are left with a conundrum: Fateh Singh aggressively pursued pig because they were necessary to Rajput masculinity,

---

[74]The Bikaner family was especially active on this front. Ganga Singh shot tigers in Alwar, Bhopal, Bundi, Danta, Datia, Dholpur, Kotah, Gwalior, Mewar, Palanpur, and Nepal. He and his sons shot in the CP in the 1920s and 1940s, and the UP in the 1920s and 1930s.

[75]Tod, *Annals*, 1:506 and 3:1477.

[76]Undated photograph in the Boheda family collection, Hotel Mahendra Prakash, Udaipur.

legitimacy, and power, and yet he did not sponsor images of himself doing so.

His predecessors, in contrast, had their boar hunts thoroughly documented alongside tiger, leopard, and bear shoots. Nor did they hesitate to be shown killing wildfowl, blackbuck, or hare.[77] Some maharanas may even have encouraged court artists to concentrate on such "lesser" pursuits. On the other hand, the artists' narrow focus may have reflected reality. Shikar miniatures produced for Bhim Singh (r. 1778–1828) almost exclusively depict him hunting boar, deer, or small game (Fig. 7). These paintings communicate his sovereignty (prominent displays of royal insignia leave no room for doubt) but they nevertheless betray his political vulnerability. A weak and nearly insolvent ruler at the mercy of his powerful nobles and threatened by Maratha incursions, Bhim Singh was as much a supplicant to his followers as their sovereign.

Blackbuck and boar, along with small game, were available well within Bhim Singh's reduced sphere of secure territorial control, centered around the Mewari capital of Udaipur. Tigers were more common somewhat further from the capital, sometimes in areas directly administered by the chiefs rather than the king, and sometimes in areas vulnerable to Maratha raids. Defended by city walls, cannon in Eklingarh, and the landscape itself, Bhim Singh preferred to hunt close to home where his safety and sovereignty were most secure. From the moment he came to the throne in 1778 at the tender age of 10, he had been reliant on his nobles' support. As he matured, he struggled to renegotiate his relationship with his chiefs. To counterbalance their influence, he sought allies even beyond the borders of Mewar. When he formally entered the Company's sphere in 1818, it was part of a strategy he had been refining over the preceding forty years of his reign.

Particularly before 1818, Bhim Singh's strained finances made it difficult to stage large, complicated, and expensive pursuits of

---

[77] For Bhim Singh hunting deer and boar, see Topsfield, *Court Painting at Udaipur*, Figs. 194, 197, and 216; Williams, ed. *Kingdom of the Sun*, Fig. 30. For Jawan Singh and Sarup Singh hunting mixed game, see Chakraverty, *Indian Miniature Painting*, 61; Topsfield, *City Palace*, Figs. 26–7, 31–2, and 34; Topsfield, *Court Painting*, Figs. 223, 229, 236, and 242.

dangerous game that could involve hundreds of beaters, each hoping to receive a token of appreciation should the hunt prove successful. Although princes often withheld remuneration on the grounds that their subjects were obliged to provide them free service (begar), the people expected generosity from righteous and legitimate rulers. Smaller and less dangerous game required fewer beaters, making it cheaper to kill blackbuck and boar than tigers. Blackbuck also repaid Bhim Singh's sporting efforts with venison, which he could distribute amongst his followers and subjects along with or in lieu of other recompense. Boar likewise provided pork, while most wildfowl and small game were considered palatable.

Depending on the season, large beats that relied on begar could draw peasants away from agricultural labor, potentially at stages critical for the future survival of crops and their cultivators. Boar and deer hunts tended to be less burdensome in this respect than tiger shikar. The maharana may also have benefited from hunting these animals because they invaded fields to feed on crops tastier and of higher caloric density than wild forage. Many wild animals are tolerated in Rajasthan, with certain species including blackbuck actively protected by communities like the Bishnoi.[78] However, wildlife cause problems for peasant farmers and landed elites. Although hunts conducted from horseback could wreak as much havoc as the most insatiable sounder of boar, the resultant quantities of dead pig partially justified the means. When Bhim Singh chose to emphasize his role as a killer of these animals, he was advertising his services in defense of local lives and livelihoods.

When Bhim Singh pursued a herd of deer or sounder of boar, he could give many participants in his royal shikar a chance at a shot or spear without undermining his own position. In the context of a group hunt with numerous available targets, the maharana was content to be first among equals. Tiger and leopard, however, are

[78] On the potential influence of tolerance alongside other factors in species survival, see Krithi K. Karanth, James D. Nichols, K. Ullas Karanth, James E. Hines, and Norman L. Christensen, Jr., "The Shrinking Ark: Patterns of Large Animal Extinctions in India," *Proceedings of the Royal Society B* 277 (2010): 1971–9.

most often found alone. Faced with a single and especially desirable target, any prince interested in proving his legitimacy and status would normally take the shot. Bhim Singh's preference for game that could be found in large numbers, or that was mundane and unburdened by royal connotation, suggests that his sovereignty was reliant on a diplomatic approach to his nobles. His hunts, and to an extent his idealized shikar miniatures—which showed him pursuing small game but made his supremacy unmistakable—allowed for a tentative equality between prince and nobility. Miniatures of tiger hunts and the messages they communicated were either too far removed from fact to appear relevant, or likely to cause offence in their portrayal of concentrated power.

As the standing of the maharanas under British patronage advanced far beyond their nobles after 1818 and through the nineteenth century, prized game like tiger and leopard increasingly shared the spotlight with, and later displaced, the boar and deer of earlier miniatures. By the end of the nineteenth century, Fateh Singh was hunting big game almost exclusively and patronizing only those images that showed him doing so. His disinterest in "lesser" scenes stemmed from a need to elevate himself unequivocally over his nobles, fellow princes, and the British. It also reveals his ambition to be known for hunting the game that British elites and European royalty pursued. The majority of British sportsmen who regularly killed boar, on the other hand, were common military men.

Fateh Singh's tactics were possible only because the *Kaulnama* agreement of 1818 with the British had normalized the centralization of princely power, reduced noble autonomy, and prevented symbolic posturing between princes from escalating into higher-stakes conflicts. Fateh Singh's Mewar was secure and centralized, allowing him to travel long distances from his capital—as far as Mandalgarh, Kuva Khera, and Bhainsrorgarh—in pursuit of tigers. Short on authority, funds, and powerful allies before 1818, Bhim Singh could not do the same and, therefore, did not hunt in the same ways.

Though most representations of Fateh Singh show him victorious over dangerous game, when artists did picture him with pigs the animals in question had to be something special. A sounder of boar attacking a leopard would do (Fig. 8), as would a prize pig battling a tiger (Fig. 9). Wild boar that failed to make their excellence known by confronting big cats did not merit special notice. When these boar shared a frame with Fateh Singh, they stayed in the background, functioning as general reminders of Mewari abundance and the maharana's righteousness.

But there was still much to gain from common pigsticking and mundane boar shoots, so long as the maharana was careful to pursue these sports only under the proper circumstances, and to memorialize them in less official ways. The pursuit of wild boar certified Fateh Singh's identity as a Rajput. It placed his sport in a continuous line of practice with that of his predecessors, as reflected in paintings, documents, and memories preserved from their times. It allowed him to practice mounted martial arts using the spear and sword, and demonstrate accuracy with a rifle on fast-moving targets. It advertised his adherence to the expected norms of righteous kingship in Mewar, as when he ensured the state's prosperity by slaying boar at particularly auspicious times—*muhurat ka shikar*. Finally, Fateh Singh could sponsor group pursuits of wild boar to adjust his relations with his nobles, without risking compromises to his status in the way he would if they participated in a tiger or leopard shoot. At the very worst, a pig hunt would return the maharana as *primus inter pares*. This was an acceptable result for the context and perhaps even a necessary one at times, but it was not worth memorializing in paint. Other kinds of shikar better communicated the maharana's aspirations for exclusive sovereignty.

Storytelling was a more ephemeral and thus suitable vehicle, often serving as entertainment for the maharana and his entourage as they ate or relaxed together during a hunting expedition. The vigorous physical activity of pigsticking proved Fateh Singh's vitality in one tale related by Tanwar about events that took place soon after the British cited the maharana's advanced age, failing faculties, and alleged mismanagement to restrict his powers in 1921. At over 70, the prince reportedly outstripped his fellow riders while pigsticking at

Nahar Magra to kill a boar with "a spear-thrust into the nape of the ... neck, which passed through its chest and stuck in the ground."[79] Familiar with the difficulty of these grounds and the singularity of Fateh Singh's feat, state subjects who witnessed or heard of this event would have interpreted it as testament to his continuing prowess and legitimacy.

Even the British recognized a correlation between hunting and power. After a 1912 assassination attempt injured Lord Hardinge, rumors predicting his imminent collapse began circulating. Talk persisted even after the viceroy, a mere ten weeks after the bomb blast and still suffering from neuritis and hearing loss, presided over a meeting of the Legislative Assembly in New Delhi. Ultimately, Hardinge "decided that the only way to put an end to these rumours was to go out and shoot a tiger!"[80] He later recalled that, after bagging the requisite cat, "nothing more was heard of my failing health!" Physical fitness proven on the hunting ground was a condition of rule. Viceroys who only sat indoors and presided over meetings were less than qualified.

Yet even as Lord Hardinge used shikar to revitalize his image in 1912, in the early 1920s it violated government policy to concede that Fateh Singh could do the same. In 1924, Lord Reading disregarded the maharana's declaration of being "still able enough ... to ride for 20 or 25 miles and take other physical exercises such as pigsticking, with the consequence that my physical constitution can easily bear the strain of work which my duties as ruler of my State impose upon me."[81] Official opinion continued to assert that "the day has gone when [the maharana] could engage in such pursuits."[82] Among Fateh Singh's loyal followers and in the eyes of sympathetic peers his well-known pursuit of tiger, leopard, and boar at places like Kumbhalgarh, Chittorgarh, and Nahar Magra up through his death in 1930 proved otherwise.

The pursuit of wild boar was integral to Rajput identity. Writing of Mewar in the 1860s, Rousselet claimed that "a young Rajpoot ... is

[79] Tanwar, *Shikari aur Shikar*, 271–2.
[80] Hardinge, *My Indian Years*, 83–4.
[81] Fateh Singh, to Lord Reading, *c.* 1924, p.4, acc. no. 27262, MMSL.
[82] Walker, *Prince in India*, 40.

not received into men's society until he has, single-handed, killed one of the enormous wild boars which inhabit the Aravallis."[83] Just shy of his twelfth birthday in 1896, Fateh Singh's son Bhupal Singh killed his first wild boar on just such a hill, the Lorya Magra. Court chroniclers recorded the happy event in some detail in the official daily register.[84] Tanwar was around 17 when he killed his first boar in another of these hills near Jaisamand.[85] Besides the importance of a young man's first kill, slaying wild boar attained greater than usual significance in Mewar at least twice each year. On an appropriate muhurat ka shikar, set in consultation with state astrologers, Fateh Singh would ride forth in the month of Phalgun at the onset of spring to kill boar, often at Nahar Magra.[86] Tod believed this spring hunt honored the goddess Gauri, whom he understood to be the Rajput Ceres, in that the boar was an enemy of cultivation.[87] At the beginning of the cold season in the month of Margashirsha, the maharana would open the hunting season on a second muhurat ka shikar, preferably by slaying a wild boar "with great fanfare" in the hills around Udaipur.[88] Success during this hunt boded well for the coming year's shikar.[89]

The importance of killing boar as a rite of passage and as a festive event on the maharana's calendar was not unique to Mewar, nor was the celebrated Sisodia Rajput taste for the animal's flesh. Boar were worthy prey and ideal food for all Rajputs because they were brave, full of vitality, and challenging to obtain.[90] British commentators

[83] Rousselet, *India and its Native Princes*, 157.

[84] Sharma, *Haqiqat Bahida*, 3:95.

[85] Tanwar, *Shikari aur Shikar*, 270–1.

[86] Tod, *Annals*, 2:660–1; Rousselet, *India and its Native Princes*, 172–3 and 181–2; Sharma, *Haqiqat Bahida*, 1:87–8.

[87] Tod, *Annals*, 2:660.

[88] Tanwar, *Shikari aur Shikar*, 288. Boar kills on the autumnal muhurat ka shikar are recorded for years including 1887, 1894, 1896, 1904, and 1908: see Sharma, *Haqiqat Bahida*, 2:190; 3:318, and 3:342; 4:458 and 4:517.

[89] Tod recorded that local nobles were summoned to "make their offerings" when the prince of Bundi killed his first boar in the early 1800s: see idem, *Annals*, 3:1746. The vernal muhurat ka shikar, which Tod calls the *ahairea*, was also celebrated in Bundi: ibid., 1:506.

[90] Tanwar, *Shikari aur Shikar*, 54.

went so far as to define Rajputs as a group in part upon their affinity for wild pork. Henry Yule and A.C. Burnell's well-known *Hobson-Jobson, a Glossary of Colloquial Anglo-Indian Words and Phrases* (1886) identified culinary habits "as a measure of the purity or degradation of the constitution of an individual Rajput," citing the example of a former Rajput prince of Alwar whose association with Muslims had led to his corruption, manifest in a refusal to eat wild boar.[91] Tod too alleged that "the wild hog, which, according to immemorial usage, should be eaten once a year by every Rajpoot, is rarely even hunted by a Shekhawut," a branch of Jaipur's Kachhwaha clan that he, in line with his Mewari informants, rated lower than Mewar's Sisodias.[92]

The Rajputs of Mewar prized wild boar flesh so greatly that they sometimes captured the animals as piglets and fattened them for consumption. One reached an impressive 400 *lbs.* before Fateh Singh's staff slaughtered it for the royal kitchen in 1907.[93] In relation to Pudukkottai, it has been suggested that Indian princes could not sustain themselves "on the dull food wrought by the plow," they required "more powerful" forest meats. In Pudukkottai, the job of procuring such meats fell to the Valaiyan or "forest people," who were generally tasked with maintaining their "king's presence in the forest domain, from which he derived his royal strength."[94] In Mewar, the maharana personally maintained his forest connections and supply of powerful meats, although his labors were supplemented by his subordinates, including shikaris drawn from the state's own "forest people," the Bhils.

Fateh Singh and his nobles frequently gave and received gifts of the strength-sustaining meat they culled from their wild boar kills.[95] When the maharana confirmed the succession of the heir to a Mewari noble estate, he presented the newly appointed *rao, rawat,* or *thakur*

[91] Jason P. Freitag, "The Power Which Raised them from Ruin and Oppression: James Tod, Historiography, and the Rajput Ideal" (PhD diss., Columbia University, 2001), 139.

[92] Tod, *Annals,* 3:1381.

[93] Sharma, *Haqiqat Bahida,* 4:379.

[94] Waghorne, *The Raja's Magic Clothes,* 170.

[95] Sharma, *Haqiqat Bahida,* 2:171–3, and 2:191.

with gifts to mark the occasion and symbolically represent the terms of their patron–client relationship. After performing Fateh Karanji's *tikka* ceremony in November 1886, the maharana presented the noble with a pig from the royal kitchen.[96] If this was Fateh Karanji of Ujwal, as seems likely, his dedication to pigsticking, which he frequently pursued as part of the maharana's entourage, may have influenced the offering. Perhaps not, however, as another noble received a gift of wild pork that same day. Presumably because the latter was merely a *sardar*, his cut came from a sow. The perceived quality of the meat, thus, matched that of its source.

It is unclear exactly where wild pork ranked in comparison with other princely gifts, but it was a common and meaningful offering. Gifts of pork could evoke a sense of shared identity among princes and nobles due to the boar's importance within Rajput culture, but eating the same food did not put everyone on the same level. In providing his subordinates with meat, Fateh Singh asserted his superior status and political authority in a courtly milieu where gift-givers outranked gift-takers. The maharana publicly enacted his nobles' dependence to put subordinates in their place, foster a sense of obligation, reward special service, and demonstrate the extent of his own resources, generosity, and good intentions. Such actions referenced the earlier familial basis of Rajput loyalty, which state nobles remained nostalgic for as a system they believed had once guaranteed their ancestors' independence and influence.[97] While the provisioning of food could be construed as a parental, fraternal, or even affinal act, by Fateh Singh's time it no longer reflected anything like parity between the maharana and his chiefs. Any Mewari noble who accepted wild boar from the royal kitchen "ate the king's salt" along with his pork.

Gifts of wild pork seem to have been especially common around mid-November, the usual timing of Mewar's autumnal *muhurat ka shikar*. Boar were the designated quarry of these hunts. Along with nobles who could maintain their own pig grounds or were privileged

---

[96] Ibid., 2:171.

[97] On earlier bases of Rajput loyalty, see Sreenivasan, *Many Lives of a Rajput Queen*, 68–70.

to hunt with the prince at Jaisamand or Nahar Magra, Fateh Singh was likely to have an abundance of pork available at this time. As an indication of the coming year's bounty, the auspiciousness of the muhurat ka shikar must have further encouraged the distribution of its fruits. It may be no coincidence that Fateh Karanji received a gift of pork to mark his succession: his *tikka* ceremony took place in November of 1886 and Fateh Singh may well have obtained the meat during this important hunt. The following November another of Fateh Singh's nobles received a pig too: a massive 184 *lb*. boar.[98]

A lively interstate exchange in gifts of pork existed too. Sending a pig across state lines communicated goodwill, as when Fateh Singh presented a boar to a party from Kishangarh State to carry on their journey home, no doubt serving also as a reminder of Mewari sport and magnanimity.[99] The maharana also received pigs. Around the time of his 1887 appointment as a Knight Grand Commander in the Order of the Star of India, the Maharaja of Jodhpur sent him the "best piece" of a "very big pig" that he had shot expressly as a congratulatory gift.[100] According to Kipling, then visiting Jodhpur as a special correspondent, the maharaja expressed his hope that Fateh Singh would "be pleased" with the offering. The pig's size and the quality of the cut rendered the meat commensurate with the maharana's importance. It would have been insulting to send the flesh of a yearling or sow to such a recipient. To guarantee its quality, which would be apparent immediately upon arrival, the meat was "pickled" before being loaded on camel-back for speedy transport.

In Mewar, the prince and his nobles commonly shared a repast of wild pork or even venison while out hunting. Fateh Singh hosted these feasts at hunting seats throughout the state, including Govardhan Vilas just south of Udaipur, Bagdara to the southeast, and near the Udai Niwas palace on the western shore of Udai Sagar.[101] Al fresco settings allowed the maharana and his followers—up to 350 at

[98] Ibid., 2:191.

[99] Ibid., 2:173.

[100] Rudyard Kipling, "Among the Houyhnhnms," *From Sea to Sea*, vol. 1, 126.

[101] Tanwar, *Shikari aur Shikar*, 187.

a time—to refresh their connections with the land as they sat on the ground and ate off plates made from leaves.[102] In combination with the anticipation of shikar and a menu featuring game, these events distantly echoed the camp experiences and rugged lifestyles of their more martial forebears. Meals were followed by relaxation or, whenever the opportunity arose, sport.

Although these royal picnics referenced a past marked by more equitable relations between former maharanas and their chiefs, Fateh Singh used them to affirm a strict hierarchy based on the more recently established, and much contested, patron–client ideal. Nobles in the sixteenth and seventeenth centuries had used Mughal alliances as a resource in their power struggles with the maharanas, and those of the eighteenth century occasionally had found the Marathas similarly useful. But after the Company assumed regional power in the early-nineteenth century, the British—with select princely input—decided the best policy was the centralization of power on the king.[103] The practical result was an invented tradition of autocracy that Tod, acting as the company's first political agent in Rajputana, helped authenticate as he "embarked on a series of measures designed to 'restore' the king's powers: powers that the latter may not have enjoyed uncontested, for any amount of time in the past."[104]

With the British helping "to empower the ruler . . . at the expense of the chiefs," Fateh Singh could arrange his feasts as he pleased to contrast his relative independence and supremacy with his nobles' dependence on his generosity.[105] On these occasions the maharana would sit with, but across and slightly apart from, an elite assemblage of high-ranking nobles, conservatively drawn from the same commensal group. Lesser notables living in the vicinity of the shikargah, whose sacrifices enabled their sovereign's sport and helped them earn the

[102] Tanwar, *Samsmaran*, 54–5. For feasts under earlier maharanas, see Topsfield, *Court Painting*, Figs. 216 and 236.

[103] Sreenivasan, *Many Lives of a Rajput Queen*, 74–5, 126, and 128.

[104] Ibid., 128.

[105] Ibid., 129.

privilege of enjoying his largesse, were served at a comfortable distance from their superiors. Servants got their share from the ample leftovers.[106] Physical proximity to the prince combined with food allotments to proclaim the participants' hierarchical relationships with one another, their degree of intimacy with their ruler, and the entire party's shared subordination to the maharana. The stakes were similar to those at a formal darbar, where "disputes over ranking, seating precedence, even of simple access ... provided a means for mobility and for challenging the rights (and power) of rival families within each Rajput state."[107]

According to Tanwar, the maharana and his staff assumed complete responsibility for every detail of the arrangements for these hunting feasts. To encourage his servants to perfect their performance, Fateh Singh dealt out "immediate punishment" if they erred.[108] Mistakes, therefore, rarely occurred. Tanwar considered these events nothing less than ideal, but certain "slanderers" maligned their sovereign's hospitality. A faction including *jagirdar* landholders and some "big nobles" reportedly submitted a complaint to officials in the Foreign Department alleging that Fateh Singh first compelled them to attend his hunts and then served inedible dishes filled with sand and stones, with no provisions for drinking water.[109] British inquiries into these claims, however, vindicated the maharana. The provisions were found to include "meat, rice, *chapati* and fried bread, sweets, green vegetables, lentils, *khichri*, etc., both vegetarian and non-vegetarian foods, made in separate kitchens, where whatever food one wanted made would be made."[110]

The complaints of these jagirdars and nobles against Fateh Singh's feasts emerged from their long-standing dissatisfaction with and desire to renegotiate the terms that bound them to the princely house of Mewar. These terms were set in 1818, when Tod negotiated the *Kaulnama* agreement between the ruling prince, Maharana Bhim Singh, and the noble families and landholding classes of Mewar.

[106]Tanwar, *Samsmaran*, 63.
[107]Haynes, "Rajput Ceremonial," 468–9.
[108]Tanwar, *Samsmaran*, 63. All translations from this source are my own.
[109]Ibid., 63–4.
[110]Ibid., 64.

Rooted in Tod's desire to reinstate what he conceived of as true and unalterable Rajput tradition, the *Kaulnama* soon proved problematic. Tod had learned his Rajput history from royal documents and inscriptions, and from bards and *charans* whose profession required them to promote the cause of their princely employers. He also assumed the normalcy of centralized power and the naturalness of permanent settlements for everything from chiefly rights and privileges through interstate boundaries. Not surprisingly, then, the *Kaulnama* was biased from the beginning in favor of Mewar's maharanas.

Discontented jagirdars and nobles reacted against the underlying assumptions of the *Kaulnama*. Earlier agreements between Mewari rulers and their chiefs had been contingent, so that "the two parties had repeatedly negotiated the terms of their mutual obligations, based on evolving assessments of their respective strengths."[111] With the British established in Mewar as a rival and perhaps even as the real power, some chiefs viewed compulsory ceremonial subordination to an increasingly impotent sovereign as a travesty and embarrassment. The most elite families cherished illustrious pedigrees, glorious histories, and noble traditions of their own. Their perceived self-importance and independence clashed with the very idea of subordination under the patron–client relationship promoted by the *Kaulnama*. They never ceased negotiating their obligations and entitlements, regularly complaining and submitting petitions to Mewar State officials and Foreign Department representatives throughout the nineteenth and twentieth centuries.[112]

Because certain families had never accepted, or had come to reject, specific courtly obligations and practices, any state ceremonial or event entailed the risk of conflict. In 1903, for example, the nobles of Kanore, Bednor, and Bijolia were "abstain[ing] from joining State processions and . . . airing their grievances," which included restrictions on their use of insignia, delays in settling boundary disputes, and required attendance on the maharana during the Dusehra festival and for three additional months out of the year.[113] Even the

[111] Sreenivasan, *Many Lives of a Rajput Queen*, 129.

[112] Ibid.

[113] Pinhey (MR), Memorandum regarding the present relations between

maharana's exclusive control over every aspect of his feasts reflected his powers as supported by the *Kaulnama*, and the hunts that followed only expanded on the theme as he assigned duties to his nobles and dictated when they could and could not shoot.

Just as Fateh Singh allegedly had feigned illness to avoid attending two imperial durbars and the Prince of Wales's 1921 arrival in Mewar, some nobles had a history of pleading poor health to absent themselves from state functions. In 1873, Nahar Singh, the Rajadhiraj of Shahpura, assured Maharana Shambhu Singh that he was "extremely anxious to be present" at an important state ceremony, but doing so was impossible "on account of itches and other complaints."[114] This noble, apparently, found service at royal hunts and hunting feasts preferable to participation in more formal functions, promising to present himself "without fail . . . when your Highness goes out for shikar."[115] Nahar Singh lived until 1932 and the disputes between his family and successive maharanas over rights and privileges were ongoing. It is unclear if "itches" ever prevented his attendance on Maharana Fateh Singh, but the *rajadhiraj* did face charges of undermining royal authority and seeking freedom from "customary service and subordination."[116] Wondering how it could be "possible for a person to be a feudatory vassal . . . and yet not to render service," Fateh Singh at least secured the noble's occasional attendance for royal hunts.[117] By 1898 Nahar Singh had bagged two boar and

---

the Maharana and his Sardars, May 10, 1903, GOI, FD, Secret I, 5–7 of October 1903, NAI.

[114] Trans. of Nahar Singh, to Shambhu Singh, September 16, 1873, in Pinhey, Memorandum, May 10, 1903, GOI, FD, Secret I, 5–7 of October 1903, NAI.

[115] Ibid. Attendance for royal shikar counted as service in Marwar too: see Hira Singh, *Colonial Hegemony and Popular Resistance: Princes, Peasants, and Paramount Power* (New Delhi: Sage Publications, 1998), 73.

[116] Trans. of MMK, to MR, February 28, 1895, GOI, FD, Internal A, 39–57 of September 1898, NAI.

[117] Trans. of Fateh Singh, to Viceroy of India, in AGG-Rajputana, to FD Secretary, April 6, 1897, GOI, FD, Internal A, 39–57 of September 1898, NAI.

one tiger in the maharana's presence, suggesting that, while he was hardly a frequent participant, he either merited special attention—or stole shots at the prince's prized cats—when he did take part.[118]

The semiotics of Mewari wildlife were especially complex where they intersected with contests between the maharana and his nobles, that is, in the field and on the plate. But Mewaris were equally attuned to the natural rivalries they saw between game animals. Fateh Singh and his followers delighted in the willingness and ability of Mewari boar to confront tigers and leopards, and to fight honorably whether they won the battle or lost. In the 1860s, Maharana Shambhu Singh had believed that wherever wild boar proliferated, they even eradicated tigers.[119] On the basis of his own experiences, Tanwar declared them more dangerous than either tigers or leopards.[120] The well-known naturalist Kailash Sankhala also later concluded that the animals had little fear of tigers.[121] On account of this famous natural animosity and the fighting prowess of wild boar, Rajput nobles liked to watch them fight big cats. The Mewari court organized contests between these animals at Nahar Magra or, more commonly, at Khas Odi.[122] Audience members would throw firecrackers to ensure the animals lived up to their reputation rather than avoiding one another by slinking off into opposite corners (Fig. 9).[123]

While they regularly observed contests between captive animals, Mewari Rajputs took special pleasure in witnessing spontaneous altercations in the wild, and recording them in paint. One miniature documents a large number of wild boar attacking a leopard shot by Fateh Singh at Kamlod ka Magra in 1888 (Fig. 8).[124] According to the detailed inscription accompanying the image, "upon seeing the

[118] *Shikar ka Naksha*, 45.

[119] Rousselet, *India and its Native Princes*, 175–6.

[120] Tanwar, *Shikari aur Shikar*, 12.

[121] Kailash Sankhala, *Tiger! The Story of the Indian Tiger* (New York: Simon and Schuster, 1977), 106.

[122] Tanwar, *Shikari aur Shikar*, 243–7; Sharma, *Haqiqat Bahida*, 1:132, 169, 190, etc.

[123] Topsfield, *City Palace*, Fig. 46.

[124] Ibid., Fig. 44.

fallen leopard, murderous intent arose and, squealing, all the boar fell on the leopard and struck it with tusks and hooves, and from this beating it tumbled down the hill and ... died."[125] Local interest in such altercations was equally on display inside Nahar Odi, where a matched set of paintings on either side of the entryway showed, on the left, two boar attacking the heels of a fleeing tiger, and, on the right, a tiger tearing into a lone boar's back. Of course, there is also the miniature of the fight in 1888 between a tiger and boar at Khas Odi.

These images of matched conflict reflect a balance in princely Mewar between admiration for wild boar and respect for tigers.[126] When Fateh Singh went pigsticking in the lowlands, he displayed a strength and reckless daring equal to that of his prey and sufficient skill on horseback to match any wild boar's speed. When he hunted tiger in the hills, he demonstrated tactical ability and foresight by successfully directing his subordinates in outwitting the animal's clever attempts to escape. He proved himself more commanding than the predator in that his word sufficed to send men against even that awesome beast. When he staged battles between wild boar and tigers in Khas Odi, he benefited from the reflected qualities of both animals.

The maharana treated European guests and visiting Indian princes to his Khas Odi shows too. By 1904, the Maharaja of Jaipur, Lord Curzon, the Grand Duke of Hesse, the Maharaja of Kishangarh, and the successive commanders-in-chief Lord Palmer and Lord Kitchener all had attended.[127] These contests were nothing new. In the 1860s, Rousselet watched a leopard lose to a particularly impressive wild boar captured locally in the Udaipur hills. At the time, he believed his hosts were "pleased ... at the victory of their favourite adversary."[128] Although Mewaris greatly admired those animals that managed to best big cats, spectators were most concerned with seeing a good fight. Each contestant had admirable characteristics and the sport

---

[125] Ibid., 167. My translation.

[126] Memory of these altercations apparently persists: a statue of a tiger attacking a wild boar is in the park on Machhla Magra above Dudh Talai.

[127] Sharma, *Haqiqat Bahida*, 1:169 and 4:180; also 4:62, 4:77, 4:104, 4:16, and 4:129.

[128] Rousselet, *India and its Native Princes*, 177.

was in seeing which would prevail. Wild boar were brave and tenacious, but tigers were forceful and awe-inspiring. Leopards, meanwhile, were ruthless and clever.

These shows continued to please Mewaris as late as the 1950s, but after the turn of the century Europeans increasingly disapproved of the fights. When Lord Hardinge saw a wild boar defeat a leopard at Khas Odi in 1912, he thought it a "cruel show" although neither animal suffered much physically.[129] The definition of sportsmanship espoused by the British in India had narrowed and, by the 1890s, the only accepted method of killing wild boar was to spear them from horseback.[130] Tigers and leopards too had to have a "sporting" chance, and shooters needed to expose themselves to a reasonable amount of danger. Caged animals at Khas Odi could not escape and seemingly posed no threat to their audience.[131] Fateh Singh's arenas also lacked the veneer of scientific inquiry that sanctified observation of animals in zoos. Instead of seeing wild boar fighting inside Khas Odi, the maharana's guests now preferred to see them feeding outside its walls. One Englishwoman noted that visitors to Khas Odi "always seem[ed] to adore" watching the animals eat.[132] This gentler spectacle was a standard item on the agenda for state guests during the latter half of Fateh Singh's reign and throughout the reign of his successor, typically scheduled after tea at Jagmandir.[133]

[129] Hardinge, *My Indian Years*, 75.

[130] MacKenzie, *Empire of Nature*, 299–300.

[131] For a leopard almost injuring spectators, see Tanwar, *Shikari aur Shikar*, 243–7.

[132] Indian Political Service Memoirs Collection (Mary Chenevix Trench), 14, Mss Eur F 226/33C, BL. For a particularly evocative account, see Walker, *Prince in India*, 44.

[133] Boar feeding at Khas Odi followed tea at Jagmandir on the 1912 vice-regal visit: GOI, FD, Secret I, 40–66 of June 1913, NAI; the 1923 viceregal visit: GOI, FPD, 1311-H of 1923, NAI; the 1932 viceregal visit: GOI, RA, PB, 471 of 1932, NAI; the 1934 viceregal visit: GOI, FPD, 15(6)-H of 1934, NAI; and the 1939 viceregal visit: GOI, RA, PB, 1-P/39-III of 1939, NAI. For photographs, see Photo 936, BL.

1. Bhupal Singh shooting the leopard in the garden, Udaipur

"Prince Bhupal Singh Shooting Leopard," by Chhagan Lal, Mewar, c. 1930, © MMCF, Pictorial Archives of the Maharanas of Mewar, Udaipur, 2012.18.0101

2. Fateh Singh with tiger, nobles, and shikaris, c. 1888

Courtesy of Boheda family and Hotel Mahendra Prakash, Udaipur

3. *Shikari and tiger with hills inside Nahar Odi,* c. 1888

4. Maharana Fateh Singh and Lord Reading with sambar stags at Dhimra Bagh Odi, Jaisamand, November 1923

© The British Library Board, Photo 10/22 (48), by Bourne & Shepherd

5. Firing from his machan in a mahua tree, Fateh Singh shoots a tigress amidst yellow-green thubar, tamarind, and other foliage near Jaisamand, c. 1888

Detail of "Maharana Fateh Singh Hunting Tiger near the Jai Samand," by Shiva Lal, Mewar, c. 1888, © MMCF, Pictorial Archives of the Maharanas of Mewar, Udaipur, 2010.T.0026

6. Beaters drive a tigress downhill and across a dry stream bed towards Fateh Singh and his nobles, including the Thakur of Sardargarh and the Rawat of Amet, near Jaisamand, c. 1888

"Maharana Fateh Singh Hunting Tiger near the Jai Samand," by Shiva Lal, Mewar, c. 1888, © MMCF, Pictorial Archives of the Maharanas of Mewar, Udaipur, 2010.1T.0026

7. Bhim Singh rides in procession with slain boar and symbols of state, c. *1810*

"Maharana Bhim Singh of Udaipur (r. 1778-1828) Returns from a Boar Hunt,"
attributed to Chokha. Harvard Art Museums/Arthur M. Sackler Museum, gift in
gratitude to John Coolidge; gift of Leslie Cheek, Jr.; Anonymous Fund in memory
of Henry Berg; Louise Haskell Daly, Alpheus Hyatt, and Richard Norton Memorial
Funds and through the generosity of Albert H. Gordon and Emily Rauh Pulitzer;
formerly in the collection of Stuart Cary Welch, Jr., 1995.89. Photo: Imaging
Department © President and Fellows of Harvard College.

8. Shooting from Mathara Mul, Fateh Singh wounds a leopard and watches as wild boar finish it off, Kamlod ka Magra, near Udai Sagar, c. 1889

"Maharana Fateh Singh Hunting Leopard at Kamlod ka Magra," by Shiva Lal, Mewar, 1889, © MMCF, Pictorial Archives of the Maharanas of Mewar, Udaipur, 2010.T.0013

9. Fateh Singh and his nobles watch a fight between a captive tiger and wild boar incited by firecrackers, Khas Odi, c. 1890

"Maharana Fateh Singh Watching an Animal Fight at Khas Odi," by Shiva Lal, Mewar, c. 1890, © MMCF, Pictorial Archives of the Maharanas of Mewar, Udaipur, 2010.T.0025

10. Famine labor dredging the dried up lake-bed in front of Gajner Palace, 1899–1900

11. Maharaja Ganga Singh and Lord Hardinge in a shooting butt, with decoy birds in the water and demoiselle crane on the wing, November 1912

© The British Library Board, Photo 592/3 (90), by Herzog & Higgins

12. "Trophies of Two Blackbuck Antelope Bagged by Maharajkumar Sadulsinghji (at no. 1) as Part of a Thinning Out Programme of Antelopes in the Vicinity of Agricultural Farms near Hanumangarh. The Junior Maharajkumar Bijey Singhji is beside Him," Bikaner, c. 1927

Courtesy of Karni Singh Parihar, Hotel Panna Vilas Palace, 758/280 Rani Road, Fateh Sagar Lake Shore, Udaipur, 313001 (Raj.) India, www.hotelpannavilas.com

It is not clear if Mewaris considered the growing British distaste for wild boar and tiger fights as evidence of foreign inferiority—perhaps even an effect of England's pastoral countryside—but Englishmen certainly fell short of Rajput standards in other ways when it came to interacting with these animals. On the walls of Nahar Odi, Fateh Singh mocked the British by impugning their abilities as sportsmen when faced with local game in the hills around Udaipur.[134] Two small but significant scenes together present an image of Englishmen as deficient in the pursuit of wild boar and tigers. In Mewari thought, wild boar and tigers set Fateh Singh and his Rajputs apart by giving them opportunities to display a masculinity that far outstripped that of visiting Englishmen.

One panel depicts three Mewaris hunting wild boar from horseback using rifle, sword, and spear. Two wear the compact turbans typical of Rajput nobility in Mewar at the time, while the third may be a Sikh. According to artistic convention, the Indians and their mounts are painted in profile, a choice that here communicates the shikaris' intense focus on their prey. Their discipline and obvious ability are underscored by intimations of their immanent success: the potential Sikh has brought his horse within half a stride of a boar and has lowered his spear in preparation for the thrust, a second rider's sword is slashing into another boar's neck, while the third horseman leans forward slightly with rifle in hand, holding the barrel safely up and away from his companions but ready for use at any moment. Their complete concentration and aura of capability are echoed in their horses, whose extended limbs, streaming tails, tucked ears, and open mouths give an impression of speed, exertion, and a desire to catch the boar matched only by their riders.

Between the two Rajputs on the left and the third sportsman on the right is an Englishman. His pith helmet, beardless face, and trimmed moustache differentiate him, as do his sharply bent knees, which mark his saddle as English in style. The third boar in the scene has surged ahead of the Rajputs on the left to charge straight at the Englishman and his mount, both of whom the artists have depicted

[134] Art and architecture have an established pedigree of redressing political humiliation in Mewar: see Joffee, "Art, Architecture and Politics."

in three-quarters view. Uncommon but not unique this early in Fateh Singh's reign, the three-quarters perspective here suggests that horse and rider are shying away from the boar in an apparent display of cowardice. The comedy of the scene is compounded by the fact that the Englishman appears to be pigsticking without a weapon, underscoring his laughable incompetence in comparison with the professionalism of the other riders. It is difficult to discern on account of water damage and flaking paint, but the Englishman may have dropped his spear in the grass behind his horse. Whatever the reason for his negligence, he now faces an angry boar unarmed; one of the advancing Mewaris will presumably come to his rescue. Significantly, the Mewari hunters excel at killing boar in numerous ways in the Nahar Odi paintings. Besides shooting, spearing, and knifing the animals from horseback, in other scenes they pursue a pair of boar with dogs and shoot a lone adult male or *ekal* from a shooting box.

On an adjacent wall, another pith-helmeted Englishman lies crumpled on the ground, ineffectually clutching his rifle as a massive tiger mauls him. Despite being appropriately armed, this Englishman was as unequal to the task of killing local game as the unfortunate pigsticker described above, showing that Mewari superiority could be proven with tigers as well as boar. A little to one side, a Rajput has dismounted to take aim at the tiger with his rifle. Even if his bullet kills the animal, it is unclear whether the Englishman will survive. While hostility and contempt towards Europeans are evident in the scene—particularly in the Englishman's dislodged pith helmet and bared head—a rescue attempt remained imperative. Leaving either Englishman to perish would have conflicted with the heroic Mewari self-image and may simply have been too extreme. It sufficed to show local Rajputs as sporting saviors who could calmly dispatch beasts that had made Englishmen tremble. The particular game species that threatened Europeans on the walls of Nahar Odi were the very ones that Mewaris considered most Rajput-like in strength and temperament. The facility with which Rajput-like wild boar and tigers defeated Englishmen further hinted that local Rajputs had the capacity to overwhelm their foreign rivals.

Had Englishmen seen this tiger attack on the walls of Nahar Odi, the scene might have brought to mind Tipoo's Tiger, the famous eighteenth-century musical organ shaped like a European soldier being mauled by a tiger. Part of the spoils taken from the despised sultan of Mysore after the Battle of Seringapatam, Tipoo's Tiger had been on display in London since 1808, first at the East India Company's own museum and subsequently at the South Kensington. Although the European victims in both representations are clad in red tops and blue bottoms with snarling tigers at their necks, there is no evidence that Fateh Singh or his painters deliberately referenced the Company's trophy. Nevertheless, just like Tipoo's Tiger at the court of Mysore, the Nahar Odi paintings were comic vignettes asserting princely superiority in comparison with European incapacity.

The inept pigsticker and mauling scene in Nahar Odi indicate that Fateh Singh did not intend his wall paintings for British eyes. It is unclear if the maharana's Indian guests ever saw Nahar Odi's interior, but Fateh Singh may have shown them to select nobles and members of his court.[135] The maharana's boldness in sponsoring mocking representations of Englishmen just half a mile from Khas Odi, where he regularly entertained viceroys, political agents, and British royalty, surely impressed any of his followers who saw the paintings. Among those privy to the secret, the knowledge would have undercut any suspicion that the maharana's hospitality towards foreign VIPs conceded anything in terms of Mewari honor and independence, or in terms of the prince's personal standing. Mewar was still holding foreign challengers at bay, aided by the animal and human products of its unique and perfectly composite environment.

While it was in Fateh Singh's best interests to appear defiant in the eyes of state subjects and fellow Rajputs, he does not appear to have aimed at excluding the British from Mewar entirely. As the middle-aged, posthumously adopted son of Mewar's previous ruler, his sovereignty remained hotly contested through the late 1880s, when his artists were completing work on the Nahar Odi paintings.

[135] Fateh Singh and his entourage visited Nad Odi, between Khas Odi and Kalka Mata, on June 20, VS 1955: see Sharma, *Haqiqat Bahida*, 3:119. Nad Odi is a variant of Nahar Odi; a Nahar Odi at Nahar Magra was variously called Nad Odi, Nar Odi, and Nahar Odi.

The prince relied on British support during these years even as he resented their interference in his affairs. What he wanted was to limit their authority. Ideally, the Government of India and its political agents would remain subordinate within Mewar's territories, but potent enough to serve any purposes the maharana needed them for, such as keeping rival states in line or guaranteeing his position relative to his nobles. The Nahar Odi paintings, which privately mocked Englishmen and delighted in but stopped short of endorsing beastly violence against them, walked the same line the maharana hoped to follow in real life.

Mewar's hunting landscapes, superior game, and excellent shooting methods set the state apart from its rivals—desert-bound prince and faint-hearted European alike. Resting on a long history of environmental distinction, Fateh Singh's thorny thuhar and rugged hills produced bigger and better boar, and braver Rajputs. At the same time, the leafy pipal trees and comparative abundance that marked the Mewari landscape fostered refinements unattainable in other lands. Ranging from elaborately decorated towers through bunker-like boxes, Fateh Singh's newly restored *mul*s and *odi*s reinforced these visions of Mewari exceptionalism, while the maharana's feasts and miniature paintings ceremoniously fixed state nobles in their proper places. And, taking their tea at Jagmandir and watching from Khas Odi as wild boar from the surrounding hills fed on Fateh Singh's corn, British VIPs visiting the state fancied themselves at long last properly honored by the stalwartly independent maharana. All the while, Nahar Odi stood nearby and quietly proclaimed local superiority with comedic visions of European incompetence, supernatural painted environments, and hyperbolic expressions of Fateh Singh's status as a righteous ruler whose royal hunting grounds were magnificent beyond belief.

4

Controlling Environments for Progressive Sport

After reports of severe famine following an extended drought led Lord Curzon to defer his 1899 tour of Rajputana to a more favorable year, the Maharaja of Bikaner, Ganga Singh, presented the viceroy with a photograph album documenting relief measures undertaken in his state.[1] Bound in maroon leather decorated with gold leaf, this album portrayed the famine not so much as a tragedy threatening the lives of humans and animals but as a golden opportunity—and one Ganga Singh was successfully embracing—to effect progressive change in Bikaner. At his leisure, the viceroy could peruse images of orderly famine camps, newly vaccinated coolies, and workers receiving rations after laboring on state projects ranging from railway diversions and road repairs to the ongoing construction at Lalgarh—a new palace in the Indo-Saracenic style suggestive of rational governance and suitable for entertaining European VIPs.

At first glance, the only evidence of the hunt in Ganga Singh's presentation album is an interior view of one of his palaces, with big game trophies on display. Upon closer inspection, it is evident that

[1] Martindale, Notes from Military Secretary to H.E. the Viceroy, September 19, 1899, GOI, FD, Secret I, 48–52 of February 1900, NAI; Curzon Collection, Photo 430/25, BL.

the best-documented famine works, and the first in the album after the usual portraits of the maharaja and his officials, were those carried out at the Gajner shooting estate. Already the site of a palace and the premier wildfowling lake in Bikaner, a series of images show Gajner receiving new infrastructure and improvements to its waterworks and access road (Fig. 10). The famine coolies who worked at Gajner were temporary participants in a much larger project that brought together state officials and shikar officers, skilled craftsmen, trained foresters, and civil engineers. The goal was to transform Gajner into a world-class shooting estate, making Bikaner a hunter's paradise in the midst of the Great Indian Desert.

It was not just for the viceroy's benefit that the scenes of Gajner in Ganga Singh's famine album depicted a perfect accord between the prince, his people, and Bikaner's environment. It was a challenging task to balance the needs and expectations of wildfowl and ungulates, peasants and state nobles, princely peers and British officials, but success was essential to Ganga Singh's self-image as a modern Rajput prince. To meet the challenges he faced, Bikaner's maharaja formulated a flexible blend of Rajput and British approaches to rulership and hospitality, sportsmanship and environment, tradition and progress, middle-class values and elite masculinity.

Like his peers in Mewar and Orchha, Maharaja Ganga Singh was a Rajput prince. But his approach to environmental management and relations with the British set him apart in important ways. Fateh Singh of Mewar and Pratap Singh of Orchha were both content, in their separate ways, to keep their distance from the paramount power and associate themselves with Rajput tradition over "foreign" standards in sport, society, and government. Bikaner's prince, on the other hand, demonstrated his progressive credentials while organizing self-consciously "modern" hunts for himself and his guests in pursuit of Bikaner's world-class wildfowl and ungulates. By 1900, burgeoning flocks of imperial sandgrouse and demoiselle crane, along with multiplying herds of blackbuck antelope and chinkara gazelle, were putting Ganga Singh's state on the map. Closely associated with his shooting estates was a series of irrigation works aimed at supporting local economies by alleviating hardship—like that caused by the

1899 famine—while simultaneously acting as watering holes where game would congregate. In step with these advances, the maharaja developed a repertoire of double-meanings wherein private pursuits complicated the meaning of public works, and meticulously ordered sandgrouse shoots advertised loyalty to the empire while quietly but firmly inverting colonial hierarchies.

Shooting impressive game substantiated Ganga Singh's membership in a peer group that measured status in part on one's ability to obtain the most exclusive sport and to kill it in the most exceptional manner. The maharaja, however, faced difficulties in getting the necessary game within Bikaner's borders. Outside the state menagerie, Ganga Singh had no tigers, almost no leopards, and certainly no lions.[2] There were no natural forests or jungles capable of supporting even sambar deer or chital.[3] To compensate, Ganga Singh struggled to turn Bikaner's environmental constraints to his advantage by touting the state's arid grounds and comparatively ordinary selection of game as exceptional. At the same time, he diverted water, regulated usage, and initiated plantings in order to transform select sites into veritable oases. Simultaneously, the maharaja pursued shooting opportunities in other states where he could obtain the prey that his own realm lacked.

Wildfowling was a long-established practice in Rajput states like Bikaner, but the princes' collective focus in the late-nineteenth and early-twentieth centuries was on big game. Themselves indisputably royal, tigers in particular bolstered the reputations of questionable sovereigns. Free of any threat besides the risk of being shot by careless fellow sportsmen, wildfowling suggested luxurious ease and courtly refinement. While these qualities too were necessary components of an ideal Rajput royal image, they were less than flattering without a

---

[2] Maharajkumar Bijey Singh shot one leopard in Bikaner in 1925. Ganga Singh shot another in 1934. These seem to have been the sole exceptions: see Ganga Singh, *His Highness' General Shooting Diary*, vol. 2 (Bikaner: Government Press, 1941), tables for 1925–6 and 1933–4.

[3] Ganga Singh partially remedied the situation by introducing chital: see PFD, Bikaner, to Secretary to AGG-Rajputana, November 5, 1935, GOI, RA, 175-P of 1939, NAI.

counterbalance of more forceful elements. On their own, they were incompatible with prevalent conceptions of "true" sportsmanship in colonial India, which called for strenuous activity and courageous endeavor. Wildfowling was vulnerable to accusations of cruelty and decadent self-indulgence: the slaughter of hundreds of defenseless birds amounted to excess and seemed to accomplish no clear public service akin to the destruction of man-eating tigers or troublesome wild boar. Yet, the sport remained respectable so long as the game birds in question presented enough of a challenge, the shooting was "sportsmanlike," and records remained to be broken. In recognition of these caveats and because he had few other options, Ganga Singh exalted the qualities of Bikaner's birds while repeatedly stressing the possibility of attaining world records in his state.

Wildfowl were Bikaner's most prolific game and figured prominently even in Ganga Singh's earliest sporting pursuits. The maharaja began hunting in 1891 at the age of 11. By 1894 he had accounted for 32 head of game, 29 of which were wildfowl.[4] His activities intensified in 1895 when he amassed a mixed bag of 825 animals following the arrival of his British tutor, the shikar enthusiast Mr (later Sir) Brian Egerton. As the product of a culture that celebrated English wildfowling practices and reveled in shoots at famous estates like Sandringham and Balmoral, Egerton's influence likely amplified Ganga Singh's appreciation for the impressive flocks available to him at Gajner, Talwara Jheel, and elsewhere.[5] Indeed, among the 825 animals that the prince killed in 1895, 786 were wildfowl, including

[4] G. Singh, *General Shooting Diary*, table for 1891–1921. He shot 28 sand-grouse, 1 houbara, 2 blackbuck, and 1 wild boar.

[5] His excellence and enthusiasm as a sportsman began under Egerton's supervision: see Karni Singh, *The Relations of the House of Bikaner, 1465–1949* (New Delhi: Munshiram Manoharlal Publishers Pvt., Ltd., 1974), 179; K.M. Panikkar, *His Highness the Maharaja of Bikaner, a Biography* (London: Oxford University Press, 1937), 42–3. On Egerton as a sportsman, see C.W. Waddington, *Indian India as seen by a Guest in Rajasthan* (London: Jarrolds Publishers, 1933), 68; see also L.S. Rathore, *Maharaja Sadul Singh of Bikaner (A Biography of the Co-Architect of India's Unity)* (Bikaner: Books Treasure and Maharaja Ganga Singhji Trust, 2005), 38.

120 duck, 59 snipe, 189 common and 389 imperial sandgrouse, besides a dozen demoiselle crane, a couple of houbara, and a bustard.[6] Also in 1895, the maharaja began hosting what would soon become his world famous wildfowl shoots at his Gajner estate.[7] Except for lapses during severe droughts and occasional absences from India in later years, the prince's annual tallies remained high for the rest of his career. He regularly bagged over a thousand head of game and sometimes nearly twice that, the vast bulk being wildfowl.

Ganga Singh greatly admired his state's wildfowl and, because his status as a sportsman was linked to the perceived quality of his game, he wanted outsiders to do so as well. According to the maharaja, the imperial sandgrouse was a superior game bird capable of giving "capital shots and sport."[8] He insisted that a great deal of skill and steady aim were required to bring down the birds because sportsmen had to shoot them precisely in the head or breast.[9] In addition, the flight of the imperial sandgrouse was vigorous and "much faster" than it appeared.[10] The maharaja found a receptive and influential audience. Lord Curzon assured the Prince of Wales in 1905 that the movement of sandgrouse on the wing was "quite unlike that of any other bird, and ... not in the least [like] that of a grouse."[11] Fifteen years later, Britain's Secretary of State for Air likened their speed to "torpedo-carrying bombers."[12]

Imperial sandgrouse, of course, were hardly the only winged game in Bikaner. Much larger than the sandgrouse but by no means

---

[6] G. Singh, *General Shooting Diary*, table for 1891–1921.

[7] Ganga Singh, October 2, 1902, BMK, s. no. 760, file 115 of 1902, RSA.

[8] Ganga Singh, "Programme, cont'd," 1901, item 25, BMK, s. no. 736, file 68 of 1901, RSA.

[9] *Detailed Instructions Relating to the Visit to Bikaner of Their Excellencies the Viceroy and the Lady Irwin. January–February, 1929* (Bikaner: 1929), 63.

[10] G. Singh, "Programme, cont'd," 1901, item 25, BMK, s. no. 736, file 68 of 1901, RSA; *Detailed Instructions* (Irwin), 63.

[11] Lord Curzon, to Prince of Wales, January 5, 1905, Mss Eur F111/216, BL.

[12] Samuel John Gurney Hoare Templewood, *India by Air* (New York: Longmans, Green and Co., Ltd., 1927), 102.

an easy target, there was also the demoiselle crane or *kunj*. Ganga Singh described these birds as strong, fast, and hard to bring down (Fig. 11).[13] Unlike sandgrouse, *kunj* were "wily and cunning" and a shoot could "easily be spoilt by ignorance of their ways and habits," or by impatience. At least one British commentator agreed with Ganga Singh's views, noting with approval that Bikaner's *kunj* inspired "man's responsive wiliness and cunning."[14] Shooting these birds was an art and a science at which the maharaja claimed to excel. The sport surpassed many other kinds of wildfowling in its difficulty and, therefore, in the merit its practitioners could accrue. In convincing most observers that he habitually pursued such challenging and stimulating prey, Ganga Singh hoped to avoid the negative associations of wildfowling.

Unlike big game, where the size of individual specimens matters most, wildfowling records are based on the number of birds shot. Accordingly, Ganga Singh could claim eminence not just by contending that Bikaner had the most challenging species, but by stressing the superlative abundance of wildfowl in his realm. It was possible to obtain record tallies in other states—most notably of duck in Bharatpur—but no other prince could boast of so many imperial sandgrouse. In the best years, Ganga Singh insisted that "when the [sandgrouse flights] begin ... the sight is most wonderful, tremendous big pack after pack come and many thousand birds drink at each tank."[15] Absolute numbers lent distinction to Bikaner's flights of duck and *kunj* too, although no other Bikaneri birds flocked in such uniquely large numbers as sandgrouse. The opportunity to shoot record numbers legitimized wildfowling by providing a reasonable explanation for massive kills that otherwise might have appeared to betray an unsportsmanlike lapse of self-restraint.

As might be expected, there were similarities between wildfowling at Gajner and at famous British estates such as Balmoral and

[13] *Detailed Instructions* (Irwin), 65.

[14] Walker, *The Prince in India*, 63.

[15] G. Singh, "Programme, cont'd," 1901, item 25, BMK, s. no. 736, file 68 of 1901, RSA.

Sandringham. Ganga Singh's intense management of birds to ensure a shoot's success would have come as no surprise to his European guests. The availability of pheasant in Britain by the mid-nineteenth century depended on rearing programs and game farms, while the maintenance of partridge stocks relied on a large staff of gamekeepers empowered to eliminate predators, improve the environment, and defend their employer's interests against competitors.[16] In Bikaner, Ganga Singh's sandgrouse required lakes and tanks, which the prince selectively made available, augmented, and blocked off to manage the birds' movements.

Ganga Singh's guests also would have recognized and accepted as legitimate his adroit bids to barter a fine day's sport for various desirable returns—social, economic, and political. It was generally accepted in Britain during the Victorian and Edwardian periods that "the ability to offer 'good' shooting ... could open doors into the highest levels of society."[17] The same principle was at work in Bikaner, where the definition of good shooting, however, encompassed bags of sandgrouse rather than English partridge. The prey, hunting grounds, shooting arrangements, and accommodations all mattered. But Ganga Singh's prospects benefited from the fact that, ultimately, at the great estates in Britain and in India, "the quality of hospitality was measured only in the quantity of birds shot."[18]

Shooting fashions and an intertwined sense of sporting and national identity helped determine what made for good sport. Just as sportsmen famously weighed the relative merits of sly fox and savage boar in the nineteenth and early-twentieth centuries, wildfowlers compared the virtues of Indian and English birds. In doing so, they discriminated not only between significantly different species like houbara and pheasant, but also between individual varieties of sandgrouse, duck, and partridge. Such debates had a distinguished pedigree among the British. Wildfowlers in Great Britain eagerly

---

[16] Alastair J. Durie, "Game Shooting: An Elite Sport c. 1870–1980," *Sport in History* 28, 3 (2008): 435.

[17] Ibid., 432.

[18] Ibid., 431.

pursued English partridge while declaring the red-legged or French partridge (*Alectoris rufa*) "a pest" on account of its "tendency to run forward rather than fly for the waiting guns."[19] Had shooting fashions favored birds on the run over those on the wing, the upstanding English bird would have been the pest rather than its unsporting French cousin.

Shooting etiquette too was fairly universal throughout the empire. Low-flying birds and those on the ground (including the sitting duck) were not fair game. Shooters were to be considerate of their fellow sportsmen, not "poaching" birds from other guns and taking care to avoid accidents.[20] So long as Ganga Singh followed these rules in Bikaner and insisted that his guests do the same, Gajner could stand in for an English shooting estate.

The style of shooting sandgrouse, duck, snipe, and demoiselle crane in Bikaner would have been equally familiar. By the late-nineteenth century the fashionable method in England was the drive or battue, which brought birds directly to the sportsman, who remained in his shooting butt. Formerly the norm, hunting on foot with dogs by "walking up to a mile for every bird shot" was now the exception.[21] With this shift in shooting practices—brought about mainly by advances in the power, accuracy, and efficiency of firearms—physical endurance as a measure of masculinity among wildfowlers no longer meant the ability to walk for miles over rough ground to take a limited number of shots. What mattered instead was a sportsman's demonstrated ability to remain perfectly still for hours in a shooting butt, stoically withstanding the impact of several hundred rifle recoils. When it came to battue hunting, whether the quarry was English partridge or imperial sandgrouse, the greatest "challenge lay in the shooting pure and simple."[22] Any further differentiation came down to the specific challenges posed by individual species, including flight pattern, air speed, distribution, wariness, and predictability.

[19] John Martin, "British Game Shooting in Transition, 1900–1945," *Agricultural History* 85, 2 (2011): 210.

[20] Durie, "Game Shooting," 436.

[21] Martin, "British Game Shooting," 207.

[22] Durie, "Game Shooting," 436.

Bikaneri wildfowl like the black-bellied or imperial sandgrouse (*Pterocles orientalis*), the houbara (*Chlamydotis undulata*), and the demoiselle crane (*Anthropoides virgo*) were exotics from a British perspective. While duck and snipe akin to European varieties did live in the state, the Grey or English partridge (*Perdix perdix*) was conspicuously absent, as was the Common pheasant (*Phasianus colchicus*), and the Red grouse (*Lagopus lagopus scotica*). Even the mixed game in the surrounding countryside failed to match up. Instead of fox and hare, Bikaner had blackbuck, wild boar, and chinkara gazelle; certainly respectable, but not the same. Different prey with correspondingly different habits and habitats resulted in substantially different shooting experiences.

In place of the English bird, a red-legged partridge called the chukar (*Alectoris chukar*) was available in Bikaner. Like French birds, chukar would "run rapidly and far at first" before taking to wing, whereas the English partridge's first instinct was to fly.[23] While sportsmen acknowledged the chukar as a game bird, its refusal to fly immediately upon being flushed made it less attractive than both the English partridge and iconic Bikaneri wildfowl like sandgrouse. Ganga Singh nevertheless experimented with partridge coverts in his state. Never a main attraction, Ganga Singh's partridge coverts made only fleeting appearances in the prince's game book. In the early 1920s, the maharaja shot at the Sheobari covert near the capital. He killed partridge there again in 1939, and repeatedly in the early 1940s.

Other partridge coverts were maintained at least from the 1920s at Dia and Kodamdesar in the Gajner area. A committee headed by the heir-apparent reviewed operations at the Dia covert in 1923, inquiring into arrangements for partridge feeding and vermin destruction in this grassy preserve.[24] The fact that the micromanaging maharaja allowed his son to take the lead in these matters reflects both the lesser status of partridge and the relative unimportance of Dia as a wildfowling site for visiting VIPs. Still, the presence of partridge at

[23] A.O. Hume and C.H.T. Marshall, *The Game Birds of India, Burmah, and Ceylon*, vol. 2 (Calcutta: A.O. Hume and C.H.T. Marshall, 1880), 35.

[24] Ganga Singh, order 275, December 28, 1922, Bikaner PWD, s. no. 2319, file B1239–46 of 1923, RSA.

Dia was desirable enough to justify the expense of their import from elsewhere in India. This was likely the norm with most partridge in Bikaner, with the possible exception of those bagged in the northern reaches near Hanumangarh, where the habitat was more conducive and the species more likely to occur naturally.

Without the right birds, Ganga Singh's shooting palaces and hunting preserves could never be exact replicas of the famed estates of Great Britain. But Bikaner's prince never fully expected that they could be. Arid and semi-arid grounds and game complicated any attempts at mimicry just as surely as did the British colonial discourse famously described as requiring "a reformed, recognizable Other, as a subject of a difference that is almost the same, but not quite."[25] Rather than attempt the impossible, Ganga Singh instead proceeded on the basis that Bikaner's environment, the state's game, and he himself were subjects of difference not necessarily the same as their British equivalents, but just as good, or perhaps even better.

The challenge Ganga Singh faced was to make his shooting parties and wildfowl acceptable to British colonial sportsmen, while also harnessing the birds' potential as emblems of a specifically Bikaneri sense of identity. While most of the credit for developing the state's environment and promoting its birds belongs to Ganga Singh himself, the maharaja's ambitions were helped along by events in Europe. World War One significantly affected shooting and game management in Britain by reducing—but not eliminating—the urge to acquire large bags, and by moderating the acceptability of what came to be viewed as a cruelly inappropriate and wasteful activity in terms of animal slaughter and misallocated funds, manpower, ammunition, grain, arable lands, and meat. Due to the economic, cultural, and environmental changes associated with the war and its aftermath, "retrenchment became the order of the day."[26] Elaborating on these

[25] Bhabha, "Of Mimicry and Man," 126.
[26] Durie, "Game Shooting," 442.

trends, World War Two brought the sport to "a complete halt" in England between 1939 and 1945.[27]

In marked contrast, wildfowling in Bikaner barely registered these trends. While there was a sharp drop in Ganga Singh's personal bag in 1939, when he shot only 194 imperial sandgrouse as opposed to 717 birds in 1938, his numbers were on the rebound as early as 1940 when he accounted for 438 birds. When he brought down another 619 imperial sandgrouse the following year, his take was not much less than his interwar average of 704 (and well within the standard deviation of 355 for those years). There were similar sudden but equally brief dips centered on 1939 in Ganga Singh's bags of houbara, duck, demoiselle crane, and quail. These reductions, however, may have been unrelated to the war: precipitation was poor in 1939, with accumulations around 50 per cent of the norm throughout Western Rajputana and no rainfall at all during the crucial wildfowling months of November and December.[28] When Ganga Singh's tanks and reservoirs dried up, his imperial sandgrouse and waterfowl were forced to go elsewhere.

A similar picture emerges from the prince's game book for World War One, with an additional dip at the end of the war reflecting his presence at the Paris Peace Conference. The major difference is that rainfall in Western Rajputana was normal, making it more certain that the reductions in 1914 were related to the onset of war than can be said of those recorded for the dry year of 1939.[29] This pattern of sudden yet brief drops, however, fails to appear for snipe and common sandgrouse, and for larger game including tiger, blackbuck, and chinkara; tallies remained steady for these in both 1914 and 1939. The numbers for relatively undesirable game, like bustard and florican, also stayed constant, at two or three, or even zero, per year.

Scholars have suggested that after World War One British wild-fowlers were better off shooting in the colonies if they hoped to

[27] Ibid., 433.

[28] *India Weather Review, 1939: Annual Summary, Part A: Summary of Weather with Tables* (New Delhi: Government of India Press, 1941), Plate A3.

[29] *India Weather Review: Annual Summary, 1914* (Calcutta: Superintendent of Government Printing, 1916), Plates 2–5.

obtain large bags at economical rates.[30] The example of Bikaner supports this. At Gajner and elsewhere in his state, the maharaja as a consummate host consistently absorbed most of the costs of his guests' shooting, and imperial sandgrouse continuously flocked in record numbers as a migratory species whose isolated and semi-arid range remained relatively undisturbed by the ravages of both world wars.[31] Rather than declining, Ganga Singh's tallies for imperial sandgrouse and duck actually peaked during the interwar years. Even when his numbers lowered during World War Two, they remained comparable to his pre-World War One levels.

All similarities aside, sport in the colonies differed dramatically from shooting in the home country when it came to the most prized game. Tiger, leopard, and record blackbuck topped many sportsmen's lists in India. Species as varied as elephant, kudu, and lion attracted the big shots in Africa. In Great Britain, "the main interest of the elite lay in winged game, the wild grouse, the managed partridge and the reared pheasant."[32] These regional preferences likewise shaped trends in trophy preservation and display. Naturalistic mounts of domestic and exotic wildfowl constituted a major portion of the market for artistic taxidermy in Europe, but major Indian firms, including Van Ingen & Van Ingen of Mysore, described themselves as big game and "*tiger* taxidermists," and they explicitly directed their customers to "send no birds."[33] Between 1933 and 1939, the number of the three most popular species processed by Van Ingen & Van Ingen—tiger, leopard, and blackbuck—was more than double that of all other species combined, including the smaller cats, bear, deer, wild boar, bison, and African game.[34]

[30] Durie, "Game Shooting," 446.

[31] *Pterocles orientalis* have "an extremely large range:" see "Black-bellied Sandgrouse *Pterocles orientalis*," BirdLife International (2012) Species Factsheet, accessed March 24, 2012, http://www.birdlife.org/datazone/speciesfactsheet.php?id=2964.

[32] Durie, "Game Shooting," 433.

[33] Joubert van Ingen, quoted in P.A. Morris, *Van Ingen & Van Ingen: Artists in Taxidermy* (Ascot: MPM Publishing, 2006), 148. Emphasis in the original. Morris, *Van Ingen & Van Ingen*, 18.

[34] Ibid., 108.

Even at Gajner, the preference for big game trophies trumped the site's identity as a wildfowling locale. Taxidermied sambar and nilgai heads lined the corridors at the estate rather than imperial sandgrouse and demoiselle crane. Likewise, tiger skins and blackbuck adorned the dining room walls. Similar decorations graced the entrance hall, smoking and billiard rooms, and the maharaja's study at Lalgarh palace in the capital. No matter how good his birds, Ganga Singh still needed tigers to embody his status and flesh out his identity.

Despite the absence of taxidermied birds in Bikaner, the maharaja did preserve traces of his wildfowling exploits. Photographs of record and routine bags appeared in souvenir presentation albums, and select images would have been displayed throughout the maharaja's palaces alongside portraits of family members, friends, British officials, and European royalty. In addition, the maharaja's *General Shooting Diary*—handsomely bound and printed for limited circulation in 1941 but likely available for perusal by guests in manuscript form from the 1890s—contained exhaustive tallies of bustard, houbara, florican, demoiselle crane, duck, snipe, imperial sandgrouse, and eighteen other kinds of wildfowl.

Somewhat predictably, given the status of wildfowling in Britain and tiger hunting in India, Ganga Singh had greater success impressing British audiences with the excellence and respectability of Bikaner's wildfowling than he enjoyed with individuals from other Rajput states. The Mewari huntsman Tanwar witnessed duck and imperial sandgrouse shoots at Gajner when he accompanied Maharana Bhupal Singh on a visit to Bikaner in 1937. Noting the vast number of birds killed and the practice of keeping the animals away from alternate water sources to concentrate them on one or two chosen tanks, Tanwar declared the sport a "cruelty."[35] The worst offenders were none other than Maharaja Ganga Singh and his heir, Sadul Singh.[36] Tanwar learned his standards of sportsmanship under the tutelage of Bhupal Singh's predecessor, Fateh Singh, who had shot birds so rarely that his lifetime bag was reportedly just two wildfowl.[37] In contrast, Maharaja

---

[35] Tanwar, *Shikari aur Shikar*, 347.
[36] Ibid., 346.
[37] The variety is unclear. Tanwar calls them *jal murg*, meaning waterfowl

Ganga Singh accounted for close to 25,000 imperial sandgrouse, nearly 23,000 duck, and over 3000 *kunj*. In Tanwar's view, wildfowling most properly was a means of putting food on the table.[38] Because it lacked any element of danger, he did not consider it much of a sport, nor did he think it a particularly suitable pastime for kings.[39] When Ganga Singh or his heir shot huge numbers in their ongoing pursuit of world records, Tanwar believed they generated more waste than glory.

Many of the same liabilities that adhered to wildfowling were associated with the pursuit of India's wide selection of wild ruminants, especially the less challenging varieties living in the plains. It was an admirably masculine sport to pursue mountain-dwelling species through Himalayan terrain. It was respectable to stalk chital and sambar stags through dense jungles. But chinkara gazelle and the ever-popular blackbuck gave little trouble to accomplished sportsmen. For many, the benefits of killing these animals peaked with the first few and rapidly declined thereafter, with the obvious exception of trophy heads. British soldiers in their youth pursued blackbuck with enthusiasm, but "antelope-shooting palls upon the taste. There is too much of it, and it lacks variety."[40] As a result, most Englishmen distanced themselves from the comparatively undemanding sport as they matured. But in Bikaner there was no better prey to advance to after securing one's initial trophies. Ganga Singh's solution was to exaggerate the qualities of his state's antelope and gazelle and the local methods of shooting them.

or moor hen: ibid., 197. They are *jangli murg* or jungle fowl in *Shikar ka Naksha*, 22.

[38] Tanwar, *Shikari aur Shikar*, 347.

[39] Ibid., 349.

[40] James Forsyth, "Game Animals and Birds of the Plains," in *The Oxford Anthology of Indian Wildlife: Hunting and Shooting*, ed. Mahesh Rangarajan, vol. 1, 42; see also V.M. Stockley, *Big Game Shooting in India, Burma, and Somaliland* (London: Horace Cox, 1913), 256.

Although blackbuck were somewhat out of fashion in the colonial period, they had a long and intimate association with kings and royal sport in India, evident both in classical Sanskritic culture and later during Mughal times.[41] Perhaps more than any other animal, blackbuck helped Hindu kings maintain their necessary connections with the forest. Like wild boar, these auspicious creatures—and more generally all deer—drew sporting kings far from cultivated areas and deep into the *jangal* or wilderness, where, like King Dushyanta of Kalidasa's *Shakuntala*, they could encounter powerful forces, reinvigorate themselves, and discover wives capable of producing lion-taming heirs. From the sixteenth century, blackbuck were also the primary quarry of the Mughal emperors' hunting cheetahs, along with chinkara and hare.[42] Mughal miniature paintings, like their Rajput counterparts, abound in antelope. Ganga Singh's later policies, however, seem independent of these noble histories. The methods used to hunt blackbuck and chinkara that the trend-setting Mughals had practiced were no longer possible. The former imperial grounds at Nagaur, Merta, Jhunjunu, and Jaisalmer that might have provided wild cheetahs were exhausted or near exhaustion by the close of the eighteenth century.[43] The species itself was presumed regionally extinct in India not long after 1947. Ganga Singh, therefore, had little reason to look back on what blackbuck and chinkara pursuits had once meant, and many reasons to look forward for his own tailor-made shooting experiences.

The maharaja was so concerned with promoting record herds of blackbuck that he inserted no provisions into his game laws that would have allowed his subjects to kill them, even if the animals were found destroying crops. This no doubt appealed to the state's Bishnoi contingent, but the primary goal was to improve Bikaner's hunting. Largely inviolate herds caused problems for cultivators

[41] See Zimmermann, *The Jungle and the Aroma of Meats*, 55–62.

[42] Divyabhanusinh, *The End of a Trail: The Cheetah in India*, 3rd ed. (New Delhi: Oxford University Press, 2006), 2 and 49.

[43] Irfan Habib, *An Atlas of the Mughal Empire: Political and Economic Maps with Detailed Notes, Bibliography and Index* (Delhi: Oxford University Press, 1982), Map 6B.

living near state shikargahs. When the prince instituted a temporary reduction scheme and began thinning herds near Hanumangarh in the late 1920s, it was probably in response to rampant public dissatisfaction: a political liability considering that the place was a favorite shooting destination for Ganga Singh and his VIP guests. The reduction program was carried out in part by Ganga Singh's two sons, the maharajkumars Sadul Singh and Bijey Singh. As seen in a commemorative photograph, they used the opportunity to obtain a pair of trophy heads (Fig. 12).[44]

In describing the animals as "trophies," the photograph's caption signals their admirable size. The omission of precise measurements invites viewers to speculate, and speculation could easily put these blackbuck at world-record length. Indeed, Bijey Singh and Sadul Singh by the early 1930s both were listed in *Rowland Ward's Records of Big Game* for blackbuck they had shot in Bikaner.[45] Even without the caption, the length of the animals' horns in comparison with the hood of the maharajkumars' mid-to-late 1920s Austin 12 or 20 touring car would have suggested that these particular blackbucks were quite large.[46] A trick of perspective enhanced the horns too: the sharp angle of the automobile relative to the edge of the field of view enlarges the apparent size of objects to the left—like the trophy heads—while diminishing everything to the right. Perhaps a pair of leopards would have been more impressive, but any prince with access to hood ornaments such as these had reason to boast.

Thanks to Ganga Singh's promotional efforts, Bikaner became famous for its record antelope and gazelle.[47] While Brian Egerton in

[44] Fig. 12 comes from a *c.* 1927 album of Bikaneri scenes, possibly meant for gifting to a state noble, princely peer, or British official.

[45] Guy Dollman and J.B. Burlace, eds, *Rowland Ward's Records of Big Game, African and Asiatic Sections, Giving the Distribution, Characteristics, Dimensions, Weights, and Horn & Tusk Measurements*, 10th ed. (London: Rowland Ward, Limited, 1935), 153.

[46] Thanks to John Baker of www.austinmemories.com, A.A. Osborne of the Federation of Austin Clubs, and Jim Stringer, ed., *The Vintage Austin Register*, for their help with this identification. The length of an Austin 12 from front to rear axle was about 9 feet.

[47] Waddington, *Indian India*, 89.

1896 had decried the unrestricted destruction of wild boar in Bikaner, his 16-year-old charge already was concerned more with protecting those species that were capable of attaining record size in his state, namely blackbuck and chinkara.[48] When preparing for the 1905 visit of the Prince of Wales, the maharaja went so far as to intimidate his taxidermists in Bombay (by accusing them of "misappropriating" his property and by threatening to publicly withdraw his patronage) into expediting the return of several locally procured blackbuck trophies, which he had sent for mounting and now wanted on hand for the upcoming festivities.[49] These included "one 25 and one 24½ inches and ... Rowland Ward's record over 25 inches." Record game distinguished Bikaner from other states and raised its status and fame. Ganga Singh worked to consolidate that reputation by doing his best to ensure VIP guests would experience sport commensurate with their heightened expectations. By 1935, *Rowland Ward's Records of Big Game* in fact listed no less than sixteen record blackbuck and ten record chinkara shot in Bikaner, often in the vicinity of Hanumangarh or Suratgarh.[50]

The Hanumangarh photograph also celebrated how the maharajkumars obtained their sport: they pursued the blackbuck from a moving vehicle, which Bijey Singh evidently drove off-roads across the northern plains. Calling for steady aim and steadier nerves, this was a favorite means of pursuing blackbuck and chinkara in Bikaner.[51] Although not actually unique to the state, Maharaja Ganga Singh boasted in 1902 that the practice was indeed "peculiar to Bikaner."[52]

[48] Brian Egerton, to Regency Council Member, April 14, [1896?], BMK, s. no. 181, file 1123 of 1910, RSA. No Bikaneri boar are listed in Rowland Ward's *Records*.

[49] Ganga Singh, to Murray Bros., telegram, November 21, 1905, BMK, s. no. 832, file 266 of 1905, RSA.

[50] Dollman and Burlace, *Rowland Ward's Records*, 153 and 161–2.

[51] Before the arrival of suitable automobiles, a six-horse carriage conveyed Sir Palmer and Lord Curzon to roadside chinkara shoots on their way to Gajner: see G. Singh, "Programme, cont'd," 1901, item 18, BMK, s. no. 736, file 68 of 1901, RSA; G. Singh, October 2, 1902, BMK, s. no. 760, file 115 of 1902, RSA.

[52] Ibid.

The state's flat landscape certainly facilitated these escapades. It also rendered them reasonably safe, at least in comparison with the dangers to life, limb, and axle posed by the broken terrain, unexpected streambeds, and inconvenient obstacles found in many other realms.[53] Nevertheless, the major attraction of the technique was that it added an aura of danger and a greater degree of challenge to the pursuit of otherwise pedestrian game.

Such vehicular sport gratified British VIPs who shot in Bikaner by treating them to a new and relatively unusual experience. The shoots impressed them with their host's prowess too. Describing the blackbuck hunts he enjoyed in 1937 along with Ganga Singh in the prince's "high-powered car," the Viceroy Lord Linlithgow wrote that "when a blackbuck appears [the maharaja] stamps on the accelerator, takes both hands off the steering wheel, and opens fire at the animal with his rifle. It is interesting for the other occupants of the car to speculate as to whether or not he will resume control of the vehicle before it disappears into a thorn thicket at 40 m.p.h."[54] Even as Lord Linlithgow expressed admiration for the sport, his letter to the King-Emperor about the experience framed it as a comic amusement. The point of his story was not Ganga Singh's marksmanship, for the viceroy never specified if the prince hit his target. Rather, the focus was the maharaja's recklessness, and hence his non-Western character and non-modern behavior.

Ganga Singh no doubt hoped to project an aura of control and competence when he took the wheel. Lord Linlithgow perceived this but concentrated instead on the equally present and far less flattering potential for chaos. The maharaja succeeded in introducing an element of danger into the pursuit of blackbuck, but the risk stemmed from his own probable incompetence and not from any threat posed by the animals. The rules of engagement required "true" sportsmen to test themselves fairly against their prey. They gained little, however,

[53] G. Singh, "Programme, cont'd," 1901, item 18, BMK, s. no. 736, file 68 of 1901, RSA.

[54] Lord Linlithgow, to H.M. the King-Emperor, November 30, 1937, no. 26 of 1937, Linlithgow Papers, Mss Eur F 125/1, BL.

from braving a fellow hunter's ineptitude. Besides, the use of a vehicle was not strictly "sporting" because it was understood as giving shooters an unfair advantage.[55] Aiming to impress and to please with his fearless pursuit of unique sport, Ganga Singh instead exposed himself to charges of irresponsibility and questionable sportsmanship.

Like the sport it documents, the Hanumangarh photograph enjoyed mixed success in establishing local superiority. The image, however, aimed at something more than illustrating the excellence of local game and hunting methods. Its caption portrays the young men's activities as benefitting the state: the initial identification of the antelopes as trophies coexists with a somewhat longer and more detailed reference to the public service occasioned by their death. The caption, in fact, is not far removed in tone from more commonly seen variations on *notorious man-eater shot dead by maharaja*. Here it is the villagers' crops rather than their lives that are heroically preserved by royalty. While defending millet and sorghum from hungry blackbuck might not be as dramatic as saving villagers from tigers, the Hanumangarh photograph presents it as similarly impressive.

Shorn of its caption, the photograph would be indistinguishable from the usual visual repertoire of late 1920s shikar photography. Somewhat less posed than many such photos, the image nevertheless conforms to standard practice in showing shooters gazing confidently towards the lens and brandishing their weapons. The bloodstains in the dirt below the animals' heads and their vaguely lifelike poses add an impression of immediacy and drama to the shot, also seen in comparable photos of tiger and leopard kills. Perfectly in line with the genre but at odds with expectations raised by the caption, this photograph provides no visual cues corroborating the maharajkumars' alleged motive of social service or explicating the supposed connection between this particular blackbuck shoot and the protection and promotion of agriculture. If anything, it raises the possibility that cultivated fields were carelessly driven over during the chase. There are no grateful peasants in view, no piles of slain antelope in numbers large enough to be of practical benefit, and no waving fields of

---

[55] MacKenzie, *The Empire of Nature*, 299.

salvaged grain. If not for the caption, the image would be no different from any other shikar photograph whose primary purpose was to glorify the shooter.

As with wildfowl, Ganga Singh of Bikaner and Fateh Singh of Mewar held divergent views when it came to shooting blackbuck and comparable game. Because he valued the sport and because the animals were available in his state, Ganga Singh killed around 800 blackbuck and 700 chinkara in his lifetime. Considering these species beneath his dignity and preferring to pursue the dangerous game in his own state, Fateh Singh reportedly contented himself with two blackbuck, twenty sambar deer, and not a single additional ruminant.[56] In contrast with Mewar's exceptional tigers, leopards, and wild boar, Maharana Fateh Singh considered Bikaner's signature sport inferior, and possibly ignoble. The Mewari ruler's perception of Ganga Singh—as a less than respectable sportsman, a second-rate prince, and an improperly ambitious upstart claiming to represent his superiors on the all-India stage—may explain why Fateh Singh never invited the maharaja to shoot in Mewar's jungles. In contrast, Fateh Singh's successor Maharana Bhupal Singh embraced wildfowling, harbored fewer resentments against Ganga Singh's assertiveness, and willingly hosted the maharaja on numerous tiger shoots beginning in 1937.[57]

Ganga Singh greatly appreciated the opportunity to engage in big game hunting in Mewar in his later years, as he did the chance to shoot as a young adult in any territory that featured wildlife not available to him in Bikaner. Impressive as they were, Ganga Singh's sandgrouse records and *kunj* tallies would not excuse mediocre entries in his game book under vital headings like Tiger, Lion, and Leopard.[58] The maharaja needed to kill unquestionably superior wildlife in order to match the achievements of other Rajput princes. He equally

[56] Tanwar, *Shikari aur Shikar*, 197. Totals recorded by Tanwar may only include animals Fateh Singh shot as maharana.

[57] Between February 1937 and May 1942, Ganga Singh shot approximately 40 tigers in Mewar: see G. Singh, *General Shooting Diary*. Bhupal Singh contracted a marriage between his heir and Ganga Singh's granddaughter in 1940.

[58] Ganga Singh's *General Shooting Diary* gives "Panther." I use the taxonomically more appropriate "Leopard" to maintain consistency.

needed to obtain a sufficient selection of animals belonging to the lesser species that his peers similarly enjoyed better access to, including chital, sambar, and four-horned antelope. A full game book defended his status as a world-class sportsman while securing his standing relative to his fellow princes. To actually improve his position, however, he required better game, more kills, and a reputation for superior shooting and novel achievements in shikar.

The maharaja from his youth had been "eagerly desirous" to shoot big game.[59] He bagged his first tiger, leopard, and bear in 1896 at the age of 16 and added more kills to his game book nearly every year thereafter.[60] In 1901, he successfully lobbied for an invitation from Maharao Raghubir Singh of Bundi to shoot "a tiger or two" in that ruler's state.[61] He had similar success the following year when he killed 3 tigers in the maharao's jungles and procured 4 live cubs.[62] By 1921, he had shot 107 tigers and 33 leopards at various locations out-of-state, in addition to 1 Asiatic lion. By 1942, he would bag an additional 159 tigers, 28 leopards, and 6 lions. Ganga Singh made the majority of his tiger kills in Mewar, Gwalior, and Kotah states, and in British territory.[63] His leopard kills were similarly distributed, but his lion trophies came from the sole remaining range of the species on the Saurashtra peninsula in and near the Gir Forest of Junagadh State.

Any sporting prince of sufficient status could shoot numerous tigers and leopards, but Ganga Singh was among the few who killed Asiatic lions. In fact, he pursued these exceptionally rare animals to

[59] Brian Egerton, "Note," in Panikkar, *His Highness the Maharaja of Bikaner*, 47.

[60] Ibid., 48. He killed 2 leopards and 5 bears in 1896. In the 1920s and 1930s young princes were shooting their first big game as early as age 11: see Allen and Dwivedi, *Lives of the Indian Princes*, 127.

[61] Ganga Singh, to Maharao of Bundi, March 5, 1901, Bundi MK, s. no. 7, file 24 of 1901, RSA.

[62] Member, Bundi State Council, to PA-Haraoti and Tonk, April 21, 1902, Bundi MK, s. no. 7, file 24 of 1901, RSA; unknown, Bikaner, to unknown, Bundi, April 23, 1902, Bundi MK, s. no. 7, file 24 of 1901, RSA.

[63] Of the 137 locatable tiger kills out of his total of 266 by 1942, 36 were in Mewar, 31 in Gwalior, 28 in Kotah, 20 in British India, 7 each in Danta and Bundi, 3 each in Bhopal and Dholpur, and 1 each in Alwar and Palanpur.

such an extent that the Nawab of Junagadh Mahbatkhanji III implied that he was a poacher.[64] When Ganga Singh tried to obtain permission to shoot a lion in Junagadh in 1913, a state representative denied his request on the grounds that few animals were left. Although encouraged to take "a sportsman's view" of the situation, the maharaja persisted and eventually obtained his first lion in 1916, possibly by luring one of the nawab's animals across the border in an inflammatory but technically legal fashion.[65] When Mahbatkhanji III refused the maharaja's request to shoot another lion in 1921, Ganga Singh again found other means to obtain his second trophy that March.[66] Most other rulers lacked the requisite power and standing to ignore the nawab's protests or weather the inevitable reprimands of locally stationed British officials. In contrast, Ganga Singh's boldness emphasized his privileged superiority as the ruler of a first-class state.

Albeit less directly, Ganga Singh also tested his sporting skills and ability to get exclusive game against the highest ranking Rajput prince of all, Maharana Fateh Singh of Mewar. When tiger hunting in Gwalior Kalan near the border between Mewar and Gwalior states in 1928, Ganga Singh particularly wanted to shoot an exceptionally large animal that he knew Fateh Singh "had failed to get."[67] If he bagged the tiger, the maharaja would succeed where the maharana had admitted defeat. Prominently displayed in his dining room, study, or billiard room, the trophy would give Ganga Singh a convenient excuse to regale guests with a stirring tale of his triumph. Unfortunately for Ganga Singh, the tiger eluded his gun just as it had Fateh Singh's.

[64] Mahbatkhanji III, to E. Maconochie, June 29, 1921, in Divyabhanu-sinh, "Junagadh State and its Lions: Conservation in Princely India, 1879–1947," *Conservation and Society* 4, 4 (2006): 543.

[65] Ibid., 531. Mahbatkhanji III claimed ownership of all Asiatic lions; today the government of Gujarat does: see Mahesh Rangarajan, "Region's Honour, Nation's Pride: Gir's Lions on the Cusp of History," in *The Lions of India*, ed. Divyabhanusinh (New Delhi: Black Kite, 2008).

[66] Divyabhanusinh, "Junagadh State and its Lions," 534. The 1921 shooting resulted in ill-will: see Sadul Singh, *Big Game Diary*, 37.

[67] Ibid., 128.

Beyond Bikaner's borders, Ganga Singh tried to co-opt the excellence of hunting grounds and game so that his foreign kills would glorify him more than his hosts. When hunting in Kotah State in 1924, he expressed his desire to shoot a tiger from a boat in that state's "novel way."[68] The Maharao of Kotah enjoyed some of the most unique tiger hunting in India along the banks of the Chambal river, but the vessels from which his guests shot failed to impress Ganga Singh and his son, Sadul Singh. In his game diary, which occasionally overlapped with his father's to the point of plagiarism, Sadul Singh commented that there was "much room for improvement" in Kotah's shikar.[69] Whereas the electric boats at Gajner were up-to-date and efficient, the ones in Kotah made shooting nearly impossible because they were "uncontrollable ... very noisy and jerky."[70] Ganga Singh might bag tigers in the admittedly beautiful Chambal river gorge, but the deplorable antiquity of the hunting craft rendered the sport substandard. Ganga Singh's superior boats helped the prince bring his sandgrouse up to the level of Kotah's big cats.

Ganga Singh shot as much big game as he could, but he would not admit that his state's shikar was in any way inferior to foreign offerings. In 1900, the maharaja learned that the officiating political agent then posted to Bikaner, S.F. Bayley, was proceeding on tour with the intention of shooting game at Hanumangarh.[71] Besides boasting some of Bikaner's finest blackbuck shooting, Hanumangarh was within reach of the Talwara Jheel, an excellent wildfowling site where Ganga Singh frequently entertained state guests.[72] Bayley had not

[68] Ibid., 46.

[69] Ibid., 11 and 47; compare with Ganga Singh, *Extracts from His Highness' Diary*, 3.

[70] Assistant Secretary, to Mechanical Engineer, November 8, 1903, BMK, s. no. 776, file 258-I of 1903, RSA; S. Singh, *Big Game Diary*, 47. Ganga Singh's boats do seem to have impressed visiting princes: see "Shikar in Bikaner 1925–1927 and Opening of the Gang Canal 1927," Maharao of Kotah Collection, 1998/133/013, 00.00.01–00.06.38, British Empire and Commonwealth Museum.

[71] K. Singh, *Relations*, 182. Karni Singh was Ganga Singh's grandson.

[72] Lord Minto was scheduled to shoot at Talwara Jheel in 1908: see Ganga Singh, to Victor Brooke (Military Secretary), October 18, 1908, BMK,

requested a game license, and so the prince wrote him inquiring if political agents in Bundi State, for example, were allowed to shoot tigers without the maharao's permission.[73] In referencing the norms of another state, Ganga Singh posited that he was entitled to exercise the same controls with the same authority as his comparably ranked Rajput peers. Bikaner's blackbuck, chinkara, and wildfowl were no less significant than Bundi's tigers.

As much as he tried to compensate by shooting wildfowl, blackbuck, and the best of big game, Ganga Singh spent his youth and young adulthood struggling for control and feeling frustrated in his ruling ambitions.[74] He endured a long minority from 1887 to 1898, during which he was subordinated to a British-appointed Regency Council. His first few years after coming of age coincided with Lord Curzon's viceroyalty, an era notorious in the states for meddling in the princes' personal affairs and administrations.[75] Most galling of all, special restrictions that effectively granted authority in all important matters to Bikaner's political agents remained on his powers until 1908, when he was 28.[76] Seeking greater independence, Ganga Singh tried to prove his administrative capabilities by subtly challenging his subordination within the colonial hierarchy. To do so, he developed a series of highly disciplined shooting programs meant to impress, and even control, British VIPs who came to his Gajner shikargah for wildfowling.

It is widely accepted that princes did not offer the best shooting in their states to British VIPs out of loyalty to the empire. Instead, they hoped to trade a tiger, sambar, or other game for political goodwill,

s. no. 138, file 926-I of 1906–10, RSA. Lord Hardinge shot there in 1912: see Ganga Singh, to Military Secretary, telegram, [November 1912], BMK, PD, s. no. 147, file FIV/218G of 1912, RSA.

[73] K. Singh, *Relations*, 193.
[74] Ibid., 180.
[75] Copland, *The Princes of India*, 21; Panikkar, *His Highness*, 55 and 91.
[76] K. Singh, *Relations*, 183.

practical concessions, or personal favors.[77] Many Englishmen in the colonial period embraced this interpretation of princely hospitality because it confirmed their suspicions that, in the end, their Indian hosts were selfish, scheming, disloyal, and inferior.[78] These conclusions conveniently excused government representatives from feeling excessive gratitude or from overly admiring their hosts' good qualities: distinct advantages considering that the first sensation raised the specter of bias in official relations with generous princes, while the second posed a threat to racial and colonial hierarchies.[79] Not surprisingly, Indian rulers saw the matter differently. The practice of exchanging shikar for various benefits did not expose princely flaws. Rather, it demonstrated their genius for managing the British and subverting unsatisfactory norms.

Considering how conveniently manipulation-based explanations suited the prejudices of both parties, it is advisable to look a little deeper. In Bikaner, Ganga Singh undoubtedly intended to ingratiate his British guests by impressing them with the state's best wildfowling. He did not expect to barter sport for dramatically expanded powers, but he did hope disciplined shooting programs would reflect well on his abilities as a modern prince invested with Western ideals. Denied full control over his own administration, he did his best to ensure his supremacy remained indisputable on the hunting ground.

Ganga Singh closely directed his guests' shooting only after 1901. Before that, circumstances were different. During Viceroy Lord Elgin's visit to Bikaner in November 1896, the maharaja and his guests had downed "<u>400 grouse</u> . . . before breakfast."[80] Although

[77] For princes gaining political concessions from hosting successful shoots, see Allen and Dwivedi, *Lives of the Indian Princes*, 140.

[78] Rajput princes prided themselves on being consummate hosts: see Sen, *Migrant Races*, 105; see also Kesri Singh, *Hints on Tiger Shooting (Tiger by Tiger)* (Bombay: Jaico Publishing House, 1975), xvii.

[79] Although happy to receive hunting opportunities, British officials worried that accepting other princely gifts would suggest corruptibility: see S.M. Fraser, August 4, 1904, GOI, FD, Internal B, 204–5 of September 1904, NAI.

[80] G. Singh, October 2, 1902, BMK, s. no. 760, file 115 of 1902, RSA. Emphasis in the original.

he claimed credit in 1902 for that tally, his role in planning this and other VIP shoots during his minority had been limited.[81] The official guidelines prepared for another VIP visit in December 1896 make this abundantly clear. In contrast to the minutely detailed eighty-page programs that became standard issue after Ganga Singh took charge, these instructions addressed a mere seventeen points in less than two pages.[82] The young maharaja had minimal influence over their composition.

Even when Lord Curzon made plans to visit Bikaner for the first time in 1899, a year after Ganga Singh's investiture, S.F. Bayley, the political agent, still blocked the maharaja's efforts to handle the arrangements.[83] Also in 1899, Bayley involved himself in preparations for the agent to the governor general's upcoming visit by insisting on reviewing Ganga Singh's plans, benignly explaining that "we both want it to be a success, and the more we work together the more successful it will be."[84] In suggesting that the prince was not equal to the task of properly entertaining a viceroy or even an agent to the governor general without assistance, the political agent implied that the ruler was incompetent to govern independently.[85] The maharaja countered such implications when he corresponded with Lord Curzon's staff in the months leading up to the viceroy's 1902 visit by stressing his long experience in organizing shikar entertainments, boasting how he had "managed two big shoots every year since '95."[86] He

---

[81] Judging by the program's style and content, the first visit Ganga Singh managed was the 1901 visit of Commander-in-Chief Sir Palmer: see G. Singh, "Programme, cont'd," 1901, BMK, s. no. 736, file 68 of 1901, RSA.

[82] H.A. and R.V., "Visit of H.E. the Commander-in-Chief to Bikaner," November 16, 1896, BMK, Regency Council, s. no. 251, file 172–80/14 of 1896–8, RSA.

[83] K. Singh, *Relations*, 180.

[84] S.F. Bayley (Officiating PA), to Ganga Singh, February 15, 1900, BMK, State Council, PD, "B", s. no. 494, file 53 of 1899, RSA.

[85] Bayley became notorious for his tendency to "encourage the belief that the real power in the State lay with him:" see Panikkar, *His Highness*, 91. See also A.P. Nicholson, *Scraps of Paper: India's Broken Treaties, Her Princes, and the Problem* (London: Ernst Benn Limited, 1930), 242.

[86] G. Singh, to Military Secretary, October 2, 1902, BMK, s. no. 760, file 115 of 1902, RSA.

neither credited Bayley's contributions nor mentioned the assistance he surely received through 1898 from the Regency Council and his tutor Brian Egerton. To impress a viceroy like Curzon, Ganga Singh needed to keep all the glory for himself.

Free of the constraints imposed on him by Bayley and the Regency Council, Ganga Singh extended his control over every detail of his guests' sport after 1901. The first impression VIPs had of shooting arrangements in Bikaner would have been formed by the palace and grounds at the Gajner shikargah. The maharaja therefore worked hard to ensure that visitors found thoroughly modern appointments and all the latest conveniences. By the time Curzon visited, Gajner had electric lighting, expanded guest quarters, and a Western-style billiard room that elicited much British approval.[87] Metaled roads and a branch of the state railway delivered visitors within steps of the palace. The estate had tennis and squash courts, croquet grounds, and a swimming pool by the 1930s. Other additions included a post and telegraph office, an automobile garage, and a power house. Ganga Singh distributed these features through the grounds, so that guest quarters fell into neat rows, service buildings were clustered at a respectable distance from the palace, and convenient walkways traversed the gardens. Popular opinion held that modern architecture and "rational" settings exerted a salubrious effect.[88] Open vistas and airy rooms promoted clarity and moral probity. Tortuous corridors, narrow chambers, and chaotic grounds facilitated intrigue, inefficiency, and short-sightedness. By adding "many details for modern comfort to the ancient establishment," Ganga Singh

[87] *Account of the Visit of His Excellency The Viceroy and Governor General of India to Rajputana. 1902* (Calcutta: Office of the Superintendent of Government Printing, 1904), xxv–xxvi, Mss Eur F112/475, BL; G. Singh, October 2, 1902, BMK, s. no. 760, file 115 of 1902, RSA; newspaper clipping, "The Duke and Duchess of Connaught, Varied Sport, Bikaner," February 16, 1903, BMK, s. no. 742, file 108 of 1902, RSA.

[88] For Indo-Saracenic architecture, see Thomas R. Metcalf, *An Imperial Vision: Indian Architecture and Britain's Raj* (Berkeley: University of California Press, 1989); for landscapes and national character, see Marjorie Morgan, *National Identities and Travel in Victorian Britain* (New York: Palgrave, 2001), 46 and 68.

transformed Gajner into a reflection of his administrative and moral competence.[89]

The desired atmosphere equally relied on an unending supply of letters and specially printed schedules, instructions, and shooting tips, alongside the informal advice he communicated in person to VIP visitors. Before his guests arrived, the maharaja would mail or telegram abstract programs indicating the proper size shot for imperial sandgrouse (no. 4 exclusively) and stressing the desirability of having two shotguns and a loader.[90] Upon their arrival at Gajner, guests received printed "hints" detailing the proper methods of shooting duck, sandgrouse, and demoiselle crane.[91] Instruction continued for the duration of their visit via a set of notice boards located near the Billiard Room, where "various forms, plans, etc.," regularly appeared to direct guests to their assigned places in accordance with Ganga Singh's strict schedule.[92] His heir carried the practice forward with little or no change, so that state guests in the mid-1940s still took direction from notice boards "plastered with plans and instructions."[93]

The maharaja's various communications repeatedly stressed the imperative of being "very punctual" when shooting imperial sandgrouse.[94] The beginning of a shoot depended entirely on the birds, and the birds arrived every morning at approximately 8:00 a.m. The regularity of their flights conveniently coincided with and even necessitated Ganga Singh's notice boards and timetables, rendering the maharaja's audacity irreproachable as he closely controlled his guests, whether they were political agents, commanders-in-chief, or viceroys.[95] The prince's consistent success in predicting the birds'

[89] "Duke and Duchess of Connaught," February 16, 1903.

[90] Kanwar Prithi Raj Singh, to guests of November 23, through December 2, 1901 shoot, November 2, 1901, items 1 and 6–7, BMK, s. no. 736, file 68 of 1901, RSA.

[91] *Detailed Instructions* (Irwin), 10.

[92] Ibid., 9.

[93] Mary Chenevix Trench, Mss Eur F226/33, BL.

[94] G. Singh, "Programme, cont'd," 1901, item 24, BMK, s. no. 736, file 68 of 1901, RSA. Emphasis in the original.

[95] British sportsmen were accustomed to following directions during a shoot, and they ideally "let the man who knows most about the game and the

time of arrival suggested an ability to coerce Bikaner's sandgrouse into following his schedule, just as he could the British. Of course, his control in both instances was illusory. The birds would arrive regardless of his timetables and British VIPs ultimately were free to do as they pleased.

The constant flood of information emanating from Ganga Singh's offices announced the maharaja's competence as a leader. His polite but firm directions reminded guests that their host was in charge. In the midst of wildfowl shoots, the maharaja remained visibly—and audibly—in a position of power. His shikaris' every action had been pre-planned, every possible portion of the shoot had been rehearsed, and his posted instructions remained on constant display— but Ganga Singh nevertheless insisted on carrying a megaphone.[96] In the interests of diplomacy he outfitted visiting viceroys with megaphones of their own, but he undoubtedly hoped they would understand that in this case being a good sport meant not using them.[97]

Modernity and efficiency were traits claimed by Englishmen. When applied to nations, they were purportedly limited to only the best Western governments. Through his precise postings, Bikaner's prince contended that these qualities belonged to his administration too. Soon after the completion of each shoot a final notice, an "Abstract Total Bag" detailing the day's successes, confirmed the maharaja's triumphs.[98] Ideally, VIP guests would draw parallels between the maharaja's successes at Gajner and his general aptitude as a modern ruler imbued with every desirable attribute and talent.

Ganga Singh also used printed shooting hints to position himself as the supreme arbiter of sportsmanship at Gajner. Distributed to

---

ground run the shoot:" J.W. Best, *Indian Shikar Notes*, 2nd ed. (Allahabad: Pioneer Press, 1922), 117.

[96] For shooting rehearsals, see G. Singh, "Programme, cont'd," 1901, item 23, BMK, s. no. 736, file 68 of 1901, RSA; for the megaphone, see Ganga Singh, Shikar Instructions to Kunwar Bhairun Singh, November 7, 1908, item 11, BMK, s. no. 142, file 926H of 1906–10, RSA.

[97] *Detailed Instructions* (Irwin), 8.

[98] Ibid., 10.

guests upon their arrival, the maharaja's leaflet on duck urged visitors to abstain from the cardinal sin of greedy shooting, reminding them that "although by not taking long shots one Gun may lose some possible chances, another Gun will obtain better shots sooner or later, and *vice versa*."[99] A similar directive appeared in the notes on *kunj* shooting, alongside a further request that visiting sportsmen keep a cool head.[100] A single gun "with patience" could cull a big bag from a small flock of demoiselle crane, but six or seven shooters succumbing to "excitement" and "firing wildly" into a much larger flight would get little sport, collectively or individually.[101] Considering that British colonial identity rested on assertions of their inborn fair-mindedness and national levelheadedness, Ganga Singh's guests easily could have taken offense at his entreaties for equitable and patient shooting.

Practical tips regarding the best size shot for *kunj*, an imperial sandgrouse's deceptive speed, and the benefits of aiming for the head, neck, or breast reiterated Ganga Singh's widely acknowledged familiarity with local wildfowling conditions. His professed expertise would not much threaten British sportsmen because many were unfamiliar with these birds; the same caveat, however, could not apply to the prince's duck-shooting tips. In daring to advise his guests on shooting etiquette, the maharaja implied he was a better sportsman and more civilized individual. By delivering his self-aggrandizing assertions in the form of "hints" that ostensibly aimed at nothing more than the facilitation of his guests' sporting ambitions, he avoided the appearance of deliberate offense and his guests were able to politely overlook their host's half-hidden agenda.

In fact, he went out of his way to ensure his guests would believe the proceedings at Gajner were meant to please them more than anything else. When preparing for a viceregal visit, he would work out the program in advance in consultation with government officials, including the military secretary and the viceroy's personal

[99] Ibid., 61.

[100] Ibid., 65.

[101] Ganga Singh requested patience in his duck shooting hints too: ibid., 61.

secretary, both of whom he would "bombard … with an endless number of questions" regarding his guests' special tastes and shooting preferences.[102] British VIPs interpreted the attention to detail as a personal compliment to them and an expression of the ruler's loyalty. They were not entirely wrong. The maharaja counted many Englishmen among his personal friends, he was devoted to the British royal family, and he generally supported the empire—even if he disagreed with specific policies and would later become a prominent lobbyist for reform in the government's relations with the princes.[103]

In his analysis of the hunts Ganga Singh hosted at Gajner, John M. MacKenzie concluded that the maharaja carefully managed his shoots to produce "a repeated statistical underpinning of the social hierarchy."[104] He surmised that it must have caused a minor scandal when Ganga Singh's heir-apparent once shot more sandgrouse than the viceroy. In fact, Sadul Singh was a famous marksman who "topped" every other gun including his father and any VIP guests, British or otherwise, on a regular basis.[105] While Ganga Singh often did his best to ensure that VIPs secured the biggest bag, his goals were not so static nor were his hunts as clear a reflection of British desires as MacKenzie suggested.[106]

The prince walked a fine line between flattery and insubordination. British VIPs might have gotten the most sandgrouse at Gajner from time to time, but Ganga Singh's wildfowling tips were there to remind them they had done so by following his lead. The maharaja may have shared his megaphones and hence his symbolic control with visiting viceroys, but his arrangements were carefully calculated to make them recognize that his was the authoritative voice.

Big bags and record shoots gratified British VIPs. Just as importantly, sizeable tallies reflected well on the maharaja's organizational

---

[102] G. Singh, to Victor Brooke, draft letter, August 17, 1908, BMK, s. no. 138, file 926-I of 1906–10, RSA.

[103] For more on Ganga Singh's efforts on behalf of the states, see Copland, *Princes of India*.

[104] MacKenzie, *Empire of Nature*, 194.

[105] Kesri Singh, *Hunting with Horse and Spear* (New Delhi: Hindustan Times, 1963), 77; Lothian, *Kingdoms of Yesterday*, 152.

[106] MacKenzie, *Empire of Nature*, 194.

abilities and conditions in Bikaner State. The expansive flocks of imperial sandgrouse and other wildfowl that big bags relied on pointed to a corresponding abundance of crops, wild forage, and water. Such proliferation indicated the soundness of Bikaner's environment, which echoed the virtue of Ganga Singh's administration. Since there were few other clear signs of fecundity in the state, massive flocks of migratory wildfowl provided evidence of Bikaner's otherwise hidden potential. Impressive bags signified all this as Ganga Singh organized his guests like pawns around Gajner, Pilap, Sugansagar, and his other wildfowling tanks.

Etiquette, however, required that Ganga Singh reserve the choicest shooting butts for his highest-ranking visitors. Along with the maharaja's other guests, viceroys and commanders-in-chief regularly received a great deal of friendly shooting advice.[107] But there was little the prince could do if a VIP proved to be a disappointing shot and unhelpful in attaining a record despite being positioned in the best butt possible. In the maharaja's opinion even good shots needed guidance when it came to downing Bikaner's birds, and he recommended a bit of target practice whenever possible. Although both were competent shots, Ganga Singh sent his close friends, Viceroy Lord Minto and his wife, a pair of targets specially designed to improve their sandgrouse shooting prior to their second visit to his state in 1908.[108]

The prince had greater flexibility when it came to lower-ranking guests, and he preferred to know the relative abilities of each sportsman before placing them. Careful preparation went into the distribution of guns for the Prince of Wales's visit in 1905. Ganga Singh made his placements using information obtained from a friend at the Indore Residency, who telegrammed that, among the expected guests, the "best shots are Keppel, Dugdale, and Wigram, average shots are Watson, Faussett, Cust, and Crichton, and Shaftesbury, and Grimston,

---

[107] Some of Ganga Singh's advice was more agreeable than prudent. Lord Linlithgow reportedly received the following guidance: "Your Excellency, if you listen to the advice of an old man and have some liqueur brandy with me, it's going to put your eye straight and you will shoot a hundred grouse this morning!" Allen and Dwivedi, *Lives of the Indian Princes*, 139.

[108] Victor Brooke, to Ganga Singh, September 8, 1908, BMK, s. no. 138, file 926-I of 1906–10, RSA.

Campbell, and Sir A. Bigge in that order."[109] Ganga Singh's later notes repeated the names in order, with the Prince of Wales added to the top and each individual numbered in sequence, 1 through 12.[110] He concentrated the best shots, and the Prince of Wales and himself, at the sites he expected to have the most birds.[111] These were Sugansagar on the first day and Gajner on both days of shooting.[112] He assigned lesser sportsmen to lesser sites the first day, including Golri, Jogiro, and Motawat.[113] When shooting was restricted to two tanks on the second day, they shot at Sugansagar rather than Gajner.[114]

Although he tried to distribute shooters according to his interests, Ganga Singh understood the imperative of giving every gun a sporting chance. Protocol required him to place certain figures in the best positions, but sporting ideals obliged him to show equal consideration to every wildfowler. If he failed, his placements ran the risk of appearing politically motivated and unduly self-interested. Such concerns led the maharaja to instruct his staff in 1905 that, if anyone did not get good sport in the first day's shooting, "special care should be taken to place them in good places" the next day, regardless of the pre-established positioning.[115] Aside from being suitably sporting, the policy reflected an awareness that low-ranking guests might advance over the years to senior positions.

Ganga Singh wanted lots of shooters to help guarantee a big bag,

[109] Harry Watson, to Ganga Singh, telegram, November 17, 1905, BMK, s. no. 841, file 304 of 1905, RSA.

[110] G. Singh, [Nov. 1905?], docs. 40–1, BMK, s. no. 841, file 304 of 1905, RSA.

[111] I define the top shooters as the first five names on Watson's list.

[112] "Butt key for 25th" and "Butt key 27th," [Nov. 1905?], BMK, s. no. 841, file 304 of 1905, RSA.

[113] Ganga Singh expected two first class places between Jogiro and Motawat, but these still would not have equaled the first day's shooting at Gajner or Sugansagar: see G. Singh, "Saturday November 25th Imperial Grouse Shoot," [Nov. 1905?], BMK, s. no. 832, file 266 of 1905, RSA.

[114] "Butt key 27th," [Nov. 1905?], BMK, s. no. 841, file 304 of 1905, RSA. The exception was the top-rated Keppel, who shot at Sugansagar on the second day.

[115] Ganga Singh, "Confidential. Detailed Instructions. Their Royal Highnesses the Prince and Princess of Wales's visit to Bikaner. 24th November,

especially when celebrating some personal achievement or special event. This was the case in 1901, when the Commander-in-Chief Lord Palmer came to Bikaner to confirm the maharaja's appointment as Knight Commander of the Order of the Indian Empire. Just as slain tigers would "properly" mark the birthdays of Ganga Singh's youngest son, the maharaja's wedding anniversary, and the festivals of Gangaur and Akha Teej in the early 1920s, record numbers of imperial sandgrouse would fittingly commemorate Ganga Singh's new rank in 1901.[116] Lord Palmer's visit therefore included a wildfowl shoot at Gajner in late November, the prime season for sandgrouse. The program the prince sent to his prospective guests prior to their visit exhorted them that "we must all try and beat the record of previous years and get a real good bag."[117] In pursuit of this goal, Ganga Singh wired a month in advance to indicate his hope that Lord Palmer would bring his entire staff and all his *aides-de-campe*, because "lots more guns" were wanted.[118] Additional shooters would bring down more birds and hordes of guests and staff at Gajner would make the logistics of Ganga Singh's entertainments more difficult, and that much more impressive.

To guarantee a good bag, Ganga Singh focused too on his own staff's performance, which he regulated through the distribution of meticulously detailed instruction booklets. These covered every conceivable aspect of the arrangements for VIP visits, including transportation, accommodation, cultural entertainment, and shikar. The prince dealt with additional minutiae, such as the eradication of wasps at Gajner prior to Lord Minto's expected arrival in 1908,

---

Friday," [Nov. 1905?], item 105, GOI, FD, Miscellaneous, 408(6) of 1905–6, NAI.

[116] For tigers killed on Maharajkumar Bijey Singh's birthday, see Singh, *Extracts*, 13–14; see also S. Singh, *Big Game Diary*, 19 and 26. For tigers killed during the Gangaur procession, see G. Singh, *Extracts*, 12 and 13. For tigers killed on Ganga Singh's wedding anniversary and Akha Teej, see ibid., 23.

[117] G. Singh, "Programme, cont'd," 1901, item 27, BMK, s. no. 736, file 68 of 1901, RSA.

[118] G. Singh, to Military Secretary, draft telegram, October 22, 1901, BMK, s. no. 736, file 68 of 1901, RSA.

in the frequent supplementary commands he sent his officers.[119] His instructions required his subordinates to make certain that no shooting opportunity was squandered. Any available game was to be marked down and kept under supervision, guests were to be situated in their wildfowling butts punctually, extra cartridges were to be provided immediately upon demand, malfunctioning weapons were to be repaired on the spot, and rifles and shotguns were to be at hand without fail whenever there was the least possibility of getting any sport.[120] After all his efforts to enhance the shooting tallies, Ganga Singh abhorred the thought of under-reported bags. He required his staff to see that every single "grouse and duck and quail" was retrieved after "each shoot at each place each day."[121]

Ganga Singh categorized his shikargah improvements under the rubric of progress by closely associating them with modern advancements in irrigation. By scientifically controlling Bikaner's harsh environment, he expected to demonstrate his administrative abilities and modern credentials while securing his status in relation to rival princes who could boast of tigers in their realms. Yet, if not managed with care, improved shooting grounds could undermine the very image of progress and responsible government that Ganga Singh intended them to project. When blackbuck and chinkara multiplied in step with expanding cultivation and the importance of wildfowling appeared to outrank the effective distribution of irrigation waters, public works lost their progressive sheen. The maharaja nevertheless counted proliferating wildlife and "progressive" shikargahs among

[119] G. Singh, to K. Bhairun Singh, [Oct. or Nov. 1908?], BMK, s. no. 138, file 926-I of 1906–10, RSA.

[120] G. Singh, "Prince and Princess of Wales's visit to Bikaner. 24th November, Friday," [Nov. 1905?], items 28, 65, 78, 81–2, 94–5, 106, and 113, GOI, FD, Miscellaneous, 408(6) of 1905–6, NAI.

[121] G. Singh, "Instructions for Shooting Arrangements for all 3 Sections of His Excellency the Viceroy's Visit Programme," item 54, [Oct. or Nov. 1908?], BMK, s. no. 142, file 926H of 1906–10, RSA.

the most effective means of attracting sporting VIPs to his state and impressing them with his talents.

When British officials visited Bikaner, Ganga Singh could display his progressive works and extol their far-reaching implications all in the course of a successful shoot. An eager participant in the ruling chiefs' conferences hosted by the viceroy in Delhi since 1913, an active member of the Chamber of Princes from 1921, and a vocal champion of states' rights, Ganga Singh made full use of these opportunities to influence British opinion, to the extent that one observer alleged "he only allowed visitors ... to see his capital and his shooting palace."[122] True enough in spirit, this was nevertheless something of an exaggeration. The prince displayed other impressive sights on a regular basis, like recently commissioned irrigation tanks and landscapes poised to benefit from proposed canals.

Ganga Singh's need to use Bikaner's arid landscape to influence and impress coincided with his desire, in the wake of the disastrous 1899 famine, to prevent further hardship in his state. It equally meshed with government policies that newly encouraged the extension of protective public works. In 1901, Lord Curzon created the Indian Irrigation Commission, a deputation of which was investigating projects for recommendation to various Rajputana states in 1904.[123] Ganga Singh already had the irrigation engineer A.W.E. Standley on loan from the government, but he arranged for the head of the 1904 deputation, Sir Swinton Jacob, to visit as well.[124] Aware from the first that new irrigation works could attract additional wildfowl, he situated his initial projects within easy reach of Gajner, near the villages of Pilap and Madh.[125] The feasibility of rainwater collection

[122] Lothian, *Kingdoms*, 153.

[123] Ganga Singh, speech at Gang Canal foundation stone laying, December 5, 1925, in *Four Decades of Progress* (Bikaner: Government Press, 1937), 93.

[124] Ibid.; PA, to Bhairun Singh, [November 1904?], BMK, s. no. 825, file 117 of 1905, RSA.

[125] On irrigation and wildfowl populations in Bikaner, see C. Sivaperuman and Q.H. Baqri, "Avifaunal Diversity in the IGNP Canal Area, Rajasthan, India," in *Faunal Ecology and Conservation of the Great Indian Desert*, ed. C. Sivaperuman, Q.H. Baqri, G. Ramaswamy, and M. Naseema (Berlin: Springer, 2009).

at these sites helped.[126] Of the two, Pilap was the greater success. After the completion of survey and excavation work by the end of 1904, construction began on a bund, or dam, and an allied irrigation tank. Pilap's planned capacity was almost 40 million cubic feet, but officials did not expect it at first to irrigate more than the few hundred acres that formed its bed, assuming the sandy soil proved capable of retaining moisture.[127] After a few years' worth of silt had accumulated, they hoped Pilap would become watertight, thus allowing for more extensive irrigation.[128] The state engineer deemed this to be the case in 1907 when he finally recommended the installation of distribution channels, which had been omitted from the original plans in the interests of economy should the tank have failed altogether.

Pilap's potential for irrigation was promising in 1907, but Ganga Singh seems to have been more enthusiastic about the tank's shooting prospects (he visited twice that year and downed nearly 200 duck between November and October) than the local population was about the water.[129] Their fields for *kharif* or autumn crops were located at an impractical distance from the tank.[130] The nearest settlements were *pattedari* properties, meaning residents would owe taxes to local landlords and the state if they used the water for their crops.[131] Furthermore, animal husbandry was more common in the area than agriculture and people preferred using the water for their cattle or to slake their own thirst.[132] The Revenue and Finance

[126] Ganga Singh, speech at state banquet for Lord Minto, 1906, in Panikkar, *His Highness*, 117.

[127] A.W.E. Standley (Executive Engineer), [1904?], BMK, s. no. 100, file 748 of 1906–10, RSA.

[128] State Engineer, to Bhairun Singh (PFD Secretary), September 3, 1907, BMK, s. no. 100, file 748 of 1906–10, RSA.

[129] G. Singh, "Note on Programme," 1908, BMK, s. no. 142, file 926H of 1906–10, RSA. See section 3, item 37.

[130] State Engineer, to Bhairun Singh, September 3, 1907, BMK, s. no. 100, file 748 of 1906–10, RSA.

[131] Raghuvar Singh, April 19, 1909, BMK, s. no. 494, file RII/19 of 1913, RSA.

[132] G. Singh, Copy of His Highness's Orders dated the Tiger-shooting Camp Palanpur, April 8, 1912, Bikaner PWD, s. no. 249, file PI/108 of 1911–14,

Secretary lamented in 1909 that the "State has spent thousands of rupees in the construction of the Bandh for the benefit of the State and its ryot [people]. The object cannot be realised unless [ways are found of] removing the drawback in the efficient working of the irrigation system" that kept cultivators from using it as intended.[133] The people's resistance to employing the bund in accordance with expectations undermined the perceived cost-effectiveness of the project, as well as threatening its progressive image.[134] Of course, none of this deterred wildfowl from embracing Pilap.

Even as his subjects' indifferent response continued to plague Pilap, the maharaja in 1912 hailed the site as an all-around success.[135] As early as 1906, the tank's wildfowling was good enough for him to consider its inclusion in the program for Lord Minto's tour. The viceroy actually shot there on his second visit in 1908.[136] Better yet, the tank secured Ganga Singh an impressive record in 1907 that the political agent, Erskine, thought "not likely to be beat."[137] Shooting "for barely 2¼ hours," Ganga Singh brought down 475 imperial sandgrouse and a duck. His companions collected an additional 349 birds that day, bringing the total bag to 825.

RSA; State Engineer, estimate, March 1916, Bikaner PWD, s. no. 1053, file 1412–23 of 1917, RSA.

[133] Raghuvar Singh, April 19, 1909, BMK, s. no. 494, file RII/19 of 1913, RSA. For continuing failures to work with local water use regimes after independence, see R. Thomas Rosin, "The Tradition of Groundwater Irrigation in Northwestern India," *Human Ecology: An Interdisciplinary Journal*, 21, 1 (March 1993): 51–87.

[134] Resistance occurred with British irrigation works too: see David Gilmartin, "Models of the Hydraulic Environment: Colonial Irrigation, State Power and Community in the Indus Basin," in *Nature, Culture, Imperialism: Essays on the Environmental History of South Asia*, ed. David Arnold and Ramachandra Guha (Delhi: Oxford University Press, 1995), 224.

[135] G. Singh, His Highness's Orders, April 8, 1912, Bikaner PWD, s. no. 249, file PI/108 of 1911–14, RSA.

[136] Ganga Singh, programme note, 1908, BMK, s. no. 142, file 926H of 1906–10, RSA. See section 1, items 11 and 13; section 3, items 27 and 30.

[137] Erskine, *Western Rajputana*, vol. 1, 312.

While the maharaja cannot have failed to recognize that Pilap was better suited to wildfowling than irrigation, he promoted the site as an example of his progressivism in speeches and state publications. His opinion flew in the face of an evaluation issued in 1911 by A.C. Davis, the new state engineer, who considered the bund a failed experiment from the public works perspective and questioned "whether it is of any use spending more money in a drainage whose yield is so small."[138] Revenue member G.D. Rudkin apparently agreed. In 1914, he recommended against diverting funds to the project, specifically condemning costly tree plantings meant to reduce water loss by evaporation.[139] The maharaja's attitude towards Pilap did not indicate indifference to the plight of his people. It indicated that he did not view the bund's evolution into a wildfowling site *first* and an irrigation tank *second* as fundamentally problematic, nor as necessarily unprogressive. Even as a shikargah, Pilap could serve the state.

Long after its foundation, Ganga Singh continued to improve the Pilap Bund. Almost yearly, he allocated funds from his privy purse to expand its hunting facilities and from the state budget to increase its irrigation potential. In 1932, he strengthened the bund and had twelve concrete wildfowling butts built on the site.[140] The following year, state workers raised these butts to provide better shooting and

[138] A.C. Davis (State Engineer), "Note of Inspection. Madh and Pilap Tanks," April 14, 1911, Bikaner PWD, s. no. 249, file PI/108 of 1911–14, RSA.

[139] G.D. Rudkin (Revenue Member), comments on State Forest Report, April 24, 1914, BMK, s. no. 101, file 754A of 1906–10, RSA. Babul (*Acacia nilotica*) seeds had been scattered around Pilap in 1907: see PWD Secretary, to F. Tarapurwala, September 23, 1907, BMK, s. no. 100, file 748 of 1906–10, RSA. By 1910, Pilap had a "fair growth of Khejra, Karil, Kakera, Beri accompanied with Jhari undergrowth:" see Rai Bahadur Bhai Sadhu Singh, Report on the Proposed Formation and Management of Forest Reserves in the Bikaner State, Rajputana, "Low lands near Pilap Madh Kotri Kolait &c," 1910, BMK, s. no. 102, file 754B of 1906, RSA.

[140] "Statement showing expenditure on Ganga Sarowar Bund (Pilap Bund) up to year 1932–33," [1934?], Bikaner PWD, s. no 1475, file B4699-4711 of

compensate for the recently expanded catchment, which had increased water levels.[141] Ganga Singh rechristened the bund as the Ganga Sarowar in 1933, underlining its ongoing importance by naming it after himself. That year, he began planning additions and expansions to prepare the Ganga Sarowar for his upcoming Golden Jubilee, when he hoped the tank would round out his glowing resumé of progressive achievements while giving his guests a bit of shooting.[142] A state publication prepared around this time, pointedly called *Four Decades of Progress in Bikaner*, boasted that the Ganga Sarowar would irrigate 3200 *bigha*s, or 2000 acres.[143] The project was in fact a mixed success. It irrigated 2061 *bigha*s in 1935–6, the following season it covered only 500 *bigha*s, and in 1937–8 it provided no irrigation whatsoever.[144] A finishing touch in 1940 then brought the focus back to wildfowling. That year, Ganga Singh erected a stone memorial at Ganga Sarowar with his guests' and his own shooting records engraved on it in letters 2¼ inches tall.[145]

At Pilap and other tanks in the vicinity of Gajner, careful research informed the placement of shooting butts. Ganga Singh's shikar officers kept track of the dates on which duck, sandgrouse, and other shoots began each year. Using gauges provided by the PWD, they

---

1936, RSA; "Government of Bikaner Notes and Orders: Shikarkhana Works to be Carried out at Gajner," March 10, 1933, Bikaner PWD, s. no. 1478, file B4791–815 of 1936, RSA.

[141] "Government of Bikaner Notes and Orders: List of Shikarkhana Works," April 2, 1933, Bikaner PWD, s. no 1478, file B4791–815 of 1936, RSA.

[142] "Notes and Orders. No. 7545 PW of 15-8-34. Extract from the report dated 6-9-33," Bikaner PWD, s. no. 386, file B3374–86 of 1934, RSA; *Four Decades*, 89.

[143] *Four Decades*, 87. This was ambitious as Pilap had never managed much more than 155 *bigha*s in a year: see note, June 17, 1907, BMK, s. no. 494, file RII/19 of 1913, RSA.

[144] *Report on the Administration of the Bikaner State for 1936–37* (Bikaner: Government Press, n.d.), 30 and 64; *Report on the Administration of the Bikaner State for 1937–38* (Bikaner: Government Press, n.d.), 34.

[145] "Making a Game Record at Sri Ganga Sarowar," November 8, 1940, Bikaner PWD, s. no. 3219, file B785–8 of 1940, RSA.

also recorded water levels for those dates.[146] Combining these data, Ganga Singh situated his butts as close as possible to the anticipated high water mark for each season's inaugural shoot, when the prince was most likely to be hosting VIP guests. These data sets could extend over a decade, like the 1933 "Statement showing the dates of first Duck Shoot of the season every year on Gajner Lake and water level on the Lake on the dates of such shoots for the last 11 years," which contained information affecting some forty shooting butts.[147] Clearly, Ganga Singh maintained the highest standards of shooting only by paying close attention to siltation rates, precipitation averages, the migratory habits of birds, and other environmental factors.

Financial concerns, on the other hand, were a lesser matter. In a 1937 report, Bikaner's chief engineer suggested that it would be best to raise the wildfowling butts at the Durbari tank "to escape level once and for all."[148] Despite the wisdom of such a move, given the costs involved and the certainty of continuing siltation, the maharaja's Shikar Officer dismissed the proposal. The state's wildfowling butts would not be raised so high because shooting suffered when guns were stationed too far from the water. Taking into account the expected advantages to be gained from good shooting, and adopting a broad view of economics, the decision may well have been sound.

The frequent raising of butts at Gajner, Pilap, Durbari, and elsewhere due to sand and silt accumulation in their beds correlated with erosion in their catchment areas. In his 1937 report, Bikaner's chief engineer wrote of Durbari that "the feeder channels bring in silt annually thus reducing the capacity of the tank and increasing the liability of giving higher gauges with the same amount of rainfall." In 1932, water levels reached just past relief level (RL) 12, where each RL marked the shoreline after an increase in depth of one foot. The

[146] State Engineer, to PWD and Revenue Secretary, September 3, 1907, BMK, s. no. 100, file 748 of 1906–10, RSA.

[147] Master of the Household, to PWD Minister, April 12, 1933, Bikaner PWD, s. no. 1478, file B4791–815 of 1936, RSA.

[148] Escape level was at relief level 17.2. Chief Engineer, Report no. S/1898 D/10-4-37 on Shikar Works at Durbari, June 3, 1937, Bikaner PWD, s. no. 2284, file B3265–8 of 1937, RSA.

following year the gauge topped RL 14. In 1935 it surpassed RL 14.5, and then RL 15.25 in 1936. Although Bikaner's engineers considered erosion when designing feeder channels, their primary concern was filling tanks, not preserving topsoil in the countryside. As unlined feeder channels worked to concentrate water, they unavoidably transferred sediment.

The number of feeder channels in the vicinity of Gajner increased rapidly after 1900. The maharaja's agents took careful note of any water pooling in undesirable locations or flowing to "waste," and they plotted ways of channeling it into the lake, palace gardens, and even into the adjacent state grasslands, which housed wild boar and provided fodder for domestic animals.[149] In deciding how to proceed, Ganga Singh relied on a basically utilitarian equation weighing the good of the many against that of the few.[150] Specifically, he assumed "the many" were generally underprivileged, "the few" overprivileged, and the state the best qualified to arbitrate between them in pursuit of the greater good, which he defined as increased state revenues, better shooting, and enhanced concentration (and thus efficiency in management and collection) in the geographical distribution of resources. The plan was to condense the state's many small, shallow, and thus evaporation-prone tanks, which were controlled locally by what he considered to be an overwhelmingly backward and exploitative rural elite, into a few large, deep, evaporation-resistant reservoirs, to be dominated by an enlightened and progressive state.

The precise impact on catchment areas and the ways local people and animals used them are unclear. If the most fertile soils and any significant proportion of local precipitation became concentrated in state-controlled tanks and their seasonally arable beds, then cultivation and perhaps even pastoral activities likely followed, possibly leading in affected areas to a shift in peasant relations with rural elites and the state. Domestic cattle and wild animals must have benefited from the development of more reliable water sources, but

[149] List of Shikarkhana Works, July 16, 1933, Bikaner PWD, s. no. 1478, file B4791–815 of 1936, RSA.
[150] G. Singh, His Highness's Orders, April 8, 1912, Bikaner PWD, s. no. 249, file PI/108 of 1911–14, RSA.

the centralization of this vital resource clearly proved a mixed blessing for game birds, and in some cases may have dried out more advantageously located ponds and tanks.

British VIPs who shot around Gajner apparently perceived signs of progressive rule in the tanks and bunds they saw, even if they suspected Ganga Singh had developed the area primarily for its wildfowling and political applications. British collusion was an appreciative response to the excellent sport and gracious hospitality they received at these sites. Waghorne has described a similar phenomenon in the southern state of Pudukkottai: while the British criticized princely excess when expenditures benefited the ruler alone, they encouraged anything that simultaneously celebrated the empire or its representatives.[151] Viceroys and political agents could hardly condemn Pilap, for example, when Ganga Singh specially flattered them with its shooting, and when they very publicly enjoyed the experience.[152] Further exploiting this angle, Ganga Singh consistently obtained the advice of British experts and government officials and scrupulously credited their contributions to his progressive works. He dotted his speeches with mentions of Sir Swinton Jacob, A.W.E. Standley, Lord Curzon, Sir James Dunlop Smith, and Sir Michael O'Dwyer, among others.[153] These efforts rendered the prince's progressive shikargahs less controversial in British eyes.

The British never viewed Ganga Singh's efforts as pure examples of progress. This may have frustrated the maharaja's ambitions, but it made his actions acceptable from an official point of view. British imperialists criticized princes for their alleged backwardness, but tended to object when rulers introduced too many innovations. The Foreign and Political Department was dominated by conservatives who doubted Indian princes were yet capable of ruling on wholly modern lines and who questioned the ability of state subjects to meet the demands of Western-style citizenship.[154] British officials

[151] Waghorne, *Raja's Magic Clothes*, 46.

[152] *The Pioneer* and *Times of India* covered VIP tours and daily bags: see *Account of the Visit of His Excellency*.

[153] For example, see Ganga Singh, speech at Gang Canal foundation stone laying, December 5, 1925, in *Four Decades*, 92–3.

[154] Ian Copland, "The Other Guardians: Ideology and Performance in the

nevertheless wanted a measure of progress in the states to validate their confidence in the benevolent effects of imperialism and its civilizing mission. To avoid conflict with political officers and appear sufficiently independent in Indian eyes, rulers needed to package progress as somehow princely. Hunting grounds were well suited to advancing Ganga Singh's modern reputation, but they could also project an aura of "tradition." The double-meanings that the maharaja developed in his state around his hunting grounds helped him *almost progress, but not quite.*[155]

The people of Bikaner did not necessarily see the Pilap Bund as part of a progressive regime. When it came to satisfying his subjects and asserting legitimacy, Ganga Singh found it as valuable to appeal to precedent and state traditions. Although Bikaner's arid landscape offered few opportunities for irrigation, artificial waterworks were not new in the twentieth century and the people would not have viewed them automatically as modern or Western. Most residents obtained their water from wells, but tanks had been established at Gajner, Kolayat, Devikund, and Sheobari between the fifteenth and the seventeenth centuries. At Gajner, "the complicated canal system . . . over a vast catchment area" that kept water levels high was the work of two former rulers, Sardar Singh (r. 1851–72) and Dungar Singh (r. 1872–87).[156] The three new canals Standley designed by 1905 were merely additions to an existing system.

Nor did the people necessarily see inherent conflicts in their maharaja's habit of building public works that doubled as shooting

Indian Political Service," in *People, Princes and Paramount Power: Society and Politics in the Indian Princely States*, ed. Robin Jeffrey (Delhi: Oxford University Press, 1978), 289. Thanks to Brandon D. Marsh for sharing insights on conservatism in the Indian Political Service.

[155] In my understanding of progress in princely states, I am indebted to Manu Bhagavan, *Sovereign Spheres: Princes, Education and Empire in Colonial India* (New Delhi: Oxford University Press, 2003) and his use of Bhabha's "Of Mimicry and Man."

[156] Hermann Goetz, *The Art and Architecture of Bikaner State* (Oxford: Bruno Cassirer for The Government of Bikaner State and The Royal India and Pakistan Society, 1950), 82.

facilities. Ganga Singh emphasized his progressive ideals when dealing with the British. With his subjects, the more important factor was the concept of *zimmedari*, generally translated as "responsibility," which among Rajput rulers did "not involve disinterest. Rather, the source of *zimmedari* as responsible authority has to do with personal identification, rootedness in place, and perpetuation over time."[157] State residents expected their prince to have a personal stake in the outcome of resource management beyond the financial benefits accruing to the state or some abstract attachment to the greater good. The people's familiarity with interventions based on personal interest made Ganga Singh's melding of public works with the extension of his shooting facilities culturally intelligible and comparatively acceptable. When he shot wildfowl at Pilap or brought VIPs to Hanumangarh, he announced his multiple connections to these places and his continuing stake in local affairs. Increases in destructive wildlife and restrictions on forest use associated with royal shikargahs were negatives, but proximity to newly attractive hunting grounds may have improved the people's chances of accessing their sovereign.[158] The people were not immune to discontent, however, and occasionally reminded Ganga Singh that *zimmedari* required him to consider their interests too.[159] But so long as they did not rebel, the prince had more to gain from impressing the British than from appeasing his subjects in every instance.

The maharaja viewed his pursuit of record bags and trophy heads in improved hunting grounds as helping rather than hurting the interests of Bikaner State and its people, but he was aware of the potential that shikar works had of sullying his progressive image. From the 1920s, nationalists and those seeking democratic advances in the states increasingly portrayed sport as a negative characteristic of

[157] Gold and Gujar, *In the Time of Trees and Sorrows*, 252.

[158] Most princes claimed their hunting gave subjects greater access to them, but Ramusack counters the evidence as "mainly hearsay:" see Ramusack, *The Indian Princes*, 158.

[159] For example, see Chaudhri Khinwsi, question, April 7, 1937, in *Bikaner Government Legislative Assembly Proceedings* (Bikaner: Government Press, 1937), 40, item 13.

Indian royalty and a sign of princely depravity and backwardness.[160] In the late 1920s and into the 1930s, it became risky to mix public works with sporting interests. Ganga Singh now grew more cautious.

While Pilap had always enjoyed a dual identity, the prince from the start billed his most ambitious public works project of the 1920s—a proposed offshoot of the Punjab's Sutlej River scheme called the Gang Canal—as a progressive measure undertaken solely for the people's benefit. It was more difficult to balance shikar and popular interests in the north around the Gang Canal than in the south near Gajner and Pilap. After its completion in 1927, the Gang Canal's waters fostered crops and increased environmental prosperity. Blackbuck, chinkara, and wild boar proliferated and damaged the newly expanded agricultural fields. By contrast, the flocks of imperial sandgrouse, duck, and *kunj* that converged on the southern shikargahs apparently caused less nuisance, primarily because agriculture was not extensive in those areas.

Ironically, record blackbuck facilitated the creation of the very agricultural wealth in the north that they now threatened to destroy. Sport played an integral part in clearing the way for the Gang Canal, which had required British consent and the government's practical cooperation. This was secured in part by hosting VIPs on hunting excursions in the region. In 1906, Ganga Singh treated the Viceroy Lord Minto to some shooting near Hanumangarh, during the course of which they together witnessed what the prince termed "the productive power of that part of the State," as occasioned by an unusually good rain.[161] The maharaja claimed that Hanumangarh had similar soil and topography to the lands along the proposed course of the Gang Canal. In addition, the shikargah was not too far removed from that area. Hanumangarh's temporary verdancy therefore proved that a proper scheme could transform a "large tract of sandy desert ... into a green garden waving with corn and grain."

In the altered political climate two decades later, Ganga Singh feared the results if the Gang Canal were linked with his hunting

[160] For example, see Jaipurian [pseud.], letter to the editor, *Hindustan Times*, July 25, 1939.

[161] Ganga Singh, speech at state banquet for Lord Minto, 1906, in Panikkar, *His Highness*, 117.

activities and those of his heir.[162] When the project was nearing completion early in 1927, Sadul Singh informed his father that he would miss a final inspection of the irrigation works and the Ganganagar canal colony due to an eye complaint.[163] The young man nevertheless remained set on joining his father's planned shooting party, which was scheduled to begin immediately afterwards. Ganga Singh warned his son via telegram that doing so would be "apt to create a wrong and undesirable impression either about you or about me in public eyes and specially [among] our own subjects and new settlers in Canal area."[164] The maharaja organized and led the hunting party himself, but first saw to Ganganagar's irrigation works. In private, Ganga Singh focused on the region's shikar as well as its potential for agriculture. In public, he carefully promoted the Gang Canal's progressive utility while downplaying its sporting attractions. The prince could not allow shikar to appear as the primary object of royal patronage, even if it was the major draw for his youthfully imprudent son.[165]

Despite his efforts to dissociate his progressive achievements from sport in the late 1920s, the link remained noticeable at the Gang Canal and other sites where the prince was less diligent in masking the connection. British VIPs perceived the bond when they shot over grounds that had benefitted from the prince's projects. State subjects noticed it when their sovereign's sporting presence increased in tandem with local irrigation facilities. Even beyond Bikaner's borders there was a widespread awareness of the connections between sport

[162] This paragraph analyzes the same evidence as Rathore, *Maharaja Sadul Singh*, 96. Rathore concluded that Ganga Singh believed it moral and proper to keep hunting within reasonable limits.

[163] Sadul Singh, to Ganga Singh, telegram, February 18, 1927, file 158, SM-MGST.

[164] G. Singh, to S. Singh, telegram, February 18, 1927, file 158, SM-MGST.

[165] Sadul Singh's lack of restraint was a continual concern. A few weeks prior to the canal's grand opening in October 1927, Ganga Singh urged his son to "cultivate at least a little less selfishness" as a sportsman and heir apparent: G. Singh, to S. Singh, October 4, 1927, in Rathore, *Maharaja Sadul Singh*, 96.

and public works in Ganga Singh's realm. Interspersed with views of the capital city and state guests, a 16mm film owned by the Maharao of Kotah sandwiched footage of the ceremonial opening of the Gang Canal between scenes of the maharajkumars Bhim Singh of Kotah and Bijey Singh of Bikaner shooting blackbuck and *kunj* near Hanumangarh and Suratgarh, and imperial sandgrouse and duck around Gajner.[166]

Successfully tempting foreign VIPs with his superlative game, Maharaja Ganga Singh of Bikaner armed his Gajner shikargah with figurative shooting blinds, lifelike decoys, and other distractions capable of keeping his more controversial aims half out of British sights. Record bags shot on schedule in eminently modern settings and in accordance with his own sage advice temporarily elevated Ganga Singh over his guests, hinting at his capacity for directing viceroys and suggesting his qualifications as a modern administrator. Meanwhile, the magnificent flocks at Gajner promulgated visions of abundance in his desert state, proving the righteousness and effectiveness of his rule. Looking out from their well-placed shooting butts, British VIPs nonetheless remained deeply invested in their notions of Western superiority, while tigers continued to outrank sandgrouse throughout the British empire.

Reaching beyond the excellence of his state's game and finely calculated controls at Gajner, Bikaner's maharaja lobbied for more influence and a better reputation by associating royal sport with public works. What began as a tactical advantage developed into a partial liability with the changing political context. In the end, the Pilap Bund morphed into the Ganga Sarowar and the prince's coveted blackbuck became a perilous scourge, destroying crops and royal reputations.

[166] "Shikar in Bikaner and Opening of the Gang Canal," Maharao of Kotah Collection, 1998/133/013, 00.00.01–00.06.38, British Empire and Commonwealth Museum.

5

Martial Pasts
and Combative Presents

I n 1912, the Viceroy Lord Hardinge enjoyed some of India's finest
wildfowling in the Jat state of Bharatpur, where he contributed
to a bag of over 3000 duck. Shooting from the maharaja's exclusive Viceroy's Bund, Hardinge was amused to discover that "instead
of dogs," he had been provided with "four naked Imperial Service
soldiers to retrieve from the water."[1] Created by Lord Dufferin in
1888 to fight "side by side" with regular soldiers, Imperial Service
Troops were deployable at government command and never entirely
at a prince's disposal.[2] Competent enough as wildfowl retrievers in
Bharatpur, Bikaner, and elsewhere, these soldiers often struck British
officials as undisciplined and unprepared for serious action.[3] The
Rajput princes, and seemingly the Jat maharaja of Bharatpur too,
rated them higher. Better armed than regular state armies and more
likely to have seen active service, especially after World War One,
Imperial Service Troops were fit for duty in any princely shikargah.

[1] Hardinge, *My Indian Years*, 78.

[2] Lord Dufferin, in *The King's Indian Allies: The Rajas and Their India*, by
Nihal Singh (London: Sampson Low, Marston, & Co., Ltd., 1916), 142.

[3] Viceroy in Council, to Secretary of State for India, June 24, 1920, GOI,
FPD, Internal, 62 of 1920, NAI; by contrast, see *Imperial Gazetteer of India:
Provincial Series, Central India*, vol. 12 (Calcutta: Superintendent of Govern-
ment Printing, 1908), 71.

Imperial Service Troops may not have been entirely under a prince's command, but they materially expanded on the possibilities offered by state armies, which Indian rulers were required to keep poorly equipped and primarily ceremonial. Under British colonialism in the late-nineteenth and early-twentieth centuries, Indian princes could no longer declare or wage their own wars. Treaties and *sanads* contracted with the British had eliminated their scope for independent conflict, territorial disputes were now adjudicated by the Foreign Department, and the doctrine of paramountcy curtailed their ability to suppress even local uprisings without attracting foreign oversight. In British India, Jats, like Rajputs, were preferentially recruited into the ranks of the Indian army as members of the so-called "martial races." Yet, while young princes had the option of joining the Indian Cadet Corps from 1888, active service remained elusive for most and no Indian could achieve promotion to the highest ranks, except on an honorary basis. By the early 1900s, the cumulative changes of the preceding century had at best transformed and at worst gutted the symbolic and practical weight of the few genuine military experiences still available to Rajput rulers, making it difficult to project the martial images they desired.

To compensate for the dearth of martial prospects, Indian princes tried to manipulate the realities and appearances of their states' military pasts and presents through the hunt and in their hunting grounds. A vast repertoire of martial places, practices, people, and paraphernalia associated variously with the glorious past and a sophisticated present allowed princes to pursue their goals through the medium of shikar. Conducted correctly, martial sports let them influence their multiple audiences as needed while acting in ways consistent with their own self-image as Rajput warriors, displaced and disrupted but still inherently gallant and martial.

A given prince's overall strategy and the weight he gave to suggestions of the past versus modern displays depended on his state's status, its historical relations with the British and earlier powers like the Mughals, and also on the availability of suitable chronotopes. Adapting the term from philosopher Mikhail Bakhtin to analyze battlegrounds and memory in the European context, Kapralski describes a chronotope as "a locus in which time has been condensed and concentrated in space … A real but symbol laden and often mythologized place in which events important for the construction of a group's identity either actually happened according to the group's vision … or are symbolically represented by—for example—monuments, the very arrangement of space, and its social functions."[4] Marked with epic events and historic relics, hunting grounds in the princely states were chronotopes constitutive of Rajput identity and legitimacy. Memories were kept fresh and adapted to present purposes through repeated visits while hunting and by the reiteration, reinterpretation, and reenactment of noteworthy feats of heroism and sport associated with these sites. Sensitized by their own military rhetoric when it came to sports like pigsticking and cognizant of the assumed tactical advantages of knowing the countryside through hunting, the British were well aware of the princes' ability to make martial claims through shikar. In response, they launched empire-sustaining counter-offensives against Rajput character, princely independence, and legitimacy by undercutting the martial overtones of princely shikar and disputing the meaning of well-known chronotopes.

Rajput identity was deeply vested in martialness.[5] In the colonial period, Rajput princes grew up hearing tales of the military exploits and legendary heroism of their ancestors from their elders. A scion of the Bundela Rajput family of Sarila in Central India, for instance, reports that when visiting his grandaunt in the 1930s in her medieval fortress home, the lady used to recite "heroic tales of … ancestors, who had held their own against the Moguls."[6] Her stories let him "slip back effortlessly a century or two in time." In addition to such

[4] Slawomir Kapralski, "Battlefields of Memory: Landscape and Identity in Polish–Jewish Relations," *History and Memory: Studies in Representation of the Past* 13, 2 (2001): 36.

[5] See Dirk H.A. Kolff, *Naukar, Rajput and Sepoy: The Ethnohistory of the Military Labour Market in Hindustan, 1450–1850* (New York: Cambridge University Press, 1990); see also Talbot, "Mewar Court's Construction of History," 20–8.

[6] Narendra Singh Sarila, *Once a Prince of Sarila: Of Palaces and Tiger Hunts, of Nehrus and Mountbattens* (London: I.B. Tauris, 2008), x.

stories were the *vamshavali*s or genealogies like the Bundela clan's eighteenth-century *Chhatraprakasha*.[7] Kings and nobles alike took pride in the fact that they were descended from the very heroes who populated their epics. They hoped to live up to the standard of legendary figures like Chhatrasal, the hero of the *Chhatraprakasha*, who had been "valiant in war, dreadful in battle, famed for heroic achievements, active, vigorous, and powerful as a tiger."[8]

Distillations of original Rajput sources, some British pronouncements on the defining features of the Rajputs and their history had by the end of the nineteenth century become as attractive and authoritative as those found in the *vamshavali*s and elsewhere. In particular, the voice of Tod dominated.[9] By the late 1800s, princes celebrated his *Annals and Antiquities of Rajasthan* as indisputable "evidence of the greatness of the Rajput."[10] They especially embraced the text's perceived ability to impress its flattering conclusions on British audiences and government officials. Although written to promote British imperialism, Tod's pleas for the resurrection of a noble Rajput race as a natural ally of the empire relied on Rajput sources. As a result, there was a broad consensus in colonial India as to the defining features of Rajput sovereigns, including innate bravery and a marked enthusiasm for shikar.[11] For the British, the accuracy of Tod's history would come into question by the beginning of the twentieth century, as would its depictions of the nobility of Rajput nature.[12] Nevertheless, Rajput elites continued to cite Tod, hoping to

[7] On *vamshavali*s, see Talbot, "Mewar Court's Construction of History," 18.

[8] Pogson, *History of the Boondelas*, 48.

[9] Lloyd I. Rudolph and Susanne Hoeber Rudolph, "Writing and Reading Tod's *Rajasthan*: Interpreting the Text and its Historiography," in *Circumambulations in South Asian History: Essays in Honor of Dirk H.A. Kolff*, ed. Jos Gommans and Om Prakash (Boston: Brill, 2003), 272–3.

[10] Jason P. Freitag, "The Power Which Raised Them from Ruin and Oppression: James Tod, Historiography, and the Rajput Ideal" (PhD diss., Columbia University, 2001), 161–2.

[11] Vishakha N. Desai, "Timeless Symbols: Royal Portraits from Rajasthan, 17th–19th Centuries," in *The Idea of Rajasthan*, vol. 1, ed. Schomer, *et al*, 313.

[12] Freitag, *Power*, 219–20.

counter negative evaluations of their character. Some even used his *Annals* as an encyclopedic reference book whenever the government called on them to argue their case in border disputes or other disagreements.[13]

Rajputs in the nineteenth and twentieth centuries knew where their predecessors had fought glorious battles through the stories they encountered in legends, family lore, and Tod's history.[14] Using that knowledge, they hoped to access the positive qualities found in martial chronotopes by engaging in warlike activities in the same places and with their thoughts dwelling on the events and legendary figures associated with those sites. Landscapes where lineage members had fought and died had held special significance for Rajputs for many generations. Wherever the blood of ancestral warriors slain in battle had seeped into the earth, the ground had incorporated their strength and virility, preserving these assets for future generations to access.[15] A popular belief among Rajputs in Rajasthan was that a slain hero continued after death to be a "protector of the land," particularly of its borders.[16] Association with such figures through their place of death benefited modern rulers who wanted to be seen as effective defenders of state territory, especially in an age when they could no longer conquer new lands and when British political agents supervised their every move and second-guessed their boundary settlements.

Reenacting battles by hunting over chronotopes allowed princes to treat old opponents as proxies of contemporary rivals who were too powerful to challenge directly. It has been suggested of Mewar State, after its capitulation to the Mughals in the early-seventeenth century, that "demonstrating the militaristic capabilities of one's family in the

[13] See Fateh Singh, to Lord Reading, *c.* 1924, p.16, acc. no. 27262, MMSL; see also Review of Documentary Evidence, final encl., GOI, FD, Secret I, 5–7 of October 1903, NAI.

[14] Portions of Tod's *Annals* were available in Hindi and other vernaculars by 1912 too: see Freitag, "Power," 232.

[15] Norbert Peabody, *Hindu Kingship and Polity in Precolonial India* (New York: Cambridge University Press, 2003), 90.

[16] Lindsey Harlan, *The Goddesses' Henchmen: Gender in Indian Hero Worship* (New York: Oxford University Press, 2003), 16.

past was especially critical when present circumstances might suggest otherwise."[17] Rajput rulers operating under British paramountcy in the late-nineteenth and early-twentieth centuries were similarly motivated. Symbolically defeating ghostly Mughals, Marathas, and rival Rajputs suggested the latent potential of hunter-kings in the present for renewed potency against the British. Hunting in this way helped Rajput princes transform their actual condition of subjugation into a more flattering mythology of overpowering but intentionally restrained power. The exercise implied princely partnership with the British rather than submission and suggested their ability to throw off, or at least lighten, the colonial yoke. As has been argued for the seventeenth century, beleaguered Rajputs preferred to portray their subordinate situation as "temporary and reversible."[18] Colonial era princes sported within martial chronotopes to achieve a similar effect.

In discussing connections between hunting, Rajput martial identity, and military history, one of the most useful sources on Mewar is the state huntsman Tanwar, who was well aware of the relevant battles and political pedigrees of the shooting grounds he visited with Maharana Fateh Singh. He esteemed hunting in part because it provided the "good fortune to see very important ... historical sites" and because it promoted historical awareness.[19] In his writings he inserted lengthy footnotes calling attention to the military histories of these places.[20] When describing a 1923 visit to Chittorgarh with Fateh Singh to hunt tiger, he recounted the history of this most famous fortress from its legendary foundation in the time of the Pandavas through the "three renowned heroic chapters in the protection of the independence and honor" of Mewar that had happened there when the place was besieged by Ala al-Din Khalji in 1303, Bahadur Shah of Gujarat in 1535, and the Mughal emperor Akbar in 1568.[21]

[17] Talbot, "Mewar Court's Construction of History," 20.

[18] Joffee, "Art, Architecture and Politics," 88.

[19] Tanwar, *Shikari aur Shikar*, author's preface and 2.

[20] Tanwar also footnotes religious sites near royal hunts: see ibid., 158 and 183.

[21] Ibid., 61.

Each time, Chittorgarh's Rajput defenders had fought to the death while the women inside the fort committed mass suicide or *jauhar* to maintain honor in the face of certain defeat. Tanwar did not provide the names and dates above: he assumed his audience would know the details because, he claimed, they were famous all over the world. In a footnote occasioned by a shooting excursion near Udai Sagar, where events had precipitated the 1576 battle at Haldighati between Rana Pratap of Mewar and Akbar's forces under Raja Man Singh of Amber, he similarly glossed that event as a "very famous battle ... of which the reader knows."[22] Tanwar's footnotes urged readers to recall a known heroic past and associate it with the maharana's sport.

Even sites that had not hosted armed conflicts could be useful if they were adequately linked to heroic figures and martial deeds. When hunting in the forests of Gogunda, Tanwar was careful to reference Rana Kakar, a place where he says two of the most celebrated heroes of the royal lineage, Rana Udai Singh (r. 1537–72) and Rana Pratap (r. 1572–97), both had taken refuge from imperial attacks.[23] Udai Singh was celebrated as the Mewari prince who was spirited away as an infant from the second siege of Chittorgarh by his nurse, for his lifelong resistance against Mughal incursions, and for shifting Mewar's capital to a more readily defensible site at Udaipur. Rana Pratap was renowned for his participation in the battle of Haldighati, which took place near Gogunda town, his refusal to submit to Akbar despite the hardships he suffered as a result, and the long years he spent as a fugitive in Mewar's Aravalli hills.

A favorite hunting ground of Fateh Singh's that Tanwar also glossed in his footnotes was in the Tikhalya and Machhla hills immediately south of Udaipur.[24] While tigers no longer frequented this convenient shikargah, leopards and wild boar remained abundant. The maharana and those close to his court would have been aware of the

[22] Ibid., 206–7.

[23] Ibid., 264–5.

[24] They are one hill divided by the city wall, called Machhla Magra to the north and Tikhalya Magra to the south. I give Machhla for Tanwar's Chhachhla, terms he used interchangeably. Chhachhla alternates with Machhla in state sources too: see Sharma, ed., *Haqiqat Bahida*, 1:93, 107, 219, and 257.

long history of royal shikar in these hills, not only because of the numerous shooting towers dotting their slopes, but also because of the miniature paintings that documented hunts held there during the reigns of former rulers including Jagat Singh II (r. 1734–51), Jawan Singh (r. 1828–38), and Sarup Singh (r. 1842–61).[25] The military associations of these hills would have been equally well known. Clearly visible from below, the city's defensive walls followed Machhla Magra's ridgeline before turning east and descending straight down the slope to the banks of the Pichola lake, sharply delineating the north–south divide between the Machhla and Tikhalya *magra*s. In miniature paintings dating to the time of Jawan Singh and Sarup Singh, observers watched royal hunts from these fortifications while armed huntsmen manned the ridgeline, the shooting boxes below, and the lookout tower perched on Tikhalya Magra's southernmost heights. On Machhla Magra's summit stood the diminutive Eklingarh fort, which housed two massive cannons and had played a central role in repelling an eighteenth-century Maratha attack enabled by disloyalty among Mewar's nobles.[26] Considering Fateh Singh's own history of troubles with some of his state's elite, a landscape evocative of their treachery and justifiable subjugation may well have appealed.

Many of Tanwar's battle-themed footnotes identified the enemy combatants as Muslims, Mughals, or Rajputs allied with Mughal emperors. In a few cases, they were Marathas.[27] Mughals, Marathas, and rival Rajputs were viewed as talented warriors and worthy opponents, rendering conflicts with them heroic. Rajputs in general and the Mewari dynasty in particular, however, valorized those clans that had been most uncompromising in their resistance to the Mughals, an empire which Tod identified as foreign/Muslim in opposition to Rajputs, whom he considered Indian/Hindu. While Mewaris had promulgated these particular divisions and measures of superiority to exalt themselves above rival clans who had intermarried with the

[25] Topsfield, *City Palace*, Figs 8, 26–7, and 31.

[26] Tanwar, *Shikari aur Shikar*, 175.

[27] Ibid., 164, 169–70, 206–7, and 218. Tanwar only inconsistently portrayed Mughals as adversaries: see ibid., 331.

Mughals, Tod's intention had been to make Rajputs appealing to British audiences, who would find easy accordances with their own prejudices.[28] What no one had anticipated were the equivalences that Indians in the late-nineteenth and early-twentieth centuries would begin to imagine between the value and feasibility of anti-Mughal resistance in medieval times and their present prospects under the British empire.[29] Battlefields and military sites in the European context, it has been argued, "stir the greatest passion and interest *if* the issues being contested by force of arms *then* are perceived as having relevance *now*."[30] Not surprisingly, places of historical significance in fights against domination by previous "outsiders" gained new resonance in the colonial period.

Fateh Singh was well positioned to pursue this angle. Mewari propaganda, with Tod's support, had established his realm as historically the most defiant and martial of all Rajput states. Conveniently, his kingdom was full of evocative battlegrounds replete with big game, and he frequented hunting grounds either at or near sites central to his state's historic episodes of resistance like Chittorgarh, Udai Sagar, Rajsamand, and Kumbhalgarh.[31] The prince's efforts to evoke a glorious past may well have impressed the British, but Fateh Singh's affirmations of Mewar's present and past independence from foreign-imposed central power, whether exercised by Mughals or Englishmen, were mostly for the benefit of state audiences. Because "several conflicting ideological landscapes may coexist at particular moments in time," it was easy for Englishmen and Rajputs to interpret the meaning of royal hunting over historic battlefields as they each preferred.[32]

[28] On Mughal–Rajput marriages, see Taft, "Honor and Alliance: Reconsidering Mughal–Rajput Marriages," 230–1.

[29] Freitag, "Power," 229.

[30] Brooke S. Blades, "European Military Sites as Ideological Landscapes," *Historical Archaeology* 37, 3 (2003): 52. Emphasis in the original.

[31] For Udai Sagar and Rana Pratap, see Tanwar, *Shikari aur Shikar*, 206–7; for Aurangzeb's attack on Rajsamand, ibid., 164–5; for Kumbhalgarh, ibid., 169–70.

[32] Blades, "European Military Sites," 47. Blades acknowledges the potential for change over time; I allow for short-term variation with context too.

Maharaja Pratap Singh of Orchha faced a more complicated situation than Fateh Singh due to the intricacies of Mughal–Rajput relations that once prevailed in Bundelkhand. Akbar (r. 1556–1605) had exerted Mughal power over Orchha in the late sixteenth century, invading the state when Raja Madhukar Shah (r. 1554–92) was on the throne. Interactions were generally cordial during Jahangir's reign (1605–27) when Raja Bir Singh Deo (r. 1605–27) preserved and protected Orchha's fortunes by remaining closely allied with the Mughals, even displaying a rare albino cheetah to the emperor—an "acknowledged naturalist."[33] The temporary peace deteriorated when Raja Jhujhar Singh (r. 1628–37) rebelled against Shah Jahan (r. 1627–58) in the 1630s, precipitating a Mughal invasion and occupation that lasted through 1641. Practical considerations and political expediency informed these Rajputs' successive decisions to collaborate or to rebel.

While there was ample precedent for collaboration between Mughal overlords and local kings in Bundelkhand, the pervasive influence in the nineteenth and twentieth centuries of the Mewari narrative that privileged non-cooperation, and Tod's authoritative repetition of that narrative, meant that Pratap Singh was interested in recalling defiance and not alliance. Suppressing the memory of Orchha's often peaceful relations with the Mughals by celebrating rebellious interludes helped establish a precedent for his efforts to achieve a high level of independence from the British.

One of Pratap Singh's largest and best game preserves was bound by the Jamni and Betwa rivers, only a few kilometers downstream from his state's abandoned former capital, the town and fort of Orchha. His small but distinguished Karkigarh island shikargah was only a few kilometers beyond. As discussed previously, the maharaja's interest in Karkigarh was based in part on its history of providing his royal forebears with tiger kills and on its natural landscape, which was suitably conducive to the norms of princely shooting. I revisit the region here to show that Pratap Singh also valued these grounds because their historical and environmental features allowed him to

[33] Koch, "Jahangir as Francis Bacon's Ideal," 293.

access the military history of his lineage, including heroic episodes that had featured defiance against challenging adversaries like the Mughals.

When Pratap Singh's ancestor Raja Rudra Pratap founded Orchha fort in the sixteenth century, he situated it in the midst of a dense forest with the expectation that the difficult approach would help secure it against military invasions.[34] After his death, these thick stands of trees succeeded in slowing the advance of Akbar's army towards Orchha in 1577, although the emperor's troops eventually did break through to defeat the Bundela defenders.[35] This was the first foray of imperial forces deep into the state and the first Mughal attack on the capital, making the incident memorable. Because the Orchha lineage again controlled the area in colonial times, Maharaja Pratap Singh could reengage this and other past battles by selectively remembering individual acts of heroism rather than collective losses, just as Fateh Singh could hunt at Chittorgarh and access past glory there. Pratap Singh hunted frequently in the area.[36] He constructed an elegant hunting lodge on the banks of the Betwa close to Orchha fort in the late nineteenth century.[37] His efforts in the 1890s to repopulate Orchha town and his successor's proud inclusion of the fort on the itinerary of visiting British VIPs is further evidence of the erstwhile capital's centrality within the royal house's understandings of Orchha State history and Bundela Rajput identity.[38]

Because Orchha's former territorial extent exceeded its borders under the Raj, Pratap Singh could look beyond his state's boundaries in his quest to hunt within attractive chronotopes. He was most interested

[34] Luard, *Gazetteer of India Eastern States*, 17.

[35] Abu al-Fazl, in ibid., 18.

[36] H.Z. Darrah, November 27, 1906, in Chief Secretary to Governor, UP, to FD Secretary, March 15, 1913, encl. 1, GOI, FPD, 32–9 of September 1914, NAI.

[37] "The Retreat," Bundelkhand Riverside, accessed April 24, 2009, http://www.bundelkhandriverside.com/ret.html.

[38] *Report on the Political Administration of the Territories within the Central India Agency for 1895–1896* (Calcutta: Office of the Superintendent Government Printing, 1896), 51.

in Dhamoni fort, once controlled by his ancestors but then included in British Bundelkhand in the Central Provinces. The layout of this stronghold—like Karkigarh's island setting—facilitated royal shoots, which led Pratap Singh to submit numerous requests to hunt there in the early 1900s.[39] He even petitioned in 1904 to build a shooting box at the site for tiger hunting.[40] Dhamoni's association with the Bundela clan's heroic military past made the place even more appealing.

Pratap Singh explained in 1905 that he coveted Dhamoni because the "ruins are . . . historically connected with [the Orchha] House."[41] British officials recognized too that the fort had been "a place of strength in the time when the power of Orchha was at its zenith."[42] Pratap Singh may have stressed his familial claims to the site to reinforce in British eyes the merits of his proposals to shoot there, but the prince's interest in Dhamoni as a historical site was genuine and the fort's connection with his lineage indisputable.

Famous for founding numerous military strongholds throughout Bundelkhand in the early-seventeenth century, the Bundela ruler Raja Bir Singh Deo had rebuilt and improved Dhamoni too.[43] The fort had figured in Raja Jhujhar Singh's doomed, yet still glorious, battles against the forces of Shah Jahan in the 1630s. The thick forests that surrounded Dhamoni at that time—like those that encompassed Orchha fort in the sixteenth century—delayed the imperial army by two days, affording the Bundela raja a temporary stay of execution as he fled through the jungles towards the next fortress.[44] Dhamoni's garrison remained behind and died a tragic but heroic death. The survival of forests at the site in the colonial period likely pleased Pratap Singh, both because they contained big game and because the

[39] For Dhamoni's history, see H.M. Elliot, quoted in Luard, *Gazetteer of India*, 27–8.

[40] W.E. Jardine, to Beville, April 15, 1904, GOI, BA, 185 of 1904, NAI.

[41] Pratap Singh, to PA-Bundelkhand, May 7, 1905, GOI, CI, 129-A of 1905–8, NAI.

[42] Beville, to Jardine, April 15, 1904, GOI, BA, 185 of 1904, NAI. See also Sleeman, *Rambles and Recollections*, 110.

[43] Elliot, quoted in Luard, *Gazetteer of India*, 27.

[44] Luard, *Gazetteer of India*, 28.

trees represented continuity with an environment that had impeded Orchha's adversaries and that (at least briefly) had sheltered his ancestors from attack. Chhatrasal, the most famous Bundela Rajput hero, had fought a major battle against imperial troops near Dhamoni in the early-eighteenth century. The *Chhatraprakasha* memorialized the engagement in stirring prose: "from side to side, like angry tigers roaring, rockets sprang. The Moosulmans advancing, boldly their utmost efforts used, and many, by the fire of Chuttur Saul, were slain."[45] The fact that sportsmen now could engage with tigers while "actually in the Fort" increased the martial significance of hunting there.[46]

Regaining Dhamoni—incompletely via hunting rights or wholly through a land exchange—would have reversed an unfortunate loss of territory in the seventeenth century. It would have constituted a modern victory over the British, and especially over British soldiers whose competing shooting interests blocked Pratap Singh's access to the site.[47] The prince's royal reputation would have benefited from dispossessing Englishmen of grounds where his predecessors had once held sway. Most Bundela Rajputs would have known Dhamoni's significance and, had the maharaja been able to hunt there, would have recognized the resurrection of Orchha's heroic past at the site through the modern proxy of shikar.

Rajput princes had long believed that geographical knowledge acquired when hunting had military benefits. Shikar familiarized rulers with their environs, revealing natural defenses against invasions in its topography.[48] Legends referring to events taking place in the sixteenth century cast sport as a mechanism leading Rajput sovereigns, including both Udai Singh of Mewar and Rudra Pratap of Orchha, to the future sites of their capitals.[49] Both Udaipur and the Orchha fort were

[45] Pogson, *History*, 86.

[46] Jardine, to Reynolds (First Assistant to AGG-CI), September 25, 1905, GOI, CI, 129-A of 1905–8, NAI.

[47] R.E. Holland, to Jardine, August 9, 1904, GOI, BA, 185 of 1904, NAI.

[48] Tanwar, *Shikari aur Shikar*, 2.

[49] Topsfield, *Court Painting*, 18; Luard, *Gazetteer of India*, 17.

originally in the midst of extensive forests. A cluster of hills additionally surrounded and protected Udai Singh's new capital. Similar
rationales regarding the practical purposes of sport in the wilderness
appear in British sources from the twentieth century, revealing
commonalities with the princes in their continued understandings
of the military advantages of knowing the countryside through hunting. Colonel W. Barrett of the Nowgong cantonment in Central India,
for example, wrote in 1911 that "good knowledge of the country is
essential for all Officers and men and the only way in which this can
be acquired is by encouraging all ranks to go into sport."[50]

Hunting landscapes had brought Rajputs into contact with individuals who provided important revelations or encouraged heroic
stands against hostile powers. According to the *Chhatraprakasha*,
Chhatrasal used shikar as a pretext to leave his own territory within the
Mughal sphere to meet a Hindu king named Sheo Raj, who inspired
him to begin his storied resistance against Aurangzeb by urging him
to "slay the Turks and Moguls."[51] The fact that Sheo Raj lived in a
forest "abounding in tigers" served as a shorthand for his heroic nature
and hinted at his kingdom's isolation from outside influence. A state's
good hunting opportunities were conceptually grouped with its ruler's
military prowess and political independence.

While rulers located tactical advantages in shikar and hunting
grounds, they historically had found themselves vulnerable to attack
when pursuing game through the wilderness.[52] Once, when Chhatrasal
was campaigning in enemy territory, he went into the forest "slightly
attended, to enjoy the pleasures of the chase ... when suddenly
intelligence was brought of the approach of the enemy."[53] A party
led by Nawab Bahadur Khan attacked, but Chhatrasal escaped. Even
ostensibly secure situations like the joint hunting expeditions the
maharaos of Bundi and maharanas of Mewar attended in the early-
sixteenth and late-eighteenth centuries offered scope for skirmishes

---

[50] W. Barrett, to F. Macdonald, February 9, 1911, GOI, CI, BA, 614 of
1910, NAI. For a contrasting view, see F. Macdonald, March 10, 1911, GOI,
CI, BA, 614 of 1910, NAI.

[51] Pogson, *History*, 52.

[52] Allsen, *The Royal Hunt*, 122 and 207–8.

[53] Pogson, *History*, 62.

and assassinations.[54] Like the battlegrounds of the Aravalli hills and the isolated forts of Bundelkhand, shikargahs presented greater dangers alongside their greater opportunities because they were situated in wild places. The risks made success that much more valuable.

The long-standing links between shikar and armed conflict relied in part on this shared geographical context of untamed wildernesses and remote military outposts. In line with the pervasive South Asian trope of hardships endured by kings in the forest as affirmations of legitimacy and masculinity, colonial Rajput princes sought to follow suit. The tribulations Fateh Singh faced in shikar were conceived as parallels to those endured by earlier warriors. According to Tanwar, Fateh Singh would walk for miles carrying his own rifle in the jungles of Mewar in the summer heat despite the many conveniences and numerous attendants on hand.[55] He added that "there were certain mountain passes ... where the maharana went on foot," suffering the thorns just as his followers did.[56] Such hardship promoted the "discipline, selfless service, courage, [and] quick reflexes" needed by genuine military men and embodied by former rulers of Mewar like Udai Singh and Rana Pratap.[57]

Tanwar credited the forest sojourns of Udai Singh, Rana Pratap, and other Mewari kings (whose signature martial landscapes at Chittorgarh and elsewhere were now Fateh Singh's hunting grounds) with having preserved Mewar from Mughal attacks over a period of 150 years.[58] A major benefit of hunting was that it taught self-protection.[59] Tanwar believed that "every maharana and Mewari ought to fully experience this kind of forest life, so that they will be able to defend themselves in times of difficulty."[60] Such references to military preparedness and defensive capabilities had a wide appeal. A member of the royal family of the nearby Dungarpur State likewise correlated the sharpened senses, quick reflexes, and general knowledge acquired

[54] Tod, *Annals and Antiquities*, 1:360 and 1:506–7.

[55] Tanwar, *Shikari aur Shikar*, 197.

[56] Tanwar, *Samsmaran*, 63.

[57] Tanwar, *Shikari aur Shikar*, 177–8 and 1.

[58] Tanwar, *Samsmaran*, 65.

[59] Tanwar, *Shikari aur Shikar*, 1.

[60] Tanwar, *Samsmaran*, 65.

through tiger hunting with the ability to defend one's people.[61] To develop these skills, kings had to enter forests as soldiers in the guise of hunters. Where no forests were available, harsh plains and forbidding deserts would do. In Bikaner, for example, official state rhetoric insisted that the arid landscape was uniquely "fitted to nurture a race of hardy warriors."[62]

As Abu al-Fazl had done in the sixteenth century, modern rulers and their associates also stressed the law-and-order advantages of intimate acquaintance with the backwoods stretches of states that could be gained through hunting.[63] Maharana Fateh Singh once came to know of a band of cattle thieves operating in Mewar near the border with Bundi State while visiting the area for sport. The maharana immediately dispatched an armed party of shikaris and noblemen who ambushed the thieves, inflicted casualties, and rescued a herd of stolen cows. Had the desire to hunt not drawn Fateh Singh to that isolated spot, the bandits would have gone unreported and unpunished. "This," Tanwar concluded, "is the importance of hunting."[64]

Hunting landscapes could establish parallels between martial episodes from India's epics and a modern prince's sport as well. In the hills around Jaisamand, Fateh Singh engaged in a variety of shikar that involved enclosing a large area within eight foot tall fabric screens, leaving only one small opening, outside of which hunters waited on shooting platforms for game animals to emerge. Tanwar compared these hunts to an episode from the *Mahabharata*. As related by Tanwar, the warrior Arjun once stationed his archers on all sides of the Khandav forest before setting the woods on fire in order to please Agni, the fire deity. The result was a slaughter so complete that not a single creature escaped alive. Tanwar claimed that, between Arjun's conflagration and Fateh Singh's screened hunts, "the difference is that we do not start a fire. The rest ... is identical."[65] While Arjun's

[61] Maharawal Lachman Singhji of Dungarpur, quoted in Allen and Dwivedi, *Lives of the Indian Princes*, 127–8.

[62] *Four Decades of Progress*, 18.

[63] Abu al-Fazl 'Allami, *The Ain i Akbari*, 282.

[64] Tanwar, *Samsmaran*, 65.

[65] Tanwar, *Shikari aur Shikar*, 312.

blaze was more a pogrom than a battle, his fame as an exemplary warrior lent martial meaning to the comparison and implied that Khandav and Jaisamand both hosted battles as much as they did infernos or shikar entertainments. The episode provided an authoritative retort to criticism of elite Indian sport as unfair or unnecessarily bloody.

By the turn of the century, the princes' collective desire to access martial glory by these means was complicated by the existence of at least two competing measures of military valor, a heroic ideal embraced by Rajput warriors and another championed by the British as modern, practical, and Western. The princes' English-style education from the late-nineteenth century at places like Rajkumar College made it clear that the "old emphasis on reckless courage had to be superseded by discipline, professionalism and a new socialization: a transition from aristocratic panache to middle-class drudgery that ... was largely complete in Britain's own military traditions by the end of the nineteenth century."[66] In most British circles, the martial values extolled in Tod's *Annals*, bardic literature, Rajput family lore, and certainly in the *Mahabharata*, were passé.[67]

Although compelling, British influence fell short of being deterministic, prompting processes of adaptation rather than assimilation. Residual tensions between the Rajput princes' continued admiration for reckless displays of courage and their recently cultivated yet genuine appreciation for measured risk-taking remained evident on the hunting ground. On the one hand, such men were required to be sensible, level-headed, and conservative. On the other, they needed to be courageous and plucky. To measure up, sporting princes with martial aspirations had to expose themselves to danger; the difficulty lay in divining the exact position of the line between Western grit and Rajput recklessness. Depending on whom they were hunting with, rulers needed to strike different balances to please Englishmen, fellow princes, or their own subordinates.[68] The illogic of the rules and the biases of the judges meant that success or failure was largely subjective.

[66] Sen, *Migrant Races*, 179.
[67] Freitag, "Power," 220 and 230.
[68] Sen, *Migrant Races*, 193.

While the playing field was far from level, the British and the princes nevertheless agreed that hunting grounds had attractive martial connotations. Lest we mistake Rajput inclinations to hunt near forts like Dhamoni or Chittorgarh as uniquely Indian in every particular, it is necessary to remember MacKenzie's observation that some European "military men seem to have enjoyed hunting over historical sites and battlefields of the past, trying to fit their own activities into a historical context."[69] A number of Englishmen, then, potentially had insights into the significance of princely activities.

Some princes, therefore, hoped to use the military associations of their hunting grounds to make positive impressions on British VIPs. Preparing for Lord Curzon's upcoming visit in 1902, Ganga Singh of Bikaner directed his subordinates to research and assemble a file of information to regale the historically-minded viceroy with as they travelled towards Gajner for wildfowling.[70] Part of the resultant narrative described how "Maharajah Sujan Singh [r. 1700–36] had once gone on a pigsticking excursion to a place about two miles to the south of the ninth mile stone on the Gajner road when an army from Jodhpur suddenly appeared to capture him, but the Baghors of Nal came to the rescue and fought a great battle … The [Jodhpur] army was compelled to retreat and the Maharaja safely returned to Bikaner."[71]

When proceeding to Gajner, it was standard practice for state conveyances to be outfitted with rifles for bagging game along the way.[72] Riding with Ganga Singh and armed to the teeth, Curzon was meant to see images of local military success superimposed upon his own pleasurable sporting achievements over the same grounds.[73]

---

[69] MacKenzie, *Empire of Nature*, 177.

[70] Ganga Singh, office note, [1902], BMK, s. no. 760, file 115 of 1902, RSA.

[71] Note on Nal, [1902], BMK, s. no. 760, file 115 of 1902, RSA.

[72] Ganga Singh, to [military secretary?], draft letter, October 2, 1902, BMK, s. no. 760, file 115 of 1902, RSA.

[73] Other sites of interest included wells, former bunds, and old tanks: Note on the Road from Bikaner to Gajner, [1902], BMK, n. no. 760, file 115 of 1902, RSA.

Bikaner's relatively tame ruminants and nonthreatening wildfowl may not have been ideal stand-ins for battle-hardened combatants, but Ganga Singh knew well enough how to compensate for perceived inadequacies in his state's distinctive wildlife.

Similarly edifying experiences awaited guests at Gajner, where the maharaja's file noted the existence of a small fort a little to the west that was linked to his ancestors, Rao Chundaji and Rao Jodhaji.[74] Gajner had been a battleground too when troops from Jodhpur State destroyed the place in 1808, but Ganga Singh would have found it difficult to use this information to glorify Bikaner and does not seem to have tried.[75] While much could be made of having bested worthy rivals, little could be gained from having lost in an undistinguished manner, as seems to have been the case at Gajner in 1808. In contrast, glory was available even in defeat when the opponents were hardy and the defense heroic.

In the end, however, Ganga Singh had relatively few chronotopes to work with: game was scarce, his ancestors had a well-documented history of cooperation with the central powers, and Bikaner had suffered little from Maratha incursions.[76] Rather than emphasizing a lackluster history of internecine warfare with his family's Jodhpuri parent lineage, Ganga Singh opted to stress the loyal support his state had given to those outsiders, like the Mughals, who had remained satisfactorily remote: just as he hoped the notoriously meddling Lord Curzon would. Official state publications therefore drew comparisons between past conditions and Ganga Singh's present devotion to the British, all the while asserting that neither he nor his ancestors had ever compromised their honor in the process.[77]

While Ganga Singh had comparatively few sites of combined military significance and sporting utility, Fateh Singh enjoyed a surplus in Mewar State. The famed Chittorgarh fort was perhaps the

[74] Rao Jodhaji (r. 1438–88) was the ruler of Jodhpur and father of Rao Bikaji (r. 1465–1504), who founded Bikaner. Rao Chundaji (r. 1383–1424) was Rao Jodhaji's grandfather.

[75] Goetz, *Art and Architecture*, 75.

[76] Ramusack, *The Indian Princes*, 23.

[77] *Four Decades*, 2.

most important of these. Sir Claude Hill, political agent from 1906 to 1908, reported that Fateh Singh began working to "restore and renovate Chittorgarh" as soon as he became maharana. His commendable efforts ultimately made it "possible to go over the whole of the ancient city and follow its history to the disastrous day of its sack by the army of the Great Moghul and the self-immolation of the women."[78]

Hill applauded improvements at the site but questioned Fateh Singh's motives. He suspected the maharana's interest was inappropriately enhanced by the tigers that inhabited Chittorgarh's jungles, and that the prince was acting in accordance with an "ancestral vow" and not out of a genuine historical interest in the site's preservation. He lamented "the apparent indifference displayed by the Maharana to the upkeep of the ancient monuments and cenotaphs commemorative of his predecessors" elsewhere in the state. Finding Fateh Singh's alleged apathy at odds with the celebrated Rajput enthusiasm for ancestral history, Hill took pains to urge the prince to repair the dilapidated funerary memorial or *chhatri* of Rana Pratap, who had fought so famously at Chittorgarh. He represented "to His Highness how regrettable it was that the memorial to one of the greatest heroes of the Sesodia Rajputs should be in [a] neglected state." Hill attributed the maharana's apparent reluctance to take action to Rajput custom, which he believed would lead a ruler to "erect a *chhatri* to his immediate predecessor, but to occupy himself not at all with earlier memorials."[79] But Fateh Singh had already commemorated Rana Pratap in 1896 in a manner commensurate with Mewari princely culture: by building a new shooting tower near his heroic ancestor's *chhatri*.[80]

Hill's appreciation for Chittorgarh stemmed from the fact that the stronghold was a place of great interest to the British. Half-ruined forts populated only by game evoked romantic reveries of "the din and clash of battle" among Englishmen as well as Rajputs. For critical British commentators, however, the dominant theme was as

[78] Claude H. Hill, *India—Stepmother* (London: Blackwood & Sons, Ltd., 1929), 85.

[79] Ibid., 85, 166, and 167.

[80] Sharma, *Haqiqat Bahida*, 3:93.

much decay as glory. Leopards and gazelle ran wild in fortresses once "rich and populous," rearing their young between "broken pillars and crumbling walls." [81] The British identified Mughal and Maratha depredations and Rajput degradation as the root causes of monumental decay. Properly restored, these places became testaments not to Rajput glory, but to the civilizing achievements of the British. Even as Hill recognized Fateh Singh's accomplishments, he credited the Viceroy Lord Curzon with "securing that the Tower of Victory at Chittor was properly repaired."[82] Conventional wisdom held that princes took action only when Englishmen provided the initiative, and when Rajput rulers like Fateh Singh did make repairs, their patent interest in sport and non-Western approach to history undermined the results.

Despite Hill's interpretation, Fateh Singh was not indifferent to Chittorgarh's past. He did, however, perceive its meaning and advantages differently than the British. Chittorgarh was not a museum piece meant only for walking over and marveling at; it was an active constituent of his sovereign identity, a place where history was still being made and where the prince could interact with his glorious past. Because of its tiger hunting, it was a site with potential power in the present and not just the past—where the British preferred Rajput authority and military might to remain.

Certain kinds of hunting, especially pigsticking, also shared military overtones among Englishmen and Rajputs. Tanwar reported that the activity was commonly taught in Mewar as a military sport and asserted that a pigsticker was akin to "a brave warrior."[83] Colonel John Vaughan, who was commandant of the Cavalry School in British India, insisted in 1909 that "pigsticking is the finest war training."[84] Yet, princes

[81] G.R. Aberigh-Mackay, *The Chiefs of Central India* (Calcutta: Thacker, Spink, and Co., 1879), iii.

[82] Hill, *India*, 85.

[83] Tanwar, *Shikari aur Shikar*, 272 and 54.

[84] John Vaughan, "Hog Hunter's Hall of the Tenth Hussars in Purneah,

deemed it characteristically Rajput to pursue boar with a recklessness deemed inappropriate in Western circles. While the British criticized them for engaging in unreasonable acts, Rajputs tended to celebrate their own approach to pigsticking and many princes did their best to uphold the difference. When Sir Pratap Singh of Jodhpur visited Fateh Singh after the maharana fell from his horse while pigsticking at Nahar Magra, Tanwar reports that the chief minister comically but movingly expressed his pleasure that Fateh Singh had fallen because the accident certified that the Mewari prince had been engaged fearlessly in "the work of Rajputs."[85] In sharp contrast were reports that Sir Pratap cautioned Prince Edward in 1921 against similar recklessness by telling him that "I know you are the Prince of Wales and you know that you are the Prince of Wales—but the pig doesn't know that you are the Prince of Wales."[86] Likewise, Fateh Singh in a speech on the occasion of Edward's visit to Mewar suggested that the British royal might like to watch some pigsticking, but clarified "I do not mean that Your Royal Highness should take part in pigsticking ... I have seen in the illustrated English papers Your Royal Highness's pictures in different games of horsemanship. Sometimes I found them dangerous and risky, hence I request Your Royal Highness not to take such risks in the future for the safety of [the] persons of exalted personages like Your Royal Highness is most important."[87]

Couched in terms of concern for Edward's wellbeing, on account of his great importance as Prince of Wales and in their feelings of affectionate devotion to the British royal, Sir Pratap and Fateh Singh managed to question British superiority while sounding acceptably submissive and loyal. Whether Englishmen were weaker or simply lacked the advantages of Rajput character, they allegedly contented themselves with calculated risks and not heroic ones while hunting. The restraint that Rajputs looked down on was something the British

---

1909," in *Modern Pig-Sticking* by A.E. Wardrop (London: Macmillan and Co., Ltd., 1914), 121.

[85] Tanwar, *Shikari aur Shikar*, 272; see also Tanwar, *Samsmaran*, 86.

[86] Allen and Dwivedi, *Lives*, 95.

[87] Fateh Singh, quoted in Laxmichand Dossabhai Shah, *The Prince of Wales & The Princes of India*, vol. 1 (Rajkot: Kathiawar Printing Works, 1923), 11.

counted in their favor. Many Englishmen would have objected to the implication that Rajputs exceeded their own abilities as pigstickers, even if it was by a different measure.

Not long after the princes of Rajputana signed their treaties and *sanads* with the British East India Company in the early-nineteenth century, Tod recorded his impressions of the martial exercises commonly undertaken by the local Rajputs:

> Riding in the ring with the lance in tournaments, without the spike, the point being guarded; defense of the sword against the lance, with every variety of 'noble horsemanship,' such as would render the most expert in Europe an easy prey to the active Rajpoot, are some of the chief exercises. Firing at a mark with a matchlock, in which they attain remarkable accuracy of aim; and in some parts of the country throwing a dart or javelin from horseback, are favourite amusements. The practice of the bow is likewise a main source of pastime, and in the manner there adopted it requires both dexterity and strength. The Rajpoot is not satisfied if he cannot bury his arrow either in the earthen target or the buffalo, to the feather.[88]

With the exceptions of accurate marksmanship with a matchlock and the combined test of "dexterity and strength" required by archery, each of these exercises prepared Rajputs to fight from horseback at close range, relying on their physical power and skill with a blade, lance, dart, or javelin. This style of combat could become quite intimate as opponents' swords crossed, their bodies came into contact, and their blood and sweat mingled. Princes found the greatest continuities between their martial pasts and sporting presents, therefore, in mounted pursuits that brought them into close physical proximity with their prey.

Even after their treaties with the British began excluding them from battle, Rajput princes and their nobles could engage in mounted war games within the bounds of their *chaugan* parade grounds and pigsticking grounds. Pursuing wild boar and killing them from horseback involved a significant risk of bodily harm, for both horse and rider. The possibility of actual contact resulting in injury, as well as the required level of horsemanship, echoed the intimacies forged

[88] Tod, *Annals*, 1:512.

between opponents, and between warriors and horses in precolonial conflicts.

Mewari game records confirmed the special skills involved in pigsticking with sword or spear by providing separate tallies for boar killed from horseback and those killed by rifle. By 1921, the Maharana of Mewar had speared 31 and shot 315 wild boar. While hunting as part of the royal party, the Rawat of Amet had speared 4 and shot 25, Fateh Karanji of Ujwal had speared 13 and shot 40, while Thakur Manohar Singh of Sardargarh had shot 6 and speared none.[89] Rajputs valorized the mounts that pigstickers and soldiers alike rode. It was in large part the equivalence of horses in warfare and pigsticking that confirmed the link between war and the pursuit of wild boar. Horses were "a matter of honor" and their qualities reflected back on their riders.[90] Fateh Singh, for example, would consider riding nothing but the best animals. For pigsticking, the prince and his peers wanted animals that were surefooted, brave, and "distinctly clever."[91]

A popular saying in Mewar held that a mature boar, a 16-year-old soldier, and a 5-year-old horse were uniquely dangerous because they never backed down once they began to fight.[92] It was the special bond between Rajputs and horses, and not the horse alone, that resulted in greatness. According to Tanwar "the pairing of horse and heroic kshatriya performs well ... At the Battle of Haldighati, [Rana Pratap's stallion] Chetak reared up and struck the head of [their opponent's] elephant and, even with an injured leg, took its master to safety on three legs before it died." Chetak could not have excelled without the example set by the celebrated Rana Pratap. Likewise, the pair of English thoroughbreds that Fateh Singh owned in the early 1900s would not have been considered so "valorous" if he had been anything less than "heroic" himself.[93]

---

[89] *Shikar ka Naksha*, 21, 31, 29, and 27.

[90] Tanwar, *Samsmaran*, 87.

[91] G.A. Robertson, March 21, 1908, GOI, FD, Secret I, 35 of July 1908, NAI.

[92] Tanwar, *Shikari aur Shikar*, 12.

[93] Tanwar, *Samsmaran*, 87. These thoroughbreds benefited from being gifts of the Prince of Wales: see Sir Louis Dane (FD Secretary), to Sir Walter Lawrence, December 8, 1907, GOI, FD, Secret I, 35 of July 1908, NAI.

When a pigsticker fell from his horse, the struggle between hunter and prey would occasionally continue on the ground. The skill and bravery needed to attack a wild boar on foot and kill it with only a knife or other blade in hand was rare even among Rajputs. During the high colonial period, one of the few men known for doing so on purpose rather than by accident was the deservedly famous Sir Pratap Singh of Jodhpur. In Mewar, state nobles earned special notice in the court records if they performed well after suddenly and unexpectedly finding themselves on the same level as their prey. A sportsman received similar honors if a severely wounded boar put up an extraordinary fight after, as was fairly common, his attacker dismounted (or descended from a shooting box) to finish the job on foot. One of Fateh Singh's most accomplished sporting nobles, Fateh Karanji of Ujwal, distinguished himself against one such boar in December 1907, which he had wounded with a rifle rather than a spear. State records indicate that after the 163 *lb.* boar "pierced his hand with its teeth and seized his shoulder, he stabbed it three or four times in the neck and eyes" before finally managing to kill it.[94]

Shooting wild boar was nonetheless meritorious and more pigs died by bullet than spear. In fact, rifles and good marksmanship were far more evocative of warfare as practiced in the early-twentieth century than the flashier exploits associated with spear, knife, and horse. It is rather ironic that the British condemned "pork butchers" when these sportsmen potentially surpassed pigstickers in living up to the middle-class values of Victorian and post-Victorian military men, including steadiness, efficiency, and accuracy under pressure. Rifle shooting requires steady hands, a good eye, and a cool head whether facing the distractions of battle or the cacophony of a hunt, with bullets flying, boulders crashing, bark chipping, and beaters shouting "ul-al-lu-lu-lu."[95]

Even so, Rajput elites who shot boar were doubly excluded by the British: first, as princes, from participating in genuine military maneuvers, and, second, as "pork butchers," from claiming

---

[94] Sharma, *Haqiqat Bahida*, 4:384. All translations from this source are my own.

[95] Kipling, "Of the Pig-Drive," 73.

membership among the ranks of modern sportsmen. The fact that Fateh Singh and his followers continued to shoot pig verifies the practice's centrality within Rajput culture and the importance placed on its martial connotations alongside the mounted sports. It is, in fact, likely that the restrained, martial qualities the British identified as modern and middle-class were understood instead by the princes as components of a specifically Rajput culture of marksmanship that complemented the better known, and rather more flamboyant, Rajput culture of horsemanship. Fateh Singh found it advantageous to keep shooting wild boar because his martial reputation rested as much on his marksmanship as on his horsemanship.

Of course, there were significant differences between the kinds of warfare the princes' predecessors had engaged in and their own sporting experiences. Perhaps the biggest disjoint was the fact of human opponents in the one and non-human quarry in the other. Rajput princes like Fateh Singh managed to resolve the tensions between past and present by employing culturally significant weapons and methods. In doing so they referenced the martial exercises and battle practices of the past more than the contemporary standards of the Indian army, with which most late-nineteenth and early-twentieth-century princes had no particular connections anyway. Resolution was an even simpler affair for the few rulers who had seen active service, like Ganga Singh of Bikaner. He excelled at marksmanship but was an indifferent horseman who failed to take full advantage of his state's pigsticking.[96] As an avowed modernizer, he could do better by amassing wildfowling records than spearing boar from horseback. For a prince who had defended the empire abroad and had the medals to prove it, hunting successes and effective shikar management functioned not as proxies of the distant past but as public reminders of an immediate and self-consciously modern military ethic.

Paralleling the self-conceptions of Rajput rulers, British commentators consistently spoke of the princes' military and sporting merits in almost the same breath. Colonel Wake, tutor to Ganga Singh's son Sadul Singh, said of his charge's father in 1937 that "we have stood by while he broke records in sport, led his troops in the

[96] His lifetime total was 98 boar: see *His Highness' General Shooting Diary*, vol. 2.

field, and took his place among the premier Princes of India round the King-Emperor."[97] Even when sporting and martial praises were not made back-to-back, few evaluations of Rajput rulers failed to include both points. An acting political agent in Bikaner characterized Ganga Singh in 1902 as an able and decorated soldier, and a few sentences later as an enthusiastic sportsman.[98] The Rajput ruler of Ratlam in Central India was "a thorough sportsman ... a capable Ruler ... a loyal Chief ... and a brave soldier."[99] Some Indian commentators followed the same convention. The author of a commemorative volume on the princes characterized Pratap Singh of Orchha as "a splendid horseman, a fine shot, and a brave and chivalrous Prince."[100] A few Indian rulers even turned this kind of language back on the British. In a speech during the Prince of Wales's 1921 visit to his state, the young Maharaja of Jodhpur praised the British royal as both "a soldier and a sportsman."[101] By applying the same terminology usually reserved for Indian princes to the British royal, the maharaja minimized the supposed differences between Rajput sovereigns like himself and Prince Edward.

Historically there has been no sharp distinction between soldiers and shikaris among Rajputs. This explains how rulers in preceding centuries, like Rana Raj Singh I of Mewar (r. 1652–80), had managed to enact military conquests "under the guise of conducting ... hunting expedition[s]."[102] Princes in the colonial period also integrated troops and military equipment into their hunts, but their most obvi-

---

[97] Rathore, *Maharaja Sadul Singh*, 135.

[98] J.N. Macleod, Bikaner, [n.d.], BMK, s. no. 760, file 115 of 1902, RSA.

[99] Walter Lawrence, *Ruling Princes and Chiefs of India. A Brief Historical Record of the Leading Princes and Chiefs in India together with a Description of their Territories and Methods of Administration* (1930; repr., Lahore: Sang-e-Meel Publications, 2005), 319.

[100] Jehangir, *Princes and Chiefs*, 2:6.

[101] Maharaja of Jodhpur, quoted in Shah, *Prince of Wales*, 29.

[102] Joffe, "Art, Architecture and Politics," 38. See also R.P. Shastri, *Jhala Zalim Singh (1730–1823), the De-Facto Ruler of Kota, who also Dominated Bundi and Udaipur, Shrewd Politician, Administrator and Reformer* (Jaipur: Raj Printing Works, 1971), 107, and Diwan Bijhe Bahadur Mazbut Singh, *A Portion of the History of Bundelkhand*, trans. and ed. C.A. Silberrad, in "A

ous goal now was to improve their chances of bagging tigers. Modern Indian rulers also considered the mingling of military personal and sporting experiences a practical measure that kept their men prepared for war. So many troops were involved in shoots in Kotah State in the early-nineteenth century that Tod characterized the proceedings as "a species of petty war."[103] Soldier-sportsmen continued to facilitate shikar in the twentieth century. For the Prince of Wales's visit in 1921, Ganga Singh of Bikaner detailed his Dungar Lancers to duck retrieval at Gajner.[104] In Mewar, Fateh Singh was known to use state troops as beaters in his tiger hunts.[105] The overlaps between soldiering and hunting were so extensive in the states that Fateh Singh even composed a poetic verse that conflated the education of youthful cadets and neophyte sportsmen:

> Mind still, heart steady, align the foresights so,
> Breath held like the dead, then pull the trigger,
> Listen huntsman's son, soldier's boy,
> This much consider, then the rifle roars![106]

Intersections with military norms appeared in the personnel and accessories princes relied on when hunting. When Ganga Singh went on summer big game shoots in the Nimach and Mewar jungles in the early 1940s, he brought along official radio equipment and trained army signalers belonging to his state's Ganga Risala regiment and Dungar Lancers.[107]

Many princes tried to obtain modern military-grade rifles for the use of their support staff and nobles. At the start of the twentieth

---

Contribution to the History of Western Bundelkhand," *Journal of the Asiatic Society of Bengal* 71, 1 (1902): 112.

[103] Tod, *Annals*, 3:1477.

[104] Maharajkumar and Ganga Singh, note for Military Member, November 24, 1921, Bikaner Military Dept., s. no. 277, file A197-264 of 1922, RSA.

[105] Topsfield, *Court Painting*, 285.

[106] Tanwar, *Shikari aur Shikar*, 38.

[107] Commanding Officer, Ganga Risala, to Army Minister, July 27, 1940,

century, however, government policy prevented princes from so arming even their state troops. At the 1918 conference of ruling chiefs in Delhi and at subsequent conferences, princes including Ganga Singh of Bikaner, Ranjitsinhji of Nawanagar, and the Maratha prince Madhav Rao Scindia II of Gwalior led the debate over upgrading state arsenals. They framed British refusals as a betrayal of the confidence placed in the princes during World War One and an insult to their honor. The difficulty in obtaining modern weapons for troops was behind what several rulers from the Kathiawar region characterized as a sad extinction of the martial spirit in the states that, incidentally, explained the difficulties they had faced in recruiting men for the war effort.[108] Without the latest arms soldiers became demoralized and a prince's followers slipped towards effeminacy.

In 1887, Fateh Singh requested permission from the Foreign Department to import fifty Martini-Henry rifles to arm his nobles for sport.[109] According to regulations in place since the Indian Arms Act of 1878, Indians could not own, among other things, any unlicensed "fire-arms, bayonets, swords, daggers, spears, spear-heads [or] bows and arrows."[110] Certain weapons, like the Martini-Henry rifle, were officially declared military grade. In theory, these were entirely prohibited. Exceptions were made, however, as many in the Foreign Department knew that "military rifles are used for sporting purposes" and some believed government restrictions were unwise and liable to alienate otherwise loyal princes.[111] The maharana's request, therefore,

---

Bikaner Army Dept., s. no. 2897, file B2412–33 of 1940, RSA; Commanding Officer, Dungar Lancers to General Commanding Officer, Bikaner State Army, April 13, 1942, Bikaner Army Dept., s. no. 3128, file B473–7 of 1942, RSA.

[108] Extracts from Jam Sahib of Nawanagar to unknown, July 10, 1918, and Chief of Thana Devli to unknown, September 8, 1918, GOI, FPD, Internal A, 63–7 of September 1921, NAI.

[109] Walter (MR), to First Assistant to AGG-Rajputana, January 14, 1887, GOI, FD, Internal B, 262–4 of March 1887, NAI.

[110] *The Indian Arms Act, 1878, as Modified up to the 1st July, 1892* (Simla: Government Central Printing Office, 1892), 4–5.

[111] Office note, April 5, 1892, GOI, FD, Internal B, 461–6 of May 1892, NAI; Walter, to FD Secretary, April 7, 1887, GOI, FD, Internal B, 63–4 of

received due consideration. Following a precedent set in favor of the Maharaja of Jaipur, they sanctioned ten Martini-Henry rifles for Fateh Singh.[112] According to the British resident, the maharana was "very deeply hurt at his request not being complied with" in full, and had concluded "that Government do not place confidence in him or trust his loyalty."[113] Alarmed at Fateh Singh's reaction, the Foreign Department promptly issued forty more licenses to settle the matter.[114]

It first came out in 1894, when Fateh Singh requested a fresh supply of cartridges for his Martini-Henrys, that the goal was not just to arm Mewar's nobles for shikar but to have them take up target practice.[115] In fact, target practice had been a regular activity for the prince and his followers at least since 1888. That year, Fateh Singh's court artists completed their wall paintings inside the Nahar Odi shooting box, including a scene showing five khaki-clad men bearing rifles (perhaps the recently purchased Martini-Henrys) watching a nobleman in courtly attire taking aim at a bull's-eye target on a stand some 225 yards away.[116] But it was only after noting further reports of target practice in the maharana's requests for ammunition in 1900 and 1909 that some Foreign Department officials raised concerns that there might be an unacceptable military dimension to the prince's agenda.[117]

Others in the department maintained that even if many of the cartridges were used in target practice, Fateh Singh still wanted them

---

June 1887, NAI; W.R. Birdwood, to Army Member, December 6, 1925, GOI, FPD, 244-G of 1926, NAI.

[112] AGG-Rajputana, to FD Secretary, February 10, 1887, GOI, FD, Internal B, 262–4 of March 1887, NAI.

[113] Walter, to FD Secretary, April 7, 1887, GOI, FD, Internal B, 63–4 of June 1887, NAI.

[114] Durand, to Walter, draft letter, May 18, 1887, GOI, FD, Internal B, 63–4 of June 1887, NAI.

[115] AGG-Rajputana, to FD Secretary, October 16, 1894, GOI, FD, Internal B, 313–17 of November 1894, NAI.

[116] The distance suggests the shooter was an accomplished marksman: Silvio Calabi, personal communication, August 12, 2011.

[117] MR, to First Assistant to AGG-Rajputana, August 3, 1900, GOI, FD, Internal B, 11–12 of October 1900, NAI.

for "sport and not military efficiency."[118] In fact, the maharana's habits were something of an open secret, long tolerated not just by the locally stationed Foreign Department officials, but also by high-ranking military men. The commander-in-chief of the Indian army himself had joined Fateh Singh for some target practice at the prince's newly-built rifle range during an official visit in March 1888, and shooting matches between Europeans, including the British resident, and the prince's followers had taken place there as well in May and August of 1894.[119] Complacency still managed to outweigh concern in government circles, even though Fateh Singh's men won both matches and the maharana saw little difference between their proficiency as marksmen for sporting purposes or for martial repute.

Princes seeking to enter into the martial spirit on the hunting ground needed to arm themselves accordingly. Mass-produced Martini-Henrys sufficed for subordinates, but Rajput rulers ordered the finest sporting rifles direct from London's top firms for their own use. Between 1908 and 1910 alone, the Maharana of Mewar imported 36 rifles. His son accounted for another 4 in addition to 4 pistols and 3 revolvers, while a select group of high officials brought in 8 more rifles and 3 pistols.[120] Originally commissioned in 1906, 4 additional sporting rifles arrived for Fateh Singh from Stephen Grant & Sons in 1911. Each of these—1 .500/.400 bore double-barrel Cordite, 1 double-barrel and 1 hammerless .303 bore, and 1 .450 double barrel—required a special license from the Government of India as prohibited bore weapons capable of firing ammunition used (and stockpiled) by the military or police.[121]

With the exception of the .500/.400 Cordite, every one of these Stephen Grants were black-powder rifles. A compound of sulfur, charcoal, and potassium nitrate in use since the tenth or eleventh century, black powder reduced visibility with every discharge by

[118] [Minchin?], office note, August 12, 1909, GOI, FD, Internal B, 62–3 of September 1909, NAI.

[119] Sharma, *Haqiqat Bahida*, 2:122, 3:207, and 3:40.

[120] Colvin (AGG-Rajputana), to FD Secretary, November 27, 1912, GOI, FD, General B, 167 of January 1913, NAI.

[121] Colvin, to FD Secretary, September 7, 1911, FD, General A, 14–23 of September 1912, NAI.

producing a cloud of dense smoke. This made rapid, accurate shooting from a rifle's second barrel a challenge, enhancing the desirability
of killing dangerous game with the first shot. Cordite had the
advantage of being "smokeless," but black powder was less corrosive
over time to the delicate rifling—from which rifles derived both
their name and deadly accuracy—found inside the barrel. Even black
powder was capable of fouling rifle bores over time, but "subjected
to Cordite ... rifling just melted away;" accuracy fell off after a few
thousand rounds and rifles were soon rendered "completely unsafe to
fire." Because cordite was so corrosive, the standard issue Lee-Metford
rifles used by many troops in the Indian army had to be redesigned
with a new pattern of rifling, as Lee-Enfields, within four years of
cordite's 1891 adoption into the service.[122]

Despite the military's change-over thirty years before, the Maharana
of Mewar was only partially embracing the new compound even
as late as 1911. British Indian soldiers may have used cordite, but
the military style Fateh Singh hoped to embody was not that of the
common subaltern, but of the royal commander. Part of the appeal of
a firm like Stephen Grant & Sons was that the company had earned
a royal warrant from Edward VII in 1901, and subsequently became
gunmakers to George V as well.[123] Fateh Singh patronized another
royal warrant holder, John Rigby & Co., gunmakers to George IV,
Edward VII, and George V.[124] The maharana's numerous "best-grade"
Rigbys were the finest to be had and, between 1902 and 1920, he
purchased two single barrel .350s and at least fourteen doubles from
the firm, in calibers ranging from .256 through .500. Some of these
used cordite, while others were designed for black powder. Many were
of prohibited grade, and thus extremely hard to come by.

British officials interpreted Fateh Singh's frequent purchases as
the self-indulgences of an avid hunter with unlimited means, such

---

[122] Patrick Sweeney, *Gunsmithing: Rifles* (Iola, WI: Gun Digest Books,
1999), 93.

[123] "Stephen Grant," Atkin, Grant & Lang, accessed August 9, 2011, http://
www.atkingrantandlang.com/our-company.php?company=15.

[124] "Royal Warrants," John Rigby & Co., accessed August 9, 2011, http://
www.johnrigbyandco.com/html/royal_warrants.html.

that "practically no new pattern of sporting rifle appears on the market which His Highness does not wish to add to his sporting armoury."[125] Even though they suspected him of amassing an excessive number of weapons, they could not accuse him of immoderate taste in rifle embellishments. The prince preferred his large bore .350, .450, and .500s without engraved barrels or carved stocks, instead requesting them "finished to London's traditional, slightly severe and ascetic taste."[126] What mattered most were quality, precision, power, and maker's marks. Choosing plain rifles over those richly figured in silver and gold, Fateh Singh aspired to be seen not as a fabulously wealthy sporting prince leading a charmed life at home and in the field, but as a discerning, infallible, effective, and pedigreed Rajput ruler and sportsman.

The British thought they could catch glimpses in princely shikar of the "true" martial spirit of the Rajputs, but they rested assured that these qualities were now happily contained. When Kipling visited Mewar in 1887 as a newspaper correspondent, he and several other Englishmen went to shoot at Kala Odi, a black hunting tower on the southern slopes of Tikhalya Magra.[127] They were accompanied by one of Fateh Singh's highest-ranking nobles, the Rawat of Amet, who happened to be carrying a Martini-Henry rifle. When the beaters flushed a leopard into the line of fire, "the face of the Rawat of Amet changed ... Looking at him as he fired, one forgot all about the Mayo College at which he had been educated, and remembered only some trivial and out-of-date affairs, in which his forefathers had been concerned, when a bridegroom, with his bride at his side, charged down the slope of the Chittor road and died among Akbar's men."[128] After bagging the leopard, the Rawat's face reflected nothing but sweetness as he politely refused credit, insisting the fatal

---

[125] Colvin, to FD Secretary, November 27, 1912, GOI, FD, General B, 167 of January 1913, NAI.

[126] Silvio Calabi, Steve Helsley, and Roger G. Sanger, *Rigby: A Grand Tradition* (Dallas, TX: Arundel Publishing, 2012), 114.

[127] Kipling, "Pig-Drive," 70–6; see also Sharma, *Haqiqat Bahida*, 2:192. For Brian Egerton's participation, see Waddington, *Indian India*, 68.

[128] Kipling, "Pig-Drive," 72 and 74–5.

bullet had come from one of the guest shooters. For Kipling and other Englishmen, the school for princes at Mayo College in Ajmer only produced the thinnest veneer of Western civilization. It easily slough-ed off when Rajputs reinhabited their natural environs and en-gaged in martial sports like shikar.

While Kipling's attempt upon returning to the British Residency "to compare the fusillade which greeted the [leopard] to the continuous drumming of a ten-barreled Nordenfeldt was ... coldly received," he was not alone in employing such language.[129] Shoots in Mewar made a martial impression on the huntsman Tanwar as well. He recalled that Fateh Singh's shikaris would be "arrayed like troops in a circular formation" and that the multitudes of "beaters on foot, horses and horsemen, elephants, camels, dogs, etc.," together achieved the look of "a massive army."[130] Indeed, as has been noted, "for both princes and British, shikar was a substitute for warfare."[131]

Englishmen often wrote about princely hunts as if they were wit-nessing battles that were impressive, but "trivial and out-of-date."[132] Having observed the Maharana of Mewar hunting in the early 1900s, Sir Claude Hill reported that he "sometimes thought, when out shooting with him, that a great soldier was lost in Sir Fatehsinghji. The consummate manner in which, from the particular station either in an *otla* [*odi*] or on the ground, he used to direct the manœuvers and advance of the line of beaters, never raising his voice, but with the utmost quietness either instructing an emissary or giving the direction with a gesture or the modification of the plan, was really impressive."[133] Hill meant to flatter, but his chosen trope would have reminded readers that the maharana was not and in fact had never been a military leader. British paramountcy had tamed and repackag-ed the martial skills of Rajputs like the maharana into sporting assets. What Hill saw, and what he wanted to see and to communicate

[129] Ibid., 76.
[130] Tanwar, *Shikari aur Shikar*, 312.
[131] Ramusack, *Indian Princes*, 161.
[132] Kipling, "Pig-Drive," 74.
[133] Hill, *India*, 86.

as an upholder of empire, was a properly contained and charming performance, not a potent reality.

In the 1930s, the veteran political officer Sir Arthur Cunningham Lothian too saw martial visions in a hunt "conducted in old-fashioned style like a military event" at Jaisamand in Mewar, where the host was Fateh Singh's son and successor, Bhupal Singh. In contrast to Hill, Lothian adopted an overtly flippant and condescending tone. Rather than focusing on military precision and quiet efficiency, he painted the events he witnessed as pleasant but farcical. It was "great fun," but "there were usually too many people about for the beats to be productive."[134] The use of modern military equipment like radio transmitters added "an amusing touch of modernity." If Mewari shoots were battles in Lothian's mind, then their tactics were outdated, their paraphernalia poorly employed, and their personnel nothing more than a collection of toy soldiers inexpertly arrayed by an unconvincing and inept commanding officer.

Visiting Bikaner State in the mid-1920s as Britain's Secretary of State for Air, Sir Samuel Templewood dotted his description of a shoot at Gajner with military terminology. Referring to Bikaner's many guests as an army moved back and forth by Ganga Singh between the capital and shooting palace, the Englishman declared that he felt himself to be "in the house of a Napoleon of hospitality."[135] Napoleon, of course, had conquered the better part of a continent and gone on to invade another. Ganga Singh was successfully stage-managing sandgrouse shoots. Templewood also made a point of noting the maharaja's "long row of service medals," but on the whole he does not appear to have taken the prince or his achievements very seriously. It seems likely that his comparison between the French emperor and Bikaner's prince was meant to amuse more than flatter. Indeed, Indian princes routinely received glowing tributes from British imperialists only to see the fine words immediately undercut by subtle—or not so subtle—intimations of the ultimate hollowness of the praise. Nevertheless, princes could and did use their public support for British

[134] Lothian, *Kingdoms of Yesterday*, 163.
[135] Templewood, *India by Air*, 100.

wars, active military service, and frequent protestations of loyalty to improve their position in the empire by making it that much more difficult for Englishmen to question their allegiance, dismiss their importance, or deny them certain political concessions.[136]

Ganga Singh pursued this angle with vigor, seeing active service in China and Somaliland and aggressively campaigning to play a part in World War Two.[137] In light of his well-known service, the maharaja's guests were quick to categorize his triumphs of hospitality as the automatic outcomes of his earlier exposure to British military discipline. In doing so, they transferred credit away from the prince and onto their own good qualities and cultural achievements. Englishmen described Ganga Singh as directing his guests via "army orders" and as carrying off shooting entertainments in "broad strategic movements."[138] Their language reduced the prince's mildly threatening usurpation of power at Gajner into an object of amusement: Ganga Singh had been trained to lead soldiers in battle against other men, but he had come into his own directing campaigns against birds. Confined within the sphere of shikar, his posturing ultimately appeared inconsequential. Despite the maharaja's best efforts, it remained impossible to wholly eliminate British biases or erase his political subjugation as an Indian prince.

The emptiness that Kipling, Hill, Lothian, Templewood, and others chose to perceive beneath the surface of princely shikar was consistent with British understandings of Rajput masculinity in an era when Tod's romanticism seemed to ring somewhat false. In the same years that the *Annals* was finding a new readership among Indian nationalists seeking to fill "a growing need for strong Indian heroes," Englishmen were rethinking the evidence and discovering an unflattering Rajput "tendency to yield to panic on the battlefield," an

---

[136] Sen, *Migrant Races*, 143.

[137] Ibid., 142; *Report on the Administration of the Bikaner State for 1938–39* (Bikaner: Government Press, n.d.), 11; *Report on the Administration of the Bikaner State for Three Financial Years 1939–40, 1940–41 and 1941–42* (Bikaner: Government Press, n.d.), 9.

[138] Templewood, *India by Air*, 99–100.

inability to maintain strategic alliances, and an excess of passion.[139] With these charges against them, princes in British eyes could have little in common with the modern ideal of sensible and steady officers, and their occasional appearance as exemplary sportsmen in military landscapes could only be chimerical.

[139] Freitag, "Power," 229; William Crooke, quoted in ibid., 220.

6

Threatened Kingdoms of
Dwindling Beasts

Not a single tiger lived within fifty miles of Dungarpur in 1909. Two decades later, only one "occasional visitor" could be found.[1] This small Rajput state just south of Mewar once boasted a respectable tiger population, supported by a prey base including plentiful sambar, nilgai, and chital. And yet, despite the last maharawal making "every possible effort" to restock the jungles with royal game up through his death in 1918, the region's sporting environment remained in a fragile state throughout his successor's minority. Frustrated by the persistent absence of tigers after ten years of Regency Council rule, Dungarpur's young Sisodia prince imported three tigers from Gwalior within a year of his 1927 investiture. He used these animals to launch a captive breeding program and soon began releasing cubs into the jungle.[2] With key prey species strictly preserved, the new maharawal's tigers did well and increased to around twenty by 1935.[3] Even so, the threat of local extinction

[1] Diwan, Dungarpur, to D.M. Field (PA-SRSA), November 15, 1928, GOI, SRSA, 261-G of 1928, NAI.

[2] Harshvardhan Singh Dungarpur, quoted in "Dept. Claims Sariska Tiger Relocation First of its Kind, Global Forum Not Impressed," *Daily News & Analysis*, April 4, 2011, Jaipur edition.

[3] Diwan, Dungarpur, Particulars of Rare Animals, in MR and PA-SRSA, to Secretary to AGG-Rajputana, January 10, 1935, GOI, RA, PB, 175-P

loomed: Dungarpur's forests were besieged by opportunistic neigh-boring princes, jealous nobles, hungry peasants, and (allegedly) poaching political agents.

The maharawal's tactics were uncommon, but the faltering wildlife, unstable environments, and political challenges he faced were familiar throughout the Rajput states. Rajput princes looked back to a happier past in which they imagined their predecessors had occupied stronger positions relative to their nobles, fewer conflicts with their subjects, and more control over foreign interference in state matters. They correlated these political advantages with the better shooting they also believed their ancestors had enjoyed. As a result, they viewed copious game and premium wildernesses as among the rights and privileges due to and constitutive of strong kings. Reductions in shooting facilities, whether documented or suspected, threw their own vulnerabilities—to British interference, noble encroachments, and popular demonstrations—into stark relief. Defending their royal prerogatives against what they considered novel threats and unwelcome innovations, princes quoted these precedents of natural order and plenitude, casting their own "invented traditions" as established practice representative of the best Rajput customs.

But by the 1910s and 1920s, every advantage Rajput rulers thought their sport and shikargahs should provide grew increasingly vulnerable to attack. State subjects seemed newly determined to violate forest and game regulations, unwilling to tolerate wild boar or blackbuck, and more disturbed than ever by tiger and leopard attacks. Princely heroics in strictly reserved grounds and inexhaustible stocks of royal game now became evidence of illegitimacy and willful negligence, not signs of righteous authority and good stewardship. At the same time, the isolation of princely India was eroding with the expansion of railroads, newspapers, progressive policies, and nationalist politics. The weakness of the princes on the all-India stage and the hollowness of their treaties with the British were increasingly obvious. The colonial state itself was cracking under the multiple strains of world

---

of 1939, NAI; M.K. Ranjitsinh, *Beyond the Tiger: Portraits of Asian Wildlife* (New Delhi: Brijbasi Publishers Private Limited, 1997), 24.

war and economic instability, government missteps and atrocities, civil disobedience, communal unrest, and popular nationalism. Not every prince acknowledged the volatile climate they were living in. Among those that did, not all were willing or able to adapt when they believed that royal shikar and all its trappings—including the maintenance of wildlife and habitat—were precedented, proper, and even necessary.

Just as eager as their sovereigns to use natural resources to establish themselves and enhance their powers, Rajput nobles also preserved game in private shikargahs and endeavored to hunt in royal style. Even as they resented the hardships that a princely superior's shikar could cause, they maintained their own right to hunt as they pleased, denying culpability for the negative consequences that landholders, cultivators, and herders faced. While princes and nobles blamed one another for the depredations of dangerous and "destructive" game, commoners were left to suffer, petition, and protest, to poach, steal, and trespass, or to exterminate local game, level small forests, and demand change.[4]

Even as reforms gained momentum and great transformations loomed, reliance on the expediency of rule by precedent, and popular respect for its validity, remained steadfast in British and princely India. Petitions for the recognition of rights and privileges were most persuasive when documents, issued by a sovereign power or recorded by recognized authorities, established their existence "from time immemorial." While Mughal *parwana* and excerpts from Tod's *Annals* carried weight with political agents and Indian princes alike, Rajput rulers sometimes relied on other sources too, which were inadmissible by government standards but authoritative in state circles. Fateh Singh of Mewar, in particular, viewed his state's paradisiac past in the miniatures of royal shikar that court artists had produced for his nineteenth-century predecessors. After coming to

[4] "Destructive" animals included boar, nilgai, blackbuck, and sambar: see E.A. DeBrett, to Commissioners of Divisions, CP and Berar, and Conservators of Forests, Northern and Berar Circles, August 14, 1911, GOI, CP Secretariat Forest Dept. B, 28 of October 1912, file 12–23 of 1911, Madhya Pradesh Directorate of Archaeology, Archives, and Museums.

power unexpectedly in 1884, he repeatedly perused the contents of the royal *jotdan* or storehouse of miniature paintings, perhaps looking for guidance on what facilities he should expect and would require to appear suitably regal in the field.[5]

Of the six maharanas who ruled Mewar in the nineteenth century before Fateh Singh, three were enthusiastic patrons of hunting miniatures. These were Bhim Singh, Jawan Singh (r. 1828–38), and Sarup Singh (r. 1842–61). Financial difficulties and other challenges restricted Bhim Singh's sovereignty for much of his reign, limiting his scope as a sportsman, artistic patron, and architect. When Tod saw the royal Nahar Magra shikargah in the early 1800s, its shooting palace "was crumbling" and the nobles' residences "all going to decay."[6] Bhim Singh's hunting seat at Udai Sagar had fallen into a similar state "for want of funds," as had other shooting facilities near Udaipur.[7] For Tod, these dilapidated palaces and shooting towers reflected the degeneration of Mewar itself. Had the state not suffered Maratha incursions and insubordinations of the nobility, its palaces and wildlife would have been preserved. Had Bhim Singh's leading artist Chokha exclusively produced "images of rulers as hunters and administrators" rather than illustrating the "women's quarters" and "eroticism of Krishna," the sovereign and his powers too would be stronger, healthier, and altogether "more male."[8]

Working within the available budget, Bhim Singh's court artists, including Chokha, nevertheless tried to produce convincing images of power and prosperity that satisfied local needs and ideals. According to Molly Emma Aitken, Chokha did so by depicting the maharana as "a massive man of appetites" whose "well-sated body ... represented that surfeit that Bhim Singh and his people were failing to enjoy."[9] Chokha's miniatures of the hunt from the early 1800s focus on the

---

[5] See Topsfield, *Court Painting*, 287. Topsfield says Fateh Singh visited the *jotdan* twice; he actually visited at least five times: see Sharma, ed., *Haqiqat Bahida*, 1:33, 1:34, 1:36, 1:37, and 1:43.

[6] Tod, *Annals and Antiquities of Rajasthan*, 2:551 and 1:85.

[7] Ibid., 1:619.

[8] Aitken, *The Intelligence of Tradition*, 278.

[9] Ibid., 204 and 220.

maharana with his prey immediately after the hunt, in camp, or in procession. Most commonly, they show Bhim Singh triumphantly riding home accompanied by servants, and sometimes camels, bearing the bulky carcasses of several slain boar, whose fleshy bodies, we may assume, will later fortify the prince's own prodigious bulk (Fig. 7).[10]

In these images, the boars' white tusks stand out against the smoky background of their massive bodies, identifying the animals as adult males. Known as *ekal*, such boar were the best game and most desirable food. They were also the rarest category of boar. By implying an abundance of *ekal* under his stewardship, these paintings feigned an unimpaired environmental status for Bhim Singh and his realm. Other miniatures featured antelope, deer, or gazelle, like one from 1799 that depicts the prince hawking amidst a small mixed herd of ruminants including two blackbucks.[11] A group of nobles pursuing boar in the background and a hare fleeing the scene in the foreground contribute to this painting's overall message of sufficiency and variety, in small game at least.

Considering Fateh Singh's particular interest in big game, even better precedents existed in paintings from the reigns of Jawan Singh and Sarup Singh. Although many were as modest as the ones produced for Bhim Singh, growing political and financial security allowed these maharanas to patronize more ambitious compositions too.[12] These miniatures featured tiger or wild boar pursuits in the midst of undulating landscapes carpeted with green trees, thorny thuhar, and dense brush, peopled with innumerable nobles, attendants, and huntsmen. In addition to the main quarry, court artists adorned the hillsides with nilgai, hare, bear, blackbuck, and deer in greater profusion than seen in illustrations made for Bhim Singh.[13] Jawan Singh and Sarup Singh are frequently depicted killing large numbers of

---

[10] Also see Topsfield, *Court Painting*, Fig. 197, and Williams, ed., *Kingdom of the Sun*, Fig. 30.

[11] Topsfield, *Court Painting*, Fig. 194.

[12] Ibid., 230.

[13] For examples, see Topsfield, *City Palace*, Figs. 31–2 and 26.

massive boar at Nahar Magra.[14] Both princes are also shown shooting tigers just south of Udaipur's city walls on Tikhalya Magra.[15] Wild boar and leopards frequented Tikhalya Magra well into the twentieth century, but Fateh Singh had to go further afield to bag his tigers.[16] Taking these paintings at face value, he could not but conclude that hunting had been far better in Mewar fifty or even twenty-five years before.

Fateh Singh could also cite several well-known nineteenth-century European authors to demonstrate his state's former abundance of game.[17] Visiting around 1870 during Maharana Shambhu Singh's reign, the French traveler Louis Rousselet wrote of "immense herds" of wild boar at Nahar Magra.[18] In Sarup Singh's day, William Rice reported chital herds of over a hundred as common, while tigers abounded around Bhainsrorgarh.[19] Rice's tallies in and around the state's eastern jungles bore out his claims. Shooting yearly from 1850 through 1854, he and his party wounded or killed almost a hundred tigers and over fifty bears.[20] Decades earlier during Bhim Singh's reign, Tod likewise found an abundance of tigers and boar in the state.[21]

Like their peers elsewhere, the sportsmen-writers of colonial India waxed nostalgic, narrating the most exciting episodes, largest trophies, biggest bags, and best settings. Blank days, inferior game,

[14] For Jawan Singh, see Topsfield, *Court Painting*, Fig. 223; for Sarup Singh, see Topsfield, *City Palace*, Figs 32 and 34.

[15] For Jawan Singh, see Topsfield, *City Palace*, Fig. 27; for Sarup Singh, see ibid., Fig. 31.

[16] Fateh Singh only once pursued a "black" tiger on Tikhalya Magra. An unusually dark tiger or melanistic leopard, it was captured elsewhere and released on the hill: see Sharma, *Haqiqat Bahida*, 4:64–5.

[17] It is uncertain if Fateh Singh's library contained Rousselet and Rice, but he was familiar enough with Tod's *Annals* to reference it in correspondence: see Fateh Singh, to Lord Reading, *c.* 1924, p.16, acc. no. 27262, MMSL.

[18] Rousselet, *India and its Native Princes*, 172.

[19] William Rice, *Tiger-Shooting in India, being an Account of Hunting Experiences on Foot in Rajpootana, during the Hot Seasons, from 1850 to 1854* (London: Smith, Elder, and Co., 1857), 54 and 81.

[20] Ibid., 22, 38, 103, 150, 192, and 218.

[21] Tod, *Annals*, 1:265.

and empty forests inevitably went underreported.[22] The hunting opportunities enjoyed in youth and by past generations were superior by default. Fateh Singh imagined Mewar's eastern districts as a hunter's paradise in the 1850s; Rice looked at the same grounds in 1854 and lamented that game was "getting very scarce in this part of Rajpootana."[23] Particularly when read alongside the paintings in the royal *jotdan*, any published shooting accounts that Fateh Singh looked to for precedents likely led him to overestimate just how much Mewar's environment and wildlife had diminished.

When responding to petitions submitted by residents of his state's Magra and Girwa districts in 1921, he relied on precedents to defend his Bagdara, Kamlod, and Hinglajya shikargahs, along with his favorite grounds at Nahar Magra. He claimed that none of these shikargahs were new, all having been "reserved places since hundreds of years." The profusion of wild boar in these places was no innovation either. Conversely, the present population was significantly smaller than that which had once prevailed. Because the grounds and his game alike were well within the bounds of established precedent, Fateh Singh insisted there could be no legitimate cause for complaint.[24]

To prove his point, the prince recounted how one beat at Kamlod ka Magra at the beginning of Shambhu Singh's reign (1861–74) had yielded twenty-five *ekal*.[25] During Fateh Singh's own tenure as maharana, not even Nahar Magra could produce such riches.[26] Earlier under Sarup Singh (r. 1842–61), "in addition to the Magras of Kamlod, Hinglajya, [and] Bagdara, in all the Magras of Saitmiri, Kolar, Moora Kherlia, Kanti Magro, Koli Wagria, Mudho, Borli, Morio,

---

[22] On why deer hunts lacked interest, see Tanwar, *Shikari aur Shikar*, 315 and 318.

[23] Rice, *Tiger-Shooting*, 218.

[24] Orders passed on Magra District petition, pp. 23–8, and Order 18320, October 12, 1921, pp. 52–71, acc. no. 27262, MMSL.

[25] Orders passed on Magra District petition, sub-order 1, p. 52, acc. no. 27262, MMSL.

[26] *Naksha Shikargah mukam Nahar Magra*, December 1907 through May 1909, docs 15, 18, 20, 39, 41, 43, 45, 47, 49, 52, 58, and 60, MMK-RD, 269 of VS 1962, RSA-U.

Dihio Mataji Walo, Chatori, Kolomagri, Saikhro, Guglo, Mormagri, Saitalio, Limbo Boro, Goderi, etc., there used to come out lone males [*ekal*] ... in one place four, in another five, as well as batches of pigs, in varying numbers resulting in a good bag."[27] Kamlod, Hinglajya, and Bagdara remained well known for their boar in Fateh Singh's day. But, while the other sites once ranked alongside the big names, little game remained by the early-twentieth century and these places had fallen into relative obscurity. Looking back even further, Fateh Singh could only speculate at the fabulous sounders of boar that must have lived in the region when Sangram Singh II (r. 1710–34) established the Nahar Magra shikargah.[28]

Beyond insisting that the past provided ample precedent for wild boar and his efforts to increase their numbers, Fateh Singh assert- ed that conditions in and around his shikargahs were akin to those found elsewhere. He claimed that every princely state in India main- tained royal shikargahs full of wild boar, and that every noble and jagirdar in Mewar kept "such reserved areas" too.[29] If Fateh Singh's peers and a multitude of nobles and landholders had the right to preserve boar, then surely the maharana did too. If peasants throughout princely India lived with pig, then so could the people of Magra and Girwa.

Princely apprehensions about the relative abundance of game were shared and exacerbated by the negative assessments and dire predictions of select British officials. In 1898, the Regency Council for Bikaner worried that "game is getting scarce day by day."[30] The Agent to the Governor General for Central India in 1905, C.S. Bayley, believed there was "no doubt that game has greatly diminished in Central India in the past twenty or thirty years," such that the only animals left worth shooting in some areas were leopards.[31] Erskine

---

[27] Order 18320, October 12, 1921, sub-order 1, p. 52, acc. no. 27262, MMSL.

[28] Ibid., sub-order 2, p. 57.

[29] Ibid., p. 61.

[30] Translation of Regency Council's proceedings, August 17, 1898, BMK, s. no. 181, file 1123 of 1910, RSA.

[31] C.S. Bayley (AGG-CI), to FD Secretary, January 17, 1905, no. 477-G,

reported in 1908 that, besides leopards, large game were not plentiful even in Mewar State.[32]

Along with the government-trained forest officers they consulted in these matters, Rajput rulers believed that recent decreases in forests and grasslands went hand in hand with declining game.[33] Fateh Singh worried most about Nahar Magra, where his newly-built and improved shooting boxes graced the eastern and western slopes of the hill while several more dotted the plains below. In former times, Nahar Magra's odis and muls had been surrounded by a continuous expanse of dense scrub, thuhar, and small trees that had provided suitable wildlife habitat. But by 1921, all the bushes in the surrounding plains had been cut down. Marked off by a trunk road, only the inner bounds of the preserve retained a thick undergrowth throughout the maharana's reign.[34] Believing that such environmental changes were possible only when the populace felt able to disobey his dictates, Fateh Singh concluded that his sovereignty was at risk along with his shikargahs and wildlife.

Rajput rulers also identified environmental degradation as an outcome of the disastrous famines their states had endured in the recent past. Whether as voluntary acts of charitable statesmanship or desperate measures to appease public opinion, princes often opened their shikargahs and reserved forests to their subjects in times of scarcity.[35] Once inside, people did their best to survive by stripping the

---

GOI, Baghelkhand Agency, 76 of 1904–6, NAI. This is not the same Bayley who clashed with Ganga Singh of Bikaner.

[32] Erskine, *Gazetteer of the Udaipur State*, 11.

[33] Rai Bahadur Bhai Sadhu Singh, "Report on the Proposed Formation and Management of Forest Reserves in the Bikaner State, Rajputana," 1910, chapter 2, no. 63, BMK, 754B of 1906, RSA. Sadhu Singh was a retired Extra Deputy Conservator of Forests, Punjab, working as a temporary Forest Officer in Bikaner. For other states employing trained foresters, see GOI, FD, Establishment B, 305–7 of February 1911 and 337–40 of November 1911, NAI.

[34] Order 18320, October 12, 1921, sub-order 2, acc. no. 27262, MMSL.

[35] This echoes the rural gentry's "moral economy" of game: see Lance van Sittert, "Bringing in the Wild: The Commodification of Wild Animals in

grounds of vegetation for fodder, extracting trees and brush for fuel, and killing wild animals including sambar and chital for food.[36] Even a decade after the great famine of 1899–1900, an "extensive wasteland of drifting sand dunes" marked the eastern portion of Bikaner State around Churu, where a preserved grassland for state horses had been before.[37] Dungarpur's tigers disappeared for want of prey after the same famine, when the state's "starving Bhils [had] destroyed every kind of deer."[38] In Orchha, the Karkigarh island shikargah was devastated during a famine in 1906. Few animals survived and the undergrowth and trees alike had yet to recover two years later, further hindered by "scanty rainfall."[39]

Englishmen added their voices to the princes' in blaming famines for damaging the environment and reducing wildlife, especially deer. Erskine reported that sambar had been "plentiful" in parts of Dungarpur before the famine of 1899–1900, but that almost a decade later they had yet to regain their former numbers.[40] In Banswara too there were fewer sambar and chital after the famine than before.[41] Aided by the protection afforded by game and forest laws, wildlife and their habitats seemed to have rebounded by the 1920s, but princely anxieties persisted and preservation remained strict in many states.

Princes undoubtedly exaggerated their worries regarding wildlife populations when it was politically expedient, but they were genuinely concerned about the availability of shikar in their states. Fateh Singh

---

the Cape Colony/Province c. 1850–1950," *Journal of African History* 46, 2 (2005): 282.

[36] Diwan, Dungarpur, to Field, November 15, 1928, GOI, SRSA, 261-G of 1928, NAI.

[37] Sadhu Singh, "Report," 1910, chapter 2, no. 41b, BMK, 754B of 1906, RSA.

[38] Diwan, Dungarpur, to Field, November 15, 1928, GOI, SRSA, 261-G of 1928, NAI.

[39] Pratap Singh, to H. Daly (AGG-CI), April 29, 1908, GOI, CI, PB, 129-A of 1905–8, NAI.

[40] K.D. Erskine, *The Mewar Residency* (1908; repr., Gurgaon: Vintage Books, 1992), 129.

[41] Ibid., 160.

actually monitored the quantity of wild boar at Nahar Magra by having his shikaris detail the presence of *ekal*, adult females or *bhundan*, sub-adults or *dagra*, and piglets at the Diwan Odi, Kesar Bagh, Bari Odi, and Rang Burj shooting towers.[42] Records covering approximately half the months from December 1907 through May 1909 and for July 1924 are available, but it is likely that Fateh Singh kept tabs on Nahar Magra's boar population at other times during his nearly fifty-year reign. Most of the available reports are from late fall, winter, or early spring.[43] These periods correspond with the hunting season and those months when Mewar's wild boar received increased rations of corn to fatten them, and to encourage their presence at known locations convenient for shooting and census taking. The information in these reports helped the maharana and his shikaris judge the efficacy of the feeding program at Nahar Magra, as measured in the hoped-for multiplication and improvement of wild boar.[44]

The existence of these tallies verifies Fateh Singh's earnestness, but the information they contain should not have exacerbated his concerns. From December 1907 through May 1909, shikaris observed up to 9 different *ekal* per day at Diwan Odi, Kesar Bagh, Bari Odi, and Rang Burj.[45] Aside from an abnormally poor showing in March 1909, when only 2 *ekal* appeared each day at Diwan and Bari *odis*, 1 at Kesar Bagh, and none at Rang Burj, the overall trend seems to have been steady.[46] Certainly there was no dramatic downturn in the wild boar population. The lone 1924 report indicates that between

---

[42] Order 7524 of *kati vid 11 samvat 1964*, MMK-RD, 269 of VS 1962, RSA-U.

[43] Besides Dec. 1907, the months are Jan., Feb., Aug., Sept., Oct., Nov., and Dec. of 1908; and Jan., Feb., March, and May of 1909: see *Naksha Shikargah mukam Nahar Magra*, December 1907 through May 1909, MMK-RD, 269 of VS 1962, RSA-U.

[44] Order 7524 of *kati vid 11 samvat 1964*, MMK-RD, 269 of VS 1962, RSA-U.

[45] *Naksha Shikargah mukam Nahar Magra*, December 1907 through May 1909, MMK-RD, 269 of VS 1962, RSA-U.

[46] *Naksha Shikargah mukam Nahar Magra*, March 1909, doc. 52, MMK-RD, 269 of VS 1962, RSA-U.

3 and 5 *ekal* came to Diwan Odi on a daily basis that July, while 1 regularly showed itself at Rang Burj, up to 2 frequented Kesar Bagh, and just 1 occasionally visited Bari Odi.[47] These numbers indicate that Fateh Singh may have had cause for concern by the mid-1920s, but the limited data and the shikaris' variable counting methods make it impossible to reach a reliable conclusion. The maharana, however, may not have been so cautious.

It is not always clear how far princes credited their own assertions that game had decreased in their states and to what extent they overstated their claims to counter the unwelcome demands of their nobles and subjects.[48] Some rulers did change their story depending on context. When responding to a request for information on the extent of game and wildlife reserves in princely India, issued in 1928 by the Society for the Preservation of the Fauna of the Empire (SPFE), rulers tailored their responses to impress their audience. Some emphasized recent increases in game, others claimed there was no need to specially preserve animals in their states on account of their natural abundance, and a few called attention to the existence of strict rules and regulations in their states.[49]

The reply from Dungarpur informed the SPFE that under the current maharawal's watchful eye, deer of all kinds were increasing, there was every prospect of reintroducing tigers, and no one could shoot without permission. Wild boar were doing so well that they even bothered cultivators—though only slightly—in a few places.[50] Along with the political circumstances, their official story would change significantly within a decade. Seeking to defend the state against newly strident popular allegations that wildlife had run amok and crops were suffering, the maharawal's representatives insisted

[47] *Naksha Shikargah mukam Nahar Magra* (*Diwan Odi, Bari Odi, Rang Burj, Kesar Bag*), July 1924, MMK-RD, 269 of VS 1962, RSA-U.

[48] For similar observations on non-Rajput Junagadh, see Divyabhanusinh, "Junagadh State and its Lions," 529.

[49] For various states' responses, see GOI, SRSA, 261-G of 1928, NAI; see also GOI, BA, General Branch, 81-D of 1928, NAI.

[50] Diwan, Dungarpur, to Field, November 15, 1928, GOI, SRSA, 261-G of 1928, NAI.

in 1937 that "wild beasts have decreased and not increased."[51] Any recent drops, however, could not have been dramatic considering that the state's ruminants and wild boar supported a steady population of approximately twenty tigers from 1935 through 1950.[52] Official boasts regarding the reach of state game laws likewise gave way to protestations that cultivators could shoot any animal found destroying their fields.[53] Genuine concerns over the present and future survival of wildlife in Dungarpur were at the root of this apparent duplicity, as was a willingness to stretch the truth to preserve the maharawal's hunting rights and privileges.

Fateh Singh's successor in Mewar, Bhupal Singh (r. 1930–55) was most concerned with his state's wild boar. Given the number of animals and sizeable specimens recorded in Mewar as late as the 1940s, it is difficult to understand why. Judging the wild stock unsatisfactory in quality and quantity and looking back with nostalgia to the time when, in 1909, he had killed an exceptionally large animal of 335 *lbs.*, Bhupal Singh was even breeding his own boar for placement in state shikargahs by the mid-1940s.[54] Yet, in 1942, he got a boar even bigger than his 1909 trophy out of a group of 200 near Jaisamand. It was 380 *lbs.*, 3 ft. tall, over 6 ft. long, and had tusks measuring a respectable 8 in.[55] The following year, he killed a similarly sized boar, the equal of which "had never before been hunted."[56] When the maharana wrote an old friend from his 1947 Christmas camp to complain about a "great scarcity of pigs" at Jaisamand, he could still report that his party had shot 37 boar, he had bagged 4 leopards, and there was every prospect of getting more of the same and a

[51] Virbhadra Singh (Musahib Ala, Dungarpur), to PA-SRSA, August 31, 1937, GOI, PD, nos 1–2, file 27(8)-P of 1939, NAI.

[52] Ranjitsinh, *Beyond the Tiger*, 24.

[53] Virbhadra Singh, to PA-SRSA, August 31, 1937, GOI, PD, nos 1–2, file 27(8)-P of 1939, NAI.

[54] Sharma, *Haqiqat Bahida*, 4:402.

[55] Tanwar, *Shikari aur Shikar*, 293–5. The 1935 world records for wild boar tusks ranged from 9.5 to over 12.5 inches: see Dollman and Burlace, *Rowland Ward's Records*, 326.

[56] Tanwar, *Shikari aur Shikar*, 297.

tiger too.[57] Whatever the actual changes had been since his youth, Bhupal Singh clearly found something lacking in Mewari boar of the 1940s.

In contrast, Tanwar looked back on his youth and early adulthood under these maharanas as a time of plenty, when Mewari boar attained such superlative excellence that Fateh Singh's personal record was a monstrous and improbable beast of 600 *lbs*.[58] In those days, there were so many boar that they overran Udaipur on a nightly basis, searching for scraps and forcing residents to hide. One even broke into the City Palace, where it was discovered in a courtyard early the next morning.[59] Hundreds lived just south of the city on Tikhalya Magra, along with herds of sambar and countless leopards.[60] Tigers had been so plentiful in the Aravallis that shikaris regularly discovered more than one per beat, so that the anticipated quarry "would turn out to be a full family: tiger, tigress, and two or three cubs, and occasionally, two tigers together."[61]

If conditions in the 1920s were anywhere near as good as Tanwar remembered, we can assume that the maharana's dictates, which inspired wide obedience among state nobles and the populace at large, were partly responsible. Because there were no formally gazetted game laws, the designation of any given act as criminal as well as the precise nature of punishment and its severity were entirely at the maharana's discretion. Fear and uncertainty, combined with the people's respect for the prince's rights and privileges, were effective deterrents: violations appear to have been rare. One well-known prohibition forbade the destruction of female game, in recognition of their breeding potential. Fateh Singh "would get angry and punish

---

[57] Bhupal Singh, to Arthur Cunningham Lothian, December 31, 1947, Mss. Eur. F144/1, BL.

[58] Tanwar, *Shikari aur Shikar*, 197. Tanwar provides no date for this trophy; his memories are as suspect as any other old shikari's. 250 *lbs*. was the acknowledged weight for a good Indian boar: see Dollman and Burlace, *Rowland Ward's Records*, 326.

[59] Tanwar, *Shikari aur Shikar*, 293 and 350.

[60] Tanwar, *Samsmaran*, 83.

[61] Tanwar, *Shikari aur Shikar*, 350.

the killer" whenever they were shot without good reason. With few exceptions, anyone wishing to shoot game of any kind required the maharana's advance permission. Tanwar recalled his own dread of Fateh Singh's wrath after slaying a charging boar and again after shooting an aggressive bear, because he had not obtained prior sanction, and despite the fact that he had acted in self-defense both times.[62] Accepting the shikari's explanations of why he had been compelled to shoot, Fateh Singh mercifully imposed no punishment in either instance. Self-defense was a legitimate excuse, but only when the maharana judged the danger as having been genuine.

Tigers, leopards, and other game had not always been strictly preserved in every Rajput state, however. While "there is no long history of state-sponsored projects to eliminate carnivores" in India, unlike in Britain and Western Europe, the Government of India from the early 1870s successfully encouraged select princes to align their rules with British Indian policies.[63] These rulers' subsequent categorization of all tigers, leopards, or any of several other species as vermin—as opposed to the identification of individual animals as man-eaters or cattle lifters—was largely an extension of British views. Government proponents of wildlife management regulations saw clear advantages in forging an all-India policy, whether for eradication or preservation: persecuting poachers and protecting game were ineffective if immunity lay just across a state or provincial border. But this was a daunting task. In the princely states alone, a wide variety of vermin-control measures took shape in line with local conditions and values, indicating that much more was going on than the simple import of British norms.

In Rajputana in the 1870s, the Rana of Jhalawar offered bounties on tigers, while the Maharao of Kotah rewarded those who destroyed tigers, along with bears, wolves, and leopards. The classification of the tiger as vermin in these states, and perhaps in Bundi as well,

---

[62] Ibid., 255 and 275.
[63] Rangarajan, "The Raj and the Natural World," 297.

was atypical for Rajputana, where "most rulers … either denied that carnivores were a major problem or claimed that sportive hunting was adequate as a means of control."[64] An explanation for this departure within Rajputana can be found in the physical proximity and linked histories of these three states in particular, which were collectively known as the Hadauti states.

Princes often consulted the rules and regulations enforced in other states when developing their own policies. States linked by geography, family ties, and shared interests, such as the Hadauti states, were most likely to do so. Likewise, Bikaner officials in 1912 had on hand the *Rules and Regulations for Shooting and Pigsticking in Marwar within the Shikar Khana Limits*. Bikaner's shikarkhana also kept a copy of the *Patiala State Game Protection Notification*.[65] While the rulers of Patiala were Jat Sikhs and not Rajputs, the state was the closest princely territory to Bikaner's northwest. Patiala furthermore enjoyed similar sporting conditions while facing comparable poaching violations from the British Punjab. Naturally, game laws also circulated between neighboring states quite unsolicited as rulers sought to defend their borders and wildlife from outsiders.[66]

The decisive factor leading to parallels within Hadauti, however, was very likely the large number of tigers in the jungles along the Chambal river valley. People living in the region appear to have been unusually troubled by these animals in the late-nineteenth century, when Kipling visited a medical dispensary in Bundi and found "loin-bite" (the local misnomer for "lion-bite," and more properly for "tiger-bite") entered in a register of "the principal complaints of the country … over and over again—three and four cases per week."[67]

[64] Ibid., 212.

[65] Bhairun Singh (Foreign Member, Bikaner), to Private Secretary to Maharaja of Bikaner, January 26, 1912, BMK, s. no. 181, file 1123 of 1910, RSA.

[66] For example, see Foreign and Home Member, Council of State, Jaipur, to Resident, Jaipur, January 10, 1928, GOI, Jaipur Agency, 15/28 of 1928, NAI.

[67] Rudyard Kipling, "The Comedy of Errors and the Exploitation of Boondi," in *From Sea to Sea; Letters of Travel*, vol. 1 (New York: Doubleday & McClure Company, 1899), 151.

With so many casualties occurring within reach of the prince's primary residence and seat of power, the maharao must have felt significant pressure to better protect his subjects.

Like the tiger, the leopard was vermin only in parts of Rajputana, but this spotted cat was widely persecuted in Bundelkhand in the Rajput states of Orchha, Bijawar, and Alipura, among others, where no restrictions limited the slaughter of leopard, dhole (*Cuon alpinus*), or even wild boar. On the other hand, no rewards appear to have been offered, suggesting that hunters either needed no encouragement to pursue these animals or princes did not deem them problematic enough to justify bounties.[68] It is possible that Bundelkhandi princes allowed their subjects to hunt leopard and wild boar not because they considered these animals vermin, but because they were sufficiently prolific to warrant classification as fair game. The balance of power between rulers and state nobles may also have been such that princes could not monopolize these animals. In contrast, the comparatively scarce and undeniably royal tiger was strictly preserved throughout the region.

Small carnivores were subject to persecution in some states but ignored in most. Interested in preserving wildfowl for his shoots, the Jat ruler of Bharatpur listed the jackal, fox, badger, wildcat, owls, birds of prey, and snakes as vermin in his *Bharatpur Game Laws* of 1924 and 1932. Yet, he set no bounties to tempt his subjects to hunt these relatively unpalatable carnivores, raising the possibility that predation was not actually much of a problem. Bikaner's wildfowling prince never declared any animals as vermin. If Ganga Singh was willing to overlook predation, it must have had no apparent impact on his massive flocks of sandgrouse, *kunj*, and snipe.

While an important goal of vermin eradication in Britain was the elimination of wild competitors for prize game like partridge and deer, in the princely states select species became vermin for vying with other carnivores. Partly because both were assumed to compete with the tiger for prey, vermin eradication in the Dungarpur State

[68] Memorandum of Replies Furnished by Political Officers, in Bayley (AGG-CI), to FD Secretary, January 17, 1905, no. 477-G, GOI, Baghelkhand Agency, 76 of 1904–6, NAI.

in southern Rajputana aimed at eliminating the dhole or wild dog and restricting the number and range of leopards. Widely despised by the British and Indians alike, a reward of Rs 25 was available for killing dholes from 1928 through at least the mid-1930s.[69] Dholes form packs to hunt chital, sambar, and other species also pursued by tigers and leopards. A study conducted in Nagarahole National Park, however, concluded that while "substantial dietary overlap" exists between tigers, dholes, and leopards in terms of the prey they consume, each specializes in different sized animals. Tigers in Nagarahole often chose large quarry, like gaur and adult sambar. Dholes preferred the medium-sized chital, as did the park's leopards. By the numbers, the "mean weights of all prey killed was 65.5 kg for the tiger, 23.4 kg for leopard and 35.3 kg for dhole."[70]

Presented with a different balance of wildlife than their Nagarahole kin, the tigers of Dungarpur in the early-twentieth century reportedly preyed most on the large and "plentiful" nilgai, although they surely targeted the state's modest numbers of sambar as well.[71] Dungarpur's leopards concentrated instead on the diminutive four-horned antelope—a species they largely ignored in Nagarahole—and on the maharawal's recently introduced and still-scarce chital and blackbuck.[72] But, along with dholes, they likely relied most on the state's miscellaneous game, chinkara, and wild boar, which were "very common indeed."[73]

While state officials recognized by 1928 that tigers killed "very many" nilgai, they made no special effort to cultivate these animals as a prey base. Maintenance of the nilgai population at around 800 struck them as satisfactory, and they were distracted by the

[69] Diwan, Dungarpur, to Field, November 15, 1928, GOI, SRSA, 261-G of 1928, NAI.

[70] K. Ullas Karanth and Melvin E. Sunquist, "Prey Selection by Tiger, Leopard and Dhole in Tropical Forests," *Journal of Animal Ecology* 64 (1995): 439–50; 443.

[71] Diwan, Dungarpur, to Field, November 15, 1928, GOI, SRSA, 261-G of 1928, NAI.

[72] Karanth and Sunquist, "Prey Selection," 445.

[73] Diwan, Dungarpur, to Field, November 15, 1928, GOI, SRSA, 261-G of 1928, NAI.

significantly smaller tallies of blackbuck (35), chital (over 50), and four-horned antelope (over 150). Lakshman Singh wanted enough of each to sustain his own shikar, and not just his tigers' needs. Nilgai, however, were not particularly prized game, even receiving protection on religious grounds in many states including Bharatpur and Jaipur, although apparently not in Dungarpur. The maharawal's interests coincided better with his tigers' tastes when it came to his "strictly preserved" sambar deer (over 200).[74]

Not just any deer, antelope, or gazelle will do for a predator when a bias towards the largest prey that can be killed successfully and safely confers distinct advantages.[75] Multiple factors are involved, but tigers in general are more likely to flourish in habitats filled with adult gaur, nilgai, and sambar, each of which yields a substantial return per kill with a live weight of 175 kg or more.[76] Dramatically smaller prey like chinkara and four-horned antelope, which weigh less than 30 kg, do not compensate as generously for the time and energy expended on their capture.[77] Although chinkara and four-horned antelope were both plentiful and on the increase in Dungarpur by the 1920s, Lakshman Singh focused his energies on yet another small ungulate, the blackbuck. In doing so he may have made Dungarpur more conducive to the already common leopard and, assuming blackbuck promotion diverted his attention from nilgai and sambar preservation, somewhat less accommodating to his hoped-for tigers. The maharawal's concurrent interest in the medium-sized chital was relatively more propitious for tigers, but would have been as beneficial, or more, to leopards and dholes.[78] Ultimately, however, there was an adequately large and diverse prey base from 1928 through 1950 to support around 20 tigers—besides the 48 more killed for sport in

[74] Ibid.

[75] Karanth and Sunquist, "Prey Selection," 447.

[76] Weights are from large-, medium-, and small-size classes as given in A.P. Andheria, K.U. Karanth, and N.S. Kumar, "Diet and Prey Profiles of Three Sympatric Large Carnivores in Bandipur Tiger Reserve, India," *Journal of Zoology* 273 (2007): 171.

[77] Karanth and Sunquist, "Prey Selection," 448.

[78] In Bandipur Tiger Reserve chital "dominated their diets (tiger=33%, leopard=39% and dhole=73%):" Andheria, *et al.*, "Diet and Prey," 169.

these years—a sizeable leopard population, and an unknown number of dholes.[79]

By the early-twentieth century, and particularly by the 1920s,
game laws in the Rajput states were moving decisively towards fining
rather than rewarding the killing of erstwhile vermin like the leopard,
likely changing in step with the contemporary trend away from
bounties in British India.[80] While the dhole remained blacklisted in
many places, the 1927 *Jaipur State Shooting Rules* imposed a Rs 50
fine for killing a leopard. The amended 1931 *Rules for the Regulation
of Shooting in the Jaipur State* increased the penalty to Rs 250. The
Jodhpur durbar's *Rules and Regulations for Shooting and Pigsticking in
Marwar within the Shikar Khana Limits* was demanding Rs 20 for
the same crime as early as 1910, and by 1931 even Jhalawar State in
Hadauti had reversed its former policies, instituting a Rs 50 fine for
killing a leopard and Rs 200 for killing a tiger in its *Akhet Niyamavali Rajya Jhalawar*.

As the twentieth century advanced, the Rajput princes of Bundelkhand and Rajputana also began replacing their strict yet largely
unwritten shikar controls with formally composed and publicly gazetted rules and regulations. Having received their education at the hands
of British tutors and Mayo College professors, the younger princely
generations included many self-described modernizers and 'true'
sportsmen only too happy to confirm their normative, empire-wide
values. Other princes faced significant pressure from locally stationed
political agents and government proponents of wildlife preservation
acts and British Indian shooting regulations to curb their arbitrary
powers with "rationalized" rules and predictable punishments.

A major wave of codification took place between 1904 and 1912,
coinciding with the government's circulation of its draft Wild Birds
and Animals Protection Act to the states and the act's final passage
in 1912. Rewah in Baghelkhand had no formal game laws in 1904,
but did by 1910.[81] In Bundelkhand, Chhatarpur had none either,

[79] Ranjitsinh, *Beyond the Tiger*, 24.

[80] Rangarajan, "The Raj and the Natural World," 296–7 and 299.

[81] Secretary to Maharaja of Rewah, to PA-Baghelkhand, October 1, 1904,
no. 477-G, GOI, Baghelkhand Agency, 76 of 1904–6, NAI; Note Regarding

but state officials forwarded a draft to the political agent in 1909. Bijawar already had "some simple rules" in 1904, but the state diwan pledged further cooperation; Datia's diwan responded similarly. In Rajputana, the only states that participated in this wave, it seems, were Jodhpur, with its *c.* 1910 *Rules and Regulations for Shooting and Pigsticking in Marwar within the Shikar Khana Limits*, and Bikaner, where revisions were drafted between 1904 and 1909 for the rules enacted by Ganga Singh's Regency Council in 1898. Jodhpur too had been governed by a Regency Council for several years after its ruler—who would be educated at Mayo College like Ganga Singh of Bikaner—ascended the throne as a minor in 1895. The 1904 government draft, then, may have offered these princes a welcome opportunity to revise rules that had been crafted without their full input, rather than representing a chance to conform more closely to British Indian norms.

Another round of revisions and codifications took place after 1928, when political agents in Rajputana and Bundelkhand forwarded a request from the SPFE for information about game sanctuaries and the condition of wildlife habitats in the princely states.[82] In Rajputana, the Jaipur State's 1927 *Shooting Rules* were succeeded in 1931 by new *Rules for the Regulation of Shooting*. Jhalawar State's revised *Akhet Niyamavali* came out that same year.

Variously remembered in Dungarpur and Mewar as an enthusiastic sportsman, suspected poacher, and thief of record sambar trophies, the political agent Donald M. Field was a driving force behind these post-1928 changes in the Southern Rajputana States Agency. He forwarded the SPFE's request to the states with a long note, in which he first proclaimed the London-based society's inquiry

---

Shooting of Game and Protection of Birds in the Rewah State, in Secretary to Maharaja of Rewah, to PA-Baghelkhand, July 12, 1910, GOI, CI, Baghelkhand Agency, 261 of 1909, NAI.

[82] D.M. Field, to Diwans of Dungarpur, Banswara, Partabgarh, and Kamdar of Kushalgarh, August 22, 1928, GOI, SRSA, 261-G of 1928, NAI; Memorandum 5988-91-C of August 11, 1928, GOI, BA, General Branch, 81-D of 1928, NAI.

"a good opportunity ... to consider the question of game preservation," and then detailed the states' many failings and how they ought
to reform their ill-considered policies. He warned that "unless remedial
measures are soon employed, the larger wild animals will before long
completely disappear from many areas where they are now supposed
to be protected."[83] Judging by the exhaustive lists of reserved areas,
closed seasons, and other information these states dispatched to
Field, many rulers in southern Rajputana, like some of their Bundelkhandi peers, had already been pursuing the work of game preservation
along "scientific" lines.

One state that remained aloof from the waves of adoption and
revision between 1904 and the early 1930s was Mewar. The closest
Fateh Singh came to issuing a formal set of shooting rules was Order
21746 of 1927, which only addressed tiger shooting and merely reiterated the maharana's existing autocratic controls in print. As before,
no one could kill a tiger anywhere in Mewar without his permission,
except one of the five or so *sardars* lucky enough to have tigers available within the bounds of their own estates.[84] Englishmen wishing
to shoot in *jagir* lands needed permission from the maharana,
through the local jagirdar, state officials, or the British Residency. If
a specific tiger took up residence near a village and began attacking
or killing people, or an animal posed a clear threat after having been
wounded but not killed during the course of some sardar's hunt, people
could submit a petition to their sovereign and await his pleasure.
In the midst of life-threatening attacks, self-defense was permissible.
The maharana retained absolute authority to determine an alleged
offender's guilt or innocence, and could impose whatever punishment
he deemed appropriate.[85]

The change in Mewar from uncodified controls based on princely prerogative did not take place until well after Fateh Singh's death.

[83] Prakash Bhandari, "1930: Story of the First Tiger Relocation," *Times of India*, July 6, 2008, http://timesofindia.indiatimes.com/archive.cms; Tanwar believed his trophy, 39 inch sambar antlers, was replaced with a smaller set while in Field's custody: see *Shikari aur Shikar*, 312.

[84] Allen and Dwivedi, *Lives of the Indian Princes*, 143.

[85] Order 21746 of October 15, 1927, MMK, author's collection.

The resultant Mewar Game and Fish Preservation Act of 1942, passed during the reign of Bhupal Singh, was no simple indication that the state's wildlife finally required protection, although it may well have. As in many other states, Mewar's new game act marked an intrusion of colonial influence, resulting in a shift to governance more in line with imperial designs and legislative processes.

Relatively powerful sovereigns of the older generations, like Fateh Singh, preferred to preserve their game without recourse to official rules. Codification restricted their options and undermined their sovereignty. The less autocratic princes of the younger generations, with their seats in the Chamber of Princes and progressive ideals, accepted or even required official justifications in print. Nevertheless, their gazetted rules could be just as strict in preserving game for themselves and their friends. Bhupal Singh's Mewar Game and Fish Preservation Act of 1942, for example, declared that "any person who willfully kills, captures or sells, or attempts to kill, capture or sell, any animal, bird, game or fish, or does any other act, in contravention of this Act or of any rules or notification under it shall be punished with imprisonment ... for a term which may extend to six months or with fine or with both." In the end, autocratic shooting rules and gazetted wildlife protection acts alike linked the preservation of state hierarchies with the conservation of princely environments and royal beasts.

Among the most contested and delicately balanced of state hierarchies were those between princes and their nobles.[86] Fortunately, both sides generally conceded that the rule of precedent sanctified age-old practices and long-standing settlements. There was far less agreement when it came to determining exactly what those practices and settlements were. Princes tried to reap the benefit of past examples by selectively remembering limitless populations of small and large game. Likewise, state nobles and landholders championed their

[86] Haynes, "Rajput Ceremonial Interactions," 471.

own preferred visions of the past. Princes and subordinates quarrel-ed over present realities too. Where sovereigns might see an alarming scarcity of game, nobles and landholders could perceive worrying proliferation. Precedents may have been the rule, but they were far more contentious and changeable than their air of conservatism and tradition suggests.

Conflicts between princes and elites over shooting grounds and hunting privileges caused no differences over the meanings of shikar, game being competed for within the bounds of a common episteme. In addition, both parties derived distinct advantages from interacting with one another as sportsmen, providing or partaking of opportu-nities to hunt, offering or receiving shikar-themed gifts, and sharing in the glory of their mutual successes. Although quick to protest any perceived encroachments on their rights and privileges, most nobles recognized that their personal authority depended on the practical support and symbolic patronage of their sovereigns. They did try to augment their status and powers by distancing themselves and their sport from their rulers, but they equally pursued beneficial connections with them. Hunting fashions that associated nobles with the often indisputable legitimacy of their princes was one way of doing so that, nevertheless, left these elites sufficient latitude to claim partial independence from and some degree of superiority over their rulers. Albeit on a smaller scale, these state nobles imitated their princes in the game they pursued, the hunting accessories they purchased, the shooting regulations they crafted, and the shikargahs they maintained.

Like their sovereigns, nobles went out of their way to obtain the sport they wanted. Princes including Pratap Singh and Ganga Singh bent British regulations and their peers' rules when especially de-sirable game was on the line (or just over the border), like tigers in British Bundelkhand or lions in Junagadh. In Jodhpur, the young Rajput noble Amar Singh violated state game laws in order to hunt wild boar.[87] Unlike their prince, Mewari nobles regularly left their personal estates, and even Mewar, in order to get the game they

---

[87] Rudolph and Rudolph, *Reversing the Gaze*, 97 and 98.

wanted. Vijay Singh of Deogarh (r. 1900–43), for example, went abroad to get 2 leopards and 50 boar in 1923.[88] The following year, he visited his peers' estates in Mewar to bag 3 leopards, 17 boar, and 3 nilgai.[89] Tigers were prized above all, but nobles in most states found few opportunities of shooting them. Only a few Mewari sardars, whose estates had tigers of their own, could hunt them without permission.[90] Others had to await their prince's pleasure, like the first-class nobles Thakur Laxman Singh of Sardargarh (r. 1912–29) and the Rao of Bedla, who each received permission to kill a tiger in the maharana's grounds in 1924. Vijay Singh of Deogarh was deeply impressed by their good fortune. As he explained in a letter to Laxman Singh, permission to shoot a tiger was the modern equivalent, in terms of the honor conferred, to the receipt of a jagir land-grant in former times.[91]

Noble sportsmen endeavored to outfit themselves like princes. At the very least, they tried to keep up with their peers. Laxman Singh of Sardargarh obtained his hunting garb by mail order from Ajmer. Patronizing the firms of Abdullah & Sons and K.J. Mehta & Bros., he purchased breeches in the popular Jodhpur fashion and others cut from "Shekari Sunproof" fabric, hunting coats in tweed, and imitation leather boots with rope soles to provide a quiet step and good traction.[92] In 1921 alone, he ordered four new hunting suits for himself and two for his 7-year-old son in a practical selection of browns, tans, and "shikari green."[93] While the maharana hunted in

[88] Vijay Singh, to Laxman Singh, March 1, 1923, *Devgarh su aya Kagaj samvat 1979*, Sardargarh *basta* (unnumbered), PSP.

[89] Vijay Singh, to Laxman Singh, March 29, 1924, *Devgarh su aya Kagaj samvat 1980*, Sardargarh *basta* (unnumbered), PSP.

[90] Allen and Dwivedi, *Lives of the Indian Princes*, 143. There may have been more opportunities after Bhupal Singh became maharana: see MJ-Shikar, s. no. 401, file 20/2 of 1939, RSA.

[91] Vijay Singh, to Laxman Singh, May 24, 1924, *Devgarh su aya Kagaj samvat 1980*, Sardargarh *basta* (unnumbered), PSP.

[92] Laxman Singh, to Abdullah & Sons, May 31, 1919; Abdullah & Sons, to L. Singh, November 30, 1921; K.J. Mehta & Bros., to L. Singh, August 1, 1922, Sardargarh *basta* (unnumbered), PSP.

[93] L. Singh, to Abdullah & Sons, June 9, 1921, Sardargarh *basta* (unnumbered), PSP.

old-fashioned achkans, Laxman Singh preferred coats and breeches, as did most twentieth-century sporting princes.[94] Whether or not the nobleman had achkans on hand for excursions with his sovereign, he could certainly match the prevailing standards of other states.

Many princes had automobiles specially equipped for sport.[95] Fully customized, a fine shikar car made by Rolls Royce or Bentley would be "fitted with compartments for weapons, a locker for cartridges, and a trunk for picnic baskets, ice chests and flasks," while more modest designs might be limited to extra lamps and a "shikari green" paint job.[96] According to their means and aspirations, the wealthier state nobles ordered custom shikar cars as well. The Sardargarh family purchased a green Citroen 5-seater saloon in 1934.[97] Unlike the Citroen convertible owned by the Maharaja of Sarila in 1933, it is unclear if the Sardargarh family used their vehicle for shikar.[98] While the green paint job makes it a possibility (assuming the shade was more olive drab than chartreuse), enclosed saloons were less popular than open touring cars for the purpose.[99] The Sardargarh Citroen was fitted with purdah curtains, but this does not disallow an association with sport any more than the zenana quarters in some of Fateh Singh's shooting towers.[100] Rather, it raises the possibility that the *thakurani* and other women may have participated in shikar excursions, as did a number of their peers in princely India, and in the royal house of Mewar.[101]

When it came to firearms, custom-made rifles like the ones

[94] Allen and Dwivedi, *Lives of the Indian Princes*, 140.

[95] Gwalior's maharaja once gifted a shikar car to Maharana Fateh Singh: see Tanwar, *Shikari aur Shikar*, 221. Ganga Singh had a whole fleet: see Sharada Dwivedi and Manvendra Singh Barwani, *The Automobiles of the Maharajas* (Mumbai: Eminence Designs Pvt., Ltd., 2003), 85 and 156.

[96] Jaffer, *Made for Maharajas*, 185.

[97] International Motor Company, Bombay, bill 19/265, January 20, 1934, Sardargarh *basta* 25, file 17, PSP.

[98] Sarila, *Once a Prince of Sarila*, 70.

[99] Dwivedi and Barwani, *Automobiles*, 156.

[100] Sharma, *Haqiqat Bahida*, 3:129.

[101] Dwivedi and Barwani, *Automobiles*, 195.

Fateh Singh used to purchase from European firms including John
Rigby & Co., Holland & Holland, and James Purdey & Sons were
beyond the means of most nobles. They could afford the eminently
functional if more pedestrian Mausers and Mannlichers.[102] Mewari
nobles paid attention to what their peers were shooting with to ensure that their own arsenals measured up. When Vijay Singh of
Deogarh expressed interest in a .256 high-velocity Mauser for sale
at Ajmer, it was because he had seen other nobles with rifles of the
same caliber in Udaipur and because he knew his frequent correspondent on the topic, Laxman Singh of Sardargarh, owned a similar
weapon.[103]

Not all of the nobles' rifles were their own carefully considered
purchases: some came as gifts from their sovereigns. By presenting
their subordinates with hunting rifles, princes gained greater influence
over their nobles' sporting activities and a controlling partnership
in their successes. Fateh Singh restricted his followers' access to
the Martini-Henry rifles he imported in bulk for their use to those
times when they accompanied him on hunting excursions or to
the rifle range.[104] When a noble or state employee shot with a weapon
presented, or lent, by his sovereign, he wielded a constant reminder
both of his dependence and the special favor he had been shown.[105]
A received or borrowed rifle helped reinforce a message already

[102] On princely sporting rifles, see Jaffer, *Made for Maharajas*, 184.

[103] Vijay Singh, to Laxman Singh, [1919 or 1920], *Devgarh su aya Kagaj
samvat 1976*, Sardargarh *basta* (unnumbered), PSP. It was easier and cheaper
to obtain cartridges for popular weapons. High velocity small caliber rifles
like the .256 were popular in the 1920s for their accuracy and power: see
Truesdell, *The Rifle*, 126-7.

[104] Walter (MR), to First Assistant to AGG-Rajputana, January 14, 1887,
GOI, FD, Internal B, 262–4 of March 1887, NAI.

[105] The Maharaja of Orchha gave or helped Diwan Madho Singh purchase
a .500 express, a .400 cordite, and a 12 bore shotgun, and used to lend him a
.395 Mannlicher for sport: see W.E. Jardine, to L. Reynolds, March 18, 1907,
GOI, BA, 456 of 1906, NAI. The Maharaja of Rewah made at least twenty-six
requests in 1903 for sporting rifles, guns, and ammunition for state nobles:
see Recommendations by Rewah State for Arms and Ammunition in the
Favor of Certain Persons, GOI, Baghelkhand Agency, 82-G of 1902, NAI.

communicated when Fateh Singh first granted permission to shoot: the means, rights, and privileges of shikar were royal monopolies.

Fateh Singh often gave sporting rifles to his followers alongside other customary presents including ceremonial *sar o pa* robes and cash.[106] As with many such gifts, the fact that the prince had briefly touched or symbolically used these weapons prior to awarding them was as significant as their monetary value. Well-known rifles that the maharana or his predecessors had specially ordered and hunted with were among the most desirable gifts, because their recipients could bask in the reflected glory of royal tiger kills whenever they used or displayed these weapons. High-quality hand-me-downs conferred great distinction on those who received them, and they maintained the maharana's enhanced position within post-*Kaulnama* hierarchies. Whatever a sardar, jagirdar, or shikari might accomplish with such a rifle was done in the shadow of Fateh Singh's earlier triumphs. Besides, accurate shooting might have been difficult with some of these rifles: if the barrel was shot out after many years of use, there was little chance of matching or surpassing feats of marksmanship achieved by the maharana while the weapon was still new.

One Mewari rifle that ultimately became a royal gift was the .577/.500 caliber rifle nicknamed the *Pratap-bar*, which Fateh Singh had used in big game hunts since the 1890s.[107] Years later, his successor Bhupal Singh passed it on to the state shikari Tanwar, who held this weapon in great esteem, illustrating the status of pedigreed sporting rifles in Rajput court culture and calling to mind the many storied swords, guns, and other weapons in museums in the former Rajput states. According to his appreciative description, the *Pratap-bar*'s most distinctive feature was that Fateh Singh had killed tigers with it. Tanwar, therefore, derived deep satisfaction from the fact that he too had killed several tigers, leopards, wild boar, and bears with it. In addition, he relished its substantial cartridge size, energy,

---

[106] Sharma, *Haqiqat Bahida*, 3:102 and 5:165.

[107] Tanwar, *Samsmaran*, 86. R.S. MacGregor's *Oxford Hindi–English Dictionary* (Oxford: Oxford University Press, 1993) defines *bar* as: "line, margin, edge; edge of a blade." More tempting is *barh*, "volley (of fire)." Pratap Singh of Idar gave Fateh Singh this rifle in about 1891, hence its name.

and velocity. Decades later, the rifle's enduring value and historical associations prompted the huntsman to keep it nearby and within sight as he composed his memoirs.[108]

While a shikari like Tanwar was satisfied with his *Pratap-bar* and the opportunities he was given to use it, higher ranking nobles aimed for more. The values and aspirations they shared with their maharana led them to demand complete control over royal game and hunting grounds in their own estates. Rajput princes, however, insisted that no one could prevent them from hunting anywhere within their state territories, even when the grounds in question were not specifically classed as *khalsa* or royal properties. Like at least one nineteenth-century raja of Pudukkottai, when Rajput princes assigned properties to their subordinates the grants did not "automatically" include hunting privileges.[109] Shikar was an assignable privilege separate from land's other divisible assets, including grazing, cultivation, occupation, and taxation. More so than other assets, it was sovereign by default.

The historically contested relationship between Rajput rulers and nobles recently has been traced through retellings of the Padmini legend.[110] Rajput polities began as coalitions of (near) equals bound by familial ties, in which the king could not make decisions without his chiefs' input. Political and technological changes beginning in the Mughal period and intensifying under British rule helped Rajput kings consolidate power by delinking their connections with elites from the bonds of kinship.[111] Their association with the king reinvented as a patron–client relationship, nobles who dared, for example, to expand their hunting grounds without permission became insubordinate and undisciplined rather than justifiably ambitious. When state nobles or lesser elites infringed on their ruler's sport, they delivered a significant challenge to their superior's status as an archetypal Rajput and authoritative sovereign.

---

[108] Tanwar, *Samsmaran*, 86–7.
[109] Waghorne, *Raja's Magic Clothes*, 180.
[110] Sreenivasan, *Many Lives of a Rajput Queen*.
[111] Ibid., 68–70 and 128–9.

In Bikaner State, one such challenge came in 1909 from the Anglo-Indian landholder Stanley E. Skinner, who disputed Ganga Singh's right to hunt in the northern village of Ratta Khera.[112] Ganga Singh had received full jurisdiction over Skinner's village in 1906 as part of a land exchange with the Government of India for outlying territories of the Bikaner State in the Deccan.[113] Surrounded on all sides by the maharaja's lands, Ratta Khera nevertheless had been part of the British district of Hissar in the Punjab. Although Skinner retained proprietary rights over the village, he was not at all pleased when government transferred jurisdiction to Bikaner over his ongoing objections, which included a fervently expressed distaste for paying taxes to any sovereign besides the British King-Emperor.[114] By 1909, Skinner's protests expanded to include indignation at having to accommodate the maharaja's hunting parties in and around Ratta Khera.[115] Most Rajput elites experienced mixed feelings ranging from gratification to resentment when called on to host princely shikar. They benefited from close association with royalty and extending hospitality, but their independence suffered when their hunting rights were suspended in anticipation of a sovereign's visit.[116] Skinner's position was not so complex.

In a 1909 notice sent to the government of Bikaner, Skinner professed his supreme right as Ratta Khera's proprietor to prevent anyone

[112] He claimed descent from Col. James Skinner of Skinner's Horse: see Stanley E. Skinner, memorial, to Lord Minto, April 13, 1908, GOI, FD, Internal B, 216–17 of June 1908, NAI.

[113] A. Latif, to W.H.R. Merk, August 27, 1906, GOI, FD, Internal A, 123 of October 1906, NAI.

[114] Skinner, to Minto, April 13, 1908, GOI, FD, Internal B, 216–17 of June 1908, NAI.

[115] Stanley E. Skinner, to RMK Secretary, Bikaner, February 19, 1909, BMK, 292 of 1906–10, RSA.

[116] The Rawat of Salumbar in Mewar received orders to suspend hunting around Seria, Toda, Thara, and Tharora in anticipation of Fateh Singh's 1895 visit: see "Translation of a communication, dated Mangsar Sudi 11, Sambat 1952, from the Foujdar and Kamdar of Salumbar to the Sarara Court," in C.H.A. Hill (MR), to C.C. Watson (First Assistant to AGG-Rajputana), December 23, 1907, GOI, RA, PB, 7 of 1907, NAI.

from shooting in his village without special permission, including Maharaja Ganga Singh. Implementing a tactic also used by the Rajput landed elite in the princely states, Skinner focused his public objections on the inconvenience royal hunts caused his tenants, alleging that state shikaris took Ratta Khera's residents away from their agricultural labors at critical plowing times to serve as unpaid beaters.[117] Focusing on the plight of peasant cultivators, Skinner and his Rajput cohort could obscure their less appealing motivations, including their personal hunting interests. Like other landholders defending their estates, Skinner's objectives probably included a wish to reserve some or all of the symbolic and practical benefits of Ratta Khera's shikar for himself. Judging by the month-long shooting excursion to Tehri-Garhwal State that he enjoyed in 1905, Skinner was as enthusiastic a sportsman as most Rajput nobles.[118] Even if he did not want to keep local sport to himself, he certainly hoped to prevent Ganga Singh from enjoying the village's sovereign perks.

While hardly Bikaner's most promising destination for shikar, Ratta Khera was not without its attractions. State records indicate that Ganga Singh and his guests occasionally did hunt there, although not as often as Skinner alleged.[119] It is unclear exactly what the landscape was like, but it may have resembled portions of the nearby Tibi *pargana* or sub-division, which boasted a "fair growth of trees, Babul, Khejra, etc."[120] Skinner's holding had grasslands good enough to

[117] Skinner, to RMK Secretary, February 19, 1909, BMK, 292 of 1906–10, RSA.

[118] Skinner, to RMK Secretary, May 23, 1905, BMK, 292 of 1906–10, RSA.

[119] The maharaja arranged for Minto's staff to shoot there in 1908: see Ganga Singh, "Instructions for Shooting Arrangements for All Three Sections of H.E. the Viceroy's Visit Programme, 1908," BMK, 926H of 1906–10, RSA. In December 1931, Ganga Singh and guests bagged over 400 imperial sandgrouse, 9 common sandgrouse, 3 duck, 2 snipe, and a demoiselle crane at Ratta Khera; six years later, the maharaja shot 21 duck and a snipe there: see *His Highness' General Shooting Diary*, vol. 2, tables for 1931–2 and 1937–8.

[120] Sadhu Singh, "Report," BMK, 754B of 1906, RSA. Like the Tibi pargana, Ratta Khera was near the Ghaggar Canal: see C.M. King, to T. Gordon Walker, May 6, 1904, GOI, FD, Internal A, 1–39 of June 1905, NAI.

tempt the residents of the nearby Surewala village, whom he accused of grazing cattle in the area.[121] Relatively high-quality vegetation, augmented as it was by the presence of standing water on at least a seasonal basis, might have attracted game.[122] Ratta Khera, in fact, was not far from some of Bikaner's more important shooting preserves. One of the state's best wildfowling locations outside the Gajner region was only a short distance away at Talwara Jheel. Hanumangarh, known for its blackbuck antelope and chinkara gazelle, was close by as well.

Despite the fact that the maharaja almost certainly could have done without Ratta Khera's limited shooting, Ganga Singh and his agents reacted strongly against Skinner's 1909 notice because his attempts to restrict hunting in the village threatened the maharaja's sovereignty. Seeking to determine the legitimacy of Skinner's claim, Ganga Singh's agents contacted an authority in the Punjab for advice on whether a landholder and subject of the Bikaner State "can or cannot assert against his Sovereign such a right."[123] Confident in the assurances they received, and perhaps especially comforted by their counsel's belief that the landholder had no legal recourse besides the maharaja's own courts, Skinner was duly informed that Bikaner shooting regulations applied to Ratta Khera and he could not keep Ganga Singh out.[124]

Restrictions on their own shooting undermined the Rajput elites' attempts to look and act like "little kings" on and off the hunting ground, and so they protested against any and all such princely

---

[121] Skinner, to RMK Secretary, February 19, 1909, BMK, 292 of 1906–10, RSA.

[122] King, to Walker, May 6, 1904, GOI, FD, Internal A, 1–39 of June 1905, NAI.

[123] Brief Statement of the Case, [1910], BMK, 292 of 1906–10, RSA. It was necessary to consult the Punjab because Bikaner was abiding by Punjab Revenue Law in dealing with the transfer.

[124] B. Mattinger, to RD, Bikaner, April 16, 1910, BMK, 292 of 1906–10, RSA; G.D. Rudkin (Revenue Member, Bikaner), to Stanley E. Skinner, January 28, 1919, GOI, FPD, Internal, 4 of July 1919, NAI. Skinner was a source of frustration through his death in 1932: see Political Member, Bikaner, office note, July 12, 1932, BMK, FPD, A053-055 of 1932, RSA.

impositions. In 1937, a consortium of nobles and landholders in Dungarpur State submitted a petition to their sovereign, Maharawal Lakshman Singh (r. 1918–89). In it, they complained that their prince and his predecessor Bijay Singh (r. 1898–1918) had confiscated jungles and cancelled their forest rights, including their freedom to hunt and kill agricultural pests like wild boar and deer.[125] The origins of their dissatisfaction extended back to 1909, when Maharawal Bijay Singh had demarcated the state's 450 square miles of reserved jungles and had instituted a "regular Forest Law ... which put an end to the destruction of ... Sambur, Cheetal and Neelgai."[126] The Dungarpur memorialists insisted that these reforms had been a sham. Bijay Singh had not appropriated their lands in the interests of the state or its people, but with the aim of creating new preserves "as a personal Shikar facility for ... himself." He had confiscated more jungles in 1918 and his successor had done the same as recently as 1936.[127]

It is difficult to determine if these successive maharawals of Dungarpur were attempting to masquerade innovations in game laws and shikargah borders as mere formalizations of established precedents, or if their nobles simply viewed the state's newly gazetted regulations and freshly demarcated boundaries as particularly vulnerable to accusations of novelty, and as uniquely threatening to their own sport, dignity, and status. Representing the Dungarpur nobles in 1937, the well-known attorney M. Asaf Ali declared that his clients asked "only ... for the *Rule of Law*, and the *Security* of their customary and legal rights within the State quite as much as the Princely Order insists on the recognition of their sovereignty in and over the States they rule."[128] Unprecedented changes in forest regulations

[125] M. Asaf Ali, to Lakshman Singh, April 27, 1937, GOI, PD, 425-P of 1938, NAI. For conflicts over Jodhpur forests, see H. Singh, *Colonial Hegemony*, 64.

[126] Diwan, Dungarpur, to Field, November 15, 1928, GOI, SRSA, 261-G of 1928, NAI.

[127] M. Asaf Ali, to Lakshman Singh, April 27, 1937, App. A, item 23–4, App. C, item 3, App. E., item 12, and App. F, item 5B, GOI, PD, 425-P of 1938, NAI.

[128] M. Asaf Ali, to AGG-Rajputana, July 1, 1937, GOI, PD, 425-P of 1938, NAI. Emphasis in the original.

violated these principles. Quite ironically, Indian sovereigns were asking government in the 1920s and 1930s to restore their dignity and powers, even as their nobles accused them of tyranny and oppression in their own states.

The Dungarpur nobles focused many of their protests on the proliferation of dangerous and destructive game that regulations now prevented them from shooting. When a prince or noble exercised clear control, an abundance of wildlife signified power, righteous or otherwise. When game proliferated because a prince or noble was incompetent as a leader, lacked talent as a sportsman, or because a higher authority prevented him from acting, excess could instead suggest impotence. As a result of the 1909 restrictions, Dungarpur State's wild boar and chinkara were "very common indeed," its leopards and nilgai "plentiful," and its sambar, chital, and blackbuck all "increasing" by 1928. Furthermore, Maharawal Lakshman Singh had introduced several tiger cubs into his jungles in an attempt to repopulate the area with this most prized game.[129]

These "improvements" suited the maharawal's interests but did not sit well with state nobles, especially *thikanadars*, who complained they had less control than ever before over wildlife living in and around their estates. Thikanadars were noble landlords holding "permanent and hereditary property rights" granted by Indian princes, who thereby ceded "direct jurisdiction over the land and the people" in *thikana* territories, although they did retain myriad rights and privileges distinct from their thikanadars' special proprietary interests.[130] In Dungarpur, they protested that "the new policy of converting forests belonging to Thikanadars into Preserves and the prohibition to kill wild beasts is resulting in considerable harm … and in many places even in the desertion of cultivable lands by tenants. In some instances wild beasts have actually mauled or killed human beings and cattle."[131] Rajput princes and state nobles alike often

[129] Diwan, Dungarpur, to Field, November 15, 1928, GOI, SRSA, 261-G of 1928, NAI.

[130] H. Singh, *Colonial Hegemony*, 59 and 61.

[131] M. Asaf Ali, to L. Singh, April 27, 1937, item 9, part A, GOI, PD, 425-P of 1938, NAI.

extended their personal sporting facilities at the expense of agriculture and animal husbandry, but they were quick to criticize one another for injuring the people's interests. Lakshman Singh's prime minister insisted in 1937 that no new game preserves had been created in Dungarpur and that it remained permissible for nobles and their tenants alike to kill animals in self-defense or in defense of standing crops.[132] If farmers were unhappy in Dungarpur, he claimed it was not the maharawal's policies that injured them.

Nobles in fact did not object to the mere presence of dangerous or destructive game in or near their estates. They promoted wildlife as far as possible in their own shikargahs and appreciated the merits of these animals as much as princes. Wild boar in particular were "popular" with the nobles, who benefited from hunting and eating them just like their princes and who likewise insisted on preserving them over their cultivators' objections.[133] Nobles primarily resented the existence of wildlife that they could not kill as needed or as desired. Game in the princely states was not the *ferae nature* of European law, but the exclusive preserve of rulers regardless of the animals' peregrinations.[134] A prince's reserved deer, wild boar, and tigers were beyond reach. The sovereign prerogatives embodied in these animals and the ease with which they trespassed on noble lands symbolized a sovereign's might and his subordinates' subjugation.

Acting the part of little kings and struggling to limit their sovereign's shikar in favor of their own, nobles found themselves confronting problems analogous to those their princes faced. Even as nobles objected to the excessive wildlife, infringements on their rights, and over-strict regulations that they associated with royal hunting grounds, petty landholders railed against wildlife in the nobles'

[132] Virbhadra Singh, to PA-SRSA, August 31, 1937, GOI, PD, nos 1–2, file 27(8)-P of 1939, NAI.

[133] D.M. Field, to Secretary to AGG-Rajputana, January 15, 1929, GOI, SRSA, 261-G of 1928, NAI.

[134] Some rulers pushed this principle to claim ownership of animals straying from their realms into neighboring states: see Divyabhanusinh, "Junagadh State and its Lions." Sovereignty over land claimed through a free-ranging animal potentially has roots in the Vedic horse sacrifice.

shikargahs. These zamindars or landholders objected when they saw their tenants' crops destroyed by game invading their fields from nearby estates. Like sovereigns contesting against their immediate subordinates, nobles and lower-ranking zamindars disputed one another's rights and privileges. When zamindars or their agents killed game or broke forest rules, nobles moved to protect their hunting grounds and their shikar in much the same way princes did.

In the Sardargarh thikana of Mewar State, Thakur Laxman Singh's son and successor Amar Singh (r. 1929–82) maintained a shikargah at Seganwas that was a source of tension with the neighboring zamindar of Dovra.[135] There was a border dispute between the zamindar and the Sardargarh thakur, and the contested grounds were situated between Dovra lands and Amar Singh's shikargah.[136] In 1930, Amar Singh complained that Balwant Singh, an agent of the zamindar, had illegally entered the Seganwas reserve to kill a wild boar. According to Balwant Singh the boar had not died in Sardargarh. Instead, he had killed one of the many animals from Seganwas that habitually invaded Dovra to feed in the zamindar's agricultural fields.[137] The precise location of the boar's death would remain disputed, but if the zamindar did violate the boundaries and rules of the Seganwas shikargah through his agent, then he temporarily asserted both his version of the border and the right to defend his crops over Amar Singh's interests.

Every Rajput prince, nobleman, and landholder had to balance the desire for wild boar against the need for crops and income. It appears that the higher ranking a Rajput, the more likely he was to promote game at the expense of agriculture, so that princes were the least interested in reducing game, nobles were somewhat more inclined towards doing so, and so on. Those at the top drew their income from the widest resource base. Their risk was spread thin

[135] This Amar Singh should not to be confused with the Rajput nobleman and diarist.

[136] MMK, to Amar Singh, order 18422, [*c.* 1939], file 32, doc. 2, Sardargarh *basta* 24, PSP.

[137] Ungar Singh, to Amar Singh, *pos sud 5 samvat 1987*, file 69, doc. 3, Sardargarh *basta* 30, PSP.

and they would have suffered little from the loss of one or two fields. Because lesser elites relied on fewer fields, the loss of one or two would represent a larger percentage of their income. Particularly low-ranking individuals like the zamindar of Dovra, with very little land to their name, would have been strongly biased towards protecting their fields and much more hostile to wild boar than comfortably situated nobles like the thakur of Sardargarh.

Precedents were as much a factor in disputes between zamindars and nobles as between nobles and princes. In 1939, the zamindars of Siyana, Sirohi, and Sumariya too complained about Amar Singh's Seganwas shikargah. Specifically, they alleged that the Sardargarh thakur had established several new shikargahs at the site. They argued that these hunting grounds were unprecedented and therefore illegitimate, and that the presence of wild boar in the area was an indefensible innovation. Previously there had been no such animals in Seganwas. Amar Singh, they claimed, had introduced the pests from some other place. Now wild boar damaged crops to such an extent that the landholders declared they could no longer realize so much as a handful of grain from their fields. They also alleged that they had lost valuable grazing grounds to the new shikargahs and faced punishment if they took their cattle into areas that had always been open to them before.[138]

The zamindars' complaints reached Mewar State authorities at Rajnagar and Udaipur, leading Revenue Department officials to demand that Amar Singh prove the antiquity of his Seganwas hunting grounds.[139] Additional shikargahs hurt cultivators, whose interests the rulers of Mewar claimed to defend against the cupidity of their nobles.[140] If the shikargah was new in 1939, then it violated not just the zamindars' interests but Mewar State's as well. Almost a decade earlier in 1928, Fateh Singh had issued an order that acknowledged the legitimacy of his nobles' existing shikargahs while making it

[138] MMK, to Amar Singh, order 18422, [*c.* 1939], file 32, doc. 2, Sardargarh *basta* 24, PSP.

[139] T. Sinha, MMK, to Amar Singh, April 2, 1940, file 32, doc. 24, Sardargarh *basta* 24, PSP.

[140] F. Singh, to Lord Reading, *c.* 1924, pp.15–16, acc. no. 27262, MMSL.

illegal for them to establish any more hunting grounds or grass reserves in their estates.[141] He suspected that his nobles attempted to
arrogate unprecedented rights and privileges to themselves when
they expanded their shikargahs, and so he moved to stop them. Fateh
Singh's policies, and apparently his suspicions, continued under
Maharana Bhupal Singh.

Suddenly required to defend Seganwas not just from hostile zamindars but from a skeptical government too, Amar Singh called on
his employees and thikana residents to attest to the antiquity of his
shikargah and the long-standing presence of wild boar in the area. In
depositions intended for the state authorities at nearby Rajnagar, a
50-year-old servant of Sardargarh named Raj Singh insisted that
Seganwas had been reserved throughout his lifetime, as did a 60-
year-old thikana employee named Man Singh.[142] One Sardargarh
official contended that the place had been established in 1863.[143]
As for wildlife, Man Singh said that wild boar had always lived there
and none had been introduced into the shikargah.[144] Unwittingly
echoing Fateh Singh's response to the analogous complaints of
people from the Magra and Girwa districts regarding wildlife at Nahar
Magra in 1921, Raj Singh added that around Seganwas "there used
to be lots of wild boars, but nowadays there are few."[145] The only restrictions the men admitted any knowledge of were against cutting
green trees and killing game. The rules were old, they claimed, and
local villagers were as free as ever to graze their cattle in the reserve.

When Amar Singh and his subordinates upheld the antiquity of
Seganwas and its population of boar, they used the rule of precedent

[141]The order was published in Circular 15081 of October 8, 1928, as
referenced in MMK, to Amar Singh, Order 18422, [*c.* 1939], file 32, doc. 2,
Sardargarh *basta* 24, PSP.

[142]Raj Singh, deposition, April 6, 1939, file 32, doc. 5, Sardargarh *basta*
24, PSP; Man Singh, deposition, April 7, 1939, file 32, doc. 4, Sardargarh
basta 24, PSP.

[143]Office note, April 8, 1939, file 32, doc. 7, Sardargarh *basta* 24, PSP.

[144]Man Singh, deposition, April 7, 1939, file 32, doc. 4, Sardargarh *basta*
24, PSP.

[145]Raj Singh, deposition, April 6, 1939, file 32, doc. 5, Sardargarh *basta*
24, PSP. My translation.

to support the greater rights and privileges of the Sardargarh thikana and its thakur over Siyana, Sirohi, Sumariya, and their zamindars. When Mewar State officials cited Fateh Singh's rule against new shikargahs, they in turn reminded Amar Singh that his own status and powers were subordinate to those claimed by the maharanas of Mewar on the basis of longstanding precedent, as formalized by the 1928 order against establishing new shikargahs. Neither princes nor nobles were inclined towards limiting their personal shikar facilities. By citing precedents and positioning themselves as putative protectors of the people, they instead tried to force one another to retrench. Princes insisted that their shikargahs, their wild boar, and their tigers were not the problem so much as their subordinates' hunting grounds and game. Princes believed nobles and landholders were less disciplined, less powerful, and less securely linked to the interests of the people through a sense of zimmedari.[146] Nobles supposedly were "lethargic, steeped in debt, backward and oppressive to their tenants ... The only thing that matters to them is their fancied rights and privileges."[147] Zamindars were no better. Princes claimed they themselves were the people's only true champions. The princely monopoly over big game subordinated lesser elites, reinforcing the princes' self-image as righteous sovereigns controlling wild animals. But when problems arose, it was easier to blame their purportedly unrighteous and unprincipled nobles and landholders than accept personal responsibility. Caught in the middle and beset by troublesome wildlife, state subjects did their best to defend themselves and their interests by submitting petitions and, occasionally, breaking forest and game laws.

Wild boar, ruminants, leopards, and tigers caused the most trouble. According to Tanwar, wild boar were second only to rats in the degree to which they damaged cultivation. While they lived only twenty-five

[146] I follow Gold and Gujar's definition: see *In the Time of Trees and Sorrows*, 252.

[147] Virbhadra Singh, to PA-SRSA, August 31, 1937, GOI, PD, nos 1–2, file 27(8)-P of 1939, NAI. The letter further maligns them as "hot headed drunk sodden jagirdars." British observers agreed nobles cared only for "their own interests:" office note, April 12, 1939, GOI, PD, nos 1–2, file 27(8)-P of 1939, NAI.

to thirty years, "in that time they troubled people up to the level of a hundred years."[148] Cultivators found it nearly impossible to keep them out of agricultural fields.[149] Wild boar could force their way through fences constructed from thorny brush. Earthen walls tended to disintegrate. Equally responsible for spoiling crops, nilgai and blackbuck were capable of jumping over most barriers. As the villagers of Bundelkhand's Lughasi estate insisted, most "wild animals were so fearless that on a blank charge being fired they ran only a few paces and began to graze again on the crops."[150]

Hoping to defend his sovereign's shikar facilities in 1928, the Maharawal of Dungarpur's prime minister contended that farmers could keep game out of their fields simply by "making a rambling [*sic*] noise with an empty kerosene oil tin with a few stones in it, or [by] putting up dummies."[151] Official representations from other states claimed that blank shots—presumably in concert with night-watchmen and due vigilance—were more than enough.[152] There could be no excuse for shooting royal prey if dissuading game from damaging crops was so easy. A published authority on the topic, David Clouston, agreed that loud noise could startle wild animals, but he countered that a moment's inattention gave them all the opportunity they needed to destroy entire fields.[153] Contrary to princely propaganda, wild boar, like deer and antelope, were quite simply "Foes of the Farmer."

[148] Tanwar, *Shikari aur Shikar*, 12.

[149] The best barrier was a 4 ft. fence of 3 in. wire mesh, with its lower edge sunk deep into the ground: see David Clouston, *Some Foes of the Farmer in the Central Provinces and How the [sic] Deal with Them* (Nagpur: Government Press, 1928), 1.

[150] Kamdar, Lughasi, to PA-Bundelkhand, September 11, 1928, GOI, CI, BA, 582 of 1910, NAI.

[151] Diwan, Dungarpur, to Field, November 15, 1928, GOI, SRSA, 261-G of 1928, NAI.

[152] *Rules for the Regulation of Hunting, Shooting and Fishing in Bundi State* (Bundi: Srirangnath Press, 1939); *Rules for the Regulation of Shooting in the Jaipur State* (Jaipur: 1931).

[153] Clouston, *Some Foes*, 1. Clouston was Deputy Director of Agriculture, Southern Circle, CP.

Tigers and leopards could pose more immediate threats to people's lives. Numerous petitions recorded their travails with big cats in Mewar in the 1930s and 1940s during Bhupal Singh's reign. In a 1938 appeal, residents of the Bhilwara district complained that several tigers had killed at least 2 men and some 900 cattle.[154] A few years later, the "poor public of Rajnagar" near the royal hunting grounds at Rajsamand sought protection from leopards that were "harassing [them] like anything."[155] Official responses were not always prompt. The 1938 complainants from Bhilwara alleged that despite their having made numerous representations, the people had been given no proper hearing.[156] The authors of a 1939 petition claimed they had submitted their complaint about a tiger killing their cattle, bullocks, camels, and goats several times, but the state had done nothing.[157]

Most shooting laws actually did allow state residents to kill animals in self-defense or in defense of their property. Any tiger found attacking people or domestic animals in Rewah could be "killed on the spot."[158] Cultivators in Fateh Singh's Mewar could pursue wild boar that invaded their fields.[159] In Chhatarpur, the mere threat of damage to life or property theoretically provided sufficient justification.[160] Princes and their representatives cited these laws when responding to complaints lodged by their subjects, or when defending local practices to the British. The people, however, do not seem to have credited such pledges of immunity. In Jaipur State, the maharaja's subjects reportedly believed in the 1930s that anyone who killed

[154] Hakim of Bhilwara, to MMK, February 1938, MJ-Shikar, 20/1 of 1937, RSA.

[155] "Poor public of Rajnagar," to Prime Minister, Mewar, [*c.* 1940], MJ-Shikar, 20/2 of 1940, RSA.

[156] Hakim of Bhilwara, to MMK, February 1938, MJ-Shikar, 20/1 of 1937, RSA.

[157] Chunilal Bisnoi, to MMK, *pos sud 11 samvat 1995*, MJ-Shikar, 20/1 of 1937, RSA.

[158] Secretary to Maharaja of Rewah, to PA-Baghelkhand, July 12, 1910, GOI, CI, Baghelkhand Agency, 261 of 1909, NAI.

[159] Tanwar, *Samsmaran*, 51.

[160] Rai Bahadur Pandit Sukhdeo Behari Misra (Diwan, Chhatarpur), to PA-Bundelkhand, August 23, 1928, GOI, BA, General Branch, 81-D of 1928, NAI.

an animal to save his own life would "have to stand his trial ... [and] to escape conviction under the plea of self-defense is difficult, if not impossible."[161]

Princes were reluctant to protect their subjects from desirable game when doing so meant that they or their guests might forfeit the pleasures and advantages of shooting the animals themselves. Cultivators living within a ten-mile radius of Jaipur city, where Maharaja Sawai Man Singh II (r. 1922–70) could most conveniently take guests to hunt when time was short, found shikarkhana employees insufficiently sympathetic in the late 1930s.[162] Jaipur shikaris allegedly refused to issue the permits people needed to destroy especially troublesome or dangerous wildlife because the animals were wanted for sport.[163] The situation in Mewar was analogous when it came to especially prized game like tigers. Responding to a 1943 complaint about a big cat near his royal hunting grounds at Chittor, Bhupal Singh instructed local authorities to kill the animal without delay if it was a leopard, but do nothing more than report back if it was found to be a tiger.[164]

Killing tigers and other big game in self-defense or for the protection of property was not illegal in Mewar, but it was discouraged. The letter of the law as late as the 1940s required subjects to report animals that had become "a danger to human life or cattle" to government authorities, who could then depute a local official or shikarkhana officer to take care of the problem.[165] Subjects found to have slain wild animals with good reason were not punished, but

[161] Jaipurian (pseud.), letter to the editor, *Hindustan Times*, July 25, 1939.

[162] "Tragedy of Forest Laws. A Harrowing Tale. Destruction of Life and Crops by Wild Beasts," *Hindustan Times*, July 24, 1939; Jaipurian (pseud.), letter to the editor, *Hindustan Times*, July 25, 1939.

[163] At least one Jaipur shikari considered state regulations "too strict:" see Kesri Singh, *Hunting with Horse and Spear* (New Delhi: Hindustan Times, 1963), 38.

[164] Bhupal Singh, January 6, 1943, MJ-Shikar, s. no. 629, file 20/1 of 1942, RSA.

[165] *Rules made under the Mewar Game and Fish Preservation Act* (Udaipur: 1942). Tanwar was among those sent to kill "problem" animals: see R. Trivedi, office note, July 2, 1941, MJ-Shikar, 20/2 of 1940, RSA; see also Tanwar, *Shikari aur Shikar*, 149.

investigations into self-defense killings were common.[166] Full-blown inquiries that focused unprecedented and possibly hostile attention on a village and obliged bystanders and character witnesses to record official depositions at the local police station may have left state subjects intimidated and skeptical of protective laws. Restricted access to suitable firearms augmented these deterrents. In practice, most shooting violations instead involved state nobles or better-positioned landholders, whose income and lives were less on the line than their dignity and privileges.[167]

It did not help that princes worried their subjects' self-defensive exploits might be acts of insubordination in disguise. The historical connections princes drew between prolific game, idyllic hunting grounds, and broader powers received reinforcement beginning in the early 1920s as *praja mandals* or people's associations formed in the states and started pushing for governmental and other reforms.[168] These groups initially asked for expanded recruitment of state subjects into government employment, wider civil liberties, and the establishment of representative assemblies. By the late 1920s, they were agitating for popular elections, restrictions on princely autocracy, and a decisive shift in spending away from activities like shikar and towards education and hospitals. Although praja mandal operatives did not question princely legitimacy *per se*, they did seek checks and balances on their powers. Royal involvement with wildlife now received increased scrutiny.

Princes blamed praja mandals, nationalist agitators, and troublemakers from British India when protests arose in their states against excessive wildlife or oppressive forest regulations. In some cases, there clearly was a connection. Condemnations of Jaipur State shooting regulations that appeared in the *Hindustan Times* in 1939 included

[166] For examples, see MJ-Shikar, No 20/1 of 1939, RSA, and MJ-Shikar, 20/6 of 1939, RSA; see also office note re: events of April 22, 1941 [July 1941], MJ-Shikar, 20/2 of 1940, RSA.

[167] For examples, see H. Khoda, August 11, 1940, 20/2 of 1939, RSA; see also MJ-Shikar, 20/3 of 1942, RSA.

[168] On praja mandals and their demands, I rely on Ramusack, *The Indian Princes*, 221–2.

a statement issued by Radha Krishnan Bajaj, who described himself as a convener of the Jaipur Satyagraha Council. In concert with a local praja mandal member named Badri Narayan Khora, Bajaj claimed to have gathered "first-hand information regarding ... the severity of the forest and Shikar laws" after hearing "reports regarding the havoc ... caused by the wild animals."[169] While Bajaj implied that the origins of the Jaipur complaints were local and that he had involved himself only upon receiving "reports," British officials and probably the maharaja as well questioned the authenticity of the protests. They believed unrepresentative, out-of-state, or transparently prejudiced sources, like newspaper reporters and praja mandals, had manufactured local discontent.[170] Had this not been the case, they insisted, the people of Jaipur would have remained content and artificial pressures would not have forced the maharaja into easing game regulations a few weeks after Bajaj's story appeared in the *Times*.[171]

Although princes and some government officials looked to British India in their efforts to trace the origins of disturbances in the states in the 1920s and 1930s, they disagreed on how disruptive forces gained entrance. Englishmen asserted that maladministration and unsatisfactory conditions in the states invited problems, and claimed it was the princes' duty to defend their borders. Deflecting responsibility onto the British, princes countered that containment was primarily the government's responsibility.[172]

A strong conviction that modern disturbances represented a break with the past reinforced princely impressions that their troubles were foreign in origin. Rajput rulers could cite precedents proving to their own satisfaction that despite occasional unrest, state nobles and subjects had once been more docile. In former times, state resi-

---

[169] "Tragedy of Forest Laws," *Hindustan Times*, July 24, 1939.

[170] Office note, July 28, 1939, GOI, RA, 175-P of 1939, NAI.

[171] Jaipur PD notification 12139-G/G-17-21, *Jaipur Gazette*, August 9, 1939, 175-P of 1939.

[172] Even when state nobles or landholders agitated against them, princes blamed "outside influences:" see Arthur Cunningham Lothian (Resident, Rajputana), to secretary to Crown Representative, March 20, 1939, GOI, PD, nos 1-2, file 27(8)-P of 1939, NAI. See also Ramusack, *Indian Princes*, 221.

dents had responded properly to the messages sent by well-stocked shikargahs and their sovereign's heroic achievements within hunting grounds. Serious agitations against wild boar and transgressions against forest laws were without precedent. Their origins were to be found in British India and in alien modern times.

Like the subjects of other Rajput states, the Mewari people did concede their sovereign's right to first-class shikar facilities. They even celebrated their prince's sporting successes.[173] They believed in the power of wild animals and wild places and wanted their ruler and state to reap the benefits of contact with potent natural forces. But they rebelled when hard times multiplied their problems or when the sheer quantity of wildlife tipped the scales from being a perceived advantage to an unbearable imposition. This was the case in Mewar in 1921, when Fateh Singh's subjects rose up in protest against rising prices, indebtedness, unreasonable taxation, the "feudal oppression" of state nobles, and unpaid compulsory labor, which was often associated with royal sport.[174] Many of their problems were compounded by strict game and forest regulations. The maharana's exclusive shikargahs and reserved wildlife bore the brunt of their demonstrations.

In the months leading up to the 1921 uprisings, Mewari residents living in the vicinity of state shikargahs had complained about an overabundance of wild boar and excessively restrictive forest use rules, which prevented them from clearing brush that harbored pig.[175] Unsatisfied by the precedents their maharana quoted and angered by his failure to respond at all in some cases, the aggrieved began attacking royal shikargahs. They demonstrated inside the borders of Fateh Singh's favorite preserves, cutting down trees and bushes, and killing wild boar at Nahar Magra, Kamlod ka Magra, and elsewhere. Apparently intending to heighten the impact of their message, they timed their initial disturbances at Nahar Magra to coincide with a

[173] For a royal hunt commemorated in song, see Tanwar, *Shikari aur Shikar*, 65–7.

[174] Hari Sen, "The Maharana and the Bhils: The 'Eki' Movement in Mewar, 1921–22," in *India's Princely States*, ed. Ernst and Pati, 157–8. On *begar* and shikar, see Gold and Gujar, *In the Time of Trees and Sorrows*, 84.

[175] Orders passed on Magra District petition, pp.23–8, and order 18320, October 12, 1921, pp.52–71, acc. no. 27262, MMSL.

royal shooting excursion there on July 6, 1921.[176] His sovereignty at stake, Fateh Singh grew desperate to quell the demonstrations and protect his reserves.[177]

Throughout the crisis, the maharana continued to insist that his subjects' first recourse against wild boar ought always to be defensive rather than offensive. One official announcement, intriguingly issued under Bhupal Singh's name rather than Fateh Singh's, informed zamindars and cultivators that they should keep pig at bay by collecting masses of spiny thuhar plants to build strong yet inexpensive fences around their fields. The announcement, however, forbade them from harvesting the generally larger and more robust *hathi* or elephant thuhar that grew on *khalsa* lands, instead directing them to cut only those thuhar that grew near their villages. If wild boar and thorny thuhar had to make way for cultivation, then Mewar's royal family would do their best to halt the forced retreat at the village lines.[178]

Fateh Singh's interpretation of the 1921 uprisings predictably placed the blame on external forces, which he believed had invaded his state to force an unwarranted break with the past. He insisted that "the words Satyagraha and non-co-operation took their rise elsewhere, and neither I nor my subjects ever knew them until they were imported into my State from outside."[179] In the maharana's view, Mewaris had not protested in former times even when there had been many more wild boar.[180] They had accepted the untold number of *ekal*, sows, and piglets that once had flourished under Sarup Singh, Shambhu Singh, and Sangram Singh II.[181] While Fateh Singh no doubt understood that even modest numbers of wildlife could cause problems, he insisted that the hardships cultivators faced were

---

[176] F. Singh, to Lord Reading, *c.* 1924, p.5, acc. no. 27262, MMSL.

[177] Fateh Singh even requested permission to deploy the Mewar Bhil Corps: see ibid., 4–5.

[178] Gaurisankara Hiracanda Ojha, *Udayapura Rajya ka Itihasa*, vol. 2 (Jodhpur: Rajasthani Granthagar, 2006), 853–4.

[179] F. Singh, to Lord Reading, *c.* 1924, p.10, acc. no. 27262, MMSL.

[180] Order 18320, October 12, 1921, sub-order 2, p.58, acc. no. 27262, MMSL.

[181] Ibid., sub-order 1, p.52, and sub-order 2, p.57.

not unprecedented and that his subjects suffered less than their ancestors. In making this argument, he ignored the possibility that fewer pigs could cause more problems if, for example, they competed with relatively more people and relatively less land lay fallow.

After the British forced Fateh Singh to devolve many of his powers onto his heir in the wake of these uprisings, the maharana may have been even more likely to correlate contracting jungles and declining wildlife with disturbing reductions in his sovereign control. "Nobody could kill a pig" in the old days, but in 1921 Fateh Singh's subjects slaughtered his game, violated his shikargahs, and cut his trees.[182] Times had once been better, his predecessors' powers more secure, and game more prolific. No one had dared shoot in the royal preserves a century ago, not even in the midst of Bhim Singh's troubled reign.[183] As recently as the 1870s, "royal edicts of the most severe nature" still had prevented anyone from hunting in reserved grounds.[184]

Fateh Singh and other Rajput rulers may have avoided taking full responsibility for problems in their states, but perhaps they were not wholly selfish in attempting to protect their personal powers and hunting interests. Admitted problems aside, royal shikar in the normal course of events was thought to benefit the people as well as the princes. In the late-nineteenth and early-twentieth centuries, "environmental well-being" in Rajput princely states came at a cost to some, but "resulted in recognizable ecological common good."[185] Rulers saw the benefits of autocracy in their states' landscapes and, rightly or wrongly, valued the advantages of denser forests, greener plains, and increased wildlife as much, and sometimes more, than their subjects' more personal and transient concerns.

[182] Ibid., sub-order 2, p.58, acc. no. 27262.
[183] Tod, *Annals*, 1:265.
[184] Rousselet, *India and its Native Princes*, 172.
[185] Gold and Gujar, *In the Time of Trees and Sorrows*, 259.

7

Leaving the Garden

The Maharajkumar Sadul Singh of Bikaner recorded a passing thought in his private game diary in 1926 that many colonial sportsmen—including Fateh Singh of Mewar, Pratap Singh of Orchha, his own father, and most Englishmen—would have deemed unconventional, even heretical: "if a real good stag or a large [leopard] or bear turned up soon after the commencement of the beat and before the tiger appeared, I think it would be worthwhile every time to have a shot."[1] With these words, Ganga Singh's youthful heir accepted the risk that premature rifle fire would turn a tiger away from his machan, or even out of the beat. The relative worth he ascribed to good stags, leopards, and bears was atypical, but his sentiments accurately convey the possibilities, explored in this book, of identifying distinction within a diverse array of species in princely India.

Sadul Singh's evaluations of game were logical progressions from his father's campaigns on behalf of Bikaner's sandgrouse and blackbuck. But they also suggest that princely shikar participated in the global trend away from rifles and towards cameras, associated in India with F.W. Champion and Jim Corbett in his later days, and throughout the empire with the SPFE's "penitent butchers." An enthusiastic sportsman who racked up numerous tigers and ventured to British Kenya and the Tanganyika Territory for African trophies too, Bikaner's

[1] Sadul Singh, *Big Game Diary*, 81.

maharajkumar was also a keen photographer. Sadul Singh (b. 1902) and his generational peers—especially the tiger-breeding Lakshman Singh (b. 1908) of Dungarpur—mark the tentative beginnings of an altered environmental consciousness in the Indian states, one that remained princely, but which became more cosmopolitan.[2]

Sporting rifles and shikargahs have now given way to cameras and wildlife sanctuaries, but heritage hotels run by royal Rajputs in their old palaces and hunting retreats preserve nostalgic traces of princely ecology and grand shikar.[3] Tourists who stay to visit nearby protected areas may view wildlife from former shooting boxes, as at Gajner Palace where scores of wildfowling butts still line the margins of the lake. They may book rooms decorated in tiger-stripes, like the Tiger Suite at Aodhi Hotel near Kumbhalgarh. They may enter lobbies adorned with taxidermy and shikar photography, as at Sariska Palace in the former Alwar State. Of course, not all princely hotels offer such amenities. At Bundelkhand Riverside, historical connections with Orchha State shikar are acknowledged but not stressed.[4] The old hunting lodge quietly serves as staff quarters. Guests are free to roam the grounds, but no established pathways or signage draw attention to the paintings of royal sport inside one isolated chhatri. There are no hunting photographs or trophies, and no themed guestrooms.

The high profile of Rajput princes even today, combined with their aggressive entry into the luxury hotel and ecotourism trades from the late 1950s, provides space for the continuing influence of their forefathers' environmental ideals. When the Rajput states first became popular destinations in the late-nineteenth century, British and American tourists aspired to "sample elements of an aristocratic way of life," including tiger shikar, ostentatiously enjoyed in India by touring European royalty.[5] Today, tourists hope to experience "the

[2] On cosmopolitan tigers, see Jalais, *Forest of Tigers*, 196–201.

[3] Taxidermy orders placed with the popular Van Ingen & Van Ingen dropped below 1000 per year by 1940, below 500 by 1970, and below 100 by 1975: see Morris, *Van Ingen & Van Ingen*, 106.

[4] "The Retreat," Bundelkhand Riverside, accessed March 14, 2012, http://www.bundelkhandriverside.com.

[5] Barbara N. Ramusack, "The Indian Princes as Fantasy: Palace Hotels,

glorious past of Rajput history and live like modern-day royalty," by staying in palace hotels once visited by Queen Elizabeth II and the Shah of Iran, or by popular celebrities such as Mick Jagger and Madonna (Lake Palace, Udaipur), or Amitabh Bachchan, Kareena Kapoor, and Dharmendra (Lallgarh Palace, Bikaner).[6]

But living fantastical Rajput pasts while indulging in modern luxuries requires isolation from disturbing facts including poverty and disease, resource scarcity (especially water and electricity), industrial development, and environmental degradation. Today's "tourists do not come to India seeking examples of modernization in the Third World; they do not want to tour the petrochemical complexes of Baroda-Vadodara or the electronic industry of Bangalore (Mysore). They seek culture and nature tourism, and the Rajput princes … have been ready to provide it."[7] Foreign tourists—and domestic ones too—expect cosmopolitan tigers on display in well-protected jungles and princely beasts mounted on the wall, with perpetual snarls curling their lips.

Looking to another field of historical European imperialism, it has been argued that "new scripts must be introduced into the global imagination of African nature, ones that replace colonial narratives of Western exploration of unspoiled, Eden-like landscapes with more realistic visions of actual African environments in their full, historical, inhabited complexity." Rather than offering opportunities "to reenact a colonial hunting safari—to be precise, the colonial safari depicted in the Hollywood blockbuster *Out of Africa*, in which Robert Redford and Meryl Streep memorably viewed wildlife in between eating gourmet meals and flirting with each other while a

---

Palace Museums, and Palace on Wheels," in *Consuming Modernity: Public Culture in a South Asian World*, ed. Carol A. Breckenridge (Minneapolis: University of Minnesota Press, 1995), 70.

[6] Ibid., 77; "India's Famous Lake Palace Hotel Loses its Lake," *The Telegraph*, July 14, 2009, http://www.telegraph.co.uk/archive/; "Guest Comments," Lallgarh Palace, accessed March 24, 2012, http://www.lallgarhpalace.com/guest_comments.htm.

[7] Ramusack, "Princes as Fantasy," 76.

fleet of crisply uniformed African servants attended to their needs," African ecotourism should challenge cosmopolitan viewpoints and global inequities, while consciously eschewing the unsustainable norms of elite consumption.[8]

Unlike African experiences, ecotourism in India is as likely to recall the exploits of colonized elites, including Maharana Fateh Singh and (beyond the Rajputs) Maharaja Madhav Rao Scindia of Gwalior, as those of colonial figures like Jim Corbett and Lord Hardinge (or Hollywood characters like Indiana Jones). Romanticized princely pasts coexist, overlap, and compete with romanticized Anglo-Indian and American ones, allowing tourists a variety of prefabricated fantasy templates to map themselves onto. Understanding the potential impact of these popular modes of experiencing Indian environments and wildlife is a precondition of making conservation work in the subcontinent.

This imperative is more obvious when we recognize that nearly every national park and wildlife sanctuary in Rajasthan State was once a princely hunting ground, from the famous tiger reserves of Ranthambor (Jaipur) and Sariska (Alwar) to the sanctuaries at Gajner (Bikaner), Mukundara (Kotah), Sitamata (Partabgarh), and Sajjangarh, Jaisamand, Kumbhalgarh, and Bhainsrorgarh (Mewar). Some Madhya Pradesh protected areas have similar pasts, including Madhav (Gwalior), Bandhavgarh (Rewah), and the eponymous Orchha Wildlife Sanctuary. In addition, select princely descendants have supported, participated in, or provided leadership for postcolonial wildlife conservation, including the Rajput ecologists M.K. Ranjitsinh of Wankaner and R.S. Dharmakumarsinh of Bhavnagar. Even granting that the persistence of vulnerable wildlife in India is the result of "more than just princely protection," the history of princely interests and influences should not be ignored.[9] Identifying the local ideals, hierarchies, and assumptions that historically underpinned

[8] Elizabeth Garland, "The Elephant in the Room: Confronting the Colonial Character of Wildlife Conservation in Africa," *African Studies Review* 51, 3 (2008): 68–9.

[9] Vasant K. Saberwal, Mahesh Rangarajan, and Ashish Kothari, *People, Parks and Wildlife: Towards Coexistence* (New Delhi: Orient Longman, 2000), 34.

influential elite interests in, uses of, and interactions with animals and environments may be a vital step towards sustainability in the present.

Because so many protected areas were once royal shikargahs, many people living in and around today's parks and sanctuaries are the descendants of princely subjects. Their opinions and practices reflect this specific heritage, and Gold and Gujar have documented lingering impacts on the environmental memories and views of former subjects of the Rajput polity of Sawar.[10] Far from being entirely modern phenomena, today's concerns over biomass extraction, poaching, and the aptness of government policies and conservation truisms that demand resettlement of protected area residents have princely antecedents too, confirming that controversy and special interests are nothing new in the forest. One historian of conservation recently noted the "brutal history" of Sariska, an Alwar State shikargah whose last rulers privileged their personal investments in shikar and state revenue over what would now be regarded as considerations of environmental justice. They forced nomadic pastoralists out while moving tax-paying villagers in, replaced usufruct rights with costly permits, and introduced lucrative commercial felling. Some villages now subject to resettlement were, in fact, introduced to the area by Alwar's most infamous prince, Maharaja Jaisingh (r. 1892–1937).[11]

Uncertain of "arbitrary changes" in the rules and suspicious of outsiders using "political pressure" to gain illegal access to local resources—and thereby damaging the park more than villagers do—Sariska's residents today "cut large branches rather than leaves, in haste, fearing discovery by forest personnel." And yet, unlike outsiders, Sariska's residents claim "emotional attachment" to the forest.[12] Akin to Rajput sovereigns from the relatively benign prince of Sawar through the notoriously unpopular Jaisingh of Alwar, these people experience a sense of zimmedari towards their environment,

---

[10] Gold and Gujar, *In the Time of Trees and Sorrows.*

[11] Ghazala Shahabuddin, *Conservation at the Crossroads: Science, Society and the Future of India's Wildlife* (Ranikhet: Permanent Black, 2010), 13 and 16.

[12] Ibid., 39–41.

which present conditions dissuade them from acting on. If popular and official conceptions of wilderness can adjust to incorporate a constitutive human presence rooted in zimmedari—a defining feature of princely ecology—then a model of parks with people, rather than the dominant and troubled conservation paradigm of parks without people, could become a natural condition. Combined with careful attention to environmental justice, this could make conservation more feasible.

Beyond the pressing issues of conservation and environmental justice, political and social engagement with animals and the environment have continued and, if anything, grown in importance since India's independence in 1947. This is evident in the efforts of the Hindu Right to promote "saffronization" or the adoption of pure and ancient Aryan traditions—including vegetarianism and cow protection—while subordinating or eliminating cultural elements identified as Muslim, Western, or otherwise allegedly un-Indian and undesirable. The chief minister of Gujarat State, Narendra Modi, promoted indigenous horse breeds at the 11th Mega Kama Horse Show and Equestrian Meet in 2008, and has obstructed conservationists' efforts to establish and populate a "second home" beyond Gujarat for critically endangered Gir lions. He is representative of a trend encouraging regional identity and pride.[13] Routinely criticized for chauvinism and anti-Muslim politics, this vegetarian chief minister has also presided over the passage of a Gujarat Animal Preservation (Amendment) Bill, increasing the penalty for cow-slaughter from six-months' imprisonment or a Rs 1000 fine to seven years or Rs 50,000.[14]

Ahimsa (non-violence) and vegetarianism are Aryan and therefore Hindu and therefore Indian; hunting, meat-eating, and other kinds of improperly motivated violence are not, making foreigners out of Muslims and national heretics out of non-vegetarian non-Muslims. The latter category includes a significant proportion of Scheduled

[13] "Modi Pitches for Horse Breeding as a Full-Fledged Industry," *Indian Express*, December 28, 2008, http://www.indianexpress.com/live-archives/.

[14] "Gujarat Assembly Passes Bill on Cow Slaughter," *The Hindu*, September 27, 2011, http://www.thehindu.com/navigation/?type=static&page=archive.

Castes and Scheduled Tribes, but potentially embraces modern and historical Rajputs as well. That is, unless recent blockbuster films can wipe the stain of princely shikar from popular memories: a pivotal scene in Ashutosh Gowariker's wildly popular *Lagaan* (2001) has one Raja Puran Singh forcefully intoning "I—am—a—vegetarian" (never mind the trophies inside his palace) to a hostile British agent offering up slices of meat. In case audiences miss the point, the film's hero Bhuvan (a commoner who accomplishes what the noble but helpless prince cannot by beating the colonizers at their own game of cricket) is portrayed as a rogue known for sabotaging British shoots.

These popular and political battles over Indian identity, along with domestic and international pressure to preserve endangered species and vulnerable ecosystems, have put contemporary descendants of Rajput princes in a difficult position. Prominent individuals like Arvind Singh Mewar and Rajyashree Kumari of Bikaner manage public opinion by carefully packaging or limiting reference to their personal and family pasts as sportsmen and sportswomen. As high-profile hoteliers also chairing their houses' charitable foundations, these two strike a delicate balance between their identities as royal Rajputs and modern Indians, their personal beliefs and civic duties, and the obvious allure that princely shikar and elite opulence hold for their foreign and domestic clientele. Both nurture vestiges of princely ecology in their present-day charitable interests and activities.

According to Arvind Singh Mewar, his duty as the "76th custodian" of the house of Mewar is to strive for "holistic sustainability; cultural, environmental, social, and economic," such that his brief includes "protecting the lakes, water bodies, and environment created" by his ancestors. In practice, he focuses less on the Mewari flora, fauna, and hills that Fateh Singh valued, and more on the region's man-made lakes, heroic history, and mythological origins. His intention of making Lake Pichola and the City Palace "fossil fuel-free" through solar energy is particularly suited to his family's *surya-vamsha* lineage.[15] Khas Odi and

[15] "Message from the 7cv. 6th Custodian" and "Focus Areas: Environment," Eternal Mewar, accessed March 24, 2012, http://www.eternalmewar.in/about/index.aspx.

the Nahar Magra palace, on the other hand, remain undeveloped and off-limits to the public. Yet, family snapshots show Arvind Singh—often in a Mewari or other hilly landscape—shooting crocodile, wild boar, blackbuck, leopard, and perhaps even tiger as a youth in the 1950s and 1960s. Clearly retaining an interest in Indian wildlife, he recently hosted and chaired a meeting of the Cheetah Reintroduction Project that was attended by Chief Wildlife Wardens from four states, Wildlife Institute of India experts, IUCN representatives, conservation geneticists, and cheetah specialists, among others.[16]

Despite Arvind Singh's mixed interests, shooting boxes still dot the hillsides and lowlands of Mewar's erstwhile hunting grounds. Over a dozen stand along the shore and in the hills immediately south of Udaipur's City Palace. Just below the ridgeline at Tikhalya Magra's southern extremity is the black, crumbling Kala Odi; down the slope is the gleaming white Maj Mul. In the plains below are the beautifully painted Nahar Odi and the elegant Khas Odi, its arena now overgrown with brush, boar and tiger cages full of rubble, and royal apartments occupied by Rajasthan State foresters. More odis and muls can be found at Nahar Magra, in the hills above Jaisamand and Udai Sagar, and in the wildlife sanctuaries at Sajjangarh, Kumbhalgarh, Bhainsrorgarh, and at other old shikargahs in Rajasthan's Udaipur, Chittorgarh, Rajsamand, and Bhilwara districts. The territorial congruence between the maharanas' old shooting grounds and today's protected areas is striking, although not absolute.

As with Arvind Singh Mewar, photographs from Rajyashree Kumari of Bikaner's childhood in the 1960s document this accomplished sportswoman shooting boar, leopard, and sambar, in addition to paper targets and clay pigeons.[17] Besides promoting "educational, medical, and sports facilities" through various foundations and trusts associated with her lineage—including one for the "welfare of animals, birds and other wild life"—she has established a new foundation to

[16] "Top International and National Wildlife Specialists Meet to Discuss Cheetah Reintroduction into the Wild in India," *Wildlife Trust of India News*, September 9, 2009, http://www.wti.org.in/news-archives/.

[17] "Gallery," Official Website of Princess Rajyashree Kumari Bikaner, accessed March 24, 2012, http://www.rajyashreebikaner.com/gallery/index.html.

support animal welfare and veterinary services, as well as pediatrics. Her foundation donates to national organizations including People for Animals and PETA-India, and to local institutions like Bikaner's Veterinary Hospital.[18] Rajyashree Kumari practices an updated version of her great-grandfather Ganga Singh's princely ecology of environmental zimmedari and Rajput sportsmanship.

Beyond Rajyashree Kumari's sphere of influence, post-colonial elaborations on Ganga Singh's irrigation works in the north-east have "resulted in large-scale ecological changes," so that formerly dry grasslands "now attract increasing numbers of woodland and wetland birds," while "desert and semi-desert birds are decreasing in some areas" along with their preferred habitat. Agricultural expansions in the wake of the Gang Canal, then the Rajasthan Canal, and now the Indira Gandhi Nahar Project have reduced the area open to pastoralists and their animals, putting stress on grasslands shared with blackbuck, chinkara, and nilgai.[19] If Ganga Singh could see Bikaner today, he would be gratified to discover more trees, water, waterfowl, and cultivation. But his pleasure would be tempered by disappointment at concomitant reductions in sandgrouse, chinkara, houbara (vulnerable on the IUCN Red List) and the recently uplisted Great Indian Bustard (critically endangered as of June 2011, with "hunting, disturbance, habitat loss and fragmentation" having reduced their numbers to around 250 individuals.)[20]

Contrary to cosmopolitan views that single out protected area residents as most responsible for the "significant linkages between forest resource use and habitat degradation," Ghazala Shahabuddin reminds us that "a large proportion of this extractive pressure ... is exerted by external towns and villages, sometimes as far as 20 km away."[21] Tigers, whether born in West Bengal's Sundarbans or transplanted into

[18] Tenth and Eleventh Newsletters, Central Office of Bikaner Trusts, December 2011, http://www.rajyashreebikaner.com/Newsletters.htm.

[19] Rishad Naoroji, *Birds of Prey of the Indian Subcontinent* (London: Christopher Helm, 2006), 38–40 and 83.

[20] "Big Birds Lose Out in a Crowded World," IUCN News Release, June 7, 2011, http://www.iucn.org/media/news_releases/.

[21] Shahabuddin, *Conservation at the Crossroads*, 57–8.

Rajasthan's troubled Sariska Tiger Reserve, are endangered not only because they suffer from local use and local conflicts, but also from seemingly remote causes. Domestic and foreign elites who donate to the cause of "cosmopolitan" tigers may be contributing—most directly through their tourism preferences and the conservation discourses their monies support—to certain challenges faced by flesh-and-blood tigers. I do not suggest that touring should cease, or that donations should stop. Rather, I believe we require "new scripts."[22]

The most recent survey found approximately 1706 tigers remaining in India.[23] Although historical populations must have been significantly higher, our sense of crisis today is not so far removed from the past, when princely tigers and other select royal game became increasingly inviolable as Indian princes grew anxious for their powers and game populations. With petitions going unanswered and seemingly arbitrary regulations compromising their very survival, it is no wonder that villagers—never able to rely entirely on avoidance strategies when it came to aggressive carnivores or hungry herbivores—resisted princes, slaughtered wildlife, and slashed forests. Conservation can emerge from princely ecology, and sustainable practices from the environmental zimmedari of erstwhile princes and princely subjects, but these alone are not enough when elite interests and cosmopolitan visions overshadow local concerns and lived experiences.

---

[22] Garland, "Elephant in the Room," 68.
[23] Jhala, *et al.*, *Status of Tigers*, xi.

Bibliography

ARCHIVAL COLLECTIONS

British Empire & Commonwealth Museum, London
British Library, London
Centre of South Asian Studies, University of Cambridge, Cambridge
Madhya Pradesh Directorate of Archaeology, Archives and Museums, Bhopal
Maharana Mewar Special Library, Udaipur
National Archives of India, New Delhi
Pratap Shodh Pratisthan, Udaipur
Rajasthan State Archives, Bikaner
Rajasthan State Archives Intermediary Depository, Udaipur
Sadul Museum, Maharaja Ganga Singhji Trust, Bikaner
Uttar Pradesh State Archives, Lucknow

PUBLISHED WORKS

Aberigh-Mackay, G.R. *The Chiefs of Central India*. Calcutta: Thacker, Spink, and Co., 1879.

Administration Report of the Orchha State for 1912–13 (July to June). Allahabad: Pioneer Press, 1916.

Administration Report of the Orchha State for 1931–32. Jhansi: Union Press, n.d.

Aitken, Molly Emma. *The Intelligence of Tradition in Rajput Court Painting*. New Haven: Yale University Press, 2010.

Akhet Niyamavali Rajya Jhalawar. Jhalawar: 1931.

'Allami, Abu al-Fazl. *The Ain i Akbari*. Translated by H. Blochmann. Vol. 1. Calcutta: Asiatic Society of Bengal, 1878.

Allen, Charles, and Sharada Dwivedi. *Lives of the Indian Princes*. New York: Crown Publishers, Inc., in association with the Taj Hotel Group, 1984.

Allsen, Thomas T. *The Royal Hunt in Eurasian History*. Philadelphia: University of Pennsylvania Press, 2006.

Altherr, Thomas L., and John F. Reiger. "Academic Historians and Hunting: A Call for More and Better Scholarship." *Environmental History Review* 19, 3 (Fall 1995): 39–56.

Andheria, A.P., K.U. Karanth, and N.S. Kumar. "Diet and Prey Profiles of Three Sympatric Large Carnivores in Bandipur Tiger Reserve, India." *Journal of Zoology* 273 (2007): 169–75.

Asher, Catherine. "The Architecture of Raja Man Singh: A Study of Sub-Imperial Patronage." In *The Powers of Art: Patronage in Indian Culture*. Edited by Barbara Stoler Miller. New Delhi: Oxford University Press, 1992.

Bernier, François. *Travels in the Mogul Empire, A.D. 1656–1668*. 2nd edition. Translated by Archibald Constable. Revised by Vincent A. Smith. Delhi: Low Price Publications, 1999.

Best, J.W. *Indian Shikar Notes*. 2nd edition. Allahabad: Pioneer Press, 1922.

Bhabha, Homi K. "Of Mimicry and Man: The Ambivalence of Colonial Discourse." *October* 28 (Spring, 1984): 125–33.

Bhagavan, Manu. *Sovereign Spheres: Princes, Education and Empire in Colonial India*. New Delhi: Oxford University Press, 2003.

Bhandari, Prakash. "1930: Story of the First Tiger Relocation." *Times of India*, July 6, 2008. http://articles.timesofindia.indiatimes.com/2008-07-06/flora-fauna/27926740_1_tiger-relocation-sariska-tiger-population.

Bharatpur Game Laws. Bharatpur: State Press, 1924.

Bharatpur Game Laws. Revised. Bharatpur: State Press, 1932.

"Big Birds Lose Out in a Crowded World." *IUCN*. IUCN News Release, June 7, 2011. http://www.iucn.org/media/news_releases/.

BirdLife International. "Species Factsheet: *Pterocles orientalis*." 2011. *BirdLife International*. 2011. http://www.birdlife.org.

Blades, Brooke S. "European Military Sites as Ideological Landscapes." *Historical Archaeology* 37, 3 (2003): 46–54.

Blane, William. *An Account of the Hunting Excursions of Asoph ul Doulah, Visier of the Mogul Empire, and Nabob of Oude, by William Blane, Esq., who Attended in these Excursions in the Years 1785 and 1786*. London: John Stockdale, 1788.

Calabi, Silvio, Steve Helsley, and Roger G. Sanger. *Rigby: A Grand Tradition*. Dallas, TX: Arundel Publishing, 2012.

Cartmill, Matt. *A View to a Death in the Morning: Hunting and Nature through History*. Cambridge: Harvard University Press, 1993.

Caton Jones, F.W. "A Glance at Udaipur." In *The Hoghunter's Annual*. Edited by H. Nugent Head and J. Scott Cockburn. Vol. 3. Bombay: Times of India Press, 1930.

Chakraverty, Anjan. *Indian Miniature Painting*. Delhi: Lustre Press, 1996.

Chatterjee, Partha. "The Nationalist Resolution of the Women's Question." *Empire and Nation: Essential Writings 1985–2005*. Ranikhet: Permanent Black, 2010.

Chattopadhyaya, B.D. "The Emergence of the Rajputs as a Historical Process in Early Medieval Rajasthan." In *The Idea of Rajasthan: Explorations in Regional Identity*. Vol. 2. Edited by Karine Schomer, Joan L. Erdman, Deryck O. Loderick, and Lloyd I. Rudolph. New Delhi: Manohar; American Institute of Indian Studies, 1994.

Clouston, David. *Some Foes of the Farmer in the Central Provinces and How the [sic] Deal with Them*. Nagpur: Government Press, 1928.

Cohn, Bernard S. "Representing Authority in Victorian India." In *The Invention of Tradition*. Edited by Eric Hobsbawm and Terence Ranger. New York: Cambridge University Press, 1992.

Copland, Ian. "The Other Guardians: Ideology and Performance in the Indian Political Service." In *People, Princes and Paramount Power: Society and Politics in the Indian Princely States*. Edited by Robin Jeffrey. Delhi: Oxford University Press, 1978.

———. *The Princes of India in the Endgame of Empire, 1917–1947*. First South Asian edition. New Delhi: Cambridge University Press, 1999.

Cronon, William. "The Trouble with Wilderness; or, Getting Back to the Wrong Nature." In *Uncommon Ground: Rethinking the Human Place in Nature*. New York: W.W. Norton & Co., 1995.

Darrah, H.Z. *Sport in the Highlands of Kashmir*. London: Rowland Ward, 1898.

"Dept. Claims Sariska Tiger Relocation First of its Kind, Global Forum Not Impressed." *Daily News & Analysis*, April 4, 2011, Jaipur edition.

Desai, Vishakha N. "Timeless Symbols: Royal Portraits from Rajasthan, 17th–19th Centuries." In *The Idea of Rajasthan: Explorations in Regional Identity*. Vol. 1. Edited by Karine Schomer, Joan L. Erdman, Deryck O. Lodrick, and Lloyd I. Rudolph. New Delhi: Manohar; American Institute of Indian Studies, 1994.

Detailed Instructions Relating to the Visit to Bikaner of Their Excellencies the Viceroy and the Lady Irwin. January–February, 1929. Bikaner, c. 1929.

Dirks, Nicholas B. *The Hollow Crown: An Ethnohistory of an Indian Kingdom*. New York: Cambridge University Press, 1987.

———. "Junagadh State and its Lions: Conservation in Princely India, 1879–1947." *Conservation and Society* 4, 4 (December 2006): 522–40.

———. ed. *The Lions of India*. New Delhi: Black Kite, 2008.

Divyabhanusinh. *The End of a Trail: The Cheetah in India*. 3rd edition. New Delhi: Oxford University Press, 2006.

Dollman, Guy, and J.B. Burlace, eds. *Rowland Ward's Records of Big Game, African and Asiatic Sections, Giving the Distribution, Characteristics, Dimensions, Weights, and Horn & Tusk Measurements*. 10th edition. London: Rowland Ward, Limited, 1935.

Durie, Alastair J. "Game Shooting: An Elite Sport c. 1870–1980." *Sport in History* 28, 3 (2008): 431–49.

Dwivedi, Sharada, and Manvendra Singh Barwani. *The Automobiles of the Maharajas*. Mumbai: Eminence Designs Pvt., Ltd., 2003.

Ellison, Bernard C. *H.R.H. The Prince of Wales's Sport in India*. London: William Heinemann, Ltd., 1925.

Ernst, Waltraud, and Biswamoy Pati, eds. *India's Princely States: People, Princes and Colonialism*. Delhi: Primus Books, 2010.

Erskine, K.D. *A Gazetteer of the Udaipur State, with a Chapter on the Bhils and Some Statistical Tables*. Ajmer: Scottish Mission Industries, Co., Ltd., 1908.

———. *The Mewar Residency*. 1908. Reprint. Gurgaon: Vintage Books, 1992.

———. *The Western Rajputana States Residency and The Bikaner Agency*. Vol. I. 1908. Reprint. Gurgaon: Vintage Books, 1992.

Falk, Nancy E. "Wilderness and Kingship in Ancient South Asia." *History of Religions* 13, 1 (1973): 1–15.

"Focus Areas: Environment." *Eternal Mewar*. http://www.eternalmewar.in/about/index.aspx.

Forsyth, James. "Game Animals and Birds of the Plains." In *The Oxford Anthology of Indian Wildlife: Hunting and Shooting*. Edited by Mahesh Rangarajan. New York: Oxford University Press, 1999.

Four Decades of Progress in Bikaner. Bikaner: Government Press, 1937.

Freitag, Jason P. "The Power Which Raised them from Ruin and Oppression: James Tod, Historiography, and the Rajput Ideal." PhD dissertation, Columbia University, 2001.

"Gallery." *Official Website of Princess Rajyashree Kumari Bikaner*. http://www.rajyashreebikaner.com/gallery/index.html.

Garland, Elizabeth. "The Elephant in the Room: Confronting the Colonial Character of Wildlife Conservation in Africa." *African Studies Review* 51, 3 (2008): 51–74.

Gauba, Khalid Latif. *H.H., or the Pathology of Princes*. Lahore: Times Publishing Company, 1930.

Gilmartin, David. "Models of the Hydraulic Environment: Colonial Irrigation, State Power and Community in the Indus Basin." In *Nature, Culture, Imperialism: Essays on the Environmental History of South Asia*. Edited by David Arnold and Ramachandra Guha. Delhi: Oxford University Press, 1995.

Goetz, Hermann. *The Art and Architecture of Bikaner State*. Oxford: Bruno Cassirer for The Government of Bikaner State and The Royal India and Pakistan Society, 1950.

Gold, Ann Grodzins, and Bhoju Ram Gujar. *In the Time of Trees and Sorrows: Nature, Power, and Memory in Rajasthan*. Durham: Duke University Press, 2002.

Gold, Ann Grodzins, with Bhoju Ram Gujar. "Wild Pigs and Kings: Remembered Landscapes in Rajasthan." *American Anthropologist* 99, 1 (1997): 70–84.

Grant, Charles. *Gazetteer of the Central Provinces of India*. 1870. Reprint. New Delhi: Usha, 1984.

"Guest Comments." *Lallgarh Palace*. http://www.lallgarhpalace.com/guest_comments.htm.

"Gujarat Assembly Passes Bill on Cow Slaughter." *The Hindu*, September 27, 2011. http://www.thehindu.com/navigation/?type=static&page=archive.

Gupta, S.R. *Shikari Dost*. Ratlam: 1903.

Habib, Irfan. *An Atlas of the Mughal Empire: Political and Economic Maps with Detailed Notes, Bibliography and Index*. Delhi: Oxford University Press, 1982.

Hardinge, Charles. *My Indian Years, 1910–1916: The Reminiscences of Lord Hardinge of Penshurst*. London: John Murray, 1948.

Harlan, Lindsey. *The Goddesses' Henchmen: Gender in Indian Hero Worship*. New York: Oxford University Press, 2003.

Haynes, Edward S. "Rajput Ceremonial Interactions as a Mirror of a Dying Indian State System, 1820–1947." *Modern Asian Studies* 24, 3 (1990): 459–92.

Hill, Claude H. *India – Stepmother*. London: Blackwood and Sons, Ltd., 1929.

Hume, A.O. and C.H.T. Marshall. *The Game Birds of India, Burmah, and Ceylon.* Vol. 2. Calcutta: A.O. Hume and C.H.T. Marshall, 1880.

Hussain, S. Sadr-Uddin, and S.A. Qadir. "An Autecological Study of *Euphorbia caducifolia* Haines." *Vegetation* 20, 5/6 (1970): 329–80.

Imperial Gazetteer of India. Oxford: Clarendon Press, 1908.

Imperial Gazetteer of India: Provincial Series, Central India. Vol. 12. Calcutta: Superintendent of Government Printing, 1908.

India Weather Review: Annual Summary, 1914. Calcutta: Superintendent of Government Printing, 1916.

India Weather Review, 1939: Annual Summary, Part A: Summary of Weather with Tables. New Delhi: Government of India Press, 1941.

Indian Arms Act, 1878, as Modified up to the 1st July, 1892. Simla: Government Central Printing Office, 1892.

"India's Famous Lake Palace Hotel Loses its Lake." *The Telegraph,* July 14, 2009. http://www.telegraph.co.uk/archive/.

Itzkowitz, David C. *Peculiar Privilege: A Social History of English Foxhunting, 1753–1885.* Hassocks: Harvester Press, 1977.

Ivory, James C. *Autobiography of a Princess, Also Being the Adventures of an American Film Director in the Land of the Maharajas.* New York: Harper and Row, Publishers, 1975.

Jaffer, Amin. *Made for Maharajas: A Design Diary of Princely India.* New York: Vendome Press, 2006.

Jain, Ravindra K. *Between History and Legend: Status and Power in Bundelkhand.* New Delhi: Orient Longman Private Limited, 2002.

Jaipur State Shooting Rules. Jaipur: 1927.

Jaipurian [pseud.]. Letter to the editor. *Hindustan Times,* July 25, 1939.

Jalais, Annu. "Dwelling on Morichjhanpi: When Tigers Became 'Citizens,' Refugees 'Tiger-Food'." *Economic and Political Weekly* 40, 17 (April 2005): 1757–62.

———. *Forest of Tigers: People, Politics and Environment in the Sundarbans.* New Delhi: Routledge, 2010.

Jehangir, Sorabji. *Princes and Chiefs of India, a Collection of Biographies, with Portraits of the Indian Princes and Chiefs and Brief Historical Surveys of their Territories.* 2 vols. London: Waterlow and Sons, Limited, 1903.

Jhala, Y.V., Q. Qureshi, R. Gopal, and P.R. Sinha, eds. *Status of Tigers, Co-predators, and Prey in India, 2010.* New Delhi and Dehradun: National Tiger Conservation Authority and Wildlife Institute of India, 2011.

Joffee, Jennifer Beth. "Art, Architecture and Politics in Mewar, 1628–1710." PhD dissertation, University of Minnesota, 2005.

Kapralski, Slawomir. "Battlefields of Memory: Landscape and Identity in Polish–Jewish Relations." *History and Memory: Studies in Representation of the Past* 13, 2 (2001): 35–58.

Karanth, Krithi K., James D. Nichols, K. Ullas Karanth, James E. Hines, and Norman L. Christensen, Jr. "The Shrinking Ark: Patterns of Large Animal Extinctions in India." *Proceedings of the Royal Society B* 277 (2010): 1971–9.

Karanth, K. Ullas, and Melvin E. Sunquist. "Prey Selection by Tiger, Leopard and Dhole in Tropical Forests." *Journal of Animal Ecology* 64 (1995): 439–50.

Kasturi, Malavika. *Embattled Identities: Rajput Lineages and the Colonial State in Nineteenth Century North India.* New York: Oxford University Press, 2002.

———. "Rajput Lineages, Banditry and the Colonial State in Nineteenth-Century 'British' Bundelkhand." *Studies in History* 15, 1 (1999): 75–108.

Keith, A. Berriedale, ed. *Speeches and Documents on Indian Policy, 1750–1921.* Vol. 1. New York: Humphrey Milford, 1922.

Kipling, Rudyard. *From Sea to Sea; Letters of Travel.* Vol. 1. New York: Doubleday and McClure Company, 1899.

Koch, Ebba. "Jahangir as Francis Bacon's Ideal of the King as an Observer and Investigator of Nature." *Journal of the Royal Asiatic Society* 19, 3 (2009): 293–338.

———. "The Copies of the Qutb Minar." *Iran* 29 (1991): 95–107.

Kolff, Dirk H.A. *Naukar, Rajput and Sepoy: The Ethnohistory of the Military Labour Market in Hindustan, 1450–1850.* New York: Cambridge University Press, 1990.

Kumari, Rajyashree. Foreword to *Maharaja Sadul Singh of Bikaner (A Biography of the Co-Architect of India's Unity).* By L.S. Rathore. 2 vols. Bikaner: Books Treasure and Maharaja Ganga Singhji Trust, 2005.

Lawrence, Walter. *Ruling Princes and Chiefs of India. A Brief Historical Record of the Leading Princes and Chiefs in India together with a Description of their Territories and Methods of Administration.* 1930. Reprint. Lahore: Sang-e-Meel Publications, 2005.

Lothian, Arthur Cunningham. *Kingdoms of Yesterday.* London: John Murray, 1951.

Luard, Charles Eckford. *Gazetteer of India Eastern States (Bundelkhand).* 1907. Reprint. Bhopal: Gazetteers Department, Government of India, 1995.

MacGregor, R.S. *The Oxford Hindi–English Dictionary.* Oxford: Oxford University Press, 1993.

MacKenzie, John M. *The Empire of Nature: Hunting, Conservation and British Imperialism.* New York: Manchester University Press, 1988.

Mangan, J.A. *The Games Ethic and Imperialism: Aspects of the Diffusion of an Ideal.* New York: Viking, 1986.

Martin, John. "British Game Shooting in Transition, 1900–1945." *Agricultural History* 85, 2 (2011): 204–24.

Marwar Shooting Rules 1921. Jodhpur: Jodhpur Government Press, n.d.

Masters, Brian. *Maharana: The Story of the Rulers of Udaipur.* Ahmedabad: Mapin Publishing Pvt., Ltd., 1990.

"Message from the 76th Custodian." *Eternal Mewar.* http://www.eternalmewar.in/about/index.aspx.

Metcalf, Thomas R. *An Imperial Vision: Indian Architecture and Britain's Raj.* Berkeley: University of California Press, 1989.

"Modi Pitches for Horse Breeding as a Full-Fledged Industry." *Indian Express,* December 28, 2008. http://www.indianexpress.com/live-archives/.

Morgan, Marjorie. *National Identities and Travel in Victorian Britain.* New York: Palgrave, 2001.

Morris, P.A. *Van Ingen & Van Ingen: Artists in Taxidermy.* Ascot: MPM Publishing, 2006.

Murray, Narisara. "From Birds of Paradise to *Drosophila*: The Changing Roles of Scientific Specimens to 1920." In *A Cultural History of Animals in the Age of Empire.* Edited by Kathleen Kete. New York: Berg, 2007.

Naoroji, Rishad. *Birds of Prey of the Indian Subcontinent.* London: Christopher Helm, 2006.

Nicholson, A.P. *Scraps of Paper: India's Broken Treaties, Her Princes, and the Problem.* London: Ernst Benn Limited, 1930.

Ojha, Gaurisankara Hiracanda. *Udayapura Rajya ka Itihasa.* Vol. 2. 1928. Reprint. Jaipur: Rajasthani Granthagar, 1999.

Pandian, Anand S. "Predatory Care: The Imperial Hunt in Mughal and British India." *Journal of Historical Sociology* 14, 1 (March 2001): 79–107.

Pandian, M.S.S. "Hunting and Colonialism in the 19th Century Nilgiri Hills of South India." In *Nature and the Orient: The Environmental History of South and Southeast Asia,* 273–97. Edited by Richard H. Grove, Vinita Damodaran, and Satpal Sangwan. Delhi: Oxford University Press, 1998.

Panikkar, K.M. *His Highness the Maharaja of Bikaner, A Biography*. London: Oxford University Press, 1937.

———. *Hindu Kingship and Polity in Precolonial India*. New York: Cambridge University Press, 2003.

Peabody, Norbert. "*Kota Mahajagat*, or the Great Universe of Kota: Sovereignty and Territory in 18th Century Rajasthan." *Contributions to Indian Sociology* 25, 1 (1991): 29–56.

———. "Tod's *Rajast'han* and the Boundaries of Imperial Rule in Nineteenth-Century India." *Modern Asian Studies* 30, 1 (February 1996): 185–220.

Pogson, W.R. *A History of the Boondelas*. 1828. Reprint. Delhi: B.R. Publishing Corporation, 1974.

Ramusack, Barbara N. *The Indian Princes and their States*. New York: Cambridge University Press, 2004.

———. "The Indian Princes as Fantasy: Palace Hotels, Palace Museums, and Palace on Wheels." In *Consuming Modernity: Public Culture in a South Asian World*. Edited by Carol A. Breckenridge. Minneapolis: University of Minnesota Press, 1995.

Rangarajan, Mahesh. *Fencing the Forest: Conservation and Ecological Change in India's Central Provinces 1860–1914*. Delhi: Oxford University Press, 1996.

———. Preface to J.H. Baldwin. "Hunting the Houbara." In *The Oxford Anthology of Indian Wildlife: Hunting and Shooting*. Edited by Mahesh Rangarajan. New York: Oxford University Press, 1999.

———. "Region's Honour, Nation's Pride: Gir's Lions on the Cusp of History." In *The Lions of India*. Edited by Divyabhanusinh. New Delhi: Black Kite, 2008.

———. "The Raj and the Natural World: The War against 'Dangerous Beasts' in Colonial India." *Studies in History* 14, 2 (1998): 267–99.

Ranjitsinh, M.K. *Beyond the Tiger: Portraits of Asian Wildlife*. New Delhi: Brijbasi Publishers Private Limited, 1997.

Rao, Velcheru Narayana, David Shulman, and Sanjay Subrahmanyam. *Symbols of Substance: Court and State in Nayaka Period Tamilnadu*. New York: Oxford University Press, 1992.

Rathore, L.S. *Maharaja Sadul Singh of Bikaner (A Biography of the Co-Architect of India's Unity)*. Vol. 1. Bikaner: Books Treasure & Maharaja Ganga Singhji Trust, 2005.

Report on the Administration of Orchha State for 1907–1908. Tikamgarh: Shri Pratap Prabhukar State Press, 1913.

Report on the Administration of the Bikaner State for 1938–39. Bikaner: Government Press, n.d.

Report on the Administration of the Bikaner State for Three Financial Years 1939–40, 1940–41 and 1941–42. Bikaner: Government Press, n.d.

Report on the Political Administration of the Territories within the Central India Agency for 1895–1896. Calcutta: Office of the Superintendent Government Printing, 1896.

Rice, William. *Tiger Shooting in India; Being an Account of Hunting Experiences on Foot in Rajpootana, During the Hot Seasons, from 1850 to 1854*. London: Smith, Elder and Co., 1857.

Rodgers, W. Alan, Hemendra S. Panwar, and Vinod B. Mathur. *Wildlife Protected Area Network in India: A Review, Executive Summary*. Dehra Dun: Wildlife Institute of India, *c.* 2002.

Rosin, R. Thomas. "The Tradition of Groundwater Irrigation in Northwestern India." *Human Ecology: An Interdisciplinary Journal*, 21, 1 (March 1993): 51–87.

Rousselet, Louis. *India and its Native Princes, Travels in Central India and in the Presidencies of Bombay and Bengal*. Delhi: B.R. Publishing Corporation, 1975.

"Royal Warrants." *John Rigby & Co.* http://www.johnrigbyandco.com/html/royal_warrants.html.

Rudolph, Lloyd I., and Susanne Hoeber Rudolph. "Writing and Reading Tod's *Rajasthan*: Interpreting the Text and its Historiography." In *Circumambulations in South Asian History: Essays in Honor of Dirk H.A. Kolff*. Edited by Jos Gommans and Om Prakash. Boston: Brill, 2003.

Rudolph, Susanne Hoeber and Lloyd I. Rudolph, eds. With Mohan Singh Kanota. *Reversing the Gaze: Amar Singh's Diary, A Colonial Subject's Narrative of Imperial India*. Boulder, CO: Westview Press, 2002.

Rudradeva. *Syainikashastram: The Art of Hunting in Ancient India of Raja Rudradeva of Kumaon*. Edited by Mohan Chand. Translated by Haraprasad Shastri. Delhi: Eastern Book Linkers, 1982.

Rules and Regulations for Shooting and Pigsticking in Marwar within the Shikar Khana Limits. Jodhpur: *c.* 1910.

Rules for the Regulation of Hunting, Shooting and Fishing in Bundi State. Bundi: Srirangnath Press, 1939.

Rules for the Regulation of Shooting in the Jaipur State. Jaipur: 1931.

Rules made under the Mewar Game and Fish Preservation Act. Udaipur: 1942.

Saberwal, Vasant K., Mahesh Rangarajan, and Ashish Kothari, *People, Parks and Wildlife: Towards Coexistence*. New Delhi: Orient Longman, 2000.

Sampson, Gary D. "Photographer of the Picturesque: Samuel Bourne." In *India Through the Lens: Photography, 1840–1911*. Edited by Vidya Dehejia. New York: Smithsonian Institution, 2000.

Sankhala, Kailash. *Tiger! The Story of the Indian Tiger*. New York: Simon and Schuster, 1977.

Sarila, Narendra Singh. *Once a Prince of Sarila: Of Palaces and Tiger Hunts, of Nehrus and Mountbattens*. London: I.B. Tauris, 2008.

Schley, Laurent, and Timothy J. Roper. "Diet of Wild Boar *Sus scrofa* in Western Europe, with Particular Reference to Consumption of Agricultural Crops." *Mammal Review* 33, 1 (2003): 43–56.

Seidensticker, John. "Tigers: Top Carnivores and Controlling Processes in Asian Forests." In *Terrestrial Ecoregions of the Indo-Pacific, a Conservation Assessment*. Edited by Eric Wikramanayake, Eric Dinerstein, Colby J. Loucks, *et al*. Washington, DC: Island Press, 2002.

Sen, David N. "Leafless Euphorbia on Rajasthan Rocks, India 1. Ecological Life-History." *Folia Geobotanica and Phytotaxonomica* 3, 1 (1968): 1–15.

Sen, Hari. "The Maharana and the Bhils: The 'Eki' Movement in Mewar, 1921–22." In *India's Princely States: People, Princes and Colonialism*. Edited by Waltraud Ernst and Biswamoy Pati. Delhi: Primus Books, 2010.

Sen, Satadru. *Migrant Races: Empire, Identity and K.S. Ranjitsinhji*. New York: Manchester University Press, 2004.

Shah, Laxmichand Dossabhai. *The Prince of Wales and The Princes of India*. 2 vols. Rajkot: Kathiawar Printing Works, 1923.

Shahabuddin, Ghazala. *Conservation at the Crossroads: Science, Society and the Future of India's Wildlife*. Ranikhet: Permanent Black, 2010.

Sharma, G.N., ed. *Haqiqat Bahida: H.H. Maharana Fateh Singhji, 24 Dec., 1884 to 24 May, 1930*. 5 vols. Udaipur: Maharana Mewar Research Institute, 1992–7.

Shastri, R.P. *Jhala Zalim Singh (1730–1823), the De-Facto Ruler of Kota, who also Dominated Bundi and Udaipur, Shrewd Politician, Administrator and Reformer*. Jaipur: Raj Printing Works, 1971.

Shikar ka Naksha. Udaipur: *c.* 1921.

Singh, Diwan Bijhe Bahadur Mazbut. *A Portion of the History of Bundelkhand*. Translated and edited by C.A. Silberrad. In "A Contribution to the History of Western Bundelkhand." By C.A. Silberrad. *Journal of the Asiatic Society of Bengal* 71, 1 (1902): 99–135.

Singh, Ganga. *Extracts from His Highness' Diary*. Bikaner: Government Press, n.d.

————. *His Highness' General Shooting Diary.* Vol. 2. Bikaner: Government Press, 1941.

Singh, Hira. "Colonial and Postcolonial Historiography and the Princely States: Relations of Power and Rituals of Legitimation." In *India's Princely States: People, Princes and Colonialism.* Edited by Waltraud Ernst and Biswamoy Pati. Delhi: Primus Books, 2010.

————. *Colonial Hegemony and Popular Resistance: Princes, Peasants, and Paramount Power.* New Delhi: Sage Publications, 1998.

Singh, Karni. *The Relations of the House of Bikaner with the Central Powers, 1465–1949.* New Delhi: Munshiram Manoharlal Publishers Pvt., Ltd., 1974.

Singh, Kesri. *Hints on Tiger Shooting (Tiger by Tiger).* Bombay: Jaico Publishing House, 1965.

————. *Hunting with Horse and Spear.* New Delhi: Hindustan Times, 1963.

————. *The Tiger of Rajasthan.* London: Robert Hale Limited, 1959.

Singh, Nihal. *The King's Indian Allies: The Rajas and Their India.* London: Sampson Low, Marston, and Co., Ltd., 1916.

Singh, Sadul. *Big Game Diary of Maharaj Kumar Shri Sadul Singhji of Bikaner, Rajasthan.* Bikaner: privately printed, *c.* 1930.

Sivaperuman, C., and Q.H. Baqri. "Avifaunal Diversity in the IGNP Canal Area, Rajasthan, India." In *Faunal Ecology and Conservation of the Great Indian Desert.* Edited by C. Sivaperuman, Q.H. Baqri, G. Ramaswamy, and M. Naseema. Berlin: Springer, 2009.

Sleeman, W.H. *Rambles and Recollections of an Indian Official.* Revised and annotated by Vincent A. Smith. London: Oxford University Press, 1915.

Sreenivasan, Ramya. *The Many Lives of a Rajput Queen: Heroic Pasts in India, c. 1500–1900.* Seattle: University of Washington Press, 2007.

Srivastava, Alok. *Orchha: An Ode to the Bundelas.* Bhopal: Directorate of Archaeology, Archives and Museums, Government of Madhya Pradesh, 1999.

Steinhart, Edward I. *Black Poachers, White Hunters: A Social History of Hunting in Colonial Kenya.* Athens: Ohio University Press, 2006.

"Stephen Grant." *Atkin, Grant & Lang.* http://www.atkingrantandlang.com/our-company.php?company=15.

Stockley, V.M. *Big Game Shooting in India, Burma, and Somaliland.* London: Horace Cox, 1913.

Sweeney, Patrick. *Gunsmithing: Rifles.* Iola, WI: Gun Digest Books, 1999.

Taft, Frances H. "Honor and Alliance: Reconsidering Mughal–Rajput Marriages." In *The Idea of Rajasthan: Explorations in Regional Identity*, Vol. 2, edited by Karine Schomer, Joan L. Erdman, Deryck O. Lodrick, and Lloyd I. Rudolph. New Delhi: Manohar; American Institute of Indian Studies, 1994.

Talbot, Cynthia. "The Mewar Court's Construction of History." In *Kingdom of the Sun: Indian Court and Village Art from the Princely State of Mewar*, edited by Joanna Gottfried Williams. San Francisco: Asian Art Museum, Chong-Moon Lee Center for Asian Art and Culture, 2007.

Talukdar, B.K., R. Emslie, S.S. Bist, A. Choudhury, S. Ellis, B.S. Bonal, M.C. Malakar, B.N. Talukdar, and M. Barua. "*Rhinoceros unicornis.*" In *IUCN 2010. IUCN Red List of Threatened Species.* Version 2010.4. http://www.iucnredlist.org.

Tanwar, Dhaibhai Tulsinath Singh. *Samsmaran: Maharana Fateh Singhji, Maharana Bhupal Singhji, Maharana Bhagvat Singhji Mewar.* Udaipur: privately printed, 1982.

———. *Shikari aur Shikar.* Udaipur: privately printed, 1956.

Templewood, Samuel John Gurney Hoare. *India by Air.* New York: Longman, Green and Co., Ltd., 1927.

Tenth and Eleventh Newsletters. Central Office of Bikaner Trusts, December 2011. *Official Website of Princess Rajyashree Kumari Bikaner.* http://www.rajyashreebikaner.com/Newsletters.htm.

"The Retreat." *Bundelkhand Riverside.* http://www.bundelkhandriverside.com.

Tod, James. *Annals and Antiquities of Rajasthan, or the Central and Western Rajput States of India.* Edited by William Crooke. 3 vols. New York: Humphrey Milford; Oxford University Press, 1920.

"Top International and National Wildlife Specialists Meet to Discuss Cheetah Reintroduction into the Wild in India." *Wildlife Trust of India News*, September 9, 2009. http://www.wti.org.in/news-archives/.

Topsfield, Andrew. *Court Painting at Udaipur: Art Under the Patronage of the Maharanas of Mewar.* Zurich: Artibus Asiae Publishers and Museum Rietberg Zurich, 2001.

———. *The City Palace Museum Udaipur: Paintings of Mewar Court Life.* Ahmedabad: Mapin Publishing Pvt., Ltd., 1990.

"Tragedy of Forest Laws. A Harrowing Tale. Destruction of Life and Crops by Wild Beasts." *Hindustan Times*, July 24, 1939.

Truesdell, S.R. *The Rifle: Its Development for Big Game Hunting.* Harrisburg, PA: Military Service Publishing Co., 1947.

van Sittert, Lance. "Bringing in the Wild: The Commodification of Wild Animals in the Cape Colony/Province c. 1850–1950." *Journal of African History* 46, 2 (2005): 269–91.

Vaughan, John. "Hog Hunter's Hall of the Tenth Hussars in Purneah, 1909." In *Modern Pig-Sticking*. By A.E. Wardrop. London: Macmillan and Co., Limited, 1914.

Waddington, C.W. *Indian India as seen by a Guest in Rajasthan*. London: Jarrolds Publishers, 1933.

Waghorne, Joanne Punzo. *The Raja's Magic Clothes: Re-Visioning Kingship and Divinity in England's India*. University Park: Pennsylvania State University Press, 1994.

Walker, David. *The Prince in India. A Record of the Indian Tour of His Royal Highness The Prince of Wales—Nov. 1921 to March 1922*. Bombay: Bennett, Coleman, and Co., Ltd., 1923.

Ward, Rowland. *Records of Big Game*. 4th edition. London: Rowland Ward, Ltd., 1903.

Welch, Stuart Cary, ed. *Gods, Kings, and Tigers: The Art of Kotah*. New York: Prestel, 1997.

Williams, Joanna Gottfried, ed. *Kingdom of the Sun: Indian Court and Village Art from the Princely State of Mewar*. San Francisco: Asian Art Museum, Chong-Moon Lee Center for Asian Art and Culture, 2007.

Woodroffe, Rosie, Simon Thirgood, and Alan Rabinowitz. "The Future of Coexistence: Resolving Human–Wildlife Conflicts in a Changing World." In *People and Wildlife: Conflict or Coexistence?* Edited by Rosie Woodroffe, Simon Thirgood, and Alan Rabinowitz. New York: Cambridge University Press, 2005.

Zimmermann, Francis. *The Jungle and the Aroma of Meats: An Ecological Theme in Hindu Medicine*. Berkeley: University of California Press, 1987.

Index